PENGUIN CLASSICS

JAPANESE NŌ DRAMAS

ROYALL TYLER, educated partly in France, graduated from Harvard and obtained a doctorate in Japanese literature from Columbia University. After teaching in Canada, the United States and Norway, he moved to Australia and taught until retirement at the Australian National University. His other books include *Japanese Tales* (1987), *French Folktales* (1989), *The Miracles of the Kasuga Deity* (1990) and, also in Penguin Classics, *The Tale of Genji* (2001).

Japanese Nō Dramas

Edited and translated by ROYALL TYLER

PENGUIN BOOKS

PENGUIN BOOKS

Published by the Penguin Group
Penguin Books Ltd, 80 Strand, London WC2R ORL, England
Penguin Group (USA), Inc., 375 Hudson Street, New York, New York 10014, USA
Penguin Books Australia Ltd, 250 Camberwell Road, Camberwell, Victoria 3124, Australia
Penguin Books Canada Ltd, 10 Alcorn Avenue, Toronto, Ontario, Canada M4V 3B2
Penguin Books India (P) Ltd, 11 Community Centre, Panchsheel Park, New Delhi – 110 017, India
Penguin Books (NZ) Ltd, Cnr Rosedale and Airborne Roads, Albany, Auckland, New Zealand
Penguin Books (South Africa) (Pty) Ltd, 24 Sturdee Avenue, Rosebank 2196, South Africa

Penguin Books Ltd, Registered Offices: 80 Strand, London WC2R ORL, England

www.penguin.com

First published 1992
Reprinted 2004
16

Selection, translation and notes copyright © Royall Tyler, 1992
All rights reserved

The moral right of the editor has been asserted

Typeset by Datix International Limited, Bungay, Suffolk
Set in 10/12 pt Monophoto Garamond
Printed in England by Clays Ltd, St Ives plc

ISBN-13: 978-0-140-44539-8

www.greenpenguin.co.uk

Penguin Books is committed to a sustainable future
for our business, our readers and our planet.
The book in your hands is made from paper
certified by the Forest Stewardship Council.

For Donald Keene

Contents

Acknowledgements

The texts of these plays have been with me for many years, but the secondary studies on them are another matter. I wish to thank Koyama Hiroshi, a nō scholar and the director of the National Institute of Japanese Literature (Kokubungaku Kenkyū Shiryōkan) in Tokyo, and his colleagues for having helped me find so much of what I needed for this book. Similar thanks are due to Professors Omote Akira and Takemoto Mikio of the Institute for Nō Research (Nōgaku Kenkyūjo) at Hōsei University, also in Tokyo.

There are two scholars to whom I owe special gratitude. The first is my wife, Dr Susan C. Tyler, without whose learning, wit, and taste my own thinking and writing would be poorer in countless ways. The second is Donald Keene, my teacher, with whom I first read a nō play (*Matsukaze*) in the original and first translated one into English. This book is dedicated to him.

Japanese Names and the Pronunciation of Japanese

All Japanese names in this book are given in the normal Japanese order, surname first. In the name of the playwright Komparu Zenchiku, for example, 'Komparu' is the surname. Likewise, 'Nishino' is the surname of the modern scholar Nishino Haruo. However, pre-modern artists and writers are referred to by their given name, which is usually a professional style. One therefore speaks of 'a play by Zenchiku'.

Japanese is easy to pronounce recognizably. Each syllable is distinct and each vowel sounds roughly as in Italian. Vowels with a macron (a long mark) over them are simply held twice as long as their shorter counterparts; the difference is approximately that between the o in 'soft' and a rather prolónged version of the o in 'sofa'. Since there are no diphthongs in Japanese, each vowel belongs to a separate syllable. There are no silent vowels. For example, the four-syllable name Sadaie is pronounced Sa-da-i[ee]-é, and the word *ue* is pronounced u[oo]-é. Japanese has no syllable stress, in which respect it is quite unlike Italian. Each syllable of the name Tadanori, for example, is equal in length and stress.

General Introduction

The Japanese nō theatre is one of the great achievements of civilization. No art is more sophisticated than this intricate fusion of music, dance, mask, costume, and language, nor does any uphold higher ideals. Nō plays, like those of other theatres, were written to be performed, but some can stand as literature beside any play ever put between the covers of a book. The aim of *Japanese Nō Dramas* is to demonstrate that this is so and to convey all that the printed page can convey of the beauty of nō.

Nō, which means 'accomplishment' or 'perfected art', is no doubt an expression of practical as well as aesthetic ambition. The actors and musicians of the early fifteenth century, when nō achieved its classic form, needed audiences and patronage. In those days, their theatre was known more often as *sarugaku* (a word that does not lend itself to useful translation), so that *sarugaku no nō* meant something like '*sarugaku* of the best sort'. Having been enshrined long ago as a cultural treasure, modern nō no longer needs to make any claims. But despite its present, rather esoteric reputation, at home as well as abroad, it was once simply the theatre of its time.

The choice of plays

Since the twenty-four nō plays in this collection were chosen for their literary interest, they are not a representative sampling of the whole modern repertoire, which includes well over two hundred works. Some plays in the repertoire make good theatre but unsatisfactory reading; others have only modest virtue of any kind; while a few – depending on one's own tastes – are deplorable. For every masterpiece of the order of *The Fulling Block*, there are several unabashed melo-dramas; for every 'warrior play' of the quality of *Tadanori*, there are several martial thrillers. Some plays have lovely dances but only a slight text. In short, not all nō plays are worth translating for a wide audience. This selection represents only those that are.

Seeing and reading

Although the introductions, notes, stage directions, etc. surrounding these translations acknowledge matters of performance, they treat the plays above all as literary texts. This approach is not self-evident. The best Japanese authorities on nō, especially before the Second World War, have held that since the plays exist only in performance, they cannot be considered literature in any sense, and this opinion remains influential. Japan has had no tradition of reading nō as literature. By now, some critics do write literary essays on various plays, but the approach is not yet fully developed. One champion of literary analysis (Tashiro Keiichirō) has cited foreign translations, and their reception as literature, in defence of his own work.

English speakers first met nō in books, thanks to Ezra Pound's beautiful paraphrases made from the notes of Ernest Fenollosa, or to the fine translations by Arthur Waley. Yeats's interest in what he knew of nō sealed the literary reputation of nō in the English-speaking world. However, the many translations published since then have been made by translators increasingly familiar with nō not only as text but as theatre. In the last twenty years or so, many English-speaking students of nō, impressed by the difference between seeing and reading, have concerned themselves especially with performance. Some have in their turn adopted the position that nō exists only on the stage. Consequently, many recent translations are meant above all to guide the spectator or the drama student. Meanwhile, nō plays by now have been done by English-speaking actors in all sorts of styles, from modern dance with electronic music to faithful reproductions (in English or the original) of a Japanese performance. One can also find 'fusion' productions that combine nō techniques with Western ones.

Anyone interested in the plays in this book should of course see them performed, if possible. However, reading does have its place, for nō texts are so difficult to follow in performance, even for the Japanese, that they must be studied separately. Besides, some performances can be disappointing and some plays (like *Komachi at Seki-dera*) are rarely performed. In any case, nō can seldom be seen outside Japan's major cities, let alone abroad. For most people, reading is the only way to approach nō at all.

For reasons like these, *Japanese Nō Dramas* provides a certain amount of technical information about the plays for those readers who need it, but leaves many technical terms undefined. It would not help to give brief definitions of musical forms or dance types and patterns. These things must be not only seen and heard, but learned in practice.

The Introductions to the Plays

Each of these translations is preceded by an introduction, often quite a long one. This is not because the plays can be enjoyed only through a commentary, for readers of English have been moved by earlier translations presented alone. However, these are complex texts, each with its own history, literary background, and theme. Pleasure in them can only be deepened by greater knowledge of them.

By the time these plays were written, in the fifteenth century, certain works of early Japanese literature had already inspired copious commentaries. However, since nō plays were not considered literature, they did not draw concerted scholarly attention until the twentieth century. With respect to the analysis of texts, authorship, and the history or background of single plays, it is really only since about 1960 that the academic study of nō has gained strong momentum. These introductions are grounded in current Japanese scholarship.

Discussion of authorship

The introductions generally begin with a discussion of authorship. It makes a difference, from the start, to know who wrote or probably wrote a certain play. Many scholars have laboured to sift through the available evidence in order to reach the present state of knowledge on the subject. Over the past thirty years, the best-informed attributions have often changed, and disagreement continues in many cases. A sign of progress is that, with the historical documents now mastered, the debate has turned more frankly towards identifying style and the playwright's voice. These plays are not the work of anonymous craftsmen, but of individual playwrights whose voices merit recognition.

Discussion of sources

The introductions and notes also treat the textual sources of the plays. Research in this area, too, has progressed in recent decades. The playwrights represented here drew many things, from short quotations to the theme of a whole play, from earlier, classical works. Poems and themes from such imperially commissioned anthologies as the *Kokinshū* ('A Collection of Poems Ancient and Modern', 905) or *Shinkokinshū* ('A New Collection of Poems Ancient and Modern', 1206) appear again and again. So do translations of lines or couplets in Chinese, especially from *Wakan rōei shū* ('A Collection of Japanese and Chinese Poems for Chanting Aloud', 1013); for Chinese poetry had much the same standing as Latin poetry in Europe. Prose classics like *Genji monogatari* ('The Tale of Genji', early 11th c.) or *Ise monogatari* ('Tales of Ise', 10th c.) gave the playwrights some exceptionally beautiful material, and for martial themes, the epic *Heike monogatari* ('The Tale of the Taira', 13th–14th c.) provided an endlessly rich source of inspiration.

Earlier in this century, it could still be said that nō plays were a mere patchwork of quotations from such sources, but detailed studies of the plays have shown this evaluation to be ill-informed and untenable. On the contrary, the playwrights' use of their sources is original, and this makes a good reason for examining it. It is interesting to see how they shaped their material. One recent discovery is that they read the classics through glosses and commentaries, just as we do today. Knowledge of the commentaries they used may change the reading of a play.

Many plays also draw on sources outside the great classics. In the fifteenth and sixteenth centuries, most educated people, including nō playwrights, cultivated a form of group versifying known as linked verse (*renga*). The practice of linked verse required a good knowledge of the literary classics, and the imagery favoured in linked verse can be seen in many of the plays in this book. Much other literature, in both Japanese and Chinese, was available too, and included historical or religious documents of a kind not generally included under the heading of *belles-lettres*. For example, a few of these plays, such as *The Diver* and *Kureha*, are based on *engi* ('sacred origins'), a genre of sacred histories of holy sites that flourished during Japan's medieval period. (The use of the terms 'medieval' or 'middle ages' in *Japanese Nō Dramas* roughly follows Japanese usage and covers the twelfth to the sixteenth centuries inclusive.)

Discussion of theme and meaning

In performance, nō plays may be, and often are, enjoyed simply as a sequence of sights and sounds – of dance and musical forms – with a general affective import (mood, emotion) but without intellectual content. Even people wholly ignorant of nō or of the Japanese language have been deeply moved by performances of which they did not understand a single word. However, in a book of translations, the text deserves particular attention. Although nō plays are works of art, not religious or poetic treatises, they evoke important religious or poetic themes.

To understand a nō text well requires a good deal of knowledge and thought, just as to translate one requires a special knowledge of language. Since these texts have greater depth and resonance than casual reading can reveal, the analyses in this book are another stage of translation. They take into account the work of Japanese critics and scholars but do not necessarily follow it, and sometimes they offer new interpretations. As already explained, the literary reading of nō plays does not have a long history. These essays are therefore a part of an effort now being made by many people to read them better as texts.

The plays' material traces in modern times

Each introduction ends by evoking, in the present, the place where the action of the play is supposed to have occurred. These plays have fed the imagination and the later literary endeavours of many people, have entered into folklore, and have had material consequences at many sites. The fame of *Takasago* at least partly supports two rival shrines, and although the two sisters of *Pining Wind* are imaginary, one can drive to visit their graves. It is fascinating to find such material traces of the plays, genuine or fictitious, all over Japan.

The Playwrights

The theatre now called nō began to reach its present form in the mid fourteenth century. It was then a provincial theatre, centred mainly in the Yamato region south of Kyoto. Four touring troupes were affiliated with Kōfuku-ji, a great temple in the old capital of Nara, in Yamato. Komparu Gonnokami (*fl.* mid 14th c.), the original author of *The Diver*, was among the actor-playwrights of the Yamato troupes. Another was Kan'ami (1333–1384), who made key contributions to early nō. Among these was his use in plays of the *kusemai*, a song and dance form that survives in the important *kuse* section of most nō plays. Another was simply that he fathered Zeami.

Zeami (1363–1443) was the genius who created classic nō. Nothing untouched by him or his influence survives from early nō, not even the plays written by his father. Certain extant plays used to be identified with Kan'ami, even though it was recognized that Zeami must have reworked them extensively. However, the most recent scholarship suggests that Kan'ami's literary traces have all but vanished.

Zeami remembered his father's acting talent with awe, as his writings show, and Kan'ami's contemporaries appear to have been similarly impressed. In 1374, Kan'ami received the signal honour of being invited to perform nō for the first time before the shogun, the young Ashikaga Yoshimitsu (1358–1408), in Kyoto. Zeami, then a boy, also appeared on stage. Yoshimitsu instantly fell in love with him, removed him from his father's care, and brought him up at his court. This son of a provincial actor was now the protégé of the most powerful man in Japan, and he received his education from the greatest men of letters of his time.

Zeami's ability was equal to the challenge. Thanks to such patronage, he developed a theatre of beauty and grace (which were not always what country audiences called for), and could stage the most elevated works. He had a superb mind and great warmth of feeling, as this collection shows. Beside his many plays (no one can say for certain how many) he also wrote penetrating treatises on the arts of acting and playwriting. Like Shakespeare or Molière, Zeami was the master of his own troupe and an all-round man of the theatre.

Later in life, Zeami suffered severe reverses. After 1429, he and his eldest son, Motomasa (*c.* 1400–1432), were barred by the shogun Ashikaga Yoshinori (1394–1441) from the shogunal palace and from all the great performance occasions in the capital. In 1430, his second son gave up nō to become a monk, and in 1432 Motomasa died. (This book includes Motomasa's most famous play, *The Sumida River*.) Then in 1434 Zeami was exiled, for reasons unknown, to the remote island of Sado. He returned to Kyoto only a few years before his death.

Despite Zeami's pre-eminence in the history of nō, his only personal successor was his son-in-law, Komparu Zenchiku (1405–1468), the grandson of Komparu Gonnokami. Zenchiku was active not in Kyoto but in Nara, where the relatively small Komparu school of nō is based even today. Zeami thought highly of him. Few plays can be attributed to him on the basis of solid documentary evidence, but there is reason to believe that *The Kasuga Dragon God*, *The Wildwood Shrine*, and *Tatsuta* are his. These show him to have been an excellent playwright. Zenchiku, like his father-in-law, left behind several critical writings.

The latest playwright represented here is Kanze Nobumitsu (1434–1516), the author of *Benkei Aboard Ship*, although the latest play in the book is probably the anonymous *The Feather Mantle*. Nobumitsu was in the lineage of Zeami's nephew, the actor On'ami (1398–1467) who, thanks to Ashikaga Yoshinori's patronage and much against Zeami's own will, continued the formal line of succession from Kan'ami. (The name Kanze is made up of the first syllables of Kan'ami's and Zeami's names.) He was a fine playwright, too, but by his time the style of nō had changed. *Benkei Aboard Ship* is more frankly dramatic, colourful theatre than the other plays in this book.

Some plays still in the modern repertoire were probably written in the sixteenth or even the seventeenth century, and at least one (*Kusu no tsuyu*) dates from the late nineteenth. However, many of the late works have little to do with those in this book, beyond the basic performance techniques that distinguish nō from other theatres. Hundreds, if not thousands of other plays exist outside the repertoire, including some by Zeami himself. Meanwhile, new ones are still being written for special occasions, and formally correct nō plays have even been written in English and other languages.

Dramatic Roles and their Language

All the roles in nō are performed by male actors. Women study nō singing or dancing and may perform whole plays as amateurs, but even now there are not many professional women actors. Most plays have at least one masked role, unless the face of a mature man – the actor – is suitable for that of the main character. Nō masks are often very beautiful, and a fine mask may be the very soul of a performance. The costumes of nō, too, are impressively lovely. Actors playing feminine roles do not 'impersonate' women in any obvious way, for acting in nō is on an entirely different plane from ordinary acting as the term is now understood. Gestures are restrained and miming highly abstract.

At the beginning of each play in this book, a list of 'Persons in order of appearance' gives the name or description of each person in the play, together with the name of the mask, when one is used. Opposite the person's name appears the name of the corresponding role-type, as defined by Japanese usage: *waki, wakizure, shite* (often subdivided into *maeshite* and *nochijite*), *tsure, kokata,* or *ai.* Modern Japanese editions of the plays all identify speakers by role-type rather than name, although some of the earliest nō manuscripts use names or descriptive words. The idea that role-type overrides the passing identity of a figure in a single play is characteristic of nō. Music, dance, and text are similarly built up of established 'modules'. Consequently, although each performer (whether an actor or a musician) learns his part separately, nō performances are hardly rehearsed. All the parts fit together precisely, because of their modular structure.

The *waki* and *wakizure*

In most plays, the first person to appear is the *waki* ('person on the side' or 'witness'). It is difficult to generalize about the *waki*'s identity or function, since these differ visibly from play to play. (In some later plays, the differences of function between all these role-types break down.) In principle, however, the *waki* watches, from the side, the display of the *shite.* The Monk in *The Well-Cradle* perfectly follows the theoretical model of a *waki.* Often, the *waki* is accompanied by companions or attendants who are called *wakizure* ('companions to the *waki*'). These generally have little to say.

Waki and *wakizure* roles are performed by lineages of actors that are quite distinct from the *shite* lineages. *Waki* actors never perform *shite* roles. In theory, the reverse is true as well, but in fact, for various reasons, *shite* actors do sometimes perform as *waki.*

Waki figures speak in both verse and prose. Verse will be covered below, in connection with the language of the *shite.* As to prose, the *waki*'s self-introduction, at the start of the play, is a good example, and Benkei's prose speeches, in *Benkei Aboard Ship*, illustrate the style at length. It is often weighty, with a high ratio of bulk to semantic content. In performance, these passages are impressive to listen to. The translator's main difficulty is to make them sound suitably formal without allowing them to become unbearably stiff.

The *shite* and *tsure*

The *shite* ('actor') is the centre of attention in any play that follows the classic form. The role may be subdivided into *maeshite* ('*shite* in part one') and *nochijite* ('*shite* in part two'). It is the *shite* who is masked, and who sings and dances. Some plays have more than one *shite*-like figure, and in these cases, one is the *shite* and the others, defined as subordinate, are called *tsure* ('companion'). *Tsure* figures, too, can be masked, although they do not normally wear so fine a mask as the *shite*. *Shite* actors also perform *tsure* roles. Their major lineages are known as the five 'schools' of nō, discussed below. An amateur who studies nō singing (*utai*) and dancing (*shimai*) studies them as they apply to the *shite* roles.

Like the *waki*, the *shite* may speak either in prose or in verse, but verse dominates. Actually, the distinction between prose and verse, in most passages that involve the *shite*, is not nearly as clear as it is in English. There are several intermediate styles of sung prose or quasi-verse.

One of these intermediate styles is epic prose of the kind found in *Heike monogatari*. Another is the style used for passages that are, or that are meant to resemble, Japanese translations of Chinese poetry. In this book, passages of such language are laid out like verse, but against the left-hand margin of the text.

Most of the *shite*'s sung passages, in most plays, are in the metre of classical Japanese poetry: alternating five- and seven-syllable phrases. As a rule, the more intense the emotion, the more regular the metre. The *waki* sometimes sings similar verse or enters into sung verse dialogue with the *shite*.

The true poetry of nō can be extraordinarily dense and complex, even though its vocabulary is relatively restricted. The difference between the lyrical prose and the poetry of nō is roughly that between the poetry of Walt Whitman and that of Hart Crane, or between Charles Péguy and Stéphane Mallarmé. Cascades of images, telescoped into one another far beyond the limits of consecutive grammar, like double and triple exposures on film, and echoing each other in an inspired play of precise conventions, render the very concept of literal translation meaningless. The translator simply does his best (I speak of myself), sometimes not even understanding how it is that he grasps the heart of such poetry. Among these translations, *Pining Wind* probably comes the closest to conveying a glimpse of this kind of language.

Only one device of nō verse has been regularly attempted in these translations, and especially in *Pining Wind*. This is the 'pivot word' (*kakekotoba*). A word, or even a part of a word, may mean one thing when taken with what precedes it and something else when taken with what follows. The meaning 'pivots' on that word. There also exist what one might call 'pivot phrases' or 'pivot lines' that go both with what precedes and what follows, although these, unlike the pivot word, do not involve a double meaning. A particularly common pivot word in these translations is 'pine' ('pine tree' and 'to pine'), since this word corresponds precisely to the double meaning in Japanese. However, there are far more pivot words than this in the originals.

In these translations, passages originally in verse, regular or irregular, are centred on the page. Passages that look like verse but are aligned against a narrower left-hand margin are, as already explained, translated from one style or another of lyrical prose. The short passages of verse which are indented to the right of the median are poems or parts of poems quoted directly from earlier sources. A full poem makes five short lines.

The Chorus

To one side of the stage sits a chorus of about eight people. It has no identity of its own, even when it sings lines that do not clearly belong to any single figure on stage. Usually, it sings for the *shite* and occasionally, especially in part two of a play, for the *waki*. The language of chorus passages is lyrical, sung prose, or verse. Members of the chorus are all *shite* actors, sometimes senior ones. The chorus may have been less prominent than now in the early period of nō.

The *kokata*

Some plays have roles for children (*kokata*). These are always boys, and as a rule they are the sons of professional *shite* actors, in training to become professionals themselves. *Kokata* may have to remain silent and immobile for a long time, but when their turn comes to speak, they deliver their lines in ringing tones.

The *ai*

Most plays include a role-type known as the *ai*. The word can perhaps be taken to mean, literally, 'interlude', since the *ai*'s major function is usually to perform the interlude between parts one and two of the play. The principal purpose of this interlude is to fill in the interval while the *shite* actor changes costume and mask in preparation for part two. Most *ai* characters are local villagers.

Ai actors are not nō actors at all. Their main speciality is performing the comedies (*kyōgen*, 'mad words') that are traditionally done between nō plays. As a result, their bearing, dress, and language are quite different from those of either a *shite* or a *waki*. In the hierarchy of the nō world, the *shite* actor is supreme, but the *waki* has his own dignity. In comparison with either, the *ai* role is on a distinctly lower plane.

The sections of a nō play that involve the *ai* are not considered a part of the text proper. They are the province of the *kyōgen* actors, and in the past, printed nō texts omitted them entirely. Nowadays they are generally included in annotated editions, but in smaller type, and the stereotyped dialogue surrounding the *ai*'s major speeches may be left out. The full text of an interlude may compare in number of words with a major section of a nō play, but it goes by more quickly and is usually far less absorbing. Since print can exaggerate the 'weight' of an interlude, the size used for interludes here is smaller than that of the main text.

The language of the *ai* lacks the formality of the *waki*'s prose but is none the less ceremoniously verbose. Moreover, most *ai* speeches are delivered in an intentionally monotonous manner quite unlike the same actor's delivery in a *kyōgen* play. A *shite* actor may scold an overly animated *ai* for upstaging him. A translation that conveyed the combined impact of the *ai*'s language and usual delivery would be unreadably dull. In these versions, the tone of the *ai* speeches follows the overall tone of the play. The colloquial tone adopted for the *ai* parts in *Chikubu-shima*, *Benkei Aboard Ship*, and *The Mountain Crone* is in keeping with the way these exceptionally lively passages are done in performance. In *Benkei Aboard Ship*, in particular, it is essential to convey a difference of weight and dignity between the *waki*, Benkei, and the *ai*, the Boatman.

Persons speaking for one another; inconsistencies of grammatical person

Japanese avoids specifying grammatical subject, verbs are invariant as to person or number, and nouns have no plural form. This may make the subject of a verb difficult to determine with certainty. Moreover, in texts like these the very concept of 'person' may at times seem to be indistinct, or at least different from what one assumes to be normal in English. Sometimes the *waki* and *shite* seem to speak for one another, although inevitable choices of grammatical person obscure this phenomenon in English. In some Chorus passages, the reader or translator must decide from line to line who is really speaking. Finally, a speaker who seems to be in a first-person mode may suddenly shift to a third-person point of view in order to narrate his or her own actions. Various explanations of this phenomenon have been offered, but the best solution is simply to accept it.

Other Aspects of Performance

The stage assistant

In several plays, a stage assistant discreetly performs an important function by assisting the *shite* at key moments. He is a *shite* actor, and may turn out to be the most senior person on stage. His expert movements are in perfect harmony with those of the *shite*.

Music

The 'orchestra' of nō, seated at the back of the stage, consists of a flute (*nōkan*), a shoulder drum (*kotsuzumi*), and a hip drum (*ōkawa*). Many plays also require a larger drum (*taiko*) that rests in a stand placed on the boards of the stage. The cries of the drummers, eerie until one is familiar with them, are a part of the music. The music of nō is unusual and complex.

The stage and props

The stage is an independent, roofed structure, even when it is placed inside a modern theatre. Pillars at the four corners support the roof, and a bridgeway leads from the rear left-hand corner of the stage towards the 'mirror room' from which the actors enter. No scenery is used. The boards of the stage are perfectly polished, and on the wall at the back is painted a single pine tree. The lighting is constant. Some plays require a special prop, such as a boat, a grave-mound, a shrine, a gate, or a loom. All such objects are elegant but sketchy representations of what they describe. Against the distinguished plainness of the stage and props, the magnificent costumes worn by the actors stand out brilliantly, and the masks may seem to come alive.

Length of a performance

Nō texts are short but performances are long. A brief performance will take about an hour, and certain plays can last over two hours. Delivery is therefore slow, and some dances can be almost indefinitely prolonged. In general, those plays that are felt to have the highest 'dignity' (*kurai*), like *Komachi at Seki-dera*, are given the most time. It is interesting that in the fifteenth century, plays were probably performed in no more than half the time they take now. The slowing down of performances is one aspect of the refining process that has gone on over the past several centuries.

The traditional classification of the plays

The 'Remarks' that follow the list of 'Persons in order of appearance' at the head of each play start by naming what customarily defined category the play belongs to. There are five of these: (1) *waki-nō*, or 'god plays'; (2) *shura-mono*, or 'warrior plays'; (3) *kazura-mono*, often translated as 'woman plays' although the *shite* in this category is not invariably a woman; (4) *yonbamme-mono*, or 'fourth-category plays', which cannot be usefully defined further in a few words; and (5) *kiri-nō*, 'concluding plays'. These categories are always cited and discussed in connection with nō, but they are not actually of critical importance to the reader. They did not exist in the fifteenth century, although others, now less well known, did.

The 'five schools' of nō

The category of the play is followed, in most cases, by the mention 'current in all five schools of nō'. These 'schools' are named Kanze and Hōshō (which can be designated together as the 'Kamigakari schools'), and Komparu, Kongō, and Kita (the 'Shimogakari schools'). They are hereditary lineages of *shite* actors, of which by far the largest is the Kanze. Some plays are current – that is, in the formal repertoire – in only one or two schools. Each school has its characteristic style, and details of music, dance, staging, and text (especially in the prose passages) may vary from school to school.

Variant performances

There are, associated with many plays, variant performance traditions known as *kogaki*. Each school has its 'normal' manner of performing a given play, but many plays, even within the same school, have recognized, named performance variants. If a variant is adopted for a performance, its name will be printed on the programme together with the title of the play and the names of the actors and musicians. Some *kogaki* are old, some surprisingly recent. They are not a trivial matter, since certain plays can be completely transformed by the choice of a *kogaki*. This book mentions only those *kogaki* that are meaningful in terms of the information provided about each play.

The subdivisions of the plays

In the translations themselves, at the beginning of certain prose speeches or immediately to the left of the first line of a passage of verse, the reader will find an italicized Japanese word, in smaller type and enclosed by parentheses. This word is the name of a *shōdan*, or standard subsection of the play. For example, *The Diver* begins with a three-line verse section labelled *shidai*. This is followed by a nine-line *sashi*, a three-line *sageuta*, and an eleven-line *ageuta*. Then comes a prose speech labelled *tsukizerifu*. These *shōdan* names, and many others, appear in each play. They recur with different frequency and generally in a different order from play to play, although certain common patterns are easy to spot. For example, many plays begin with a *shidai* and end with a *noriji*.

The *shōdan* names provide precious information for those concerned with the musical structure of the plays. Prose *shōdan* like *nanori* ('self-introduction'), *tsukizerifu* ('arrival speech') or *mondō* ('dialogue') are easily understood, but the verse *shōdan* are musical in nature and therefore difficult to describe usefully. All passages shown as verse in these translations are sung, and each verse *shōdan*, for instance a *shidai* or an *ageuta*, has a musical form that remains constant from play to play. *Shōdan* sequences can effect comparisons between plays or conclusions about the historical evolution of a play.

The *shōdan* indications need not concern most readers, but they remain generally useful for two reasons. First, they are convenient when one wishes to refer to a specific passage of a play. In the case of *Eguchi*, for example, the *kuri–sashi–kuse* section (a section in part two made up of a *kuri*, a *sashi*, and a *kuse*) is critically important and is discussed in the introduction to that play. Second, the *shōdan* that label discrete verse passages should remind any reader that the verse is not really as continuous as it looks. At the beginning of *The Diver*, for example, four different *shōdan* are indicated during a verse passage of twenty-six lines. Even if one knows nothing about them, a new *shōdan* clearly indicates a change of topic or mood.

The stage directions

A nō play in translation needs some stage directions, yet full information on movement and gesture would be impractically bulky, and in any case, would represent only one 'school' or style. The directions included here tell what happens on stage at important moments and keep track, except during dance passages, of where the persons of the play are situated on the stage. Vital yet wordless passages are indicated in upper-case letters so that the reader should not miss them. Most are marked 'dance' or 'quasi-dance'. A dance, in particular, can last twenty minutes or more, even if it comes between two consecutive lines of verse. Other important, wordless events include a woman's donning of her lover's robe, or the dropping of a curtain around a 'hut' or 'shrine' to reveal the figure seated within.

The Religion of the Plays

As a matter of convention, all writers who discuss Japan in English speak of Shinto 'shrines' and Buddhist 'temples'. In this book, Buddhist temples are referred to by their Japanese names only. For example, Hōryū-ji means 'Hōryū Temple' ('Temple of the Law Ascendant'). In most temple names, the character read *-ji* means 'temple'. In a few, however, the same character is read *-dera*. An example is the title of the play *Komachi at Seki-dera* ('Komachi at Seki Temple').

In medieval Japan, as in medieval Europe, religion coloured all of life. Religion meant Buddhism above all, but not a Buddhism with which many people are now familiar. Zen, although present in a few plays, is unimportant beside the legacy of an older, richly complex Buddhism that embraced, more or less closely, nearly every conception of the sacred held in Japan. Even Shinto (the roster of cults of the 'native' Japanese deities) was then continuous in most respects with Buddhism, and neither excluded the other. God plays like *Takasago* may seem free of Buddhism, but the patterns of Buddhist thought are there beneath the surface, as occasional references to Buddhist matters show.

God plays evoke a perfect world that has no need of the Buddhist teaching, since Buddhism is concerned with spiritual or psychological wholeness; in a perfect world wholeness is not lost or threatened. In other kinds of plays, however, one Buddhist issue is often central: attachment, or clinging, to the objects of sense and desire, and the need to renounce this clinging. Since Buddhism teaches that this clinging is a grievous error, it is called *mōshū*, 'wrongful clinging'. In many plays, the *shite* is a spirit still clinging to some aspect of its earthly life and eager for the *waki*'s help to renounce·this clinging. When the *waki* is a monk, he normally begins by offering the spirit 'comfort and guidance' (*tomurai*) by reciting scriptural texts so as to bring the spirit peace and guide it towards the light. Later on, he confronts the spirit more directly, in a vision or dream.

An important religious issue for thinking people in medieval Japan was the relationship between art (especially dance, music, and poetry) and enlightenment, since art actually creates objects of sense. Several plays, among them *Eguchi* and *The Mountain Crone*, touch on this issue, which naturally concerned a playwright like Zeami.

The Ideal of the Capital

Although grounded in some ways in obstinate human reality, the world of nō is in other ways a world of the imagination. This is clear, for example, from the way these plays evoke the figure of the sovereign. One would never guess from them that in the fifteenth century, the emperor had no significant political or any other kind of power. The line of emperors survived, it is true, and imperial sanction was essential if a new shogun was to claim legitimacy. However, the emperor was in no position to refuse this sanction to the Ashikaga lord who asked it of him; and as the fifteenth century wore on, even the Ashikaga shogunate began to crumble. In the time of the playwright Nobumitsu, Kyoto was all but destroyed by civil war. Nevertheless, the sovereign of *Kureha* or *Takasago* presides over a halcyon world in which 'the provinces all enjoy peace and ease'. Even if the image of the sovereign includes at times that of the shogun, as some writers have suggested, it is only an ideal.

The model for the ideal reign, as *Takasago* makes clear, was that of Emperor Daigo (r. 897–930). It was more a poetic than a political ideal, since 905 is the year when the *Kokinshū* ('A Collection of Poems Ancient and Modern'), the fountainhead of the classical poetic tradition, was compiled. The Japanese preface to the *Kokinshū* (there is also one in Chinese) describes all the sounds of the world as 'song' (*uta*), which is the generic word for poetry. It is therefore one source of legitimacy for all song and music, including the art of nō. That is why, in these translations, words like 'song' or 'to sing' are often associated with matters of poetry. The significance of poetry went far beyond words.

The capital, often called Miyako, is the seat of the ideal sovereign. In *The Diver*, Miyako is Nara, the imperial capital from 710 to 784. Elsewhere, it is Kyoto, the imperial capital from 794 to 1868. Kyoto enjoyed the same sort of reputation as other royal or imperial capitals have in other countries. It was acknowledged to be the centre of civilization, and, as several plays suggest, people from Miyako were assumed to be more cultivated than those from the provinces. The plays in this book are an art of the capital.

Form, Meaning, and the Mind of Heaven and Earth

In conclusion, it is worth returning to the issue of meaning. All the longer introductions in the pages that follow assume meaning in the plays, and set out to translate something of this meaning into rationally ordered, expository language. In Japanese terms, however, the validity of doing so is not self-evident. As already noted, nō plays are often watched as sequences of dance and musical forms, without thought of intellectual content. This matter deserves further comment.

In Japanese artistic practice, form generally precedes meaning. Once form is correct, appropriate content appears. Training in the performing arts generally stresses mastery of form over theoretical knowledge; the student learns forms without a word of theoretical explanation.

Differences in talent and achievement are recognized, but talent, however brilliant, is not the foundation of accomplished performance. That foundation is form.

The same principle applies to classical poetry. There certainly were inspired poets, but for the basic practice of poetry, 'inspiration' was neither here nor there. The task was to combine learned poetic vocabulary into correct forms. From childhood on, one studied models to this end. Classical poetic manuals catalogued matters of form and vocabulary, and glossed obscure words. What poetic criticism discussed was the affective quality of a poem. The question of intellectually conceived meaning did not arise. This is not to say that the poems had no meaning; far from it. Rather, meaning transpired naturally from the appropriate choice of words and the proper execution of the form, and was not an issue in itself.

The forms of nō are more diverse in kind than those of poetry, but otherwise nō works in the same way. Most people who have read about nō are familiar with the term *yūgen*, which has a range of meaning between 'graceful elegance' and 'subtle mystery'. First used in poetic criticism, it was later applied to nō. Many writers have described nō as a theatre of *yūgen*, or treated *yūgen* as the goal or pure essence of nō. *Yūgen* arises, when it does, like the scent of a flower: from the harmony of countless perfectly realized, cellular forms. The text of a play makes up only one subcomplex of these forms. This is why nō is often held to exist only in performance. *Yūgen* transcends words.

Seen from this standpoint, the 'meaning' of a play is a sort of by-product of accomplished form – form the goal of which is *yūgen* – and not an issue in itself. Some Japanese scholarly writings on nō, including very valuable ones, leave a similar impression. Reading them, one comes to feel that meaning is an accidental by-product of history – of the evolution of an inherently meaningless motif through countless practices, documents, legends, poems, and stories.

Zeami wrote about nō in the same spirit. Intensely concerned with form, he never made interpretive comments about the plays or betrayed any wish to give them a depth reachable through language alone. None the less, his plays, above all others, give the careful reader almost inexhaustible riches. *Japanese Nō Dramas* is an acknowledgement of those riches. Whether accidental or intentional, they deserve to be seen. It is difficult to believe that Zeami himself did not carefully put them there.

Working within extremely sophisticated conventions, the classical poets and the playwrights who followed them had a wonderful freedom. Since no element of their poetry was their own, they were unencumbered by the need to be original. Zeami merely put words together in the service of his theatre. Yet as he wrote down what he hoped would make good plays, the conventions of the literature ranged themselves, through his brush, into marvellous patterns. He once wrote:

That which creates seed and blossom of the full range of nō is the mind playing through [the actor's] whole person. Just as the emptiness of crystal gives forth fire and water, ... the accomplished master creates all the colours and forms of his art out of the intention of his mind ... Many are the adornments of this noble art; many are the natural beauties that grace it. The mind that gives forth all things, even to the four seasons' flowers and leaves, snows and moon, mountains and seas – yes, even to all beings, sentient and insentient – that mind is heaven and earth.

If he danced in that spirit, surely he wrote in that spirit too.

List of Terms Used in the Stage Directions

Stage locations and features of the stage

base pillar	*shitebashira*
base square	*jōza*
before chorus	*jiutaimae*
before drums	*daishōmae*
before flute	*fueza*
bridgeway	*hashigakari*
centre	*shōchū*
chorus position	*jiutaiza*
corner	*sumi*
corner pillar	*metsukebashira*
curtain	*agemaku*
first pine, second pine, third pine	(small pine trees placed along the bridgeway, outside the railing)
flute pillar	*fuebashira*
front	*shōmensaki*
mirror room	*kagami-no-ma*
side	*wakishōmen*
side door	*kirido*
stage assistant position	*kōkenza*
witness pillar	*wakibashira*
villager position	*kyōgenza*
witness position	*wakiza* (the spot where the *waki* normally sits)
witness square	*wakiza* (the square area around the witness position)

Actions or gestures

sit   *shita ni iru* (to sit in formal
                                   Japanese posture)
weep   *shiori* (the actor brings his right
                                   hand or both hands slowly to a
                                   position before his eyes)

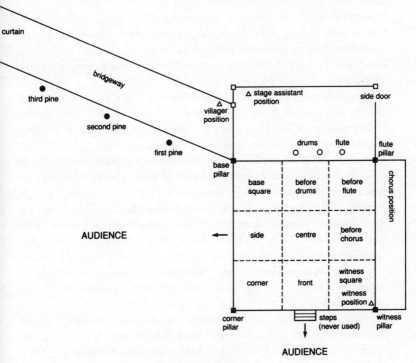

Plan of the Nō Stage

Ama · THE DIVER

The Diver is an old play. Komparu Gonnokami (*fl.* mid 14th c.), the grandfather of Komparu Zenchiku, probably wrote the original version; but part two, and especially the Dragon Princess's dance, must have been added later, perhaps by Zeami. The play is strongly flavoured compared with some others in this book, and its pious message stands out as well. In fact, *The Diver* is something of an advertisement. It urges devotion, hence pilgrimage, to a temple on the north coast of Shikoku, on Shido Bay in old Sanuki province: Shido-ji, in the present Kagawa Prefecture.

The Diver tells this temple's legendary history in the 'dream vision' form characteristic of nō. Its source appears to be *Sanshū Shido dōjō engi* ('The History of the Holy Place at Shido in the Province of Sanuki'), an example of the medieval *engi* ('sacred origins') genre.

The Fusazaki of the legend is Fujiwara no Fusazaki (681–732) who founded the so-called 'Northern House' of the Fujiwara, a lineage that, after the ninth century, dominated the imperial court. In his time the capital was Nara, whence he sets out, in the play, for Shido Bay. His purpose is to honour his mother, a diver who once lived there on the shore. Woman divers could be found all along the coast of Japan, gathering seaweed and shellfish such as abalone. Fusazaki's mother died after retrieving a priceless jewel from the deep at the request of Fusazaki's father, and the spot where she died was named, like her son, Fusazaki.

Historically, the legend is absurd, not least because Fusazaki's mother actually belonged to the powerful Soga clan. However, it has a strong logic of its own: one that affirms, first of all, the centrality not just of the Nara court, but of Fusazaki's own clan temple, Kōfuku-ji. In fact, it brazenly implies that the court and Kōfuku-ji are identical. Actually, although Kōfuku-ji had been built by Fuhito, Fusazaki's father, the institution evoked in the play is less the historical one of Fusazaki's time than Kōfuku-ji at the height of its pretensions and glory, some five centuries later. Two centuries later still, when its might was waning, Kōfuku-ji fostered early nō, and supported the troupe headed by Komparu Gonnokami. The legend of Shido-ji hints at political victories then far in the past of Kōfuku-ji, but still nostalgically remembered.

According to the legend, Fuhito's daughter (Fusazaki's sister or half-sister) was sought in marriage by no less a suitor than Kao-tsu, the founder of the T'ang dynasty in China. Once Kao-tsu (in Japanese, Kōso) had his bride, he sent three precious gifts back to Kōfuku-ji, of which one was the jewel. The *engi* describes him as willing enough to relinquish the two lesser gifts, but not the jewel. The lady wanted it desperately for her own country, and when her husband refused to part with it, she sat like one struck dumb. Sleep did not touch her eyes, nor food pass her lips, until Kao-tsu, after seeking counsel from his entire court, gave in. An ambassador bearing the gifts was despatched to Japan. But the Dragon King of the sea, too, wanted the jewel. Off the coast of Shida Bay the ship met a fearful storm, and to save it the ambassador had to throw the jewel into the waves. Dragon hands reached up to clutch it and the storm melted away.

Although *The Diver* omits the contest between Fusazaki's sister and Kao-tsu, one notes that this lady wrested the jewel from her husband just as Fusazaki's mother wrested it from the 'Dragon Palace'. Such contests for gain mark each phase of the legend. Kao-tsu desired Fuhito's daughter because she was rumoured to be an astonishing beauty, and what he got was a wife who knew how to look after her own. After the jewel's loss, Fuhito came down to Shido Bay and married a diver to get it back. In short, he used her. And when Fuhito asked her to dive for the jewel, she refused unless he named their son his heir. The dive cost her her life, but Fusazaki rose to be the Minister in Miyako. Her sacrifice had not been in vain.

The key to the legend is no doubt the jewel. Since the Buddha was visible in it, it signifies the Buddha's presence; and its difficult passage from the T'ang capital to Nara refers to Nara's acquisition, from the continent, of the Buddha's teaching and enlightenment. The *engi* claims that once the jewel was in Fuhito's hands, the Dragon King himself moved to Sarusawa Pond at Kōfuku-ji in order to protect it. The claim that the Buddha is now fully manifest in Japan, but no longer on the continent, is made plainly in *The Kasuga Dragon God*, also a Kōfuku-ji play.

It is on the shore of Shido Bay, meanwhile, that Fusazaki (so the legend says) built Shido-ji. What does Shido-ji actually have to do with the jewel that Fuhito carried off to Nara?

The Buddha in the jewel is Shaka (Shakyamuni) who preached the *Lotus Sutra*. Since the Sutra leaves no doubt that he preaches outside space and time, no particular place can plausibly claim his presence. Yet it is true, in practice, that his voice is not equally heard everywhere. For it to be heard by a sentient being at a certain spot, a sort of empowerment must occur. The transfer of the jewel to Nara empowered Miyako. *The Diver* is about the empowerment (reflected back, as it were, from Nara) of a spot on the shore of Shido Bay.

The empowerment requires, on the one hand, a being who thirsts for comfort, and, on the other, a follower of the Buddha through whom the comforting Teaching can be heard. In a nō play the suffering being is typically a spirit because the *Lotus Sutra* was chanted to guide and comfort the spirits of the dead. The spirit in a nō play appears in response to the Monk's (or, as here, the lay devotee's) presence, and hears the voice of the teaching with joy.

The model for this encounter is found in the 'Devadatta' chapter of the *Lotus Sutra*. The Buddha, who could if he wished remain silent and unseen, has instead appeared before a vast assembly to give them his teaching. In the sea, the Dragon King's youngest daughter – the lowest of beings – hears his voice. In response, she rises from the deep, bearing a jewel beyond price; gives the Buddha the jewel; and passes on (through an inevitable flicker of rebirth as a man) to the highest goal, Buddhahood. This is the Buddhist meaning of the moon reflected in the water: the moon aloft is the Buddha, the moon in the deep is any sentient being endowed – as all beings are – with the jewel of inherent Buddha-nature.

In part two of *The Diver*, the diver's spirit is this canonical Dragon Princess. She appears at the sound of the *Lotus Sutra*, chanted for her by Fusazaki or by monks acting for him. (In the *engi*, he is accompanied by the great saint Gyōki.) The moment of her enlightenment is at hand.

This moment has been prepared through two stages of the legend. First, the jewel comes down to the sea from the T'ang imperial capital, in the west, but the Dragon King rises towards it only to snatch it for himself. Second, this benighted act brings Fuhito down from Miyako, in the east, with an interested motive of his own: he wants the jewel for Kōfuku-ji. It is his descent that, in the end, brings the diver up with the jewel. She, however, is moved not by the Buddha's word, which Fuhito lacks anyway, but by the promise of advantage for her son. Both stages have hinted at the *Lotus Sutra* encounter, but with something critical missing. Fuhito and the diver are karmically bound to one another, but not in love.

Love is what Fusazaki brings down from Miyako and what brings him down: the love that informs the Buddha's word, and a son's care for his mother's repose. At last, the full *Lotus Sutra* encounter can take place. Without this love, there would be no temple and enlightenment would not be present on the shore of Shido Bay. The play says so plainly.

According to the *Lotus Sutra*, the Buddha's power to save sentient beings from the abyss of mortal peril is manifest in the compassionate bodhisattva Kannon. The divinity of Shido-ji is Kannon in his eleven-headed form. The temple is the eighty-sixth station on the venerable pilgrimage circuit of the Eighty-Eight Holy Places of Shikoku. An old pine beside the main hall spreads its branches over a 'diver's grave'. Nearby, a sacred mound enshrines the buried scrolls of the *Lotus Sutra*.

THE DIVER

Persons in order of appearance

The minister Fujiwara no Fusazaki	*kokata*
A Courtier under Fusazaki	*waki*
Two or three Attendants	*wakizure*
A woman Diver (*Fukai* mask)	*maeshite*
A Villager	*ai*
A Dragon Princess	
(*Deigan* mask with dragon headdress)	*nochijite*

Remarks: A fifth-category play (*kiri-nō*) current in all five schools of nō. Among many variant performance traditions (*kogaki*), one in the Kongō school presents the *nochijite*, in the process of achieving enlightenment, as a male dragon king; another, in the Kanze school, presents her as an enlightened being, dressed in white with a white lotus crown.

*   *   *

*To shidai music, enter Fusazaki, followed by Courtier and Attendants. They face
each other at front.*

COURTIER and ATTENDANTS

(*shidai*)   Sad to leave, we follow the new moon
              sad to leave, we follow the new moon
              out of Miyako, towards the west.

COURTIER

(*sashi*)   Heaven and earth parted aeons ago,   *They turn to audience.*
             leaving to all an eternal blessing.
             See, then, the scion of Amenokoyane: [1]

FUSAZAKI   for I am the Minister Fusazaki.
             Know, then, that my own honoured mother
             has passed away in Sanuki province,
             on Shido Bay, at the spot named Fusazaki:
             so I am informed. Now with all speed,
             I will go and pray for her repose. [2]   *Face each other.*

COURTIER and ATTENDANTS

(*sageuta*) New to the road, we climb Nara slope
             and turn for a last glance at Miyako;
             but spring mists rise, alas, to hide the hills.

(*ageuta*)   O Mount Mikasa! [3]
             Now this shore shall prosper ever more
             now this shore shall prosper ever more;
             and we who hasten to the southern sea [4]
             are swiftly come to the land of Tsu,   *Monk mimes walking.*
             pass Koya Pond and cross to Awaji

---

1. The ancestral deity of the Fujiwara, Fusazaki's clan; he was honoured at the Kasuga
Shrine in Nara.
2. Although Fusazaki may have learned of her death only recently, she actually died
thirteen years ago, as the play later makes clear. Fusazaki is now about sixteen years old.
3. A hill (283 m), celebrated in *The Dragon God of Kasuga*, that rises close to Kōfuku-ji
and the Kasuga Shrine. It is sacred to the Fujiwara ancestral deity.
4. These three lines (one is repeated) allude to a poem uttered by the Fujiwara deity as a
blessing upon Fusazaki's own lineage. The expression rendered as 'southern sea' refers
to Fudaraku, the paradise of Kannon. Like Shido-ji itself, Mount Mikasa and the
Nan'en-dō, a hall at Kōfuku-ji dedicated to the Fujiwara ancestral cult, were identified
with Fudaraku; in fact, the Shido-ji *engi* suggests it was because Fusazaki founded Shido-
ji that his line flourished so greatly. Here, the 'southern sea' no doubt refers also to the
'Spotless World in the South' where, in the *Lotus Sutra*, the Dragon Princess was reborn
in enlightenment.

that was the first land in all Japan,[5]
till we near the sea off Naruto,
loud with clashing tides, and hear afar
cries from little boats that roam the waves
cries from little boats that roam the waves.

They turn to audience.

COURTIER (*tsukizerifu*) His Excellency has travelled so swiftly that we have already reached Shido Bay. Ah, I see in the distance someone coming this way, although whether man or woman I cannot tell. I will wait for the person to approach, and inquire about the history of this place.

All proceed to witness square, where Fusazaki sits on a stool. Courtier sits upstage of him, and Attendants still further upstage, before Chorus.

To issei *music, enter Diver. In her right hand she holds a sickle and in her left a bunch of green cryptomeria fronds to evoke seaweed. She stands in base square.*

DIVER (*issei*) The sea-tangle that the divers reap

harbours a creature said to shed salt tears.

I am not one; but I too, alas,

have welling sorrows that soon wet my sleeves.

(*nanorizashi*) You see before you one who knows nothing of higher things, even though our temple is nearby. I am a diver from the hamlet of Amano, on the shore of Shido Bay in Sanuki.[6]

(*sashi*) The seafolk of Ise, so widely sung,

wait among evening waves to watch the moon

rise above the Inner and Outer Shrines;

and wind through the reeds, for them, speaks of fall.

Elsewhere, the seafolk on Suma shore

---

5. The island of Awaji, between the Kyoto-Nara region and Shikoku, was identified with the first island created by the world-creating pair in the early myths. The Naruto whirlpool (below) is off Awaji.
6. Like other, similarly humble figures in other plays, she claims to be 'without heart', that is, insensitive to the truth of the Buddha's teaching and the beauty of the turning seasons. In the passage below, she evokes other places (Ise, Suma) where seafolk like herself are sensitive to poetic pleasures, only to declare that no such pleasures are to be had on Shido Bay. This is so probably because Ise and Suma are places whose poetic value is established in the literary tradition, whereas Shido Bay is without literary associations. (The seafolk sisters of *Pining Wind*, who live at Suma, have no such disadvantage.) The twin Inner and Outer Shrines of Ise stand near Ise Bay. As for the Young Cherry Tree of Suma, it figures in *Tadanori* and is discussed in connection with that play.

break off sprays from the Young Cherry Tree
to fuel their salt fires, so honouring spring.
But we of this coast have no consolations.
Seafolk we are, but not like those others;
among our poor grasses, no flowers bloom.
Knowing no pleasures, we merely cut seaweed.

(*sageuta*) Yet, all uncut, the drifting reeds run on
yet, all uncut, the drifting reeds run on
down the streams that cut across our beach,
and into the sea; so we ourselves,
our labours done, at last meet our end.
Yes, we too grasp some truths, in our way.
Now I will start for Amano and home
now I will start for Amano and home.   *Courtier rises.*

COURTIER (*mondō*) Pardon me, my good woman, but are you one of the seafolk from this shore?

DIVER Yes, I am one of our divers.

COURTIER If you are a diver, then please do His Excellency the favour of cutting the seaweed that grows there on the bottom.

DIVER Oh dear, you are all worn out with travelling, and now, I suppose, you are hungry. My home is so poor and remote – how strange it is to see here you gentlemen from the court! Please have some seaweed! [*Holds out her 'seaweed'.*] Never mind my going to cut more. Take what I have here!

COURTIER No, no, good woman, we have no wish to consume your seaweed. It is just that the seaweed is very thick there, you see, and it prevents His Excellency from watching the moon in the water. He wishes you to remove it for him.

DIVER He wants me to cut away the seaweed so that he can see the moon? Why, yes, something like this happened long ago.[7] A

7. The Diver, once asked to bring a jewel up from the sea into the light, is now being asked to make the moon-in-the-sea visible by cutting away the seaweed that obscures the moon's reflection. This idea is at first puzzling because, optically, the moon's reflection from the surface has nothing to do with the sea floor. In any case, how could the sea be so glassy calm as to reflect a clear, round moon? And how could Fusazaki, from his low viewing angle, see a round reflection even in a mirror? However, such images are not really 'natural' ones at all, but mental abstractions. The moon's reflection corresponds to the jewel, and the seaweed that obscures it to the darkness of the 'Dragon Palace'. This seaweed also corresponds to the clouds that may hide the moon in the sky.

priceless Jewel was swallowed by the sea off our shore and claimed by the Dragon Palace.

      One of us, it was, who brought it up

CHORUS (*shidai*) round and full the moon, the tide is high

Diver gives her 'seaweed' to stage assistant and starts towards side of stage.

      round and full the moon, the tide is high,

      and for him I shall gladly cut seaweed.

COURTIER (*mondō*) A moment, please. Did you say it was a diver from here who retrieved the Jewel?

DIVER Yes, one of us dove for it and brought it up. The hamlet you see is called Amano, and that was the diver's home. Shinju Island, the island just over there, is where the Jewel was first brought back to the light. That is why its name means New Gem.[8]

COURTIER But what was the name of the Jewel itself?

DIVER Inside it you could see the Buddha Shaka, and whatever direction you looked at Him from, He always faced you. That is why the Jewel was called the Jewel That Never Turns Away.

COURTIER Why did the Chinese court send our land so marvellous a Jewel?

DIVER (*katari*) The younger sister of Lord Fuhito, who was Minister then, became Empress to Kōso in Cathay. In return, Emperor Kōso sent three treasures to Kōfuku-ji, his wife's ancestral temple: a gong of Kagen stone, another of Shuhin stone, and the Jewel That Never Turns Away. The two gongs reached the Capital, but just off this coast the priceless Jewel was claimed by the Dragon Palace. The Minister then disguised himself, came down to our shore, and took up with one of our diver girls. The pair had a son, the present Minister Fusazaki.

FUSAZAKI (*mondō*) But *I* am the Minister Fusazaki! [*Courtier sits before Fusazaki and bows low.*] What tender feelings flood me now! Good woman, please continue your story!

DIVER This is astonishing news! I never imagined the tale might concern anyone present. I have been terribly indiscreet!

                          Sits at centre.

FUSAZAKI (*kudokiguri*) I myself was born that Minister's son,

      and prosper with the Fujiwara clan;

8. Or 'true gem', i.e. pearl. Offshore islands named Tama-shima ('Gem Island') appear in passing in other plays that evoke the edge of the sea, and the sacred isle of *Chikubu-shima* resembles them. Among the treasures presently owned by the temple on Chikubu-shima is a Jewel That Never Turns Away.

          but there lingers still, in this heart of mine,
          grief that my own mother is strange to me.   *Weeps.*

  (*kudoki*) For once, a man of mine at court
          intimated to me that my mother
          belonged to the seafolk at Fusazaki
          on Shido Bay in Sanuki province,
          though discretion let him say no more.
          Then even I am of lowly birth,
          having lodged in a very humble womb!

CHORUS (*ageuta*) But never mind, for just as the moon
          but never mind, for just as the moon
          shines, still the moon, within the dewdrop,
          I am her son, and enjoyed her blessing.
          It was such thoughts that brought me here.

   Diver and Fusazaki turn to face each other.

          O how I long for that sea-mother!
          And with these words, he sheds warm tears.   *Weeps.*

DIVER   I too, who care not for higher things,

CHORUS   and whose sleeves all day are wet with brine –
          do you wish me to wet them again?   *Weeps.*
          O how your kind words have touched my heart!

  (*kuse*) That so great a lord should seek the womb
          of a girl so humble, by the sea,
          proves their bond was from lives long past.
          Just so, the sun or moon, in a small pool,
          shines brighter still. But I may not say
          that such a man is a diver's son.
          That would be madness, though it does seem,
          my lord, that you and I are linked.
          No, your noble gate, wistaria-twined,[9]
          is not for me. I shall keep my peace.   *Turns to audience.*
          These lips are sealed, and for love of you
          I shall not sully your great name.

COURTIER (*mondō*) Now that you have spoken to His Excellency of the Jewel, please show him, as well as you are able, how the Jewel was brought up from the bottom of the sea.

DIVER Very well, I will show him how it was done.

9. Wistaria (*fuji*) is the emblem of the Fujiwara clan.

(*katari*) The diver then declared, 'If I do retrieve the Jewel, please acknowledge our son as your sole heir.' The Minister soon agreed. 'Very well,' thought she, 'this is all for my son, and never mind if it costs me my life.' Round her waist she wrapped a rope a thousand fathoms long. 'Once I have the Jewel,' she said, 'I shall tug on this rope. All together you must then pull me back up.' And this the others promised to do.

Diver thrusts her fan forward like a knife, then rises. She dances and mimes vividly throughout the long passage below.

Then she drew a sharp-edged dagger,

CHORUS (*dan-uta*) leaped, and dove to the ocean deep.
Sky fused with sea, the waves were clouds
as spray beat upon her. Down she went
through the vast bulk of the rolling waters,
down and down, yet still saw no bottom.
Then, nearing the unknown sea-floor realm,
she feared that one without magic powers
could never hope to seize the Jewel.
Upon reaching the Dragon Palace,
she saw a jade tower three hundred feet high
where the Jewel now glowed, enshrined,
among offerings of incense and flowers.
Divinities there mounted strong guard:
the fellowship of the Eight Dragon Kings,
horrible fishes, and monstrous sea-beasts
whose jaws she surely would not evade.
As a woman will, she found her thoughts
flying homeward to those she loved.
'There is my child, beyond the waves,
and beside him his noble father,
but now I shall never see them again!
I cannot bear the pain of parting!'
Dissolved in tears, she turned to go,
but then bravely joined her palms in prayer:
'All hail, Kannon of Shido Temple,
in this trial, lend me your aid!'
To her forehead pressing the blade of mercy
she burst straight into the Dragon Palace.
To left and right the guards recoiled,

and in that instant she seized the Jewel.
Now she was fleeing, the guards behind her.
For this peril, she was prepared:
shifting her grip upon the dagger,
she cut herself open under the breast,
concealed the Jewel in her own body,
dropped the blade, and fainted away.
Now, the Dragon Palace abhors a corpse.
No baleful creature dared to approach,
and when the rope jerked, as agreed,
those above hauled away with joy.
Up came the diver to the sea's surface,
though at first no one knew about the Jewel.

DIVER (*kudoki*) Yes, up she came, and they pulled her out.
It seemed the monsters had done their work,
for her broken body was covered with blood.
The Jewel itself was no doubt lost,
and the diver, too, as surely dead.
At the sight, the Minister groaned aloud.
But then she whispered, under her breath,
'Look carefully just beneath my breast.'
He saw there the mark of a wound
from which he took the radiant Jewel.
And that is why, as your father promised,
you are a Minister, and your name
is Fusazaki, the name of this shore.[10]
And I myself – for why should I hide it? –
am that diver's ghost, your mother!

Fan held upright, she approaches Fusazaki, then hands him the fan: it now represents her letter.

CHORUS (*uta*) Look, then, at what I have written here,
and have no doubt. Only comfort me!

Restraining tears, goes to base square.

Now I must go back under the sea,
for I came by night, as one in a dream,
and day, alas, will be breaking soon.

10. The name Fusazaki might also be taken to mean 'at the breast'; and *saki* can mean 'cape' or 'point'.

Turns back to look at Fusazaki.

> Yes, the spell is broken; mother and child
> are sundered once more. As first light dawns,
> she slips deep under the morning tide,

Spreads arms wide, meaning that she has disappeared.

> she has vanished beneath the waves.   *Exit.*

*   *   *

Courtier goes to base pillar, looking towards curtain.

COURTIER Is any villager nearby?

Villager, who by this time has slipped in to sit at villager position, rises and stands at first pine.

VILLAGER He is asking for a villager. I will go and see what he wants. [*Turns to Courtier.*] What is it you wish, sir?

COURTIER I have something to ask of you. Please come closer.

VILLAGER Certainly, sir.

Courtier sits near Attendants, Villager at centre.

COURTIER This is no doubt a curious request, but I understand that a diver from this shore once died after bringing up a priceless jewel. Would you be good enough to tell me her story, as well as you can?

VILLAGER That certainly is a curious request, sir. I live here, it is true, but I really know very little about such things. Still, it would be too bad of me, the very first time we meet, to claim that I know nothing at all. So I will tell you the story as I myself have heard it told.

COURTIER I will be very much obliged.

VILLAGER Yes, one of our divers did retrieve a jewel, and this is how it all happened. [*He faces front.*] In Nara, the Capital, Lord Kamatari had a daughter – the younger sister of Lord Fuhito – and her name was Lady Kōhaku. They say all the world acknowledged her beauty. When Emperor Kōso heard of her, he fell hopelessly in love without even having laid eyes on her. One way or another, she ended up as Kōso's empress. And since Kōfuku-ji in Nara was her ancestral temple, the Chinese court sent it three treasures: a gong of Kagen stone, something else of Shuhin stone, and the Jewel That Never Turns Away. The gong of Kagen stone, you see, was a musical instrument. Once you struck it, it would ring on and on for ever. If you wanted to stop it ringing, you only had to hang a ninefold ecclesiastical stole over it, and then it would stop. The Shuhin stone treasure was an inkstone.[11] Whenever you wanted to write something, it would make ink

---

11. The inkstone is from a variant tradition. The *engi*, like the nō text, speaks of two musical stones.

for you even if you had no water – as much as you wanted. As for the Jewel That Never Turns Away, you could see the Buddha inside it, and whichever direction you looked at it from, He was always facing you. That was how the Jewel got its name. When the Dragon God heard about it, he wanted it for his own Dragon Palace. He thought up all sorts of schemes, too, but the ship's captain, a man named Banko, never let him get at it. The ship was near our shore when the Dragon Palace finally managed to swallow the Jewel. The Minister Fuhito was extremely disappointed to see only the other two treasures reach the Capital. He disguised himself then, came down here, and took up with one of our diver girls. The pair had a son, and after he had promised her one thing and another, she agreed to retrieve the Jewel. That island over there is where she brought it up, and that is why it is called New Gem Island. As a result, the boy became Lord Fuhito's heir, and since this spot is called Fusazaki, that is the name he was given. [*Turns again to Courtier.*] That, sir, is the way I have heard the story told. But why did you ask? I am a bit puzzled.

COURTIER Thank you very much for your account. You see, this gentleman is the Minister Fusazaki himself.

VILLAGER Is he really? Lord Fusazaki in person? Why, sir, I had absolutely no idea! And to think how I told that story! Oh, I am so embarrassed. Please, sir, do forgive me!

COURTIER No, no, you need not worry. His Excellency has come here only to pray for his mother's repose. He wishes to offer a ceremony of music for her comfort and guidance. Please assemble the musicians.

VILLAGER I understand, sir.

COURTIER And please announce that for seven days hence, all along this coast, nets are to be removed from the water. There will be no taking of life.

VILLAGER Very well, sir. [*Stands at base pillar.*] Hear me, good people, hear me! Lord Fusazaki, the Minister, has come to our shore to comfort and guide the diver who retrieved the Jewel. He has decreed that there will be a ceremony of music for her. The musicians are to assemble immediately. And he has ordered that for seven days hence, all along this coast, nets shall be removed from the water. There will be no taking of life. Please hear what I say! Hear what I say! [*Bows before Courtier.*] I made the announcement, sir.

COURTIER That is excellent.   [*Exit Villager.*]

*   *   *

Courtier sits at centre and bows to Fusazaki.

COURTIER (*mondō*) I beg your pardon, Your Excellency. It is an extraordinary tale we have just heard. You should look at the letter she gave you.

Fusazaki opens the fan he received from Diver and holds it before him in both hands.

FUSAZAKI (*unnamed*) This, then, is my late mother's writing![12]

I open the letter out and read:
'Since my spirit left for the afterworld,
thirteen years have gone by,
and the white sands have buried my body
these endless months and days.
The road of death is blacker than night.
There is no one to comfort me.
My son, if you wish to honour your mother,
then help me towards the light!'
It really was thirteen years ago!

CHORUS (*uta*) It is not possible to doubt.   *Closes fan.*
Come then, for her spirit's repose,
this temple shall have heartfelt offerings:
the Wonderful Sutra of the Lotus,
and good things from me, of every kind
and good things from me, of every kind.

To deha *music, enter Dragon Princess, carrying a sutra scroll in her left hand. Chorus starts singing as she reaches first pine, but she continues on to base square.*

(*unnamed*) *If one in a silent place, apart* . . .[13]

PRINCESS (*sashi*) O the welcome music of those words!
Thanks to this Sutra's precious teaching,
the worst of villains, Devadatta,
received the Buddha's promise of Heaven,
and the Dragon Princess, in her eighth year,
was born in the Spotless World to the south.
O go on! Go on chanting the Sutra!

Dragon Princess sits at centre, opens out her sutra scroll, and reads.

CHORUS (*unnamed*) *He grasps in depth both good and evil,*
He illumines all worlds in the ten directions

PRINCESS *and His Buddha-Body, perfectly pure,*
displays the Thirty-two Fortunate Signs.

---

12. This letter, in ornate prose rather than verse, is still voiced as song.
13. A line of verse in Chinese from the 'Merit of the Teacher' chapter of the *Lotus Sutra*. The passage a few lines below is from the 'Devadatta' chapter.

CHORUS (*noriji*) *In truth He has eighty excellent marks*
PRINCESS *with which He adorns His Dharma-Body,*
CHORUS *such that beings in Heaven adore Him*
    and Dragons and Gods are struck with awe.

    To iroe-gakari *music, Dragon Princess rolls up the scroll and hands it to Fusazaki.*
    After gazing at him a moment, she turns away and moves to base square.

    (DANCE: *hayamai*)

    She now does a hayamai *and continues dancing as text resumes.*
PRINCESS (*noriji*) By the Lotus Sutra's wonderful power
CHORUS   by the Lotus Sutra's wonderful power,
            the Eight Tribes of Celestial Dragons
            and beings both human and non-human
            all come from far away to behold
            the Dragon Princess reach Buddhahood.
            Yes, at Shido Temple in Sanuki,
            each year, the Eight Lectures on the Lotus,[14]
            and sacred services morning and evening,
            mark a holy spot where the Teaching lives:
            and all, we hear, thanks to a son's love.

    Facing side from base square, she stamps the final beat.

---

14. A course of sermons, standard in form, that was a widespread feature of *Lotus Sutra* devotion.

Atsumori

Zeami, who wrote *Atsumori*, developed in it a particularly touching passage of the epic *Heike monogatari* ('The Tale of the Taira'). The Taira clan had lorded it in Kyoto for a generation when, in 1183, the approach of the rival Minamoto forces put them to flight. The next year, they were routed from their camp on the shore at Ichi-no-tani by a daring Minamoto attack. Taking to their ships, they sailed away towards the scene of *Yashima*. Alas, one Taira youth, the gentle Atsumori, was left behind on the beach, there to be challenged by the seasoned Minamoto warrior Kumagai no Jirō Naozane. Kumagai took Atsumori's head, though he would gladly have spared him, and at the young man's waist he found a flute. To think that this noble youth had gone into battle with a flute! Disgusted with the warrior's calling and with all the crassness of the world, Kumagai entered religion and became the monk Renshō (or Rensei) of the play.

In sober fact, Atsumori may have been killed by someone else, and Kumagai became a monk some twenty years after the battle, probably in disappointment after losing a dispute over land. However, the tale told in *Heike monogatari* lived on as the truth, inspiring popular fiction, more nō plays by later playwrights, and plays for the bunraku and kabuki theatres of Edo times (1600–1868).

Zeami evoked in *Atsumori* the contrasts between Atsumori and Kumagai-Renshō. Atsumori was little more than a boy and Kumagai a mature man when they fought, but Atsumori was also a noble from Miyako while Kumagai was a rough warrior from the East. A social gulf yawned between them, even as Kumagai wept for Atsumori's youth. The flute brought home to Kumagai all the uncouthness of his own kind, and the fineness of that almost celestial world, Miyako. Yet, as Renshō, a follower of the Buddha, it is Kumagai who is in touch with higher things, while Atsumori, a restless shade, is deep in suffering. From these contrasts springs the conflict of the play: a conflict less of the battlefield than of the mind. The conflict is resolved not in victory for one side or the other, but in mutual sympathy.

Moreover, Zeami conveyed, especially in the passage on music and flutes, a concern with art that is still clearer in his *Tadanori*. He seems to have cared no more than Renshō for war.

The battlefield of Ichi-no-tani lies now within Suma-no-ura Park in Kōbe. Near a railway station that serves the park stands an old and imposing funerary monument to Atsumori. Not far away, roughly where the young mower of *Atsumori* played his flute, stands Suma-dera. This temple prospered thanks to Atsumori's legend and for centuries has exhibited a flute identified (implausibly) as Atsumori's own. Elsewhere, in Saitama Prefecture, one can still see Yūkoku-ji, the temple founded by Kumagai in 1205 on the site of his own residence. And in Kyoto, at Kōmyō-ji where Renshō is said to have trained under the great saint Hōnen, a Kumagai Chapel contains a statue of Atsumori purportedly carved by Kumagai, a painting of Atsumori, and votive monuments dedicated by the faithful to both men.

Atsumori

Persons in order of appearance

The monk Renshō, formerly the Minamoto warrior Kumagai	*waki*
A Youth (no mask)	*maeshite*
Two or three Companions to the Youth	*tsure*
A Villager	*ai*
The phantom of the Taira warrior Atsumori	
(*Atsumori* or *Jūroku* mask)	*nochijite*

Remarks: A second-category or warrior play (*shura-mono*) current in all five schools of nō.

* * *

To shidai *music, enter Renshō, carrying a rosary. He stands in base square, facing rear of stage.*

RENSHŌ (*shidai*) The world is all a dream, and he who wakes
　　　　　the world is all a dream, and he who wakes,

casting it from him, may yet know the real.

He turns to the audience.

(*nanori*) You have before you one who in his time was Kumagai no Jirō Naozane, a warrior from Musashi province. Now I have renounced the world, and Renshō is my name. It was I, you understand, who struck Atsumori down; and the great sorrow of this deed moved me to become the monk you see. Now I am setting out for Ichi-no-tani, to comfort Atsumori and guide his spirit towards enlightenment.

(*ageuta*) The wandering moon,
            issuing from among the Ninefold Clouds [1]
            issuing from among the Ninefold Clouds,
            swings southward by Yodo and Yamazaki,
            past Koya Pond and the Ikuta River,   *Mimes walking.*
            and Suma shore, loud with pounding waves,
            to Ichi-no-tani, where I have arrived
            to Ichi-no-tani, where I have arrived.

(*tsukizerifu*) Having come so swiftly, I have reached Ichi-no-tani in the province of Tsu. Ah, the past returns to mind as though it were before me now. But what is this? I hear a flute from that upper field. I will wait for the player to come by and question him about what happened here.   *Sits below witness pillar.*

To shidai *music, enter the Youth and Companions. Each carries a split bamboo pole with a bunch of mowed grass secured in the cleft. They face each other at front.*

YOUTH and COMPANIONS

(*shidai*) The sweet music of the mower's flute
            the sweet music of the mower's flute
            floats, windborne, far across the fields.

YOUTH (*sashi*) Those who gather grass on yonder hill
            now start for home, for twilight is at hand.

YOUTH and COMPANIONS

            They too head back to Suma, by the sea,
            and their way, like mine, is hardly long.
            Back and forth I ply, from hill to shore,
            heart heavy with the cares of thankless toil.

(*sageuta*) Yes, should one perchance ask after me,

1. The moon suggests the monk Renshō himself. The 'ninefold clouds' refer to Miyako. 'Ninefold', an epithet for the imperial palace, hence for the capital, refers to the nine gates of ancient Chinese palaces.

my reply would speak of lonely grief.[2]

(*ageuta*) On Suma shore

the salty drops fall fast, though were I known

the salty drops fall fast, though were I known,

I myself might hope to have a friend.[3]

Yet, having sunk so low, I am forlorn,

and those whom I once loved are strangers now.

While singing, Youth goes to stand in base square, Companions before Chorus.

But I resign myself to what life brings,

and accept what griefs are mine to bear   *Renshō rises.*

and accept what griefs are mine to bear.

RENSHŌ (*mondō*) Excuse me, mowers, but I have a question for you.

YOUTH For us, reverend sir? What is it, then?

RENSHŌ Was it one of you I just heard playing the flute?

YOUTH Yes, it was one of us.

RENSHŌ How touching! For people such as you, that is a remarkably elegant thing to do! Oh yes, it is very touching.

YOUTH It is a remarkably elegant thing, you say, for people like us to do? The proverb puts the matter well: 'Envy none above you, despise none below.' Besides,

the woodman's songs and the mower's flute

YOUTH and COMPANIONS

are called 'sylvan lays' and 'pastoral airs':[4]

they nourish, too, many a poet's work,

and ring out very bravely through the world.

You need not wonder, then, to hear me play.

RENSHŌ (*kakeai*) I do not doubt that what you say is right.

Then, 'sylvan lays' or 'pastoral airs'

YOUTH   mean the mower's flute,

RENSHŌ   the woodman's songs:

YOUTH   music to ease all the sad trials of life,

RENSHŌ   singing,

YOUTH   dancing,

2. These and the following three lines allude to the poem by Ariwara no Yukihira (818–893) that figures so prominently in *Pining Wind*. Yukihira was exiled to Suma.

3. Yukihira's poem alludes to a friend in Miyako; and the Youth is probably longing for a similar friend, in the Miyako now lost to him, who would know his true quality. In fact, his only possible friend, Renshō, is already present.

4. In a line of Chinese verse by a Japanese poet, included in *Wakan rōei shū* ('Collection of Japanese and Chinese Poems for Chanting Aloud', 1013).

RENSHŌ   fluting –

YOUTH   all these pleasures

Below, Youth begins to move and gesture in consonance with the text.

CHORUS *(ageuta)* are pastimes not unworthy of those
who care to seek out beauty: for bamboo,
who care to seek out beauty: for bamboo,
washed up by the sea, yields Little Branch,
Cicada Wing, and other famous flutes;
while this one, that the mower blows,
could be Greenleaf, as you will agree.[5]
Perhaps upon the beach at Sumiyoshi,
one might expect instead a Koma flute;[6]
but this is Suma. Imagine, if you will,
a flute of wood left from saltmakers' fires
a flute of wood left from saltmakers' fires.

Exeunt Companions. Youth, in base square, turns to Renshō.

RENSHŌ *(kakeai)* How strange! While the other mowers have gone home, you have stayed on, alone. Why is this?

YOUTH You ask why have I stayed behind? A voice called me here, chanting the Name. O be kind and grant me the Ten Invocations![7]

RENSHŌ Very gladly. I will give you the Ten Invocations, as you ask. But then tell me who you are.

YOUTH In truth, I am someone with a tie to Atsumori.

RENSHŌ   One with a tie to Atsumori?

Ah, the name recalls such memories!

Presses his palms together in prayer over his rosary.

'Namu Amida Bu,' I chant in prayer:

Youth goes down on one knee and presses his palms together.

YOUTH and RENSHŌ 'If I at last become a Buddha,

5. It was felt that bamboo washed up by the sea yielded particularly fine flutes. Atsumori's own was in fact the one named Little Branch (Saeda). The divine music of Greenleaf was legendary.

6. Because Sumiyoshi (celebrated in *Takasago*) was where ships from Koma (Korea) once used to put in. The *koma-bue* ('Koma flute') is used in the ancient court music known as *gakaku*.

7. The Name is that of Amida, the Buddha of Infinite Light, whose invocation goes *Namu Amida Bu* ('Hail Amida Buddha'). The Ten Invocations (ten callings of the Name for the benefit of another) were often requested of holy persons even by the living. Renshō's teacher, Hōnen, was an outstanding Amida devotee. In *Pining Wind*, too, the Monk invokes Amida for the spirits of the dead, although the dead are comforted more often with passages from the *Lotus Sutra*.

then all sentient beings who call my Name
in all the worlds, in the ten directions,
    will find welcome in Me, for I abandon none.'[8]

CHORUS (*uta*) Then, O monk, do not abandon me!
One calling of the Name should be enough,
    but you have comforted me by night and day –
    a most precious gift! As to my name,
    no silence I might keep could quite conceal
    the one you pray for always, dawn and dusk: *Youth rises.*
    that name is my own. And, having spoken,
    he fades away and is lost to view
    he fades away and is lost to view.   *Exit Youth.*

*   *   *

Villager entered discreetly during the ageuta *above, and sat at villager position. He now comes forward to base square.*

VILLAGER You see before you one who lives here at Suma, on the shore. Today I will go down to the beach and pass the time watching the ships sail by. [*Sees Renshō.*] Well! There's a monk I've not seen before. May I ask you, reverend sir, where you are from?

RENSHŌ I came from Miyako. Do you live nearby?

VILLAGER Yes, I do.

RENSHŌ Then would you please come nearer? I have something to ask of you.

VILLAGER Very well, reverend sir. [*Sits at centre, facing Renshō.*] Now, what is it?

RENSHŌ Something rather unexpected, perhaps. I hear this is where the Minamoto and the Taira fought, and where the young Taira noble, Atsumori, died. Would you tell me all you know of the way he met his end?

VILLAGER That certainly is an unexpected request, reverend sir. I do live here, it is true, but I really know very little about such things. Still, it would be too bad of me, the very first time we meet, to claim I know nothing at all. So I will tell you the story as I myself have heard it told.

RENSHŌ That is very kind of you.

8. The canonical vow made by Amida, before he became a Buddha, to save all beings by his grace. These lines, in Chinese, are from the sutra known in Japan as *Kammuryōju-kyō*.

VILLAGER [*Turns to audience.*] It came to pass that in the autumn of the second year of Juei, Minamoto no Yoshinaka drove the Taira clan out of Miyako. This is where they came. Then the Minamoto, bent on destroying the Taira for ever, split their army — sixty thousand and more mounted warriors — into two wings and attacked without mercy. The Taira fled.

Now one among them, a young gentleman of the fifth rank named Atsumori, was the son of Tsunemori, the Director of Palace Repairs. Atsumori was on his way down to the sea, meaning to board the imperial barge,⁹ when he realized that back in the camp he had forgotten his flute, Little Branch. He prized this flute very highly and hated to leave it behind for the enemy's taking. So he turned back, fetched the flute, and again went down to the beach. But by this time, the imperial barge and the rest of the fleet had sailed. Just as he was riding into the sea, hoping to swim his horse out to the ships, Kumagai no Jirō Naozane, a warrior from Musashi province, spread his war fan and challenged him to fight.

Atsumori wheeled his horse and closed fiercely with Kumagai. The two crashed to the ground between their mounts. But Kumagai was a very powerful man. He instantly got Atsumori under him and ripped off his helmet, meaning to take his head. He saw a youth of fifteen or sixteen, with powdered face and blackened teeth — a young man of high rank, there was no doubt about that.¹⁰ Kumagai wanted to spare him. Then he glanced behind him and saw Doi and Kajiwara riding up. A good seven or eight other warriors were with them. 'I do not wish to kill you,' said Kumagai, 'but as you can see, there are many men from my own side behind me. I will take your head myself, then, and afterwards pray with all my heart for the peace of your spirit.' So he cut off Atsumori's head. On examining the body, he found a flute in a brocade bag attached to the waist. When he showed the flute to his commander, all present wet the sleeves of their armour with tears. To think that he had been carrying a flute at a time like that! Even among all those gentlemen from the court, he must have been an especially gentle youth! Eventually, Kumagai found out that his victim had been Atsumori.

I wonder whether it's true, as they say, that Kumagai made himself into a monk to pray for Atsumori. If he was that sort of man, though, he wouldn't have killed Atsumori in the first place. But he did kill him, so the

9. The Taira had fled Kyoto with the child emperor Antoku. Antoku drowned in the final Taira defeat at Dan-no-ura, the battle evoked at the end of *Yashima*.
10. Courtiers of both sexes wore white powder and blackened their teeth. Teeth in their natural state (like Kumagai's, no doubt) were felt to be unsightly.

story must be wrong. I'd like to see that Kumagai here now! I'd kill him myself, just to make Atsumori feel better.

Well, that is the way I have heard it told. But why did you ask? I am a bit puzzled.

RENSHŌ Thank you very much for your kind account. Perhaps there is no harm in my telling you who I am. In my time I was Kumagai no Jirō Naozane, but now I am a monk and my name is Renshō. I came here, you see, to give Atsumori's spirit comfort and guidance.

VILLAGER *You* are Kumagai, who fought in the battle here? Why, I had no idea! Please excuse all the silly things I said. They say the man mighty in good is mighty, too, in evil. I'm sure it's just as true the other way round. Anyway, do go on comforting Atsumori's spirit.

RENSHŌ I assure you, I am not in the least offended. Since I came here to comfort Atsumori, I will stay on a while and continue chanting the precious Sutra[11] for him.

VILLAGER If that is your intention, then please accept lodging at my house.

RENSHŌ I will do so gratefully.

VILLAGER Very well.   [*Exit.*]

*   *   *

RENSHŌ (*ageuta*) Then it is well: to guide and comfort him
              then it is well: to guide and comfort him,
              I shall do holy rites, and through the night
              call aloud the Name for Atsumori,
              praying that he reach enlightenment
              praying that he reach enlightenment.

To issei *music, enter Atsumori, in the costume of a warrior. He stops in base square.*

ATSUMORI (*shimo-no-ei*) Across to Awaji the plovers fly,
              while the Suma barrier guard sleeps on;
              yet one, I see, keeps nightlong vigil here.
              O keeper of the pass, tell me your name.[12]

---

11. The *Lotus Sutra*. Perhaps an inconsistency introduced by analogy with other plays (this dialogue is not a part of Zeami's text), since Renshō actually chants the Name of Amida. However, it is not impossible, in practice, that he should have chanted both.

12. The barrier on the pass through the hills behind Suma was well known in poetry, as was its nameless guard. In the language of poetry, an older man seen at night at Suma can only be this guard; so that Atsumori's playful challenge, 'O keeper of the pass, tell

(*kakeai*)	Behold, Renshō: I am Atsumori.

RENSHŌ   Strange! As I chant aloud the Name,
           beating out the rhythm on this gong,
           and wakeful as ever in broad day,
           I see Atsumori come before me.
           The sight can only be a dream.

ATSUMORI   Why need you take it for a dream?
           For I have come so far to be with you
           in order to clear karma that is real.

RENSHŌ   I do not understand you: for the Name
           has power to clear away all trace of sin.
           Call once upon the name of Amida
           and your countless sins will be no more:
           so the sutra promises. As for me,
           I have always called the Name for you.
           How could sinful karma afflict you still?

ATSUMORI   Deep as the sea it runs. O lift me up,

RENSHŌ   that I too may come to Buddhahood!

ATSUMORI   Let each assure the other's life to come,

RENSHŌ   for we, once enemies,

ATSUMORI   are now become,

RENSHŌ   in very truth,

ATSUMORI   fast friends in the Law.

Below, Atsumori moves and gestures in consonance with the text.

CHORUS (*uta*) Now I understand!
                'Leave the company of an evil friend,
                cleave to the foe you judge a good man':
                and that good man is you! O I am grateful!
                How can I thank you as you deserve?
                Then I will make confession of my tale,
                and pass the night recounting it to you
                and pass the night recounting it to you.

Atsumori sits on a stool at centre, facing audience.

(*kuri*) The flowers of spring rise up and deck the trees
          to urge all upwards to illumination;
          the autumn moon plumbs the waters' depths

---

me your name,' seems intended to remind the more rustic Renshō of his place. His
words, based on a twelfth-century poem, are as elegant as the music of his flute.

to show grace from on high saving all beings.

ATSUMORI (*sashi*) Rows of Taira mansions lined the streets:
we were the leafy branches on the trees.
Like the rose of Sharon, we flowered one day;

CHORUS but as the Teaching that enjoins the Good
is seldom found,[13] birth in the human realm
quickly ends, like a spark from a flint.
This we never knew, nor understood
that vigour is followed by decline.

ATSUMORI Lords of the land, we were, but caused much grief;
CHORUS blinded by wealth, we never knew our pride.

Atsumori rises now, and dances through the kuse *passage below.*

(*kuse*) Yes, the house of Taira ruled the world
twenty years and more: a generation
that passed by as swiftly as a dream.
Then came the Juei years, and one sad fall,
when storms stripped the trees of all their leaves
and scattered them to the four directions,
we took to our fragile, leaflike ships,
and tossed in restless sleep upon the waves.
Our very dreams foretold no return.
We were like caged birds that miss the clouds,
or homing geese that have lost their way.
We never lingered long under one sky,
but travelled on for days, and months, and years,
till at last spring came round again,
and we camped here, at Ichi-no-tani.
So we stayed on, hard by Suma shore,

ATSUMORI while winds swept down upon us off the hills.
CHORUS The fields were bitterly cold. At the sea's edge
our ships huddled close, while day and night
the plovers cried, and our own poor sleeves
wilted in the spray that drenched the beach.
Together in the seafolk's huts we slept,
till we ourselves joined these villagers,
bent to their life like the wind-bent pines.

13. It is only rarely, and by great good fortune, that a sentient being is able to hear the
Buddha's teaching; and it is only as a human being that one can reach enlightenment.

The evening smoke rose from our cooking fires
while we sat about on heaps of sticks
piled upon the beach, and thought and thought
of how we were at Suma, in the wilds,
and we ourselves belonged to Suma now,
even as we wept for all our clan.

Atsumori stands before drums.

ATSUMORI (*kakeai*) Then came the sixth night of the second month.
My father, Tsunemori, summoned us
to play and dance, and sing *imayō*.[14]

RENSHŌ Why, that was the music I remember!
A flute was playing so sweetly in their camp!
We, the attackers, heard it well enough.

ATSUMORI It was Atsumori's flute, you see:
the one I took with me to my death

RENSHŌ and that you wished to play this final time,

ATSUMORI while from every throat

CHORUS rose songs and poems
(*issei*) sung in chorus to a lively beat.

(DANCE: *jo-no-mai*)

Atsumori performs a lively chū-no-mai, *ending in base square. Below, he continues
dancing and miming in consonance with the text.*

ATSUMORI (*unnamed*) Then, in time, His Majesty's ship sailed,

CHORUS (*noriji*) with the whole clan behind him in their own.
Anxious to be aboard, I sought the shore,
but all the warships and the imperial barge
stood already far, far out to sea.

ATSUMORI (*unnamed*) I was stranded. Reining in my horse,
I halted, at a loss for what to do.

CHORUS (*noriji*) There came then, galloping behind me,
Kumagai no Jirō Naozane,
shouting, 'You will not escape my arm!'
At this Atsumori wheeled his mount
and swiftly, all undaunted, drew his sword.
We first exchanged a few rapid blows,
then, still on horseback, closed to grapple, fell,

14. The popular songs (much appreciated at court) of the late twelfth century.

and wrestled on, upon the wave-washed strand.
But you had bested me, and I was slain.
Now karma brings us face to face again.
'You are my foe!' Atsumori shouts,   *Brandishes sword.*
lifting his sword to strike; but Kumagai   *Drops to one knee.*
with kindness has repaid old enmity,   *Rises, retreats.*
calling the Name to give the spirit peace.
They at last shall be reborn together
upon one lotus throne in paradise.
Renshō, you were no enemy of mine.

He drops his sword and, in base square, turns to Renshō with palms pressed together.

Pray for me, O pray for my release!
Pray for me, O pray for my release!

Facing side from base square, stamps the final beat.

This is a frightening play if one acknowledges that desire can make a fool and far worse out of any mortal this side of the grave. No one knows who wrote it, but a revised version entitled *Koi no omoni* ('Love's Heavy Burden') is by Zeami, and perhaps the original is Zeami's too. *Koi no omoni* may not be one of Zeami's most successful experiments, but *The Damask Drum* is difficult to forget.

It is also strange. Although some other plays (for example, *The Fulling Block*) take place in distant Kyushu, the setting for this one seems particularly remote in space and time. 'His Majesty's Log Palace in the province of Chikuzen' (built as a temporary residence in the mid-seventh century, at Asakura in present Fukuoka Prefecture, by Empress Saimei) might almost be in Central Asia, compared with the Suma of *Atsumori* or even the remote setting of *The Sumida River*. Perhaps this impression of alienness is due to the behaviour of the Consort in the play. Her mockery of the old man is extraordinarily harsh.

No source for the play has been found. One can point to nothing closer than an Indian story in *Hōbutsu-shū* ('A Collection of Treasures') a tenth-century compendium of Buddhist tales. There, a young fisherman, hawking his fish at the palace, catches sight of the queen and falls sick with love. His mother gets the truth from him and arranges a conclusion to the matter, with the queen's compassionate help. There is no compassion in *The Damask Drum*.

The cloth of the title is really twill (*aya*), not damask, but 'damask' is far more evocative – and suitably so – in English. Moreover, the title in this form is already well known thanks to Arthur Waley's earlier translation, and it would be a pity to change it. In any case, there are all sorts of figured twills. The *aya* of *Kureha*, for example, seems to be a figured twill so elaborate that only 'brocade' will do. Here, one imagines something fairly plain, since the old gardener mistakes it for skin.

The false drum of the play hangs in the branches of a laurel tree, the tree that grows in the moon. The drum itself stands for the moon, as motifs in poetry and in other plays attest, but this moon, like the Consort, is false. In poetry, separated lovers take comfort from the thought that both may be watching the same moon. A false moon, however, unites hearts not in love but hate. The old man drowns in the pond that should have reflected the Consort's beauty. The Consort's falseness plunges her into torment and the hapless old man into Hell.

THE DAMASK DRUM

Persons in order of appearance

A Court Official	*waki*
An Attendant to court official	*ai*
An Old Man, a gardener (*A kobujō* mask)	*maeshite*
An Imperial Consort (*Ko-omote* mask)	*tsure*
The old man's angry Phantom (*Ōakujō* mask)	*nochijite*

Remarks: A fourth-category (*yonbamme-mono*) play current in the Hōshō and Kongō schools. The Kita school performs a recent (1953) play with the same title. The Kanze and Komparu schools perform the similar *Koi no omoni* instead, although *The Damask Drum* has recently been revived in the Komparu school.

*   *   *

Stage assistant places a small laurel tree, with the drum in its branches, in a stand at front of stage.
Enter Consort, to sit on a stool at witness position. Enter then Official, followed by Attendant.
Official stops at first pine; Attendant sits at second pine.

OFFICIAL (*nanori*) You have before you an official in service at His Majesty's Log Palace in the province of Chikuzen. This residence boasts a lovely pond, known as Laurel Pond, where His Majesty is often pleased to stroll. And by this pond, the old man who sweeps the garden saw the Imperial Consort, with whom he fell desperately in love. Her Highness was moved to pity when she learned of his feelings, for love strikes where it will, high or low. In the laurel tree beside the pond, she has therefore hung a drum. She would have the old man beat upon it, and wishes him to know that when the drumbeat reaches her in the palace, she will graciously condescend to let him see her again. I will summon the old man and convey to him Her Highness's words.

(*mondō*) Are you there, my man?

ATTENDANT [*Rises.*] At your service, sir.

OFFICIAL Have that old gardener come here immediately.

ATTENDANT Very well, sir. [*Official sits at stage assistant position, with his back to audience. Attendant calls towards curtain.*] Do you hear me, old man? My master has a message for you from Her Highness. Come here this minute.

Attendant withdraws to villager position. Enter Old Man, carrying a broom. He stops at third pine.

Official then rises and returns to first pine.

OFFICIAL Well, old man, there you are. It has come to Her Highness's ears that you are now in love with her. And since she wishes to take pity on you, she has hung a drum in the laurel tree by the pond. You are to go and beat that drum. When the sound reaches her in the palace, she will graciously condescend to let you see her once more. Quickly now, go and beat the drum.

OLD MAN Yes, sir. Thank you, sir. Then I will venture to go and beat the drum.

OFFICIAL Follow me, please. [*Official stands before chorus, Old Man in base square.*] This is the drum, you see. Beat it now. Quickly!

OLD MAN Why yes, a laurel grows, or so they say, in the Palace of the Moon, and that one is a far-famed tree. But this laurel stands beside the pond. Were the drum to sound, that hangs among its branches, love might find some solace.

To the tolling of the evening bell
I shall then add the drumbeat of the days,

CHORUS (*shidai*) loud with a promise: come at sundown, come
loud with a promise: come at sundown, come.
Yes, I shall beat the drum that cries the hours.[1]

---

1. Here and below, the old man often treats the drum in the laurel tree and the palace drum that announces the time of night or day as though they were the same.

Official sits. Old Man drops his broom, takes up his fan.

OLD MAN *(issei)* To think a poor old man,
                    an aged crane already lost in night,[2]

CHORUS   must suffer yet the agonies of passion!   *Weeps.*

OLD MAN   That time goes by, I know not: all I care

CHORUS   is that a beaten drum must surely sound.

Old Man sits at centre, facing drum.

OLD MAN *(sashi)* The afterworld approaches, yet I sleep:
                     an autumn tinged with lust burdens my years.

CHORUS   Dew and tears in showers wet me through,
            and blossom-drops issued from my heart
            add new colour to these humble sleeves.[3]
            Helpless victim of love's tangled coil,

OLD MAN   I would as soon forget her, yet that wish

CHORUS   afflicts me more than all remembering.

       (kuse) So it is: in this world of ours,
            all goes for us as, for that man of old,
            went possession of a handsome horse:
            it brought him turn by turn both good and ill.[4]
            Days speed past, years fly, the future comes,
            yet where the road will lead our dewdrop life,
            we can ask of no one. O cruel fate!
            And if we know that much, why then, O why,
            must we always go so sadly wrong?   *Weeps.*

OLD MAN   Wake! calls out the lightening sky of dawn.

CHORUS   The Keeper of the Hours breaks my sleep,
            beating rapid strokes upon his drum.
            Startled awake, I leap to look abroad,   *Rises.*
            to glimpse, perhaps, the one for whom I burn,
            not knowing hers to be a damask drum,
            and feel strength gather in my aged arm.

Goes to drum, mimes beating it.

            My blows make no sound!

---

2. The crane is an emblem of longevity; in *Takasago*, too, the old couple refer to themselves as aged cranes.

3. Someone in desperate misery could be said to weep red tears of blood.

4. A Chinese story. A man had a horse, but it ran away. Searching for it, he found a magnificent steed. His son then rode the steed, fell, and broke his arm. But this misfortune let the son escape military conscription.

Can it be old age has turned me deaf?
Listening, listening now,
I hear the pond's waves, rain upon the window,
each beating as they will.
Then it is this drum that will not beat!
Is it this drum?
But why does it not sound?

Sits at centre, weeps. Below, moves and mimes in consonance with text.

(*rongi*)   Perhaps she hoped I might at last forget her.
Perhaps she is there waiting,
wondering whether I will come to her,
waiting to hear a damask drum beat loud.

OLD MAN   No one will come, this night of rain.
There will be no moon, no longed-for light
to drive the darkness from my heart.
Never will the drum beat out this hour.

CHORUS   The hours sound, and the days.
Only yesterday, it was, and then today,
I thought to behold her; yet time runs on,

OLD MAN   and she whose word I trusted will not come,

CHORUS   no, not in dream or ever. That one truth
will never leave me.

OLD MAN   Never will the drum resound,

CHORUS   nor she appear.
What will happen now?
They say the very thunder god
cannot part true lovers:[5] what explains
the gulf that cleaves me from her?   *Weeps.*
But there is no sense in living on,
angry at my fate and hating her.
Thus, into the waters of the pond,
he has cast himself and passed away,

                              Drops to one knee in base square.
cast his blighted life and passed away.   *Exit.*

*   *   *

5. A motif from an anonymous *Kokinshū* poem.

Attendant rises and comes to base square.

ATTENDANT What a sad and dreadful thing! The old man who sweeps the garden, desperate because the drum would not sound, has thrown himself into Laurel Pond and drowned. Even I, a simple man, can well imagine what was in his heart and mourn him with my tears. He was just a poor old gardener. And then, one day, he chanced to see Her Highness and conceived for her a fearful passion. Apprised of this, the lady hung, among the branches of the laurel tree beside the pond, a drum stretched with damask; and she instructed the old man to beat that drum. She let him know that should the drum resound, she would grant him his desire. The old man, overjoyed, and never imagining it to be a damask drum, went and beat upon it; but of course it gave no sound at all. Distraught then, he died. Why, even an ordinary drum, beaten by someone unused to doing so, may hardly speak. Obviously, a drum stretched with damask was bound to make no noise. As far as I can see, Her Highness meant all along to break that old man, lowly as he was, of an impudent passion. But rather than chatter on like this, I should instead announce the old man's demise. [*Sits before drums.*] I beg your pardon, sir. The old gardener, distraught that the drum would not sound, has thrown himself into the pond and drowned.

OFFICIAL What? You say the old man, distraught that the drum would not sound, has thrown himself into the pond and drowned?

ATTENDANT That is correct, sir.

OFFICIAL Then I must convey the news to Her Highness.

Attendant withdraws to villager position.

*　　*　　*

Official sits at centre, facing Consort.

OFFICIAL I beg your pardon, Your Highness. The old man whom you know was so distraught, when the drum failed to sound, that he cast himself into Laurel Pond and died. Such a being's clinging passion is very much to be feared. Do go discreetly to the pond and see for yourself.

Official and Consort rise. Consort turns towards drum.

CONSORT Good people, do you hear?
Why, the beat of waves upon the shore
sounds like the beating of a drum!
What can this mean?
How curious, this beating of a drum!

OFFICIAL	O strange, strange!
	Her Highness seems not herself.
	What can have possessed her?
CONSORT	No wonder I am not myself.
	Can it sound, a drum stretched with damask?
	When I had him beat what could not sound,
	my own wits turned!
OFFICIAL	And as she speaks, from the pond's face,
	clamorous with waves,
CONSORT	loud above the rest, there breaks
OFFICIAL	a cry:

To deha music, enter Phantom, leaning on a staff and with a demon's mallet in his sash. He stops at first pine.

PHANTOM	The waters claimed me for their sport,
	a poor old man
CHORUS	whom now a wave of clinging and of hate
	sweeps yet again into the world,
PHANTOM	though hate and grief are pale words
	beside all this I feel.
CHORUS	Single-minded rage and lust-fuelled hate *Stamps beat.*
	cloud my heart, and will forever more, *To base square.*
	for I am now a demon, haunted.
PHANTOM	Ever deeper flood
	the little fields
	of green seedling rice,
	yet my heart's waters
	spill no word abroad.[6]

That was my own wish. Yet, cruelly,
you would have had me wrest a beat
from your drum, one that could not sound.
Why did you do that? Did you then hope
to rob my heart of strength, till I should die?

Steps menacingly towards Consort and raps the stage with his staff.

Through the branches shines a heartless moon:

| CHORUS | a damask drum hung in the laurel tree. |

Gazes at the drum, palms pressed together.

6. In this anonymous poem from the *Gosenshū* (c. 951), the speaker resolves never to reveal his love.

PHANTOM   *Will* it sound, then? *Will* it?
               Try, madam. Beat the drum yourself!
Drops staff, advances towards Consort.
CHORUS   Beat, O beat, he cries, a loud tattoo,
               as when armies clash: beat, madam, beat!
Seizes the breast of Consort's robe, drags her to the laurel tree.
               and threatens her, hellish whip raised high.
*At side, brandishes mallet. Below, circles stage, then from base square calls to
Consort.*

               The drum is silent. Only her own voice
               bursts forth, wailing: Horror, horror!
               What have I done? And, in answer, his:
               Repent, repent your cruelty!
Below, continues dancing as Chorus sings.
               The Ahōrasetsu, fiends of hell
               the Ahōrasetsu, fiends of hell,
               shriek such reproaches as they strike,
               shattering bone, or driving sinners on
               to board the hideous chariot of fire.
               Their torments could not be worse.
               O terror! Where must this karma lead?
CONSORT   Retribution looms before my eyes.
CHORUS   Retribution looms before my eyes,
               whole and plain. There in the laurel tree,
               beside the tossing pond, she hung a drum
                                    Approaches laurel tree, mallet lifted high.
               that he beat, obsessed, till he grew weak
               and could bear no more. Into that pond
               he threw himself and drowned,   *Sits in base square.*
               the plaything of the waves.
               That instant he turned vengeful ghost,
               possessed her, laid a curse upon her,
                                    Rises, brandishes mallet.
               and lashed her as waves lash the shore.
               The pond freezes now, and the east wind
               sweeps in, bringing sheets of rain.
               The cold Scarlet Lotus Hells grow real.
               All one's hair bristles; and as from the waves
               a carp leaps, he, a fell serpent, leaps,

now a true demon from the afterworld,
crying, I hate you, lady, how I hate you!
and sinks in the abyss of desire.

In base square, sinks to one knee.

Chikubu-shima

No one knows who wrote *Chikubu-shima*. The play is not as deep as some, nor as literary, but its happy vigour is cheering and the sacred island it celebrates is a jewel of its kind. The interlude, with its amusing enactment of 'the mystery of our island', is particularly appealing.

Chikubu-shima ('Chikubu Isle') lies off the north shore of Lake Biwa, not very far from Kyoto. It rises to an altitude of 120 metres above a two-kilometre coastline of lava cliffs. Old stands of pine and cryptomeria, and tall bamboo groves, clothe the heights. Seen on a fine day from an approaching boat, as the Court Official sees it, Chikubu-shima inspires delighted awe.

The only landing is below the island's two temples, of which the first, dedicated to Kannon in his thousand-armed form, is a station on the pilgrimage of the thirty-three Kannons of the Western Provinces. The second enshrines the goddess Benzaiten, who appears in the play. Most of the island is closed to visitors, and the few people who live on it belong to the temples.

Like the Shido-ji of *The Diver*, Chikubu-shima has a medieval *engi*, or 'sacred history', filled with drama and rivalry. However, the playwright did not draw on the *engi* directly. Instead, he adapted similar lore (even the *engi* could not have included all the legends and fancies current about the island) to achieve a new, felicitous tone.

The island was born from a volcanic eruption. In the eighth lunar month of 82 A.D. (so runs one legend), there was an earthquake, the waters of the lake burst into flames, and the island emerged in a single night, spouting fire. The *engi* says it arose from the 'golden disc' at the bottom of the world, and describes it as a jewel for which the visible cliffs and crags are only a sheath. It also records a festival observance in which a model of the island was sunk in the lake as a jewel-offering to the Dragon God. Chikubu-shima therefore resembles the jewel recovered from the Dragon Place in *The Diver*.

Chikubu-shima features two deities: Benzaiten and the Dragon God. Benzaiten is derived from the Hindu goddess Sarasvati, whom Buddhism introduced to Japan, and like Sarasvati she is a patron of music and eloquence. She is also a water deity, which is why her shrines are found not only on islands, but on peaks and watershed ridges. Therefore she has a serpent aspect, despite her celestial form in the play. The *engi* says that after Chikubu-shima erupted from the deep, 'a goddess established her seat upon the summit of the island and a white snake wrapped itself around the island's slopes'. Medieval paintings of the island show the goddess as Benzaiten, seated upon the coiled snake. By now, official Shinto (Benzaiten counts vaguely as 'Shinto') has purged itself of snakes and dragons, and so the serpent has been banned from Benzaiten's main shrine hall. However, a White Serpent Shrine near the hall was built only recently by those who perform the traditional music and dance known as *nagauta* and *buyō*.

The Dragon God is like several others in nō, but in one passage of the *engi* he has a striking counterpart: a gigantic catfish (*namazu*), or leviathan, whose coils reach seven times around the base of the island. The *engi* narrates the meeting of this leviathan with a serpent from the heights:

In the sea off Naniwa [Osaka Bay] there is a great serpent . . . that moves up the Uji River [towards Lake Biwa, reaches the lake,] and ascends to the island's summit. It swallows humans who land on the island. Now and again it wraps its tail around a great pine tree, lowers its head to the edge of the lake, stretches forth its neck, and drinks. At this, the leviathan lifts its head, opens its mouth, seizes the serpent's head in its jaws, and tugs sharply, upending the pine and tossing it far away . . . The snake is no match for the dragon's [i.e. the leviathan's] might . . .

Perhaps this passage describes how water rises from sea to sky and then descends from the mountains as torrents that are swallowed up again by the lakes and seas. But it suggests, above all, the 'rawness' from which even a Benzaiten can spring, and the animal struggles that may underlie, somewhere in the corresponding legend, even a god play's good cheer.

The Benzaiten and Dragon God of *Chikubu-shima* are as much a pair as the serpent and leviathan of the *engi*. The nō play *Enoshima* even has Benzaiten and a Dragon God marry. One is of the heights and one of the depths. Their meeting by the lake, once purged of the *engi*'s violence, is a simple play of reflections. Therefore the interlude concerning 'our island's most sacred treasure' and 'the mystery of our island' is easy enough to understand.

'Our island's most sacred treasure' is a length of forked bamboo. The one in the Chikubu-shima Museum is labelled 'The Staff of En no Gyōja'. This wizard of the Japanese mountains is said to have meditated in a cave on Chikubu-shima. After having an awesome vision of Benzaiten, he planted his bamboo staff in the ground and declared, 'If Buddhism is to flourish here, let this staff grow!' It divided into a length of forked bamboo, sprouted leaves, and grew.

The staff then resembled the twin-trunked evergreens that are still commonly honoured at sacred sites in Japan. They show how the dualities of the world (male and female, sky and abyss, etc.) resolve themselves in union. The meeting of Benzaiten and the Dragon God does the same. And so when a shrine attendant jumps off a rock into the lake, to display 'the mystery of our island', he is not really being obscure. In fact, he may only be entertaining his guest, since at other spots around the lake, men jumped from rocks (for a fee) to amuse passing travellers. But here on the sacred island, he is probably miming non-duality, as well as one good fellow can. His leap deserves the merriest laughter of the wise.

Chikubu-shima

Persons in order of appearance

An Official from Emperor Daigo's court	*waki*
Two Companions	*wakizure*
An Old Man, a fisherman (*Warai-no-jō* mask)	*maeshite*
A Young Woman (*Ko-omote* mask)	*maetsure*
A Shrine Attendant	*ai*
A Dragon God (*Kurohige* mask, dragon headdress)	*nochijite*
The Goddess Benzaiten (*Ko-omote* mask, celestial crown)	*nochitsure*

Remarks: A first-category or god play (*waki-nō*) current in all five schools of nō. A variant performance tradition (*kogaki*) in the Kongō school reverses the *shite* and *tsure* roles throughout the play; another in the Kita school reverses the roles only in part two.

*   *   *

Stage assistant places a dais before the drums, and on it a 'shrine' surrounded by a
curtain. To shin-no-shidai *music, enter Court Official and Companions. They face*
each other at front.

OFFICIAL and COMPANIONS

> (*shidai*) Yonder, the warbler is born from bamboo
> yonder, the warbler is born from bamboo:
> to Chikubu Isle, come, hasten away![1]   *Turn to audience.*

OFFICIAL (*nanori*) You see before you an official in the service of our
most holy sovereign, His Majesty of the present Engi age.[2] Now,
since the Divine Presence upon Chikubu-shima is wonderfully
endowed with sacred power, I have obtained leave from His Majesty
and am setting forth for the island without delay.

OFFICIAL and COMPANIONS

> (*ageuta*) Ah, Shi-no-miya:[3]   *Face each other.*
> along your stream, past a noble shrine, swiftly,
> along your stream, past a noble shrine, swiftly,
> by Rushing Spring, bright with a moon
> unsullied, we pass, in this happy reign,
> on to Ōsaka Barrier, bow to the god,   *Mime walking.*
> and down from the mountains to Shiga, at last
> we reach Lake Niho and stand on the shore
> we reach Lake Niho and stand on the shore.[4]   *To audience.*

OFFICIAL (*tsukizerifu*) Having come so swiftly, we have already reached
the shore of Lake Niho. I see a fishing-boat coming our way. Wait
here a moment. I will ask the boatman to ferry us across.

COMPANIONS Please do so.

All sit in witness square. Stage assistant places a light framework representing a
boat in base square.

To issei *music, enter Young Woman followed by Old Man. They take their places*
respectively in the middle and in the stern of the boat. The Old Man carries a pole.

---

1. The characters used to write 'Chikubu-shima' suggest the meaning 'born from
bamboo', although in fact their use is probably only phonetic. One explanation of their
meaning refers to the leafing-out of En no Gyōja's bamboo staff, while another is
explained in the interlude. It is not clear how the warbler got into these lines.
2. Emperor Daigo (r. 897–930), the emperor whose reign also is the present of *Takasago*.
3. A spot on the way over Ōsaka Pass (the scene of *Semimaru*) from Kyoto to Lake
Biwa: Shinomiya-kawara, along the modern Keihan electric rail line to Ōtsu. It is near
Moroha Jinja, the shrine mentioned below.
4. Shiga refers to the southern coast of the lake, near Ōtsu; Lake Niho is the old name
for Lake Biwa.

OLD MAN (*sashi*) How lovely a scene!
          With the third moon now halfway spent,
          calm has smoothed the lake's broad face,
BOTH   misted over in morning light.
OLD MAN (*issei*) Peacefully, fishing craft ply to and fro –
BOTH   no dreary toil, ours, amid such beauty!
OLD MAN (*sashi*) We whose home is this shore village,
          morning and evening take fish of all kinds,
BOTH   in uncounted numbers, simply to live:
          for poverty keeps us ever tossing
          among the waves – ah, the sad fate,
          so to struggle through life!
BOTH (*sageuta*) Yet for all that, we fishermen
          still have this lake,
     (*ageuta*) richer than elsewhere in sights far-famed,
          richer than elsewhere in sights far-famed.
          See, then, there against hill and shore,
          Shiga, long ago the Capital;[5]
          Hanazono park and Nagara hill
          abloom as of old with mountain cherries;
          Mano inlet, where, as we sail by,
          a traveller calls:
          come, put in and see what he needs,
          come, put in and see what he needs.
Old Man mimes sculling. Court Official rises.

OFFICIAL (*mondō*) Excuse me, there in the boat! Would you take on
some passengers?

OLD MAN Do you imagine we are a ferry? Then look again. This is a
fishing-boat.

OFFICIAL I see quite well you are a fishing-boat. That is just why I
asked you whether you would take some passengers aboard. I am
on my first pilgrimage to Chikubu-shima, you understand.
          I would gladly board now the ship of the Vow.[6]

5. The site of the ancient capital of Emperor Tenchi (r. 668–671), along the Shiga coast,
continued even in the time of nō to evoke poetic nostalgia. The places mentioned below,
well known in poetry, are all in or near modern Ōtsu.
6. Usually, the Buddha Amida's vow to save all sentient beings; the ship of his Vow
ferries souls to his Western Paradise. But here the reference is also to the same
'compassionate vow' of Benzaiten, mentioned later on. Thus the 'ship of the Vow' is

OLD MAN   Indeed, indeed, this is a holy place,
                 and those who come here may well find
                 testiness like mine offends their faith;
                 nor should one trifle with the Gods' will.

YOUNG WOMAN   Our boat, then, is at your disposal.

OFFICIAL   Ah, what a pleasure! The ship of the Vow
                 surely calls me aboard at the Teaching's own prompting.[7]

OLD MAN   The air today being wonderfully calm,
                 no breeze stirs to arouse forebodings.

CHORUS (*sageuta*) Yes, the lake is perfectly smooth.
                 You who stand now on Shiga coast:
                 why, are you then from Miyako?
                 Forgive me, I beg, and please come aboard.
                 See the beauty of each stretch of shore!

Court Official sits in boat; his Companions, though with him in the mind's eye,
remain in witness square. Young Woman sits too.

   (*ageuta*) The Lake spreads its broad waters before us
                 the Lake spreads its broad waters before us,
                 here in Ōmi, happiest of lands,[8]
                 as, mountain by mountain, spring's quickening touch
                 calls forth blossoms so dazzling white,
                 they might well be snow –
                 no, one cannot tell, when, like Fuji,
                 Mount Hiei, yonder, towers to the heavens![9]
                 The lingering chill this fine spring day
                 (cold breath, surely, from Hira's peak)
                 will never stop boats sailing these waters.

   (*kuse*) Strange indeed, the fortunes of travel
                 that bring you here, far from Miyako,
                 to sail with us now in company.
                 But see! The shore has dropped behind us,
                 and ahead, Chikubu-shima looms!

bound specifically for Chikubu-shima. A sacred site like Chikubu-shima was understood
to be a paradise on earth.
7. The Teaching is the Buddhist teaching of enlightenment.
8. The old province in which the Shiga coast and Lake Biwa are situated. The gentle
beauty of its landscape was often acknowledged in poetry.
9. Mount Hiei (848 m), which rises between Kyoto and Lake Biwa, could be called 'the
Fuji of Miyako'. The Hira mentioned below rises north of Hiei, above the western shore
of the lake.

OLD MAN Shapes of green trees sink down,

CHORUS as fishes climb to sport among their branches;
  a buoyant moon swims upon the lake,
  while the moon-rabbit dances on the waves.[10]

OLD MAN (*mondō*) We have arrived. Please disembark. [*All do so. Court Official stands at witness position and Young Woman before Chorus. Stage assistant removes the boat.*] This old man will be your guide. [*Turns to shrine.*] You see here the Celestial Goddess Benzaiten. Please pray as your heart moves you to do.

Old Man sits at centre; Court Official and Companions sit in place.

OFFICIAL The place is yet more holy than I had been told. [*Bows towards shrine.*] But how very strange! [*Turns to Young Woman.*] They say this place is forbidden to women. Why is a woman with us before the shrine?[11]

OLD MAN Your question betrays your ignorance. This goddess, awesome to tell, is an incarnation of eternal enlightenment; therefore women are particularly welcome at her shrine.

YOUNG WOMAN Ah, but why mention matters so lofty?

CHORUS (*ageuta*) Benzaiten has a woman's form
    Benzaiten has a woman's form
    and her divine power is truly wondrous.
    Since she appears as a Celestial Lady,
    she and all women are really one.
    Your question shows how little you know.
  (*kuse*) She conceived her compassionate Vow,
    and reached perfect enlightenment,
    countless aeons ago.
    Since the ancient days of Lion-Power King,[12]
    she forever works all beings' weal.

OLD MAN Yes, in truth, you may feel secure,

CHORUS with our fishing craft now safely moored
    on the isle's rocky coast, beneath these pines,

---

10. This passage of Chinese, or pseudo-Chinese, verse evokes the reflections seen by one who approaches the island. (The rabbit in the moon is a Chinese motif.) Such a play of reflections may foreshadow the appearance of Benzaiten and the Dragon God.

11. Women, whom Japanese religion generally held to be impure, were barred from most sacred sites.

12. Unknown elsewhere; perhaps a previous form of Benzaiten, or the Buddha under whom she made her vow to save all beings.

for I in fact am no human being.
And having spoken, she flings wide
the Shrine's closed doors,   *Enters shrine.*
enters, and vanishes.
And the old man plunges (it seems)
into the deep, with this parting cry:
I am this Lake's own lord!
Such are his words, before the waves
conceal him and he is gone.

To raijo *music, exit Old Man.*

*   *   *

To kyōgen raijo *music, enter Shrine Attendant. He stands in base square.*

SHRINE ATTENDANT I am a priest in the service of the Celestial Lady of Chikubu-shima. Now, it was in the reign of Keikō, twelfth in the line of Human Sovereigns, that a bamboo stalk grew up in one night all the way from the Golden Disc, there at the bottom of the cosmic ocean, and formed this island. That is why the island's name is written 'Bamboo-born-island': because the island *was* born from bamboo. As for our Celestial Lady, she confers peace upon each reign in turn, and ample prosperity upon all the people. Therefore pilgrims make their way here in great numbers, filled with faith, from every corner of the land. And now, Your Excellency, you yourself, who serve our present Majesty, are here on pilgrimage to the island. That is why I have come out to thank you. Please allow me to express my thanks. [*Bows to Court Official.*] Thank you, Your Excellency, thank you. And please note, Your Excellency, that people on their first visit here generally inspect our shrine's sacred treasures. Would Your Excellency care to see them too?

OFFICIAL The treasures of the shrine? Yes indeed, I have heard of them. I should be very happy to see them.

SHRINE ATTENDANT As Your Excellency wishes. Please excuse me while I open the storehouse where they are kept. [*Goes to stage assistant position, where stage assistant hands him the 'treasures' in the lid of a large round lacquer box; then comes out to centre.*] Here, you see, is the storehouse key. Now, this is the Rosary that the Celestial Lady holds every morning and evening while perusing the Scriptures. Do examine it, Your Excellency, with all due reverence. [*To Companions.*] You too, gentlemen, please have a look. And *this* is the Forked Bamboo which is our island's most sacred treasure. Do inspect it, please. [*Shrine Attendant returns to base square.*] Well now, those are the treasures of our shrine.[13] But I must mention also the Mystery of our island. It is called the Rock-Leap. Shall I perform it for you? Would that please Your Excellency?

OFFICIAL I would be most grateful if you would perform the Rock-Leap.

SHRINE ATTENDANT Very well, Your Excellency. [*Tucks up the sleeves of his outer robe and begins to dance.*]

> Here we go now, the Rock-Leap's coming
> here we go now, the Rock-Leap's coming!
> cries he, racing to a rocky spur.
> A glance to the east: sun and moon are shining.[14]
> A glance to the west: soon the day will be done.
> Up with him, then, to that perilous pinnacle
> up with him, then, to that perilous pinnacle,
> and down he plummets to the watery deep!

[*Drops to one knee, then stands back up as though re-emerging from lake.*]
Ah, ah, ah-choo! Ah-choo!   [*Exit.*]

*   *   *

Musicians play deha *music.*

CHORUS (*kuri*) Furiously, the sanctuary quakes![15]
> Sun and moon shoot forth brilliant rays
> while, as though rising from the rim of the mountains,
> the Celestial Lady dazzles our eyes!

(BENZAITEN APPEARS)

Stage assistant drops the curtain from the shrine, revealing Benzaiten seated within on a stool.

GODDESS (*nanori-guri*) I am the Goddess Benzaiten. I make my dwelling upon this island to protect all sentient beings.

CHORUS (*noriji*) Aloft in the heavens, sweet music resounds
> aloft in the heavens, sweet music resounds,   *To base square.*
> flowers float down, and, this mild spring night,

---

13. A 'jewel that gathers both fire and water' has been omitted here; not all versions of the interlude have it. One version replaces it with 'an ox's balls and a horse's horns'.
14. A painting of such a sacred site would normally show both sun and moon in the sky.
15. Well-attested evidence of divine approbation.

moonlight gleams on the Maiden's sleeves,
as they toss and billow. O lovely vision!

(DANCE: *tennyo-no-mai*)

Goddess performs a 'dance of the heavenly maiden' and continues dancing as Chorus resumes.

CHORUS (*noriji*) On and on she dances, until in time
on and on she dances, until in time,
moon-illumined, the lake's vast waters,
whipped up by a brisk breeze, tremble and shake,
for now, from the nether depths of the world,
the Dragon God bursts forth!

Goddess sits near Court Official in witness square.
To hayafue *music, enter Dragon God, bearing a red 'fire jewel'. He also carries an* uchizue, *or 'demon mallet'.*

(*noriji*) The Dragon God rises from the lake
the Dragon God rises from the lake,
offering the visitor a glorious jewel,
all a-glitter with silver and gold: *Gives Official the jewel.*
a wonder in this world, supremely rare!

(DANCE: *mai-bataraki*)

Dragon God dances a simple but powerfully vigorous dance. He continues dancing as text resumes.

DRAGON GOD (*noriji*) Many are the Vows made to save sentient beings
CHORUS   many are the Vows made to save sentient beings:
sometimes Enlightenment displays the form
of a Celestial Lady, to answer the prayers
of beings so attuned; and sometimes the form
is a Dragon God from the nether world,
bringing peace to the realm.
Now the Celestial Lady retires to her shrine,

[*Exit Goddess; the Dragon God watches her go.*]

while the Dragon God, soaring over the lake,
tosses the waves high, churns the waters,
swarming in the mid-heaven: a mighty serpent
swarming in the mid-heaven: a mighty serpent,
to his Dragon Palace now flown and gone.

With a last flip of his sleeves, the Dragon God drops vigorously to one knee.

Eguchi

The earliest extant manuscript of *Eguchi*, dated 1424, is in Zeami's own hand. Did he then write the play? In one of his treatises he noted that the music for the *kuri–sashi–kuse* section in part two was his father's, and his manuscript lacks musical information for this section, suggesting that the passage was already known. Therefore Zeami probably wrote *Eguchi*, except for the important passage mentioned; and he probably gave the play its final form in 1424.

Eguchi dramatizes a paradoxical vision: a harlot gives a monk a sermon on human subjection to desire, points the way to liberation, then rises into the sky as the bodhisattva Fugen. No doubt Kan'ami wrote the *kuri–sashi–kuse* section, the harlot's sermon, but parts of it may have existed already as singing girls' songs. Japan in medieval times was so thoroughly Buddhist that a lady of pleasure (so one gathers from *Ryōjin hishō*, a late twelfth-century song collection) could sing poignant devotional songs and even sutra texts. Since Fugen is prominent in the *Lotus Sutra*, the vision adapted by the playwright for *Eguchi* sums up, in its way, centuries of widespread and diverse *Lotus Sutra* faith.

The vision in question appears in such medieval tale collections as *Kojidan* (early thirteenth century) or *Senjūshō* (mid thirteenth century). There, the seer is Shōkū (910–1007), not the Saigyō who figures so prominently in part one of the play; and the place is not Eguchi but Muro, a similar port further along the coast. Although the villager tells the story sketchily in the interlude, it deserves better. Here is a summary of the *Senjūshō* version:

By chanting the *Lotus Sutra*, the saintly Shōkū had freed himself from the tyranny of the senses, yet he still yearned to behold Fugen in the flesh. At last, his prayers were answered by this message: 'Look at the chief harlot of Muro: she is the true Fugen.' Shōkū went to the harlot's house, though not in his monk's habit. She served him wine, then danced while she and her girls sang him a song: 'Down in Suō, among the marshes of Mitarashi, the swift winds blow, and waves are dancing: look the pretty waves!' 'So this is the living Fugen!' thought Shōkū, and closed his eyes. Now he saw Fugen, perfectly real before him, mounted on the bodhisattva's white elephant and singing, 'On the great sea of truth unsullied, how brightly the moon of pure insight shines!' When he opened his eyes again, there was the harlot singing about waves dancing in the wind. When he closed them, there was Fugen. Awed, he took his leave. He had hardly gone when the harlot passed away.

'Yes,' added the *Senjūshō* author, 'in the presence of enlightenment, the sound of the wind and the noise of waves are all the wondrous teaching.' And he exclaimed, 'Oh, I would have loved to look upon her with eyes touched by illumination!'

Zeami knew this story, but it appears that when he set about incorporating the *kuri–sashi–kuse* section into a complete play, he did not immediately think of it. He was more concerned with writing part one, and so concentrated on the poetic exchange that is its main theme. This conclusion arises from recent research on the manuscript, which has shown that, originally, the harlot at the end of the play became not Fugen but a vague 'bodhisattva of song and dance'. Zeami chose Fugen at the last moment and edited his manuscript to accommodate the change. This stroke of genius connected the *kuri–sashi–kuse* section explicitly with Shōkū's vision and made the play unforgettable.

The poetic exchange developed in part one also appears in *Senjūshō*. It involves the great monk-poet Saigyō (1118–1190), a fascinating figure for many poets of the middle ages and beyond. Saigyō often touched on the dilemma of one who renounces the world yet cannot but love its beauty. He met the harlot of Eguchi on his way through the town. Rain drove him to seek refuge at her house, and when she would not let him in, he reproached her in a poem. Her answering poem reminded him that a monk should neither seek admission to a bawdy house nor be disappointed at being turned away from one.

In phrasing her message, the harlot played on the higher meanings of the 'moment's refuge' Saigyō desired. This refuge is less an anecdotal shelter from the rain than the body, that temporal lodging with which the spirit so mistakenly identifies its interests; and less the body than whatever object of desire arrests the mind and blinds it to the truth that all things pass. In the play, the harlot speaks clearly of desire. What she does not say as clearly, but what her own person declares, is that the model of desire is erotic love, and, of each 'moment's refuge', the other for whom one burns. One source gives her name as Tae, written with the first character of the title of the *Lotus Sutra*.

Actually, once the harlot had given Saigyō her poem, she let him in, and the two spent hours talking of the trials of life and the solace of religion. In time, Saigyō heard that she had become a nun. Nothing in the original story about her suggests she was more than human, but the play's vision of Fugen is on a quite different level: that of the harlot's highest aspirations, and Saigyō's as well.

The harlot's sermon to the monk was a popular motif in the prints of the Edo period (1600–1868). Eguchi itself was in present Higashi Yodogawa ward, Osaka. One finds there now, in the grounds of Jakkō-ji in Minami Eguchi-chō, amid factories and congested highways, a chapel named Fugen-in and carefully tended memorials to Saigyō and the harlot.

Eguchi

Persons in order of appearance

A Monk	*waki*
One or two Companions	*wakizure*
A Woman (*Waka-onna, Zō-onna* or *Ko-omote* mask)	*maeshite*
Two Singing-Girls (*Waka-onna* or *Ko-omote* mask)	*tsure*
A Villager	*ai*
The Harlot of Eguchi (*Waka-onna, Zō-onna* or *Ko-omote* mask)	*nochijite*

Remarks: A third-category play (*kazura-mono*) current in all five schools of nō.

*   *   *

To shidai *music, enter Monk and Companions. They face each other along front of stage.*

MONK and COMPANIONS

    (*shidai*) The moon has always been to me a friend
             the moon has always been to me a friend:

where then truly lies outside the world?[1]   *Face audience.*

MONK (*nanori*) You have before you a monk from the north. Lately I have been in Miyako, but now I wish to go on and see the whole land. First of all, I mean to make my way around the holy temples and shrines of the Inner Provinces.[2] Therefore, in the company of two or three companions, I am off this very day.

MONK and COMPANIONS

(*ageuta*)   With Miyako still deep in night,   *Face each other.*
we start, our Yodo River craft
gliding on by Cormorant Hall,
amid the reeds half lost in haze
pines rise above the wave-washed shore
at Eguchi, where we now arrive
at Eguchi, where we now arrive.   *Face audience.*

MONK (*tsukizerifu*) They call this place the village of Eguchi. Over there under that tree, beneath that banked rock seawall, I see a cairn. It must be a monument to someone important. I will ask a villager about it.

Companions sit before Chorus. Monk calls from near base pillar.

(*mondō*) Is a villager of Eguchi nearby?

Enter Villager. He stands at first pine.

VILLAGER You are asking for a villager, reverend sir? What is it you wish?

MONK I am a monk from the north and have never been here before. This cairn clearly commemorates someone important. Could you tell me who it is?

VILLAGER This cairn marks the grave of the famous Lady of Eguchi, a harlot who lived long ago. She was a poet, although they say that in reality she was a manifestation of the bodhisattva Fugen. Even the Venerable Saigyō made a poem for her, and I gather she gave him a lively reply. People who honour her memory give her comfort and guidance. You, too, reverend sir, should do the same.

MONK Thank you for all you have told me. I will do as you suggest.

---

1. The moon of enlightenment, the monk's companion, also recalls to the watcher all of life's sorrows, so that one who has 'left the world' finds, in the moon's company, that he has gone nowhere new. It was widely acknowledged in medieval times, on the basis of Buddhist doctrine, that suffering and enlightenment are non-dual.
2. Kinai: the central provinces surrounding Kyoto and Nara.

VILLAGER Please call on me, reverend sir, should you need anything at all.

MONK Thank you, I will.

VILLAGER Very well.

Villager retires to villager position. Monk stands at centre.

MONK (*unnamed*) This, then, is the grave of the Lady of Eguchi, so celebrated long ago.

> Here she lies, buried in the earth,
> yet her name lingers on, till even now
> her grave calls an old tale to mind,
> and I am privileged to give her comfort!

Yes, once when Saigyō asked her for a night's lodging and she was unwilling to let him in, he gave her this verse:

> To scorn the world
> and all its ways:
> *that* is hard – but you,
> the least moment's refuge
> you cling to as your own![3]

And the refuge in question was this lady's! Oh, it is a witty poem!

Monk starts towards witness square. Woman calls to him through the curtain, then slowly enters bridgeway while the Monk continues to stand at witness position.

WOMAN (*mondō*) Excuse me, traveller! What moved you to sing that poem just now?

MONK How strange! From yonder where no house is to be seen a woman has appeared, and she wants to know why I sang the poem. But why do you ask?

WOMAN   I had forgotten through the years,
    but now find my heart tinged
    by leaves of speech[4] from long ago,
    dewdrop words: *On bridgeway, faces audience.*

3. Saigyō's poem and the harlot's reply (below) appear in the imperial anthology *Shinkokinshū* (1206). They play upon the two expressions *kari no yado* ('temporary lodging', also used as a metaphor for the body) and *oshimu* ('to cling to, be unwilling to part with, withhold'). The way they do this makes the poems, and the dialogue about them, very difficult to render at once accurately and naturally; in any case, they are more witty (in the original) than beautiful. It is typical of medieval verse and of medieval readers to find higher philosophical meanings in concrete images.

4. A literal translation of *koto no ha*, 'word'. According to a canonical work on poetry (the *kana* preface to the *Kokinshū*, 905), poetry grows from its 'seed' in the heart into the 'ten thousand leaves of speech'. Saigyō's poem has filled the speaker's mind with memories.

> To scorn the world
> and all its ways:
> *that* is hard – but you,
> the least moment's refuge . . .
> Yes, so he sang – I am ashamed!
> And quite frankly to explain
> she clung to nothing as her own,
> I have now come before you here.

As the Monk speaks, the Woman comes to stand in base square.

MONK I do not understand. 'The least moment's refuge you cling to as your own!' is what Saigyō sang for the lady buried here. And while I happen to be giving this lady comfort, you come forward to assure me that she herself clung to nothing. Who are you, then?

WOMAN You see, I am ashamed of what he thought when he wrote of her clinging to a moment's refuge as her own. Tell me, then: why do you not sing her reply, which said that she did nothing of the kind?

MONK Yes, I remember. Her answer ran:

> You are one, I hear,

WOMAN
> who scorns the world,
> and my sole care
> is to say: Set not your heart
> upon a moment's refuge.

> Set not your heart, she counselled him,
> who had cast the world away,
> and would not have him look for refuge
> in a woman's house. Was she not right?

MONK
> Undoubtedly, for Saigyō, too,
> long since had scorned the moment's refuge,

WOMAN
> while she, a known woman of pleasure,
> harboured in her house forgotten troubles,
> secrets disowned by all. Upon that house,

MONK
> set not your heart, her poem warned,

WOMAN
> only because she cared for him
> who had renounced the world.

MONK
> Yet those words,

WOMAN
> 'cling to as your own',

CHORUS (*ageuta*) were a pity. After all,
> I cling to no refuge as my own
> I cling to no refuge as my own.

                    Why say I do, when evening waves[5]
                    come not again, nor the old days,
                    for now, O you who scorn the world,
                    set not your heart on worldly tales![6]

MONK and COMPANIONS

    (*rongi*)   The tale is a worldly one indeed
                the tale is a worldly one indeed,
                and as I listen to you, your own form
                grows shadowy in the twilight.
                Whoever can you be?

WOMAN   Twilight shadows
                veil the sight of me, as dimly
                veil the sight of me, as dimly
                glimmering, I am soon gone
                among the river's sinuous bends:
                a lady of the winding stream,[7]
                she of Eguchi.
                O you have seen me now!
                I am ashamed!

MONK and COMPANIONS

                There is no doubt, then: it is you
                who long ago passed away,
                a wave on the wild shore!

WOMAN   Here where I have lived a while,
                    At this my home,

MONK and COMPANIONS

                    the plum's tall sprays
                    no doubt show bravely:

WOMAN   quite unlooked for,

CHORUS   friend, you have come![8]
                Perhaps the same tree sheltered us,

5. Nō poetry often puns on the homophonous *iū* ('say') and *yū* ('evening'), even when 'evening' seems far from inevitable. Several passages in these translations omit the 'evening'.

6. That is, do not believe the gossip you hear about me – the gossip suggested by Saigyō's poem.

7. Behind the lady, the mind's eye sees the bends of the Yodo River. *Nagare* ('flow') means a stream, but *nagare no kimi* means a prostitute. A great deal of lore links women not only with water but with snakes. The goddess Benzaiten, in *Chikubu-shima*, is also a water deity, serpentine in form.

perhaps we drank from the same stream: [9]
for you see me now, the phantom
of the Lady of Eguchi! So she cries,
only her voice remaining, and is gone
only her voice remaining, and is gone.   *Exit.*

*   *   *

Villager rises and stands in base square.

VILLAGER   It was some time ago I told that monk about the Lady of Eguchi's grave. I think I will go and see whether he is still there. [*Sees Monk.*] Ah, reverend sir, there you are!

MONK   Yes, I am still here. Are you the man I talked to before?

VILLAGER   Yes, I am the one who told you about the grave.

MONK   Are you? Then please come closer. I have something to ask of you.

VILLAGER   Certainly, reverend sir. [*Sits at centre.*] Now, what is it you want?

MONK   Something a bit surprising, perhaps. In connection with this grave, would you tell me all you know about the lady herself?

VILLAGER   Your request *is* a surprise, reverend sir. I live nearby, it is true, but I really know very little about such things. Still, it would be too bad of me, the very first time we meet, to claim I know nothing at all. So I will do my best to tell you what I myself have heard.

MONK   That is very good of you.

VILLAGER   [*Faces audience.*] Now, they say the lady known as the chief harlot of Eguchi was from the village of Naka-no-mitarai-e, in Suō province.[10] For one reason or another she decided to set sail for Miyako and landed here. She liked the place when she heard its name, because Eguchi and her home village of Naka-no-mitarai-e share the same 'e' for 'river mouth'. Besides, Eguchi is quite close to Miyako. So this is where she set up her house. And they say she was the living bodhisattva Fugen. This is the story. A holy

---

8. The female speaker in this classic poem (by a man) takes it that the blossoming plum tree in her garden has caught the eye of the lover she has waited for so long, and brought him to her. In the play, this lover is the Monk, a friend in the teaching.

9. Even such fleeting contact in a past life may explain a much deeper bond in this one. A common thought in nō.

10. The *Senjūshō* version of Shōkū's vision, told in the introduction, has the harlot and her girls singing a song about Mitarashi in Suō province, in the far south of Honshū. Here, the harlot has become a native of that place, which is better known as the harbour of Murozumi. (Mitarashi and Mitarai are the same name.) The *engi* of the temple at Murozumi claims that Shōkū came there after his vision, and that a local fisherman then brought up from the sea a statue of Fugen that Shōkū kept as his own.

monk named Shōkū prayed to Kannon that he might worship the living Fugen, and one night he received, in response, a sacred dream: if he wished to worship the living Fugen, he was to look upon the chief harlot of Eguchi. So he went to Eguchi, and when he arrived, he found the lady sailing on the river with ten of her women, singing a song. Closing his eyes in peaceful contemplation, Shōkū saw the harlot revealed as Fugen. Astonished, he opened his eyes again and the vision vanished. As before, he only saw the harlot. By this he knew that the harlot was, sure enough, the living Fugen. At last, the harlot's boat turned into Fugen's white elephant and she rode off into the heavens. With longing in his heart, the Venerable Shōkū watched her vanish into the distance and rejoiced that his heartfelt prayer had been answered.

MONK Thank you very much for your account. This is why I requested it. A short while ago I was contemplating the Lady of Eguchi's grave, having just chanted the poem Saigyō gave her, when a woman appeared from nowhere, or so it seemed to me, and chanted the lady's reply. She then declared herself the lady's phantom and vanished.

VILLAGER What an extraordinary thing to have happen! Since the Lady of Eguchi allowed you to see her a moment, reverend sir, and exchanged words with you as well, you must stay on here and chant the precious Sutra for her. If you do, I am sure you will witness another wonder.

MONK My companions and I are convinced you are right. We will stay here, chant the precious Sutra, and prepare ourselves to witness a second wonder.

VILLAGER If you are staying on, I will be glad to have you at my house.

MONK That is very kind of you.

VILLAGER You are welcome.   [*Retires to villager position and soon slips out.*]

*   *   *

MONK (*unnamed*) Making my way, as I do, all around the provinces, I reach every corner of the land; and that is how it happens that I can witness such a wonder. No doubt this is all made possible by the merit one gains from becoming a monk.[11]

> Tonight, through all the moon-illumined hours
> here by the Lady of Eguchi's grave,
> for her comfort I will chant the Sutra.

11. The Monk thinks the moment a reward for his own virtue. The lady and her companions will have to speak sharply to him to open his eyes.

MONK and COMPANIONS

> (*ageuta*) Hardly have I spoken when, strange to tell
>
> hardly have I spoken when, strange to tell,
>
> a boat appears, with girls singing aboard,
>
> and lit up by the moon. Astonishing!

Monk and Companions sit in witness square. Stage assistant then places the boat (a light framework with a roof amidships, where the Lady will stand) in base square. To issei music, enter Lady of Eguchi, between two Singing-Girls. They enter the boat. The girl at the stern slips the outer robe off her right shoulder, takes a pole in hand, and mimes sculling.

LADY and SINGING-GIRLS

> (*ageuta*) Our craft, stream-borne,
>
> we moor for fleeting love, pillowed on waves
>
> we moor for fleeting love, pillowed on waves.
>
> Dreaming this sad world's familiar dream,
>
> light of body and mind, we never wake.
>
> Matsura shore, where Lady Sayo pined,
>
> still recalls her sleeves, spread all forlorn,
>
> wet with tears as her love sailed for Cathay;[12]
>
> while the poor Lady of Uji Bridge[13]
>
> pined away for one who never came.
>
> O sad to think that their lives are our own!
>
> (*ageuta*) Alas, Yoshino![14]
>
> Alas, Yoshino: all those dazzling blossoms,
>
> the loveliest snows, the clouds and the waves –
>
> all are foam on the water, and love is in vain!

MONK (*kakeai*) The night grows late, while the moon aloft

> shines down on the broad river waters,
>
> on a boat gliding by. A glance within:
>
> harlots lift their voices loud in song,
>
> most seductive in their gay finery.
>
> To whom, then, does this craft belong?

12. Matsura was a port in Kyushu. In early times, a courtier on an official mission to the continent spent some time there before he sailed, and formed a liaison with Sayo-hime, probably a singing-girl. Her grief when he left is the subject of another play, *Matsura*, that exists in Zeami's own hand and is presumably by him. It is no longer performed.

13. A mysterious figure from the poetic tradition, usually described as the deity of Uji Bridge (south of Kyoto), but probably also a kind of prostitute.

14. The name of Yoshino, a mountain village south of Nara, is practically synonymous with cherry blossoms, and the snows of Yoshino were famous too.

LADY   You wish to know whose craft this is?
            Shameful to tell, she of long ago,
            the Harlot of Eguchi, sails the stream
            by night on her boat, bright in the moonlight:
            see her before you now!
MONK   The Harlot of Eguchi – do you mean
            she who, in times gone by . . .
LADY   No, no, not times gone by! For look:
            the moon as ever shines, unchanged!
SINGING-GIRL And we, too, whom your eyes behold,
            are not the past, but wholly real!
LADY   Ah, never mind. You may well ask,
SINGING-GIRL but we shall pay no heed, we shall not tell!
LADY   Spare us your questioning![15]
LADY and SINGING-GIRLS
  (*kami-no-ei*) The waters of autumn overflow,
            sweeping our light craft along
            in moonlight, come now, bend the oar
            and merrily our sculling songs
CHORUS (*uta*) sing on, O sing! Foam on the stream,
            we sing of yearning for long ago,
            even now, harlots sailing for pleasure,
            we make our lives with a measure of song.
            Come, come, sing and play!

  *In Zeami's time all remained in the boat, but at present they step out. Singing-Girls
  sit before Chorus, Lady on a stool at centre or before drums. As Chorus sings, stage
  assistant removes the boat.*

CHORUS (*kuri*) So the Twelve Dependent Links revolve[16]
            as a coach turns round a park,
LADY   or birds sport in a wood.
CHORUS   Past lives precede past lives,

15. The Monk misses the point of what he sees. He thinks he is doing the dead a good
deed, when the living truth is before him. No wonder the ladies speak to him impa-
tiently.
16. A twelvefold, circular causal chain that brings forth from ignorance form, the senses,
desire, becoming, birth, suffering, and death: in short, the miseries of endless transmigration. This *kuri*, which is based on passages from hymns written in Chinese by the great
Japanese monks Genshin (942–1017) and Jōkei (1155–1212), may actually have been
sung by singing-girls at Eguchi and elsewhere. The same is true for much of the *sashi*
below.

LADY	till the start of all these lives
	lies beyond our knowing;
CHORUS	new births follow future births,
	and where these births will end
	there is no telling.
LADY (*sashi*)	Some enjoy the happy fruits
	of the Human Realm, or Heaven,
CHORUS	yet, distracted and confused,
	still plant no seed of Liberation.[17]
LADY	Some fall among the Evil Realms
	of the Three Paths, the Eight Agonies,
CHORUS	and, prisoners of suffering,
	conceive no Aspiration.
LADY	We ourselves have indeed received
	human bodies, ever hard to win,[18]
CHORUS	yet were born immersed in sin,
	and became, a fate most rare,
	bamboo-pliant women of the stream.
	What sorrow attends this pondering
	our reward for lives lived long ago!

Lady weeps, then rises and begins to dance and mime.

(*kuse*)	One crimson-blossoming spring morning,
	mountains in crimson brocade
	deck themselves as we look on,
	yet evening winds lure their hues away;
	one autumn dusk, all golden leaves,
	the forest's glowing, tie-dyed stuffs
	burst with colour
	that in the morning frosts will turn and fade.
	As fall winds tinge the moonlit vines,
	gentle guests sweetly converse:
	they too, once gone, will come no more.

17. There are six realms (or 'paths') of transmigration: Hell, starving ghosts, beasts, warring demons, humans, and Heaven. Rebirth among humans or in Heaven is a reward for good actions in the lower realms, but is not yet sufficient for release from transmigration. The 'three paths' (below) are the three lower realms of this scale; the 'eight agonies' attend the passage of all beings from birth to death; and 'aspiration' means aspiration to enlightenment.

18. Buddhahood can be attained only from birth as a human being, and this birth is supremely rare.

Green-curtained in their scarlet room,
lovers lie, their pillows twinned:
they all too soon will go their ways.
Yes, plants and trees that have no heart,
human beings, endowed with feeling:
which can ever evade sorrow?
This we know all too well,

LADY   yet, at times, stained with love's colours,
still harbour desires by no means shallow;

CHORUS   or hear, at times, a welcome voice,
and find love's longing runs very deep.
The heart's fond pangs, the lips' own words
lead us on to wrongful clinging.[19]
Alas, all humans wander, lost,
the realm of the Six Pollutions,
committing the Six Senses' sins; [20]
for all things seen, all things heard,
turn to the heart's confusion.

(*waka*) Fascinating!

(DANCE: *jo-no-mai*)

Lady dances a quiet jo-no-mai, *then continues to dance and mime throughout the concluding lines.*

LADY (*waka*) Fascinating!
On the vast sea of Truth Perfectly Sealed,
winds of the Five Dusts and the Six Desires
can never blow,

CHORUS   yet waves of the Real in Causal Sequence
rise each and every day
rise each and every day.[21]

LADY (*unnamed*) And the waves rise for what reason, pray?
We set our heart

19. Injurious attachment to the objects of sense perception.
20. Esoteric Buddhism defines consciousness as a sixth sense. The 'six pollutions' correspond to the six senses.
21. This *waka* was probably an independent song (*imayō*). The unchanging truth behind shifting phenomena is untouched by any turbulence, yet the chain of causation calls forth discrete sense objects, like waves on a calm sea. Desire is the wind that drives these waves.

(*noriji*)   on a moment's refuge.

CHORUS   Did we not, no sad world would be.

LADY   Lover would never yearn for lover,

CHORUS   never suffer nights of pining;

LADY   ways would never part, storm-swept,

CHORUS   O blossoms, O autumn leaves,
O moon, O snows forever falling
through the old songs, in vain refrain!

LADY   (*uta*)   Yes, all things are a moment's refuge

CHORUS   yes, all things are a moment's refuge.
Never set your heart upon them:
that was my own warning to him.
I will leave you now, she cries,
revealed as the bodhisattva
Fugen, the All-Wise.
Her boat is a white elephant:
in glory she mounts dazzling clouds
and sails off westward through the skies,[22]
leaving behind her gratitude and joy
leaving behind her gratitude and joy.

22. A white elephant is Fugen's canonical mount, and she sails away westward as though she and her mount were the moon. *Bodaishinron* ('A Treatise on the Mind of Enlightenment'), an essential Buddhist treatise, compares the mind of Fugen to the disc of the moon.

Funa Benkei · BENKEI ABOARD SHIP

Benkei Aboard Ship, by Kanze Nobumitsu (1434–1516), differs from most of the plays in this book by being relatively late and unabashedly theatrical. The 'villager' (a boatman) is integral to the action, and the *shite* of part two contrasts thrillingly with the *shite* of part one: the actor who has just played a grieving beauty now takes the role of a warrior's vengeful ghost. Poetic depth and resonance are not the issue. *Benkei Aboard Ship* is richly varied entertainment.

The Benkei of the title fought under Minamoto no Yoshitsune, the late twelfth-century commander who routed the Taira forces at Ichi-no-tani (see the introduction to *Atsumori*) and again at Yashima and Dan-no-ura. Yoshitsune appears in many nō plays, including Zeami's *Yashima*. But in *Yashima* he is a mature warrior. Why, in *Benkei Aboard Ship*, should he be played by a child and seem smaller than life, while Benkei – who does not figure in *Yashima* at all – seems so much larger?

For one thing, between the events of *Yashima* and those of *Benkei Aboard Ship*, Yoshitsune met with misfortune. He had won his battles on behalf of Yoritomo, his elder brother, who was soon to become Shogun. Yet Yoritomo did not reward him. Instead, he heeded the slander of Yoshitsune's villainous rival – or so it is said – and sought to have him killed. *Benkei Aboard Ship* starts as Yoshitsune, suddenly reduced to flight, slips out of Kyoto for ever. The time is late in 1185.

However, the greater difference between the two Yoshitsunes has to do with the playwrights and their sources. Zeami's is from the epic *Heike monogatari* ('The Tale of the Taira'). For *Benkei Aboard Ship*, however, Nobumitsu looked to the much later *Gikeiki* ('Record of Yoshitsune'), a fantastic work that tells how Yoshitsune, as a child, learned the art of arms from a supernatural master; how he then bested the awesomely powerful warrior-monk Benkei; and how Benkei swore service to him. The Benkei and Yoshitsune of *Gikeiki* are mythical types: Benkei a paragon of loyalty and Yoshitsune a sort of eternal youth, curiously dependent on his brawny retainer. None the less, the custom of having Yoshitsune played by a child seems not to date from

Nobumitsu's own time. At the expense of dramatic interest (how could a boy be a great general and Shizuka's lover?) it throws the roles of Shizuka and Tomomori into sharper relief as pure spectacle, and leaves Benkei as the uncontested master of the play.

Nobumitsu followed only the spirit of *Gikeiki*, for he freely adapted its content to his own purpose. For example, *Benkei Aboard Ship* has Yoshitsune send his mistress, the dancer Shizuka, back to Kyoto, then sail from Daimotsu shore to his victorious encounter with the ghost. In *Gikeiki*, however, Yoshitsune and Shizuka flee together, from the same Daimotsu shore, towards the Yoshino mountains. Tomomori, the Taira ghost, is largely a fantasy too, though one Taira commander did bear that name. The fantasy is not frivolous, however. Japanese religion fears the spirits of those who died violently or in the grip of rage, and the wrath of the Taira ghosts is a theme that lasted in folklore and the theatre into the present century.

Daimotsu shore was north-west of present Osaka. The area is now an industrial zone built largely on reclaimed land. A faded sign in a vacant lot marks the imagined spot where Shizuka danced her farewell.

BENKEI ABOARD SHIP

Persons in order of appearance

Musashibō Benkei	*waki*
Two or three Warriors under Yoshitsune's command	*wakizure*
Minamoto no Yoshitsune	*kokata*
A Boatman	*ai*
Shizuka Gozen (*Waka-onna*, *Ko-omote* or *Fukai* mask)	*maeshite*
Taira no Tomomori (*Mikazuki* or *Awa-otoko* mask)	*nochijite*

Remarks: A fifth-category play (*kiri-nō*) current in all five schools of nō.

*   *   *

To shidai *music, enter Yoshitsune, Benkei and Warriors. They stand facing each other along front of stage.*

BENKEI and WARRIORS

    (*shidai*) Boldly today we don travel wear

             boldly today we don travel wear:

             and when shall we set eyes on Miyako again?   *Face audience.*

BENKEI (*nanori*) You see here before you one whose home is near the Western Pagoda on Mount Hiei.[1] Musashibō Benkei is my name. My noble lord, His Honour the Magistrate,[2] has on Yoritomo's order led an army westward and destroyed the Taira, who once were so proud; and the two brothers should therefore be as close as the sun and moon in the sky. Yet a despicable villain's slander has made them enemies to one another. No words can describe the tragedy of this misunderstanding. And now my lord, in deference to his older brother, has hastily withdrawn from Miyako and set out for the Western Provinces. The better to make plain his perfect innocence, he has slipped away in the dead of night towards Amagasaki in the province of Tsu, and Daimotsu Shore.

    (*sashi*) The time is the first year of the Bunji era;[3]

             Yoritomo and Yoshitsune now stand at odds.

             Yes, the die is cast: what must be will be.

YOSHITSUNE Prudently, the Magistrate abandons Miyako

             before all roads are barred against him,

BENKEI   bound away for the lands of the west.

YOSHITSUNE By dark of night,

             with a rising moon aloft in the heavens,

BENKEI and WARRIORS

             he arises to flee the Capital we love.

             Only last year, it was,

             he bravely rode forth to quell the Taira.

             How different his leaving now,

             sadly disappointed, with a mere dozen men,

             all trusted companions, in boats down the river,[4]

    (*sageuta*) adrift on the stream like clouds and waters,   *Face each other.*

1. The religious community on Mount Hiei, near Kyoto, included a force of warrior-monks, thousands strong, who were not fully ordained. Benkei was one of them. The Western Pagoda defined one of the three main areas on the mountain.

2. Yoshitsune's modest court title, Hōgan, designated the third-ranking officer in the Imperial Police.

3. 1185.

4. The Yodo River, the same one as in the corresponding passage of *Atsumori* and several other plays. It was the main route from Kyoto down to Osaka Bay.

our lives, like all lives, the sport of fate.

(*ageuta*)   Let all the world
whisper as it will: He of Iwashimizu [5]
whisper as it will: He of Iwashimizu
knows full well, with insight divine,
the pure at heart. Before His lofty form
we bow and pass by until, soon,   *Benkei mimes walking.*
waves and tides draw us on, heart-weary,
to Daimotsu shore: we have arrived
at Daimotsu shore: we have arrived.   *Face audience.*

BENKEI (*tsukizerifu*) Having come so swiftly, we have already reached Daimotsu shore in the province of Tsu. Someone I have long known lives nearby. I will go and ask him to give my lord lodging.

WARRIORS   Very well.

BENKEI [*To Yoshitsune.*] In the meantime, my lord, please wait here.

Yoshitsune sits on a stool at witness position, with Warriors upstage of him. Benkei goes to base square. Boatman has meanwhile slipped in to sit at villager position.

BENKEI (*mondō*) I beg your pardon! Is the owner of this house at home?

BOATMAN Who's there? Ah, Master Benkei, it's you! Do tell me, please, what brings you here.

BENKEI I am accompanying my lord and he needs lodging for the night.

BOATMAN I understand. Then please conduct him into my inner room.

BENKEI As my lord will then be going on to the Western Provinces,[6] we will also need a ship.

BOATMAN Very well. I'll see to it.

Boatman returns to villager position.

Benkei, at centre, goes down on one knee facing Yoshitsune.

BENKEI (*mondō*) I beg your pardon, my lord, but I find myself obliged to raise a delicate subject. Mistress Shizuka seems to have come here with you. I am afraid, however, that under the circumstances, her presence beside you is most unsuitable. With all due apologies, I simply must ask you to have her return to the Capital.

YOSHITSUNE In this matter, Benkei, do as you think best.

5. Hachiman, a powerful divinity claimed by the Minamoto as the deity of their clan. From Iwashimizu, his shrine on Otoko-yama along the river, he protected Kyoto.
6. The provinces along the Inland Sea.

BENKEI Very well, my lord. [*Returns to base square.*] Now I must go and announce his decision. [*Goes to first pine.*] Excuse me, but may I ask whether Mistress Shizuka is within? I, Benkei, have a message for her from my lord.

Shizuka enters through curtain and stops at third pine.

SHIZUKA This is a great surprise, Master Benkei. What is this message you have brought me?

BENKEI The lord whom I serve sends you these words. 'I am deeply touched that you should have wished to come so far with me. Under the circumstances, however, your presence beside me is unsuitable. I must ask you to return to Miyako.' That is the message he would have you heed.

SHIZUKA I had not thought ever to hear such words from him. No, I had meant to stay by him even to the ends of the earth. Oh, I trusted him, but there is nothing firm to trust in one faithless at heart. Alas, alas, what am I to do?

BENKEI I quite understand your feelings. But please tell me the answer I should take to my lord.

SHIZUKA Why, if by going on with him I place him in any danger at all, I will gladly stay behind.

BENKEI No, no, you exaggerate. Danger is not the issue. What matters is that you should stay behind and not follow him.

SHIZUKA Having given this message of his a little more thought, Master Benkei, I believe it comes from no one but yourself. I shall go to see him and give him my reply in person.

BENKEI That, madam, must be as you wish. Permit me to accompany you. [*Both come on stage. Benkei, before drums, kneels and bows towards Yoshitsune.*] I beg your pardon, my lord, but Mistress Shizuka is here to speak with you.

YOSHITSUNE Please have her come to me. [*Benkei sits before Chorus, Shizuka at centre.*] Dearest Shizuka, to my consternation I find myself a hunted man, and you have already come far with me on my flight. This touches my heart deeply. However, you must not accompany me further on my journey across the sea. I beg you, return to Miyako and wait there for happier days.

SHIZUKA Then it was, after all, my lord's own idea that I should go! Master Benkei, it was wrong of me to speak angrily to you, and I apologize. Oh, when I think how I talked to you, I am sorely ashamed.

BENKEI No, no, it was nothing, nothing at all. But people will talk, and our lord is concerned for his honour.

        Do not imagine his love has changed,
        cries Benkei, shedding tears of sorrow.

SHIZUKA   Alas, do not grieve for me!
        I, who count for naught,
        feel no bitterness, no anger at all.
        Here my love is setting forth far across the sea,
(*ageuta*)   and wind and wave
        (may they speed him on!)
        for Shizuka now must bar the way
        for Shizuka now must bar the way,
        she cries, in tears.
        By the sacred charms of all powers divine
        he swore that his heart would always be true.
        How quickly he changed!
        Ah, but more precious in my sight, by far,
        than my own love, is this life of mine,
        for surely one day,
        I will be with him once more.

YOSHITSUNE (*mondō*) A word, Benkei.

BENKEI At your service, my lord.

YOSHITSUNE Give Shizuka a cup of wine.

BENKEI Most willingly, my lord. [*Opens his fan and mimes pouring wine.*]

(*kakeai*)   A chrysanthemum promise of pure happiness[7]
        through ages everlasting fills the noble cup
        Benkei now offers stricken Shizuka.

SHIZUKA   For myself, as my love leaves me,
        I feel wholly lost: my sight grows dim,
        tears choke my speech.

BENKEI   No, no, lady, do not grieve so!
        Only sing, instead, to honour his sailing
        far across the sea, a happy song!
        And, so encouraged,

SHIZUKA   Shizuka rises, barely catches
        the hour's right mode[8] and begins to sing:

(*ei*) The ferry sails from port in a now kindly breeze;

---

7. The chrysanthemum being the flower of long life, 'chrysanthemum wine' conferred longevity.
8. The proper musical mode depended upon time, season, and setting.

Across the waves my place of exile stands under a clear sky.[9]

Stage assistant gives Benkei an eboshi *hat. He lifts it with both hands.*

BENKEI (*mondō*) Here are a dancer's hat and robe. Please put them on.[10]

To ashirai *music, Shizuka retires to sit in flute square. Benkei sits beside her, but it is the stage assistant who places the hat on her head. She then rises and begins to dance. Benkei goes to sit before Chorus.*

SHIZUKA (*issei*) I who have no heart to rise and dance,

CHORUS   wave my sleeves now in sorrow and shame.

(QUASI-DANCE: *iroe*)

To music, Shizuka performs an iroe *circuit round the stage.*

SHIZUKA (*sashi*) They tell the tale of how Lord Tōshu[11]
               took his king, Kōsen,

CHORUS   to Mount Kaikei, and there hid away,
               revolving in his mind many a deep plan
               to regain Kōsen his throne;
               then at last destroyed the King of Go,
               accomplishing what Kōsen had dreamed.

    (*kuse*) In this way Kōsen, a second time,
               took in hand his kingdom,
               and cleared the shame he had known at Kaikei:
               all because Lord Tōshu was so wise and brave.
               Thus a minister of Etsu, loyal to his king,
               could himself have seized the reins of government,
               gaining from his deed both lofty renown
               and all the wealth his heart could have desired.

---

9. Lines in Chinese by a Japanese poet, from the *Wakan rōei shū* ('Collection of Japanese and Chinese Poems for Chanting Aloud', 1013). They evoke the gallant spirit of one condemned to unjust exile.

10. Shizuka was a *shirabyōshi* dancer, a kind of female entertainer that flourished in the late twelfth and thirteenth centuries. A *shirabyōshi* danced wearing a man's hat and robe, and this costume was assimilated as a motif into plays like *The Well-Cradle* or *Pining Wind*.

11. This story from ancient Chinese history was quite well known in Japan. For this climactic scene of part one, it provides a decorative (although approximate) example for Yoshitsune's own situation. The states of Wu (in Japanese, Go) and Yüeh (Etsu) were at war, and Kou-chien (Kōsen), the King of Yüeh, was ignominiously defeated by Wu at Mount Hui-chi (Kaikei). Kou-chien and his minister T'ao-chu (Tōshu) then hid in the Hui-chi wilderness for twenty years until T'ao-chu's stratagems allowed Kou-chien to defeat Wu after all. T'ao-chu then retired from the world.

Yet he knew full well
that with fame now won and honour secure,
wisely to withdraw was the way of Heaven,
and instead plied the oar in his little boat
to enjoy the Great Lake and its noble waters.

SHIZUKA Such cases have been known, for as dawn came,
CHORUS my lord abandoned Miyako under a bright moon,
bound now for the billows of the western sea,
innocent in thought and word of the least misdeed.
Should he voice his complaint,
Yoritomo at last must surely yield,
for as willow fronds twine around one another,
so the brothers' love can never, never die.
(*waka*) Only trust in me . . .

(DANCE: *jo-no-mai* or *chū-no-mai*)

Shizuka now performs her major dance: depending on the performance, either a jo-
no-mai *or a slightly faster* chū-no-mai.

SHIZUKA (*waka*) Only trust in me,
although misfortune
bring you great pain,
CHORUS as long as I remain
as saviour in the world.[12]

SHIZUKA (*noriji*) So sang Kannon, whose words, unless false,
CHORUS so sang Kannon whose words, unless false,
mean that our lord soon will rise again.
(*ageuta*) Then come, lads, come!
Make haste! Loose the moorings and let us be gone
Make haste! Loose the moorings and let us be gone!
cries Benkei's great voice. The Magistrate, too,
leaves the poor shelter where he had sought lodging,
SHIZUKA while Shizuka in tears
CHORUS removes hat and cloak, drops them at her feet,
speechless with weeping, and bids him farewell.
All who look on fully share her grief
all who look on fully share her grief.   *Exit.*

Boatman comes forward to stand in base square.

12. A poem spoken by the Kannon of Kiyomizu-dera in Kyoto.

BOATMAN [13] (*shaberi*) What a sad, sad scene! Seeing Shizuka just now, so stricken as she said goodbye to her lord, brought tears even to *my* eyes, though the likes of me aren't generally that sensitive to people's troubles. No wonder Shizuka wanted to go with him, wherever he might wander. But he decided that tongues would wag if she did, and he was certainly right. When I think how both of them must feel, all I can do is cry. He's destroyed the Taira for ever, and as far as everyone knows, he and his older brother ought now to be as close as the sun and moon in the sky. But it seems this isn't so at all. Instead, the two brothers are at odds, and his lordship is fleeing towards the western provinces. It's all very strange. At any rate, a short while ago, Master Benkei ordered a ship placed at his lordship's disposal, and I have a stout ship ready now. I will let Master Benkei know. [*Sits at centre, facing Benkei.*]

(*mondō*) Excuse me, Master Benkei.

BENKEI What is it?

BOATMAN Seeing Shizuka just now, so stricken as she said goodbye to her lord, brought tears even to my eyes, though the likes of me aren't generally that sensitive to people's troubles. I wonder how *you* feel about it, Master Benkei.

BENKEI Just as you do, I assure you.

BOATMAN A short while ago, Master Benkei, you ordered a ship to be placed at his lordship's disposal. I have a good, stout ship ready now. We can sail whenever you wish.

BENKEI Then let us do so soon, by all means.

BOATMAN Very well, Master Benkei.

Boatman returns to villager position. Benkei rises and goes to base square.

BENKEI What a pathetic sight! Sympathy for Shizuka has made him weep! We must sail without delay.

A Warrior rises.

WARRIOR I beg your pardon, sir, but our lord wishes me to tell you that in his judgement, the wind and waves are at present much too high. He means to remain here.

BENKEI What? He means to remain here, you say?

WARRIOR That is so, sir.

13. Although the Boatman is integrated into the action of the play, he still must fill in time, like the *ai* in the interlude of other plays, while the *shite* actor changes costume and mask. This is the functional purpose of his prominent role in the pages that follow.

BENKEI Aha, my lord, I understand![14] You have issued this order simply because you cannot after all bear to bid Shizuka farewell! Please calm yourself a little and listen to me. As I understand things, when a man in your position takes that attitude, he will never enjoy good fortune again. Besides, a year ago, when we sailed from Watanabe in the teeth of a tremendous gale, it was you who insisted on pressing ahead and who went on to destroy the Taira. The situation today is just the same.

> Make haste, make haste, let us put to sea!

WARRIORS How right you are! Who would not agree?

> Enemies are everywhere, the rolling waves

BENKEI raise their clamour before us. Come, my lads, come,

CHORUS (*issei*) pull away now,   BENKEI (*mondō*) Come, captain,
for as the tide runs   let us get this vessel under
our good ship is launched   way!
and takes to the sea!   BOATMAN Aye, aye, sir!

While Chorus sings above, Boatman runs down bridgeway with the 'boat' and places it in witness square. Seizing his oar, he stands in the stern.

BOATMAN Please, gentlemen, take your places aboard! [*Yoshitsune sits on stool in the bow. One Warrior sits in stern, the others aft of amidships.*] You too, Master Benkei, please take your place aboard! [*Benkei sits amidships. Boatman mimes rowing.*] Pull, pull away! Pull, pull away! [*Continues rowing as he talks.*] I beg your pardon, Master Benkei.

BENKEI What is it?

BOATMAN The weather today is perfect, isn't it![15]

BENKEI Yes, the weather today is just right. I myself could hardly have wished for better.

BOATMAN We've not had any weather like this lately. Surely it's a sign his lordship is setting out towards the best of good fortune. And speaking of good fortune, Master Benkei, there's a certain subject I'd gladly discuss with you, if I may make bold to do so.

BENKEI What is it, then? Please speak freely.

BOATMAN Really, sir? May I ask you my question?

---

14. Benkei's sudden, direct address to Yoshitsune is a bit jarring. In the verse passage below, variant versions distribute the lines differently. In giving the last one to Benkei, I have followed the Itō text.

15. Earlier, Yoshitsune complained of high wind and waves, but now the weather is perfect. The discrepancy is hard to explain except as a device to set off the storm that follows.

BENKEI Of course.

BOATMAN Oh, thank you, sir, thank you so much! Then I *will*. You see, sir, my lord may be gone from Miyako a while, but he certainly will be back soon. And when that happens, I wonder whether you'd be good enough to put in a word with him, and have me appointed overseer of shipping between here and the west. Could you see your way to doing that, Master Benkei?

BENKEI Captain, I see no reason why you should not entertain such hopes. Yes, I will do my best to see to it.

BOATMAN I am very, very grateful, Master Benkei. With you on my side, the thing is as good as done. But please, sir, don't forget your promise. It so often happens that people forget their promises when something else comes up to claim their attention.

BENKEI Never fear, captain, I will not forget.

BOATMAN Pull, pull away! Why, now there's a cloud hanging over Mount Muko.[16] There wasn't any cloud there before!

BENKEI What is that you are saying, captain?

BOATMAN That I see a cloud over Mount Muko, sir. It's nothing really to worry about, but still, if that cloud comes our way, we'll be in for some wind. Yes, just as I thought, here it comes! Pull away, lads, put your backs into it! And here's the wind now, sure enough! Take care, gentlemen! [*Goes down on one knee and bares right shoulder to do battle with the elements, then rises and wields the oar lustily.*] But never fear, Master Benkei, never fear. I've picked for his lordship's voyage an outstanding crew, and with myself at the helm, we can cut straight through any storm. So please don't worry.

BENKEI We all count on you, captain.

BOATMAN The fine weather today was enough of a surprise. Now it's suddenly taken a turn for the worse, we must look lively. [*Dramatic music.*] Oh, I knew it, I knew it! The waves are rising! [*Rows frantically.*] Oh my, oh my, oh my, oh my, oh my, oh my! [*Soothing the waves.*] Hush, hush, hush! Pull, pull away! Oh, this is no ordinary storm! I just don't understand it! Heavens, here come those waves again! [*Dramatic music.*] Oh my, oh my, oh my, oh my! Hush, hush, hush!

WARRIOR (*mondō*) How very strange! The wind has shifted!

BENKEI So it has! With a gale like this howling down from Mount

16. The old name of Mount Rokkō, which rises behind modern Kōbe.

Muko and Yuzuriha Peak, our ship has no hope of ever reaching land. Pray, everyone! Pray with all your heart!

WARRIOR Master Benkei! An evil spirit has possessed our ship!

BENKEI Hold your tongue! Never say that aboard a ship at sea! Just leave everything to me!

BOATMAN Hey, you! I spotted you the moment you stepped on board, with that look on your face! I knew you'd be blabbing some sort of nonsense! And now, sure enough, you've gone and done it! Don't ever say a thing like that aboard ship! Just leave everything to Master Benkei and me!

BENKEI Never mind, captain. This man is no sailor. He has no idea how to behave at sea.

BOATMAN That's all too obvious, sir. Heavens, here they come again! [*Dramatic music.*] Oh my, oh my, oh my, oh my, oh my! Hush, hush, hush! Oh, we're in for it now!

BENKEI (*unnamed*) Ah, this is eerie! I see upon the ocean the whole host of the Taira, who not long since perished in the west, all of them riding the uproarious sea! For them, the moment is perfect to vent upon us all their pent-up wrath!

YOSHITSUNE (*mondō*) A word, Benkei.

BENKEI At your service, my lord.

YOSHITSUNE There is no need to be alarmed. Though evil spirits resolve to destroy us, what harm could they possibly do?

    (*kuri*) They whose sins, whose crimes are many,
            who raised dismal rebellion against Buddhas and Gods,
            who at Heaven's command drowned: all the Taira,

CHORUS (*uta*) their own Sovereign the first among them,[17]
            and all their great nobles gathered like clouds,
            wave-borne, now swarm before our eyes!

To hayafue *music, enter Tomomori, carrying a halberd and with a sword at his waist. From third pine he glares at the ship, then rushes on stage and stops in base square. Below, he continues to move around stage, miming as appropriate.*

TOMOMORI (*nanori-guri*) You see before you the phantom of one in the ninth generation from Emperor Kammu. Taira no Tomomori is my name.

    (*unnamed*) Aha! A marvel indeed!

---

17. The child-emperor Antoku, whom the Taira took with them when they fled Kyoto. He and most of the Taira nobles drowned in the battle of Dan-no-ura.

What say you, Yoshitsune?
I had not imagined the thundering waves

CHORUS (*noriji*)   might lead you to me as you sailed the sea
might lead you to me as you sailed the sea

TOMOMORI   where Tomomori drowned! Just so, today,

CHORUS   I will drown Yoshitsune in the blue abyss!

TOMOMORI   And with this cry, on the glowering waves,
he grips his halberd for battle,
in the 'curling wave' pattern sweeps it wide,
kicks high the salt foam, belches noxious vapours,
till all sight grows dim, all hearts quake with terror.
Each man, dumb-struck, stares, wide-eyed.

(QUASI-DANCE: *mai-bataraki*)

Tomomori does two mai-bataraki *circuits round the stage, threatening Yoshitsune.
As text continues, the figures on stage mime and dance as appropriate. When at last
repelled, Tomomori flees onto bridgeway.*

KOKATA   At that moment Yoshitsune, wholly untroubled

CHORUS   at that moment Yoshitsune, wholly untroubled,
draws his sword as though true flesh and blood
challenged him to fight,
trades words with the phantom and closes in combat.
Yet Benkei thrusts between them, crying,
No skill at arms can ever best this foe!
Rasping his prayer beads against one another,
he summons the Five Mantra Kings: [18]
in the east, Gōsanze, in the south, Gundari-yasha,
in the west, Daiitoku, in the west Kongō-yasha,
in the centre Lord Fudō:
the Mantra King whose noose binds evil powers!
Fiercely he prays until the baleful spirit
step by step falls back.
Benkei lends his strength to the straining crew,

18. Benkei quells the ghost just as other monks in other plays quell similar apparitions.
He rasps his rosary beads rhythmically together rather as a Christian might display the
Cross. The 'Mantra Kings' (*myōō*) whom he summons are a mandala of wrathful,
protector divinities: Fudō ('The Unmoving') in the centre, surrounded by a guardian for
each of the four directions. They belong to the Esoteric Buddhist tradition and are still
invoked in Japan.

rowing the ship on towards yonder shore,
while the evil spirit, pursuing them still,
is ever repelled by prayer and the sword,
till the ebbing tide bears him, tossing and rocking
till the ebbing tide bears him, tossing and rocking,
far across the waves: he is gone.

At third pine, Tomomori leaps into the air, then comes down with a crash, kneeling with one knee raised: he has disappeared. He then rises and stamps the final beat.

Hagoromo · THE FEATHER MANTLE

The Feather Mantle, often performed and a favourite of amateurs, is among the most popular of all nō plays, yet no one knows who wrote it. Since existing records first mention it in 1524, it must date from long after Zeami's time. The play's celestial maiden conveys all the charm of the 'swan maidens' so common in world folklore, and its dances are lovely. As to its sources, they are unusually diverse. An attempt to understand their significance led to the discussion that follows.

In *The Feather Mantle*, a celestial maiden descends to the seashore and hangs her mantle on a pine, where a fisherman finds it. At first he threatens to keep it, but then gives it back so that she can dance for him. Her dance is the climax of the play, and once it is over, she returns to the sky. The play treats her dance as the origin of the *Suruga-mai* ('Suruga Dance'): one of the six pieces of the *Azuma asobi* ('East Country Songs') that still are performed in the imperial palace and at certain shrines.

One source of the play is a poem, with its preface, by the eleventh-century poet Nōin:

Composed when Shikibu no Taifu Sukenari, then Governor of Iyo, offered the *Azuma asobi* to the Mishima Deity in that province: 'Of old, the celestial feather mantle descended upon Udo Beach, and ah, the dancers wave today the sleeves that she waved then!'

According to *Shūchūshō* ('Remarks on Poetry', *c.* 1180), the maiden dancing in her feather mantle was seen by a 'rustic old man' who passed on her dance to others.

Udo Beach adjoins the shore at Mio, the scene of the play. Both are on a spit that juts out into western Suruga Bay, in old Suruga province (now Shizuoka Prefecture). The playwright simply assimilated one to the other, and although this seems reasonable, it is a surprise. Place names are crucial in classical poetry, and if the *Suruga-mai* was first danced on Udo Beach, the playwright should have left it there.

In several early Japanese legends, a heavenly maiden (or maidens) comes down and dances to music played by a mortal. For example, an emperor's *koto* playing brought down five maidens whose dance became the Gosechi Dance of the court. Such maidens return to Heaven without incident. At Mio, however, the maiden of the play takes off her mantle as soon as she arrives. She gets a bad fright when the fisherman finds it and refuses to give it back.

Her encounter with the fisherman helps to make *The Feather Mantle* a play, and it also brings in the 'swan maiden' motif. In a typical swan maiden tale, a band of celestial maidens come down to a pool, remove their mantles, and bathe. A young man sees them, steals a mantle, and hides it. He then marries the mantle's owner, who can no longer fly away, and has children by her. Many years later, the maiden recovers her mantle and returns to the sky. In *The Feather Mantle*, just one angel comes down to the sea, not a freshwater pool. She does not bathe, does not marry the mortal, and soon returns to Heaven. Still, the playwright used the motif consciously.

He knew (because anyone able to write *The Feather Mantle* would have known) two patterns of swan maiden tale. The first, the type recognized by folklorists, is the marriage pattern just described. In Japan, the earliest surviving example of it is a fragment of *Ōmi fudoki* ('Report on the Province of Ōmi', early eighth century). The second pattern involves adoption instead of marriage, and the earliest example of it is a fragment of *Tango fudoki* (also early eighth century). Folklorists do not class this pattern with swan maiden tales, but the *Tango fudoki* fragment none the less gave the playwright his swan maiden. Nōin, who evoked the angel's descent to Udo Beach, quoted it in one of his works, and *The Feather Mantle* refers directly to it twice. A childless old couple take the maiden's mantle and ask her to become their daughter. When she assents but asks for her mantle back first, they accuse her of deceitful intent, and she defends herself. The passage is just like its counterpart in the play. The maiden makes them rich, but eventually they drive her away without returning her mantle. Then, in her despair, she speaks the poem 'O celestial plains', quoted in the play. In the end, she becomes the deity of a village shrine.

The Feather Mantle turns the *Tango fudoki* tale of adoption into something closer to a marriage. In fact, there existed a Suruga legend that had the fisherman marry the maiden. Hayashi Razan quoted it in his *Honchō jinja kō* ('Researches on Our Shrines', *c.* 1640). When the maiden flies away, the fisherman rises after her to the realm of the immortals. Razan took the legend from a purported fragment of the lost *Suruga fudoki*, but since the fragment is probably spurious, the legend may well be derived from the play.

Many later marriage and adoption tales concern Mount Fuji, which dominates Mio and Suruga Bay. A fourteenth-century marriage tale in *Shintō shū* ('Collected Histories of the Gods') calls the maiden the deity of the mountain; so does *Fujisan engi* ('The Sacred Origins of Mount Fuji', 15th–16th c.?), in an adoption tale; and a puppet play, *Nippon Hōraizan* ('The P'eng-lai Mountain of Japan', 16th c.?), expands the adoption motif into an interminable account of the deity's agonies in the world below.

Like *The Feather Mantle*, the Fuji legends evoke the descent of spirit into the world, but they also suggest a counterpart ascent. The mortal husband or foster parents may themselves become mountain deities (*Shintō shū*, *Fujisan engi*, *Nippon Hōraizan*). *Fujisan engi* also says that when the maiden returned to the mountain, men set out to follow her, and that this is how the Fuji pilgrimage began. Medieval paintings of Mount Fuji show pilgrims disembarking on the coast of Suruga Bay, to wind their way up towards a summit clearly marked as paradise.

Does the fisherman in *The Feather Mantle* ascend to such a realm? No, not really. Once the angel dances, he says nothing more, but when at last she vanishes over Mount Fuji, his yearning heart no doubt follows her. Moreover, his own name suggests a rising movement of the spirit. Hakuryō is an improbable name that means 'White Dragon'. Its implications, if taken seriously, are as follows.

A passage in the Chinese *Shuo-yüan* ('A Garden of Tales', 1st c. B.C.) describes how a white dragon (*hakuryō*) descended from Heaven into an earthly pool, where it changed into a fish. The reason why Hakuryō is now a human, and no longer a fish, transpires from the complete story, which concerns a king who wished to mingle with his people. His adviser used the white dragon's example to warn him against doing so, for once the dragon was a fish, a fisherman shot it in the eye with an arrow. The dragon flew away to complain to the King of Heaven, but the King of Heaven declared that mortals normally shoot fish and refused to condemn the fisherman. The Chinese king listened attentively and decided against playing at being a commoner.

This story predates Buddhism in China, but the playwright read it as a medieval Japanese Buddhist. In the white dragon and the fish, he saw man's dual nature, intrinsically enlightened yet temporarily in darkness. Then, in his imagination, he seems to have prolonged it according to the principles of karma. Having been shot as a fish, the dragon so hated the fisherman that he was reborn as the object of his hatred. Nothing otherwise requires that Hakuryō should be called so precisely a fisherman (*gyofu*). A more natural term would have been *ama*, which often refers in poetry and nō to someone who lives from the sea.

Being a fisherman left Hakuryō stranded on earth and in danger of Hell, since in Buddhism the sin of taking life is very grave. Yet he did have a human body (the only one from which enlightenment is possible), and residual good karma had given him birth at a lovely spot (Mio) and a heart not quite closed to higher things.

As the play begins, the beauty of spring transports Hakuryō with delight and his spirits rise. Just then, the maiden descends. Perhaps he has felt her coming, or perhaps (to risk a trite expression) she has heard the music in his heart. But no doubt she really responds to more than music. The fisherman's heart may be singing, but, as his behaviour soon shows, it is not wise. He is still benighted and so needs compassion.

The maiden herself may not mean to 'save' a poor fisherman. She is simply one of the thirty maidens who dance the moon's phases around the Palace of the Moon. In the play, she pauses in her dance to salute 'almighty Seishi, source of the Lord of the Moon'. This lord (a Chinese figure) rules time and the seasons, but his higher 'source' in medieval Japan was the bodhisattva Seishi. As the moon swings westward, Seishi draws the spirit on to enlightenment in Amida's Western Paradise. Thus Seishi's compassion sends the maiden, like a moonbeam, down. She does not really need to think about it. A bodhisattva's compassion works as naturally as a stream descends from the hills, and, in the world of nō, may easily take the form of dance.

However, to touch the mortal Hakuryō deeply, the angel must meet him as a mortal. That is why she removes her feather mantle; the play gives her no other reason to do so. Her risk is his great chance. Now she is at Hakuryō's mercy, just as he, a fish in a pool, was once at a fisherman's. The fishrman shot the fish. If Hakuryō now 'shoots' the maiden by keeping her mantle, he will sink himself so deep in dire karma that this time he will lose even his human birth. But if he is generous, he will rise.

Happily, kindness and the sweetness of spring prevail. Hakuryō lets himself be tempted in the right direction: he returns the mantle so that the maiden can dance. His reward is beauty beyond imagining, for her dance is 'Rainbow Skirts and Mantle of Feathers' (in Chinese, *Ni-shang-yü-i*), which the play treats as the source-dance for the *Suruga-mai*. Lines by the poet Po Chü-i (772–846) had made it famous in Japan. In legend, the T'ang emperor Hsüan-tsung ascended to the moon on the fifteenth night of the eighth lunar month (the great full-moon night of the year) and saw the moon-maidens dance it there. It was he who brought it back down to earth.

About 150 metres back from the beach at Mio, a sacred fence still surrounds a *Hagoromo no matsu* ('Pine of the Feather Mantle'). The original pine is said to have stood at a spot now nearly an equal distance out to sea, and to have been lost in the earthquake caused by the great eruption of Mount Fuji in 1707.

THE FEATHER MANTLE

Persons in order of appearance

Hakuryō, a fisherman	*waki*
One or two Companions	*wakizure*
An Angel (*Zō-onna* mask and an elaborate headdress with a white bird in it)	*shite*

Remarks: A third-category play (*kazura-mono*) current in all five schools of nō. The several performance variants (*kogaki*) of this play adopt different dances and may also require cuts in the text. In one (Kanze school), no pine is placed on the stage; instead, the mantle is hung on the first pine, along the bridgeway.

*   *   *

Stage assistant places a small pine tree near front of stage. A robe (the angel's mantle) hangs in its branches.
To issei music, enter Hakuryō and Companions, each carrying a fishing pole over his right shoulder. They face each other along the front of stage.

HAKURYŌ and COMPANIONS
          (*issei*) Swift winds blow
                    at Mio down the curving shore
                    small craft row,
                    and fisherfolk
                    call over the sea-lanes![1]   *Face audience.*

HAKURYŌ (*sashi*) You have before you a fisherman named Hakuryō,
     from the pine woods of the coast, at Mio.

HAKURYŌ and COMPANIONS
     Above endless leagues of lovely hills,   *Face each other.*
                    suddenly, clouds rise;
     a bright moon over the pavilion
                    proclaims the clearing of the rain.[2]
                    Yes, this is a time of peace and calm.
                    Spring has touched the pine woods,
                    wave on wave washes the shore
                    as mists rise, and the moon
                    loiters in the plains of Heaven:
                    even for such as we,
                    beauty to transport the heart with keen delight!
                    beauty to transport the heart with keen delight!
          (*sageuta*) How could I forget?
                    By mountain trails we came to Kiyomigata
                    and spied afar the pine woods of Mio:[3]
                    now, my friends, let us journey there
                    now, my friends, let us journey there.
          (*ageuta*) Wind-billowed,
                    clouds drift aloft:
                    do you see waves
                    clouds drift aloft: do you see waves,
                    men – why, no fishing done,

1. Slightly adapted from a poem in the *Man'yōshū*, a great eighth-century poetry collection, that refers to a Mio in the province of Kii (Wakayama Prefecture). Some linked verse (*renga*) manuals confused it with the Mio of the play.
2. Lines from a thirteenth-century Chinese anthology. The original second line has the clouds clearing instead of rising, which makes better sense. The discrepancy is curious.
3. Three lines based on a poem in the imperial anthology *Shokukokinshū* (1265). They establish the poetic value of Mio. Kiyomigata, the name of a stretch of shore, is across the water from the spit where Mio is situated. Its name suggests the meaning 'pure sight'.

              will you hurry home?[4]
         Stay, for spring is here: the morning breeze
         surely will be kind, singing with gentle voice *Mimes walking*.
         through pines ever green, while in the calm of dawn,
         fishermen crowd forth in teeming craft
         fishermen crowd forth in teeming craft.

During the passage above, Hakuryō puts down his fishing pole at the stage assistant position while Companions go and sit in witness square. Hakuryō now stands in base square.

HAKURYŌ (*unnamed*) Just as I reach the pine woods of Mio and stand gazing out over the shore, blossoms fall from the sky, music resounds, and a wondrous fragrance pervades all the air. This is nothing ordinary. And, in fact, I see an exquisite mantle hanging on this pine. Yes indeed, it is astonishing in both colour and scent. Surely this is no common mantle. [*Takes it and moves towards witness position.*] I will take it home with me, show it to the elders, and make it an heirloom in my house.

Angel calls through curtain, then comes down bridgeway.

ANGEL (*mondō*) Forgive me, but that mantle belongs to *me*. Why have you taken it?

HAKURYŌ It was hanging there and I found it. I am taking it home with me.

ANGEL But this is an angel's feather mantle. It is not something lightly given to a human. Please put it back where it was.

HAKURYŌ If I understand you correctly, this mantle belongs to an angel. Why, in that case, I must secure it as a wonder in this latter age and make it a treasure of the realm. No, I certainly cannot return it.

ANGEL Oh no! Without my feather mantle, the pathways of flight are closed to me. Never again will I return to Heaven! Please, please, give it back!

HAKURYŌ   Rather than heed her desperate plea,
           Hakuryō waxes stubborn.
           When was I ever kind, I, a fisherman?[5]

---

4. A slightly modified version of a poem (perhaps by Reizei Tamesuke, 1263–1328) on one of the 'eight views of Hsiao-hsiang', an important subject in Chinese or Chinese-style painting. The confusion of banks of cloud in the sky with waves on a lake (Hsiao-hsiang) or the sea is a conventional motif.

5. A thought already found in *The Diver*: a humble person such as one who lives from the sea is without 'heart', and does not understand higher human or religious values.

	he cries, and hides the feather mantle.
	No indeed, he says, and turns to go.
ANGEL	In her desperate plight, the angel now,
	like a wingless bird,
	moving to rise, still lacks her mantle,
HAKURYŌ	yet the earth to her is the nether world.
ANGEL	What then shall I do? in distress she cries,
HAKURYŌ	and when Hakuryō still withholds the mantle,
ANGEL	helpless,
HAKURYŌ	hopeless,
CHORUS	the dewdrop tears fall;

her jewelled crown, the flowers in her hair,
wilt and droop:
the five signs of an angel's decline [6]
are plain to see, heart-breaking!

ANGEL (*shimo-no-ei*) O celestial plains:
as I gaze aloft,
mists rise before my eyes,
the cloudways blur,
the path is lost! [7]

CHORUS (*sageuta*) My dear home, the sky: when shall I go
there, the clouds roam free
while I look on in envy and sorrow.

(*ageuta*) The kalavinka's voice [8] I loved to hear
the kalavinka's voice I loved to hear
dies away; and the fading cries
of wild geese on the wing,
down the skyways homeward bound,
recall to me all I have lost!
Seagulls, plovers, speed across the waves,
diving and soaring in the winds of spring
that blow so free –
they too quicken my yearning!

HAKURYŌ (*mondō*) Please excuse me, but I can easily see how much you are suffering. I cannot bear it. I will give you your mantle back.

6. In Buddhist writings, the five signs of a heavenly being's approaching death.
7. A poem from the *Tango fudoki* fragment discussed in the introduction.
8. The kalavinka (a Sanskrit word) is a bird that sings in paradise.

ANGEL Oh, how happy you have made me! Then please bring it to me.

HAKURYŌ A moment, though. I will return it if you will dance for me, here and now, the angel dance that people tell of.

ANGEL How glad I am! Then I *shall* be able to go home to Heaven! And in thanks I will gladly dance, for those who inhabit this sad, lower world, a dance to commemorate my visit among them: the one we do around the Palace of the Moon. But I cannot dance without my mantle. You must give it back to me first.

HAKURYŌ Oh no! If I give you your mantle back,
you will not dance at all.
Away you will soar, straight up to Heaven.

ANGEL No, no, suspicion is only for humans.
In Heaven, falsehood is quite unknown.

HAKURYŌ I am ashamed.
Very well, says he,
returning the feather mantle.   *Does so.*

(THE DONNING OF THE ROBE)

Angel retires to stage assistant position, where stage assistant dresses her in the robe.

ANGEL (*kakeai*) Clothed in her mantle, the maiden dances
'Rainbow Skirts and Feather Cloak'.[9]

HAKURYŌ Her own celestial mantle moves with the wind,

ANGEL moist with rain, the blossom sleeves

HAKURYŌ sway and flutter

ANGEL as she dances on!

CHORUS (*shidai*) The Suruga Dance from the East Country Songs
the Suruga Dance from the East Country Songs:
this, surely, is how it began!

(*kuri*) Why are the heavens called boundless, everlasting?[10]
When the Divine Pair, long, long ago,
laid out the world in its ten directions,

9. A dance known at the court of T'ang China. It may have come from Central Asia. (See introduction.)

10. 'Boundless' and 'everlasting' are two meanings attributed in medieval manuals of poetry to *hisakata*, the poetic epithet (*makura-kotoba*) conventionally associated with 'heaven', 'sky' or, by extension, 'moon'. These five lines simply quote from one of these manuals. The Divine Pair are Izanagi and Izanami, the primordial pair of Japanese mythology. The ten directions are the four main compass directions, the four intermediate compass directions, and up and down.

they found the sky went on without end
and so named it boundless, everlasting.

ANGEL (*sashi*) How does it look, the Palace of the Moon?
Hewn with glittering axe it stands, for all eternity,

CHORUS   while angel maidens robed in white or black,
twin bands, each of fifteen,
night by night all month long,
faithfully serve out their role.

ANGEL   Of these I am one,
a celestial maiden of the moon-laurel tree,
now divided in two,[11]
and present here briefly: for so the world learned
the East Country's Suruga Dance!

Angel dances throughout the passage below.

(*kuse*) Mists of spring
veil all the hills:
in the everlasting
moon the laurel tree
surely is in full bloom.[12]

This crown of blossoms, so gay in hue,
declares spring has come.[13] Ah, beautiful!
Although not Heaven, the earth is lovely too.
O sky-coursing breezes, close with your breath
the passageways through the clouds!
Let the angel maiden linger a while
here by the pine wood, to show us spring
touching Mio Cape, the moon so clear
over Kiyomigata, the snows of Fuji –
peerless, all, like this spring dawn:
the waves, wind in the pines, the tranquil shore!
Heaven and earth, why, are they not one?
Simple spirit-fences part Inner from Outer

---

11. The laurel tree of the moon appears also in *The Damask Drum*. 'Divided in two' (*mi o wakete*) suggests that while appearing below, the angel has never actually left the moon. In Japan, a deity's presence may be multiplied indefinitely by ritual 'division of the body', without diminishing the original divine presence. In short, the angel is like the moon reflected below.

12. A poem by Ki no Tsurayuki (d. 946).

13. The angel's springtime loveliness is that of the Fuji divinity herself: Konohanasakuya-hime, whose name means 'Lady All-the-Trees-Are-Blooming'.

Shrine, whose Gods' offspring still rule
our moon-illumined land, source of the sun![14]

ANGEL
In our Sovereign's reign,
the celestial feather mantle
rarely descends

CHORUS
to brush the rocks below:
unworn, they endure,[15]
O happy news!
Songs of the East swell from countless throats
as drone-pipes, flutes, harps, and zitherns
resound through the heavens
from the Cloud of Welcome[16]
as the sun sinks, the red of Mount Sumeru;[17]
blue the waves towards Ukishima Moor,[18]
swept by storm winds that scatter blossoms,
like swirling snow, the dancing sleeves
whirl, like clouds, so white, so pure.

Angel goes down on one knee in base square, with palms pressed together.

ANGEL (*ei*) Hail to the refuge, almighty Seishi, source of the Lord of
the Moon![19]

---

14. The Inner Shrine of Ise is that of the Sun Goddess, Amaterasu, whose 'offspring' are the line of emperors; the Outer Shrine is that of the deity of increase, Toyouke. An influential view in medieval times held that the two shrines were a non-dual pair, here distinguished from one another, but not separated, by the sacred enclosure (*tamagaki*) around the sanctuaries. The presence of sun and moon together evokes a paradisal realm. 'Source of the sun' is *hi no moto*, equivalent to Nihon, the name of Japan.
15. This poem from the *Shūishū* (*c.* 1006) is related to the one that became the Japanese national anthem. It celebrates the eternity of the imperial realm, which will last as long as it takes an angel's mantle, brushing every few thousand years the rocks of the mountains, to wear those rocks away.
16. The music of the *Azuma asobi* has become the music that resounds from the cloud on which the Buddha Amida comes forward, surrounded by the host of his bodhisattvas and saints, to welcome the soul of the dying into his paradise.
17. The central mountain of the Buddhist cosmos. It is red on the west (here, the colour of the setting sun), white on the east, yellow on the north, and blue on the south.
18. From Mio one looks north-east across Suruga Bay towards Ukishima-ga-hara, a strip of land along the south side of Mount Ashitaka, itself a lesser volcanic peak (1505m) just south-south-west of Fuji. The blue of the waves corresponds to the blue of the south side of Mount Sumeru.
19. A Chinese line like a passage from a Buddhist litany. The angel declares her devotion to the moon-lord and, beyond him, to the bodhisattva Seishi. Seishi is, with Kannon, one of the two bodhisattvas who accompany Amida, and has the 'supreme power' (*seishi*) to lead the soul to Amida's paradise. The moon is the visible sign of this power.

CHORUS   A dance, then, from the East Country Songs.

(DANCE: *jo-no-mai*)

Angel dances a jo-no-mai *and continues dancing as text resumes.*

ANGEL *(noriji)* Now you see the blue mantle of the lofty heavens,

CHORUS   now the mantling mists that rise in spring:

ANGEL   a wonder in scent and hue, the maiden's train

CHORUS   sweeps and sways, rustling,
          flowers in her hair nod while feather sleeves
          billow, coil and turn, the dancing sleeves!

(DANCE: *ha-no-mai*)

Angel dances a ha-no-mai *and continues dancing as text resumes.*

    (noriji) The East Country Songs play on and on
          the East Country Songs play on and on
          as she whose loveliness is the moon's own,
          this fifteenth night, aloft in the heavens
          shines again, the face of accomplished truth,
          showering riches – all prayers fulfilled,
          the realm replete, and the seven treasures –
          on our land below.
          As time goes by, the celestial feather mantle,
          wind-borne, floats on down the shore,
          above the pine woods of Mio,
          the moors of Ukishima,
          Mount Ashitaka, Fuji's soaring peak,
          and, mingling with the mists,
          fades into the heavens,
          lost for ever to view.

Angel stamps a final beat.

Hanjo · LADY HAN

There is no doubt that Zeami wrote *Lady Han*, a play that resembles an old love ballad with a haunting tune. Hanago, a singing-girl at a provincial inn, entertains a passing guest from the capital and then, hopelessly lost in love, starts out to look for him. At a shrine in Kyoto, where he has gone to pray that he may find her, the two meet again.

The literary levels of *Lady Han* are comparable to those of a ballad: anecdote, rhyme, and melody. As anecdote, Hanago's troubles, like the story told in many a ballad, are affecting but easily forgotten. The inn madam, in her opening speech, treats Hanago's predicament as vexing but quite ordinary. In poetry, however, the very name of Nogami (the location of the inn in question) evoked a mood of romantic sorrow, and this mood might be likened to a ballad's metre and rhyme. Finally, the haunting melody is Chinese. For well over a thousand years, Chinese poets, and Japanese poets after them, had celebrated a Han Dynasty emperor's abandoned concubine: Han Shōyo (Pan Chieh-yü, 'Pan the Favourite Beauty'). Hanago, in her distress, is assimilated to Han Shōyo (Hanjo, or 'Lady Han').

The story of Lady Han was first recorded in the *Han shu* ('History of the Early Han Dynasty', 206 B.C.–24 A.D.), and then, having been taken up by poets and painters in China, was developed in Chinese and Japanese verse by the nobles of the Heian court (794–1180). From there, it passed into *enkyoku*, long songs popular among warriors and aristocrats alike after about the mid thirteenth century. In the play, once Hanago has reached the shrine in Kyoto and has been provoked, in her troubled state of mind, to 'rave', her speech becomes a tissue of allusions to such poems and songs.

A medieval commentary on the *Wakan rōei shū* ('A Collection of Japanese and Chinese Poems for Chanting Aloud', 1013) explains the story of Han Shōyo as follows.

Han Shōyo was a consort of Emperor Sei (Ch'eng) of Kan (Han), who showered his favour upon her. Then Hiran (Fei-luan, or Fei-yen) of the Chō

(Chao) family danced very beautifully, and the emperor fell in love with her and forgot Shōyo. Shōyo was deeply hurt, and the flames of jealousy coursed so unbearably through her breast that she made a round hoop, stretched it with silk, and had herself fanned with this fan. That is why, in [Chinese] poetry, the fan is called 'white silk'. Further, being round and white, it is compared to the full moon. Since it is white, it is likened to snow and called the 'round snow' fan. Fanned with such a fan, Han Shōyo forgot her heat.

In poetry, as in the play, the key image of the story is therefore a round, snowy, moon-like fan: the fan Han Shōyo herself evoked in a poem of grief, when she compared herself to a fan abandoned in autumn, after summer is past. The same fan in all these guises adorns the poetry of *Lady Han*, although the fan Hanago treasures is actually unlike Han Shōyo's. When Hanago's lover left, the pair, like many lovers before them, exchanged fans ('fan-shaped' ones). Hers had on it a painting of moonflowers (*yūgao*), his a painting of the moon.

Nogami, where Hanago met her gentleman, was in old Mino province (Gifu Prefecture), on the road from Kyoto to what were then the wilds of the East. The spot is near the present Sekigahara station on the 'bullet train' line to Tokyo. Throughout medieval times, Nogami was in poetry just what it is in the play: a place where a gentleman traveller and a lady of pleasure might fall in love, only to suffer afterwards the pangs of longing. (Alas, the poet Shōtetsu, passing through Nogami in 1408, found the village a dreary place where 'there was nothing going on'.) Hanago's lover, a courtier named Yoshida, would have been on some official mission to the East when he broke his journey there. Other plays associated with Zeami, set at other provincial spots, spring from similar encounters (*Higaki*, *Matsura*). *Eguchi*, too, alludes to the theme.

The fate of Hanago in Edo times (1600–1868) is a surprise, for popular fiction and theatre (bunraku and kabuki) based on the nō play immediately confused her with the tragic mother of *The River Sumida*. Perhaps this happened simply because the name Yoshida is shared by the gentleman in *Lady Han* and the dead boy in *The River Sumida*, and because both plays involve a journey to the East. At any rate, on the grounds of Shinnen-ji at old Nogami, now sandwiched between a noisy highway and the 'bullet train' tracks, a sign before a 'Lady Han's Kannon Chapel' reads:

This place is called Nogami. Of old . . . the Yoshida Minor Captain [a modest court rank] . . . stopped here and formed a bond with Hanago, the girl who served him. When he left, he told her that if their child was a boy she should name him Umewaka-maru, and as a keepsake he left her his fan . . . When Umewaka-maru grew up a little he travelled east to look for his father, and in time, his anxious mother followed him. On reaching Mokubo-ji in Edo [which did not yet exist in Zeami's time], she learned that Yoshida had gone up to Miyako, and that Umewaka-maru had died and was now buried at the temple. Distraught, Hanago returned to Nogami, where she worshipped the image of Kannon on Kannon-yama and died insane . . .

Not far from Shinnen-ji, a fine old house is said to occupy the site of the Nogami brothel. The family there preserve a statue of Umewaka-maru, and a statue and several paintings identified as 'Lady Han'.

LADY HAN

Persons in order of appearance

A post-station Madam	*ai*
Hanago, a post-station courtesan (*Zō-anna* or *Ko-omote* mask)	*shite*
The Yoshida Minor Captain, a gentleman of Miyako	*tsure*
A Gentleman, friend of Yoshida	*waki*
Two or three Attendants to Yoshida	*wakizure*

Remarks: A fourth-category (*yonbamme-mono*) play current in all five schools of nō. The text translated here is dated 1543. In modern performances, the Yoshida Minor Captain is defined as the *waki* and the Gentleman is assimilated to one of his attendants, the *wakizure*.

*   *   *

Enter Hanago, fan in hand – the standard fan of nō, and not in fact the one described in the play. She sits before drums. Enter then Madam, to stand in base square.

MADAM (*nanori*) You have before you the madam of the inn at Nogami in the province of Mino. One among the many girls in my service, Hanago, has been with me ever since she was small. This Hanago is forever toying with her fan, which has a special meaning for her, and that is why everyone calls her Lady Han. This spring, you see, a gentleman known as the Yoshida Minor Captain spent the night here, on his way down from Miyako towards the East. It was Hanago I had entertain him, and he exchanged fans with her before continuing on his way. Ever since, she has done nothing but stare at his fan. It is no use my telling her to go and entertain a guest: she will not do it. She just stays in her room. Guests are constantly accusing me of providing poor service. That is why I am now going to have Hanago clear out.

Madam steps towards Hanago. (In modern performances, Madam goes to first pine and calls to Hanago, who is not yet on stage.)

(*mondō*) So Hanago, there you are! Time and again lately I have had to speak to you, yet you never listen to a word I say. I have had enough. I will not have you stay in this room a moment longer. Clear out now and go wherever you please. [*Notices Hanago's fan.*] Oh, you make me so angry! Look at you, mooning over that fan again! The very sight of it drives me to distraction! [*Snatches the fan and throws it down.*] Now, clear out, do you hear? Clear out! Clear out!

Exit Madam. Hanago picks up the fan and weeps.

HANAGO (*kudoki*) O the world does play us false,
             and always will; yet many sorrows
             break her days' swift flow – she whom fate
             bends to be a woman of the stream.[1]

  (*sageuta*) Now I go wandering,
             knowing nothing of what lies ahead;
             robe wet with weeping,   *Weeps.*
  (*ageuta*) Nogami I abandon and set forth   *Slowly rises.*
             Nogami I abandon and set forth
             along the Ōmi Road[2] – to him, perhaps,
             that cruel man – for since he left,
             dew forever lingers on my sleeves.
             O that I might vanish with my grief!   *Weeps.*
             O that I might vanish with my grief!

To ashirai *music, exit Hanago.*

1. A prostitute, as in *Eguchi*.
2. The province of Ōmi, around Lake Biwa, lies between Nogami and Miyako.

Enter Gentleman, who sits before chorus.

To shidai *music, enter Yoshida and Attendants; they stand along the side of stage.*
(In modern performances, Gentleman does not appear, his part being taken by an Attendant.)

YOSHIDA and ATTENDANTS

    (*shidai*)   Sad is our farewell to towering Fuji[3]
               sad is our farewell to towering Fuji,
               whose snows we shall praise in Miyako!

YOSHIDA (*nanori*) I whom you see before you now am the Yoshida Minor Captain. You must know that last spring I travelled down to the East, and that with autumn now so soon upon us, I am making my way back up to Miyako.

YOSHIDA and ATTENDANTS

    (*ageuta*)   Forth from Miyako
               we sallied as the spring mists rose
               we sallied as the spring mists rose,
               lingered a while, and now the fall winds blow,
               sweeping through the gate at Shirakawa,[4]
               whence, in travel wear, we start for home.
               By shore and mountain, on to Mino province
               we have come, and to the village of Nogami
               we have come, and to the village of Nogami.

YOSHIDA (*mondō*) Are you there, my man? [*An Attendant goes down on one knee.*] Having come so swiftly, we have already reached the inn at Nogami in Mino province. This is where I pledged my love to a young woman whom people quickly dubbed Lady Han. Please go and find out whether she is still here.

ATTENDANT Sir, I have inquired about Lady Han. It appears that she and the madam had a falling-out, and I am sorry to report that she has left.

YOSHIDA I see. Then perhaps I made too much of what passed between her and me. None the less, make sure that word reaches me in Miyako if Lady Han ever returns.

---

3. Mount Fuji, far beyond Nogami on the road to the East, was naturally a major attraction for a traveller, and had been poetically consecrated as such by its presence on Narihira's path in *Ise monogatari* ('Tales of Ise', 10th c.).

4. The Shirakawa Barrier (a tollgate and checkpoint) in Iwashiro province (the present Fukushima Prefecture) was exceedingly famous. No poetic evocation of a journey like this one could fail to mention it.

(*tsukizerifu*) Having travelled so swiftly, we are already here in Miyako. A certain matter preoccupies me greatly. I will therefore go straight to Tadasu,[5] to pray. All of you, follow me, please!

Yoshida sits on a stool at witness position, while Attendants sit directly on the stage nearby. To issei music, enter Hanago. Her right shoulder is bared to the under-robe and she carries a spray of dwarf bamboo (sasa) *stems: these are signs that she is mad. She stops at first pine.*

HANAGO   (*sashi*) Where snow is gone,

the new shoots, love,

upon Kasuga meadow,

spring: slender and few,

those glimpses I had of you![6]

He was untrue, who took my love with him.

Now day follows day, the months wheel round,

while wearily I listen to the wind,

for no one else will speak to me of him.

Before the banners of the sunset clouds,

I grieve, longing to reach beyond those skies,[7]

and lost to any thought of present need.

O Gods, O blessed Buddhas, pity me!

O bring to pass what I so desire!

The Gods of Ashigara and Hakone,   *To base square.*

Tamatsushima, Kibune, and Miwa,[8]

graciously have vowed to lend their aid

and protect the love of men and women.

Should I address my prayers to all of these,   *Kneels in prayer.*

surely they will send an answering boon.

Accept with profound respect obedience renewed . . .[9]

---

5. The name of the sacred wood around the Lower Kamo Shrine, still one of the major shrines of Kyoto. Yoshida will pray to be reunited with Hanago.

6. A poem by Mibu no Tadamine, from the imperial collection *Kokinshū* ('Poems Old and New', 905). Very early in spring, in the time of the Nara court (8th c.), ladies and gentlemen went into the meadows near the Kasuga Shrine to pick new shoots amid the lingering snow, and the occasion became established in poetry. A gentleman might glimpse a lady and fall in love.

7. From a *Kokinshū* love poem: the words of a woman of humble station who longs for her noble lover in far-off Miyako.

8. These are all deities of mountains or of the streams that flow from them, and several are associated (like the Kamo Shrine where Yoshida and Hanago finally meet again) with marriage myths.

9. These opening words of a formula for addressing the gods occur also in *Tatsuta*.

(QUASI-DANCE: *kakeri*)

To music, Hanago performs a kakeri *tour of the stage. Though short, her* kakeri *changes rhythm several times, thus conveying her disturbed state of mind. As text resumes, she is in base square.*

<table>
<tr><td></td><td>(issei)</td><td>The lady is in love:</td><td></td></tr>
<tr><td></td><td></td><td>everyone knows,</td><td></td></tr>
<tr><td></td><td></td><td>and so quickly, too.</td><td></td></tr>
<tr><td>CHORUS</td><td></td><td>He never knew,</td><td></td></tr>
<tr><td></td><td></td><td>when he first stole my heart.[10]</td><td></td></tr>
<tr><td>HANAGO</td><td></td><td>The faithless man! O he is hateful, hateful!</td><td>Weeps.</td></tr>
<tr><td></td><td>(sashi)</td><td>Simply pray and let a sacred stream</td><td></td></tr>
<tr><td></td><td></td><td>cleanse you, till you love no more:[11]</td><td></td></tr>
<tr><td></td><td></td><td>whoever said that lied. The human heart</td><td></td></tr>
<tr><td></td><td></td><td>truly is a shallow, turbid pool;</td><td></td></tr>
<tr><td></td><td></td><td>and if we, impure, entreat the Gods,</td><td></td></tr>
<tr><td></td><td></td><td>it is no wonder they reject us!</td><td></td></tr>
<tr><td></td><td></td><td>I only know that he has not divined</td><td></td></tr>
<tr><td></td><td></td><td>the tears of love</td><td></td></tr>
<tr><td>CHORUS</td><td>(sageuta)</td><td>that leave me unconsoled.</td><td></td></tr>
<tr><td></td><td></td><td>O where will my sad journey end?</td><td></td></tr>
<tr><td></td><td>(ageuta)</td><td>Only let your heart</td><td></td></tr>
<tr><td></td><td></td><td>come into accord</td><td></td></tr>
<tr><td></td><td></td><td>with the true Way</td><td></td></tr>
<tr><td></td><td></td><td>come into accord with the true Way,</td><td></td></tr>
<tr><td></td><td></td><td>and you need not pray:</td><td></td></tr>
<tr><td></td><td></td><td>the Gods will keep you.[12]</td><td></td></tr>
</table>

Even for such as me, the moon of truth
might shine bright and clear, but time goes by,
and nothing comes from him, who is unkind.
The jewel of love is mine, yet I must weep
as he withholds it.[13] Ah, what can I do?
I only pray we two should share our life.

10. A poem from the imperial collection *Shūishū* ('Poetic Gleanings', *c.* 1006) by Mibu no Tadami.

11. A *Kokinshū* poet cited this method, only to lament that it did not work.

12. An old poem of uncertain origin, often cited in medieval literature.

13. The 'jewel of love' is, more literally, the 'jewel in the robe' that figures in a parable in the *Lotus Sutra*. It refers to the jewel of Buddha-nature with which all beings are endowed, although most do not know they have it.

> I only pray we two should share our life. *Prays.*

Gentleman rises.

GENTLEMAN (*mondō*) You, the mad girl! Why are you not raving today?
Come, rave and entertain us![14]

HANAGO You are too cruel! Why, see there!
Those boughs, till now, had looked firm enough,
yet at the wind's touch, one leaf falls.
For once I have my wits, you gentlemen
would have me rave. It is you, I think,
the wild wind turns. That flying autumn leaf
spins my heart away to storms of love.
O please, do not ask me to rave!

GENTLEMAN Well, what have you done with Lady Han's fan?

HANAGO You are quite mad! Are you now calling me Lady Han?
This fan, you see, was his – that cruel man's
whose faithlessness I mourn. It was his gift,
and once I touch it, I cannot put it from me,
though my tears fall like rain.
Ah, I recall the words of an old song:

In Lady Han's chamber, whiteness of an autumn fan;
on the So King's terrace, music of an evening ch'in.[15]

Hanago takes a few steps forward. Gentleman sits before Chorus.

CHORUS (*uta*) With summer done,
the fan and autumn's
pale, pale dews –
O, of these two,
which will be first to fall?[16]
Day and night, upon a desolate bed,

---

14. This apparently callous utterance is typical of nō plays that feature a mad person.
People hardly distinguished between the ravings of the mad and the antics of entertainers, and it appears that Hanago (who is an entertainer anyway) has been entertaining people here for some time. Women entertainers often travelled the roads in medieval Japan, but if any other kind of woman had done so, alone like Hanago, she probably would have had to pretend she was an entertainer in order to escape notice.
15. A couplet in Chinese included in the *Wakan rōei shū*. The *ch'in* belongs to the zither family, like the Japanese *koto*. Its music here, like the fan, is meant to evoke the whiteness of snow.
16. A Japanese poem, also from the *Wakan rōei shū*, and attributed elsewhere to Mibu no Tadamine. It suggests that Lady Han was abandoned like a fan in the cool of autumn. The 'dews' are also her tears. The passage below, through the *waka*, alludes repeatedly to lines by Chinese and Japanese poets included in the *Wakan rōei shū* and other such works.

	I lie alone, downcast and forlorn,	
	from my chamber gazing on the moon.	*Sits at centre.*

(*kuri*) Now the moon has sunk behind Mount Chō,
I lift my fan to double for the moon.

HANAGO   Flower petals scatter on brocade:

CHORUS   I gather snow and weep for fleeting spring.

HANAGO (*sashi*) Evening storms and the morning clouds:
how could either stir no troubled thoughts?

CHORUS   A bell tolling in the lonely night
echoes from the heights of Cockcrow Hill
as dawn comes on, urging love away.

HANAGO   O that at least moonlight, slanting in,

CHORUS   might linger on my pillow! Yet it leaves,
and, as before, I lie here alone.   *Weeps.*

(*kuse*) Green the curtains, red the dainty room
where he and I lay, our pillows twinned,
warm all night under welcoming quilts;
but those sweet dreams of bliss fled long ago.
Yet he lives and I live. The day must come,
so my heart says, when we two shall meet.
Might it be soon! O how *they* hastened, too,[17]
to whisper each to each enraptured vows
to share as birds one wing, as trees one root,
there in his fair palace at Ri-san.
Whoever could have heard them and passed on,
to people even now, what they said then?

Hanago rises and begins to dance.

Ah, but my own love promised me
he would return before autumn came,
and still the nights go by: so many nights
that prove he lied, he with his false heart!
I believed him, and he never comes.
Evenings I spend leaning on the railing,
gazing out towards far distant skies.
Autumn wind at twilight, rushing gales,
chill air from the heights, the late fall storms,
all come calling on that pine nearby.

17. The celebrated lovers Hui-tsung (the T'ang emperor) and Yang Kuei-fei.

	When will I hear from him, for whom I pine?
HANAGO	At least I have his gift: the fan I hold,
CHORUS	that its breeze might whisper me some word.

Yet summer now is past, and through my window
the autumn wind sinks, cold. Round Snow, my fan,
so frosty white, starts me shivering
merely to hear its name. O autumn wind,
I would quarrel with you.
Yet well I know, to meet means to part,
and loss follows from past happiness.
No, I should not blame him or the world.
But how can I forget my unloved state?
That is all that matters. He is gone,
and Lady Han's poor room is desolate.

Hanago pauses a moment near base pillar.

(*waka*) The painted moon

(DANCE: *jo-no-mai*)

She now does a jo-no-mai *dance, or, in many modern performances, a slightly faster* chū-no-mai. *As the text resumes, she continues dancing and abstract miming.*

HANAGO	I slip beneath my robe,
	the fan I hold,
CHORUS (*noriji*)	my bright sleeve, make three –
HANAGO	so pretty, too –
CHORUS	his most earnest vow,
HANAGO	to return by fall. Yet suns and moons
CHORUS	in procession pass, while fall winds blow,
HANAGO	and still no word breathes to stir the reeds.[18]
CHORUS	The belling of the stag, shrill insect cries
	recede and lapse. So too his promise fades.
	Better, then, if he had never made it!
HANAGO (*uta*)	His gift to me, this fan
CHORUS	his gift to me, this fan,

with its back and front, is less two-faced
than the giver's heart. Oh yes, he lied.
I shall not see him, nor will my love die
I shall not see him, nor will my love die.   *Weeps.*

18. The rustling of the reeds might announce his coming.

YOSHIDA (*mondō*) Are you there, my friend? Please tell that mad girl
   that I wish to see her fan.

Gentleman rises and turns to Hanago, who is in base square.

GENTLEMAN Come, Lady Han, the gentleman in the palanquin says he
   wants a look at your fan. Do let him have it.

HANAGO This fan was my love's parting gift, and that is why I keep
   it with me always. Oh, it is true,

> His parting gift:
> that is my enemy.
> Were it gone from me,
> a moment of forgetfulness
> might even now be mine.[19]

(*uta*) That is my own thought. Yet, all the same,
   at times I feel him with me.
   Then, how I would miss my fan!   *Turns to Gentleman.*
   No, I cannot show it to another.

Hides the fan protectively in the fold of her robe and turns away. Gentleman sits.

CHORUS (*rongi*) I myself remember well that keepsake
   and her lover's words, yet do not speak
   or make her any sign. How could she know?
   Yet, one look, and she will know my fan.

HANAGO You want a look at it, you say – but why?
   Why should you require, so urgently,
   a fan painted with an evening moon?
   What can your purpose be?

CHORUS (*rongi*) Ah, then perhaps you have forgotten
   all those ardent promises you heard
   at Nogami, while beside you lay
   a traveller, to return by fall:
   do they mean nothing to you now?

HANAGO Nogami, yes – why, Nogami lies
   far along the highway to the East
   where seas have overwhelmed the pine-clad hills[20]
   in reproach to one who went away
   and never came again.

19. A poem from the *Kokinshū*, also quoted in *Pining Wind*.
20. In a *Kokinshū* poem, a lover swears that if he is ever false, waves will sweep over a
mountain named Sue-no-matsuyama ('Pine Mountain of Sue') in the far north of Japan,
and the oath became proverbial.

Are you that man?

Peers at his face. Gentleman takes Yoshida's fan and starts towards her.

CHORUS (*rongi*)   O do not reprove me with those waves

that may have swept the hills, for I am true,

HANAGO   and you, too, preserve a keepsake fan

Sits at centre and receives Yoshida's fan.

CHORUS   that never leaves my side: a treasured fan

HANAGO   now offered me,

CHORUS   for you to take,

and examine in the gathering dusk:

Hanago opens the fan, with both hands lifts it reverently, and gazes at it.

Yes, I glimpse a painting of moonflowers.

Takes out her own fan, rises, and gives it to Yoshida. She then sits at centre.

Then why delay? Koremitsu, come,

bring me a lamp, that I may see *her* fan![21]

Each, holding an open fan, compares it with the other's. They look into each other's eyes.

Each in the other's fan knows that lost friend

who now is found. For each, these gifts

sealed after all the bond of steadfast love

sealed after all the bond of steadfast love.

In base square, Hanago stamps the final beat.

21. With a last, literary flourish brought on by the mention of 'moonflowers', Yoshida speaks (through the Chorus) as though he were Prince Genji in the 'Yūgao' chapter of the *Tale of Genji*; for the lady Yūgao sent a maid to offer Genji white moonflowers (*yūgao*, 'evening faces'), which the maid held out to Genji on a fan. Koremitsu, who had escorted Genji to the spot, was his confidant.

Izutsu · THE WELL-CRADLE

Since the term 'well-cradle' does not properly exist, the first thing to explain about *The Well-Cradle* is its English title. It refers to a 'well-curb' (the railing round the mouth of a well), and 'well-curb' would have been good enough were it not for one of the poems in the play: 'Cradle, well-cradle, well-cradle that told who was the taller: I've grown up, love, since I saw you last.' In Japanese, the poem starts with the musical, repeated syllables *tsutsu izutsu izutsu ni*, and it has to do with the love of two children who grew up to marry one another. They used to measure their heights against the 'well-cradle'. 'Well-curb' would have destroyed the euphony of the poem, and 'cradle', so suitable in sound and meaning, proved impossible to set aside.

Zeami wrote *The Well-Cradle* in his sixties. Many people believe it is his greatest play, and one authority (Kōsai Tsutomu) called it frankly 'a masterpiece among masterpieces'. It is admired as a model of the *yūgen* (depth and grace) that was Zeami's own ideal and that the modern schools of nō proudly uphold. Post-war scholars have therefore examined it carefully, and have given special attention to its history. Their discoveries are very interesting.

The Well-Cradle draws openly on episode no. 23 of *Ise monogatari* ('Tales of Ise'). This tenth-century work, a collection of some 125 short episodes or anecdotes centred on poems, is one of the pillars of the classical tradition. It evokes the many moods of love. Episode no. 23 tells of two children, a boy and a girl, whose houses were side by side. Before the two gates there was a well. They played by the well, as just described, until they grew up and 'knew modesty one toward the other'. The young man courted the girl and they married, but then his heart wandered, until, with a moving display of devotion, she recaptured his love. Part one of *The Well-Cradle* tells this story.

However, the anonymous *Ise monogatari* is an enigmatic work. Its title is arbitrary, no one in it is named, no episode is dated, and not a word links any episode to any other. Episode no. 23 therefore does *not* say, as the play does, that the man was Ariwara no Narihira (825–880) and the woman the daughter of one Ki no Aritsune (815–877); nor does it suggest any connection between itself and any other passage of the work. Moreover, *The Well-Cradle* assumes that Narihira and the daughter of Aritsune figure also in episodes nos. 17 and 24. Scholars having long ago dismissed such notions as fantasy, Zeami's use of *Ise monogatari* seems a bit free, even though cavalier use of sources is unlike him.

Ariwara no Narihira has always been linked with *Ise monogatari* because several dozen poems in the work are identified elsewhere as his. An outstanding poet, he seems also to have been an enterprising lover, and for these traits he became immortal. *Ise monogatari* promoted his legend because it left readers (who desperately needed help in making sense of the work) free to connect any or all of it with Narihira and his amorous adventures. In short, *Ise monogatari* tended to be read as a sort of encrypted biography of Narihira.

By the Kamakura period (1180–1333), the work of restoring largely spurious names, dates, and coherence to *Ise monogatari* was well advanced, and people read the work through commentaries. So did Zeami. *The Well-Cradle* is therefore based on these medieval commentaries. Since different lines of commentary disagree with one another minutely, one can even tell which texts Zeami used. His treatment of his sources, though brilliant, was not cavalier. The commentaries assured him that episodes nos. 17, 23, and 24 are all about Narihira and Aritsune's daughter. Zeami simply read continuity into the three, in the order 23, 17, 24.

All this helps to explain the difference between sixteenth-century and more recent performances. Nowadays, the *shite* wears a young woman's mask (*Waka-onna*) throughout the play, and one scholar (Yashima Masaharu) has shown that Zeami's own conception of the play may have corresponded to the gentle refinement this mask suggests. In the sixteenth century, however, the *shite* in part one wore *Fukai*, the face of a woman of about forty. (This is the mask in part one of *The Diver*.) Then, in part two, the 'Well-Cradle Lady' often appeared wearing *Masugami*, the face of a similarly mature woman touched by madness; and she danced not an elegant *jo-no-mai*, but a disturbed *kakeri*. (*Masugami* can be worn by the wildly perplexed princess in *Semimaru*.) In other words, the modern interpretation of the play differs from the sixteenth-century one.

The medieval commentaries were forgotten in the Edo period

(1600–1868), and it is easy for one who does not know them to see *The Well-Cradle* almost entirely in terms of episode no. 23. The allusions to nos. 17 and 24, in part two, seem then to lack weight, and in any case, their significance is not spelt out in words. Episode no. 23 evokes childhood friendship, youthful courtship, a first threat to conjugal happiness, and the triumph of a young wife's tender concern. It is no wonder that the phantom of this young wife should wear the *Waka-onna* mask. To the extent that the play is hers, it resembles a touching song of lost, still innocent love.

The 'Well-Cradle Lady' of part two is the same person as in part one, but her mind is concerned with trials the young wife never dreamed of. That is why, in the sixteenth century, she could change from *Fukai* into a different, more troubled mask. Her opening words are a poem from episode no. 17: 'Fickle they are, or so people say, these cherry blossoms, who have yet been pining for one rare all year round.' The woman in *Ise monogatari* speaks this poem when a man who has long neglected her suddenly appears at her door in cherry blossom time. Assuming this woman is Aritsune's daughter, Narihira has been wandering again, leaving her once more forlorn. By this time, however, she is no longer the innocent young wife. According to the commentaries, she does not mean, 'These cherry blossoms are said to be fickle, since they fall so soon, but even they, and still more so I, have been faithfully awaiting your coming.' Instead, she means, 'I know they call me fickle, just like these blossoms, but still, I have been waiting for you after all.' And the man's reply amounts to this: 'Perhaps you have been waiting, but then, if I had not come today, you no doubt would have taken up with someone else tomorrow.' She is therefore an older, more experienced woman. She, too, has stumbled. Perhaps she deserves no blame for that, since Narihira treated her intolerably, and no doubt she remained true to him in her heart. Still, she has learned more than she once knew about the world.

More time passes while this now wiser lady suffers from her husband's continued neglect. This is presumably when Narihira was pursuing his famous and disastrous affair with an empress. In episode no. 24, he has been gone three years and she has at last given up. Someone else has been courting her, and she has finally admitted him to her room. Just then Narihira knocks at the door. She explains the situation in a poem, and he replies: 'The days, the months, the years have passed while I loved you: so do you love him.' Then he leaves.

She calls out after him, in another poem, that she has always loved him alone, but he does not turn back. Desperate, she then sets out to catch up with him. Alas, the effort is beyond her strength. By a clear spring she collapses, with blood from her finger writes a last poem on a rock, and dies.

This is the lady of *The Well-Cradle*. The *Waka-onna* mask conveys her tender constancy, and the play certainly dwells on her childhood. Yet it is no wonder that she once wore *Fukai* and *Masugami*. Her sisters in Zeami's plays are not only the young women of *Pining Wind*, but the distraught singing-girl of *Lady Han* and the tragic wife of *The Fulling Block*. To see *The Well-Cradle* through *Ise monogatari* no. 24 is to see for the first time the force of her clinging to the place where she and Narihira were so happy as children, and to understand why she treasures the old victory – her only one – that briefly made him hers again. Looking back through depths of experience and time, she dances under the moon in Narihira's clothes, still calling him; and when she begins the poem *he* sang to lament his own great love, the empress ('Is this not the moon, this spring not the spring of old . . .?'), one hardly knows who is speaking. A few lines later, she looks into the well and sees him as in life, though she also knows he is a reflection – her own.

The site of *The Well-Cradle* is Ariwara Temple (Ariwara-dera) at Isonokami, below the hills a short way south of Nara. According to the play, although not to *Ise monogatari*, Narihira built it where he and the lady had lived as children. The temple no longer exists, if it ever did (the only confirmed Ariwara Temple is Futai-ji in Nara), but three sites at Isonokami claim it. For example, a stone pillar inscribed 'Ariwara-dera' stands at the entrance to a croquet ground for old people, and on the croquet ground itself one finds a little shrine to Narihira and his father. A well nearby is identified as the one in the story, although actually it is new: its predecessor fell victim to road construction. But apart from all this affection for old legends, Narihira could well have had a tie with Isonokami. It is a venerable locality and boasts one of the oldest and most sacred shrines in all Japan. A play on the Isonokami deity (*Furu no nō*), although not in the current repertoire, survives in Zeami's own hand.

THE WELL-CRADLE

Persons in order of appearance

A Monk	*waki*
A young Woman (*Waka-onna* mask)	*maeshite*
A Villager	*ai*
The 'Well-Cradle Lady' (*Waka-onna* mask)	*nochijite*

Remarks: A third-category play (*kazura-mono*) current in all five schools of nō. A variant performance tradition (*kogaki*) in the Kanze, Hōshō, Kongō, and Kita schools retains the Woman on stage, at the stage assistant position, at the end of part one; there she is clothed in the hat and robe that she wears in part two. In this case, the interlude is dropped. (The differences between sixteenth-century and modern performances is discussed in the introduction.)

*   *   *

Stage assistant places a 'well-cradle' (the square railing round the mouth of a well) at front of stage. A few stalks of tall plume grass (pampas grass) rise from one corner.

To nanori-bue *music, enter Monk. He stands in base square, facing the audience.*

MONK (*nanori*) You have before you a monk who is seeing all the provinces. Lately I visited the southern capital, and now I am on my way to Hatsuse.[1] Someone told me, when I inquired, that this temple is called Ariwara Temple. I will go to it and have a look. [*Moves to centre.*]

(*sashi*) Why, this Ariwara Temple can only be
at Isonokami, where, long ago,
Narihira and the daughter of Ki no Aritsune
lived together as man and wife.

> Let the wild wind blow,
> and at sea white waves
> rise, O Tatsuta! . . .[2]

---

1. The site of Hase-dera, in the mountains south-east of Nara. Hase-dera, one of the most famous Kannon temples in Japan, has been a pilgrimage centre since at least the tenth century. The 'southern capital' is Nara.

2. This poem appears in full later on. See note 12, below.

No doubt she spoke that poem here.

      (*uta*) Now I have reached this storied spot,   *Sits in place.*
             where Narihira and his chosen friend,
             Aritsune's daughter, tarried,
             I will comfort those two lovers,
             I will comfort that fond pair.   *Sits at witness position.*

To shidai *music, enter Woman, carrying a rosary and a leafy twig. She stops in base square, facing back of stage.*

WOMAN (*shidai*) Dawn after dawn, holy water[3]
             dawn after dawn, holy water
             refreshes both heart and moon.

      (*sashi*) Yet it is true, a loneliness   *Faces audience.*
             pervades the autumn nights,
             and at this ancient temple,
             callers are rare.
             Wind through the garden pine
             sighs through long, wakeful hours;
             the sinking moon gleams through grasses
             fringing the eaves,[4]
             while the old days, once forgotten,
             flood a troubled mind.
             How long must one live on
             in this world, all hope gone,
             when every thought is of *him*?

    (*sageuta*) But ceaselessly, with pure devotion,
             I trust Amida's proffered cord:[5]
             guide me, I beg, voice of the Teaching!

    (*ageuta*) Even the lost
             He shall illumine, for so He promised
             He shall illumine, for so He promised,
             and He surely will: the moon
             at dawn sets in the western hills,[6]

---

3. *Aka no mizu*, water placed as an offering on a Buddhist altar. The offering gladdens the giver's heart, and the pure water reflects a pure moon. The flowers mentioned later on are probably *shikimi* (star anise), the normal offering to the dead.

4. *Shinobu* grasses that grow in the thatch. *Shinobu* also means 'to remember with longing'.

5. The Buddha Amida was often shown holding a cord, the other end of which could be grasped by the devotee. With this cord, Amida was believed to draw the devotee's soul into his Western Paradise.

6. The moon's westward course recalls the journey of the soul towards Amida's Western Paradise.

though autumn fills the sky
and pines' sighing all the air
as storm winds sweep abroad:
a shifting world that seems a dream.

She places the leafy twigs as an offering before the well-cradle and joins her palms in prayer.

What sound will bring on awakening
what sound will bring on awakening?

She returns to base square and stands facing audience.

MONK (*mondō*) As I pause a while at the temple, quietly collecting my thoughts, a beautiful lady comes to draw water from the garden well. She then offers the water, with flowers, to the Buddha. All her prayers seem to be for the benefit of this grave-mound. Lady, please tell me: who are you?

WOMAN I am simply one who lives nearby. Ariwara no Narihira, whose vow founded this temple, left his name behind, and no doubt his remains lie beneath this mound. I myself do not know for certain, but I give him comfort, as you see, by offering flowers and water.

MONK Narihira did indeed leave us his name. Yet he whose memory still lingers here lived so very long ago. Why is it, then, that you, a woman, tend him and give him comfort? Do you and Ariwara no Narihira have some deeper tie?

WOMAN Have I some tie with Narihira, you ask, who even then was called 'A Man of Old'?[7] Why, it was all so long ago! No one now could have any tie with him at all.

MONK   One cannot argue with what you say,
                but still, his grave preserves the past.

WOMAN   The man is gone, yet Narihira's

MONK   trace[8] still lingers, even now

WOMAN   his fame lives on the lips of those

MONK   who speak of him,

---

7. Many episodes of *Ise monogatari* start with the words *mukashi otoko*, 'Once upon a time, a man . . .'. In the commentaries used by Zeami, these words appear as a name for Narihira.

8. *Ato*, a reminder of the continuing presence or memory of the deceased. Despite the use of the English word 'grave', Narihira's body is not necessarily buried here. The notion of *ato* requires a physical 'trace' of some sort, but it is quite different from the idea of a tomb.

WOMAN   'A Man of Old':

CHORUS *(ageuta)* the name, at least, is with us still,

           while Ariwara Temple, his own, grows old

           while Ariwara Temple, his own, grows old,

           and a pine springs from the mound's grasses.

           Seek him here, then, by a grave   *Moves towards well.*

           nodding with grasses in full plume . . .[9]

           that call to mind what times now gone?   *Gazes at grasses.*

           Wild, wild the weeds,

           deep, deep the dews

           that moisten the ancient grave.

           O, it is true! Out of the past,

           his present trace holds my love still   *To base square.*

           his present trace holds my love still.

   During the passage above, the Villager has slipped in to sit at villager position.

MONK *(unnamed)* Please go on speaking to me of Narihira.

   Woman sits at centre.

CHORUS *(kuri)* Of old, the Ariwara Middle Captain[10]

           lived long years in this ancient village,

           Isonokami,

           for its spring blossoms and its autumn moon.[11]

WOMAN *(sashi)* Then he courted Aritsune's daughter,

           and their love was far from shallow;

CHORUS   yet in Takayasu, in Kawachi province,

           he had yet another lady,

           so that his loves led him two ways.

WOMAN   Then she sang, the lady here,

               Let the wild wind blow,

               and at sea white waves

               rise, O Tatsuta!

CHORUS   Love, will you by night

               cross those hills alone?[12]

9. In poetry, the tall, nodding plumes of *susuki* resemble beckoning hands – the hands of those one knew in the past.

10. Narihira's court rank.

11. Blossoms and moon sum up the delights of all the seasons.

12. A poem from episode no. 23 of *Ise monogatari*. The Tatsuta hills had to be crossed on the way from Nara to Kawachi province, along Osaka Bay. The meaning of the opening lines, which ornament the place name Tatsuta, has long been debated. One theory, still cited, appeals to a motif from Chinese literature and holds that the 'white waves' are

	being anxious where night might take him:
	till that other left his heart
	and his bond with her dissolved.
WOMAN	Yes, her song, so naturally,
CHORUS	told of a love delicate and true.
(kuse)	There lived in this province, long ago,
	two families, house by house
	and, at their gates, a well.
	To the well-cradle their two children came
	fondly to talk and watch each other
	in the mirroring water,
	cheek to cheek and sleeve on sleeve;
	and their hearts' waters knew no soundings.[13]
	But as the moons and suns passed by,
	they grew up, and knew modesty
	one toward the other.
	In time, that good man wrote in gemmed tracery
	words given hue by his heart's flower:
WOMAN	Cradle, well-cradle,
	well-cradle that told
	who was the taller:
CHORUS	I've grown up, love,
	since I saw you last.
	He sent her the poem, and she, in turn:
	The girlish tresses
	I'd hold to yours
	hang past my shoulders:
	and if not you,
	who will put them up for me?[14]

bandits; so that the lady is afraid her husband may be attacked. However, most critical opinion over the centuries has rejected this explanation as out of keeping with the spirit of the poem. The lines probably evoke the traveller's loneliness in a desolate landscape.

13. The water and the children's 'hearts' (their bottomless love) are one and the same. Most of this *kuse* passage is faithful to episode no. 23 of *Ise monogatari*, but Zeami added the picture of the children watching each other in the water of the well. The 'water mirror' (*mizu kagami*) motif occurs in one form or another in other plays attributed to Zeami, including *Pining Wind* and *Semimaru*.

14. Putting up a girl's hair meant marriage. Since information from the Heian period (794–1180) indicates that her hair was put up by the ceremonial sponsor of the marriage, most commentators reject the idea that the groom himself could do it, and prefer something like, 'If not for you, for whom will I have my hair put up?' Yet this is not

Perhaps their exchange is the reason why
one hears of the 'Well-Cradle Lady':
an old name for Aritsune's daughter.

Chorus now sings for Monk.

   (*rongi*) Yes, it is an old tale you tell,
and, listening, I wonder still
at how strange you are.
Please let me know your name.

WOMAN   Ah, if I am, love-wrapt so,
Aritsune's daughter, I little know,
yet white waves rise, O Tatsuta!
by night I have come to you.

CHORUS   Astonishing! Then Tatsuta
hill bright with the hues of fall

WOMAN   leaves Ki no Aritsune's daughter [15]

CHORUS   or, it may be, the Well-Cradle Lady,

WOMAN   disclosed, to my shame, as I!

CHORUS   When we two vowed love's long-coiled strand
should bind us always, we were children   *To base square.*
so near the cradle, the cradle, well-cradle,
into the well-cradle she slips and is gone
into the well-cradle she slips and is gone.   *Exit.*

*   *   *

[The Villager, who previously had come in to sit at villager position, now comes forward, notices the Monk, and asks him who he is. The ensuing dialogue culminates in his recital of the story of Narihira and Aritsune's daughter. All this rather interrupts the mood of the play, at least for a reader, and conveys little that one does not already know. It is therefore omitted. This passage is typical.

   . . . Yes, those two were deeply in love. Later on, Narihira had a mistress in Takayasu, in the province of Kawachi, and he used to go to see her every night. But Aritsune's daughter showed no sign of jealousy. Narihira concluded that she must have another lover of her own. One evening, he

<hr/>

what the original says, and as Takeoka Masao has pointed out, the literal meaning better suits the intimacy of the exchange.
15. 'Leaves' is a 'pivot word'. These autumn leaves are the goddess who figures in *Tatsuta*.

pretended to set off for Kawachi as usual, but actually he hid nearby in a clump of plume grass and from there spied on the house. He saw her pick flowers and light incense, and heard her lament that he was gone. Then she spoke this poem: 'Let the wild wind blow, and at sea white waves rise, O Tatsuta! Love, will you by night cross those hills alone?' When Narihira heard that, he remembered the saying that a sage minister does not serve two sovereigns or a chaste woman two husbands, and he marvelled that any man could have so true a wife. They say that after that, he gave up his visits to Kawachi for ever.

In the closing dialogue, the Villager urges the Monk to stay on and 'comfort those two lovers'. The Monk promises to chant the *Lotus Sutra* for them.]

*   *   *

MONK (*ageuta*) The night hour grows late:
               above the temple hangs a moon
               above the temple hangs a moon
               to restore the past: with robe reversed,
               I prepare to dream,[16] and, briefly pillowed,
               lie down upon a bed of moss
               lie down upon a bed of moss.

To issei *music, enter the 'Well-Cradle Lady', wearing the hat and robe left her by Narihira.[17] She stands in base square, facing audience.*

LADY (*sashi*) Fickle they are,
               or so people say,
               these cherry blossoms,
               who have yet been pining
               for one rare all year round.[18]
               Yes, that poem being mine as well,
               they call me, too, the Pining Lady.[19]
               Since those old well-cradle days,
               the days, the months, the years have passed,[20]

16. Gazing at the moon brought back memories of the past, and sleeping with one's robe inside out brought dreams of one's beloved.
17. This is the costume worn by Shizuka as she dances in *Benkei Aboard Ship* and by the *nochijite* in *Pining Wind*.
18. From *Ise monogatari*, episode no. 17. (See introduction.)
19. The medieval commentaries give her this name.
20. A line from a poem in episode no. 24 of *Ise monogatari*, discussed in the introduction.

```
                  till now, in a life long lost,
                  I take upon me that same robe
                  Narihira left me,
      (issei)     O shame! to dance the Man of Old,
CHORUS            blossom sleeves swirling snow . . .²¹
```

(DANCE: *jo-no-mai*)

The Lady now dances a quiet jo-no-mai, *ending in base square, and continues dancing as text resumes.*

LADY (*waka*) Come hither now, I bring again
               the days of old; in Ariwara
CHORUS   Temple's well, round and clear,
               a radiant moon shines
               a radiant moon shines.
LADY   (*unnamed*) Is this not the moon,
                        this spring
                    not the spring of old . . .?²²
                So he once sang – but when, I wonder?²³
               (*noriji*) Cradle, well-cradle,

She circles stage, approaches the well-cradle, parts the plume grasses, and peers into the well.

CHORUS   cradle, well-cradle,
                    well-cradle that told
LADY   who was the taller,
CHORUS   I've grown up, love . . .
LADY   I've grown old, yes!
CHORUS   Just as he looked, the Man of Old,
               his robe and headdress,
               conceal the woman, show me a man,
               Narihira:

Gazes at her reflection, then backs away, weeping.

LADY   (*uta*) there before me, and so dear!
CHORUS   I see myself, yet still I love him!
               Departed lover in phantom form,
               a flower withered, all colour gone,

21. Flying cherry petals were often likened to snow and the dancer's tossing sleeves to cherry blossoms.
22. The beginning of Narihira's most famous poem (*Ise monogatari*, episode no. 4): 'Is this not the moon, this spring not the spring of old? Am I alone the one I ever was?'
23. Grammatically, this line can just as well mean, 'So I once sang . . .'.

but fragrant yet, Ariwara[24]
Temple bell tolls in the dawn:
an ancient temple, loud with pines
where the wind sighs. Plantain-leaf frail,[25]
the dream has broken into waking,
the dream breaks into day.

Facing side from base square, stamps the final beat.

24. The *ari* of Ariwara is intended in the original to mean also 'he remains'.
25. The immensely long, graceful leaves of the *bashō* tree (a species of banana or plantain) tatter easily in the wind.

Kantan

The theme of *Kantan* is surprisingly familiar. A young man goes off in search of a master; meets on the way an innkeeper with a magic pillow; dreams on the pillow a dream of worldly glory; realizes on awakening the vanity of all things; and goes home again, his questions answered. It is not only the young seeker who is familiar, for so, in a general way, is the play's attractively spiritual message. Moreover, *Kantan* is excellent theatre.

No one knows who wrote the play. The earliest mention of it is dated 1456, thirteen years after Zeami's death, and the first record of a performance dates from 1464. Some writers have suggested that since Zeami wrote plays towards the end of his life, *Kantan* could be one of them. Still, important authorities (Itō Masayoshi, for example) refrain from attributing it to him, and one shares their reluctance. Curiously enough, no one seems to have suggested that the playwright might be Komparu Zenchiku, Zeami's son-in-law. Judging from the other plays in this book that are linked to Zenchiku (*The Kasuga Dragon God*, *The Wildwood Shrine*, *Tatsuta*), the idea does not seem far-fetched.

Kantan is not the only nō play set in China, for Chinese literature and art were important to many fifteenth-century patrons of nō. Its ultimate source is *Chen-chung-chi* (Japanese *Chinchūki*), a fictional work of the T'ang dynasty, but several other, widely varied versions of the story intervened between *Chen-chung-chi* and the playwright, who in any case used his own imagination as well. Perhaps his single most direct source was the 'Dream of Ōryō' chapter of *Taiheiki* ('A Record of Great Peace'), a long, half-fictional chronicle completed by the late fourteenth century. In *Taiheiki*, however, the seeker sets out in search of wealth and success, not wisdom; a Taoist adept offers him the pillow at an inn; and the seeker wakes from his dream when his empress suddenly drowns with their heir in her arms. Further, the play's description of the dream palace is based on the 'Kan'yō Palace' chapter of the war epic *Heike monogatari* ('The Tale of the Taira', *c*. fourteenth century). In truth, there is no need to analyse the sources of *Kantan* at length because knowledge of them adds nothing to one's understanding of the play. It is more interesting simply to know that the Innkeeper is the playwright's invention and that the playwright himself made enlightenment the object of the seeker's quest.

Kantan seems originally to have been the capital of the ancient Chinese state of Chao, but this historical fact has nothing useful to do with the story of the pillow of Kantan.

Kantan

Persons in order of appearance

A woman, the Innkeeper	*ai*
Rosei, a young man (*Kantan-otoko* mask)	*shite*
An Imperial Envoy	*waki*
Two Palanquin-Bearers	*wakizure*
Three Imperial Ministers	*wakizure*
A Dancer	*kokata*

Remarks: A fourth-category play (*yonbamme-mono*) current in all five schools of nō. In the Kanze and Kongō schools, the palace may be replaced by a straw hut. The moment (near the end of the play) when Rosei races to lie down on the pillow before he wakes is now famous, but pre-nineteenth-century staging was much less dramatic.

*   *   *

Stage assistant places a 'palace' (a roofed dais) in witness square.
Enter Innkeeper, carrying the Pillow of Kantan. She stands in base square.

INNKEEPER (*nanori*) You see before you one whose home is the village of Kantan, in China. Ryōsen'ō is my name.[1] For a long time now I have been giving lodging to those who pass by on the road. A

---

1. In modern performances (the text of this speech dates from the eighteenth century) the Innkeeper does not have a name. Ryōsen'ō is actually one of the names of the Taoist adept who gives the seeker the pillow in some of the source versions of the story.

monk who once stayed here was practising the arts of the Immortals and he gave me a wondrous pillow. One who merely dozes off on this pillow awakens to the truth of past and future. I call it the Pillow of Kantan, and I offer it to travellers for their use. If a traveller comes by, I will invite him to stay. Take heed, good people! I will have him in to stay!

She places the pillow on the dais and withdraws to villager position.

To shidai *music, enter Rosei, carrying a 'Chinese' fan in his right hand and a rosary in his left. He stands in base square, at first facing back of stage, then turning to face audience to say his name.*

ROSEI (*shidai*) Lost on the journey of this dreary life
　　　　　　　　lost on the journey of this dreary life,
　　　　　　　　how long have I to tread the path of dreams?

(*nanori*) You have before you a young man named Rosei. My home is in the land of Shoku. Although born as a human being, I do not aspire to follow the Buddha, but instead only fritter my life away.[2] However, I understand that a holy sage resides upon Flying Sheep Mountain in the land of So. I am therefore hastening toward Flying Sheep Mountain, to seek enlightenment from him.

(*ageuta*) The home I know so well
　　　　　　vanishes behind me in the clouds
　　　　　　vanishes behind me in the clouds,
　　　　　　while I cross the mountains, range on range,
　　　　　　unsure what lies ahead. In travel wear,
　　　　　　I lodge where night finds me, in the fields,
　　　　　　among the hills or in a lonely village,
　　　　　　till Kantan, once simply a name,　　　　　*Mimes walking.*
　　　　　　lies before me, for I have arrived
　　　　　　lies before me, for I have arrived.

(*tsukizerifu*) Having come so swiftly, I have already reached the village of Kantan. The sun is still high in the sky, but I will none the less seek lodging here.

(*mondō*) I beg your pardon!

Innkeeper rises and comes to first pine.

INNKEEPER Are you a traveller? Where are you going?

ROSEI My name is Rosei and I am from the land of Shoku. Although

---

2. Buddhahood can be attained only from birth as a human being, and this birth is supremely rare.

born as a human being, I do not aspire to follow the Buddha, but instead only fritter my life away. So I have come to find the holy sage who resides upon Flying Sheep Mountain. I wish to seek enlightenment from him.

INNKEEPER My goodness, you have certainly come a long way! Well, once a monk stayed here. He was practising the arts of the Immortals, and he gave me a wondrous pillow called the Pillow of Kantan. One who dozes off a moment on this pillow awakens to the truth of past and future. Rest your head upon this pillow, then, and wait to dream.

Rosei steps on to the dais, goes down on one knee, and gazes at the pillow.

ROSEI (*unnamed*) So this is the celebrated Pillow of Kantan!

     Now I shall set out to know the truth,
     testing this pillow and the sacred dream
     that Heaven no doubt will vouchsafe to me.

  (*ageuta*) Refuge I sought, from a passing shower [3]

CHORUS refuge I sought, from a passing shower,
     at a wayside inn, though day remained;
     and now, to sleep a while and dream,
     I lie down on the Pillow of Kantan
     I lie down on the Pillow of Kantan.

Rosei lies down on his back, head on the pillow, and covers his face with his fan.
Enter Envoy, followed by Palanquin-Bearers. Envoy kneels, raps dais near the pillow with his fan, then retreats to centre where he kneels again and bows low.

ENVOY (*mondō*) Pardon me, Rosei, if you please. I have a message for you.

Rosei rises.

ROSEI Who are you?

ENVOY Sir, I am a royal envoy, and it is my duty to inform you that the King of So wishes to cede you his throne.

ROSEI What astonishing news! Why in the world should I occupy his throne?

ENVOY How should I fathom his reasons, sir? You are to rule the kingdom. No doubt you are endowed with certain auspicious signs. Please lose no time. Enter this palanquin.

3. A reference to the story of Saigyō and the Harlot of Eguchi, explained in the introduction to *Eguchi*.

ROSEI	How it gleams and sparkles, as though dew
ENVOY	shone in slanting sun! This palanquin,
ROSEI	wholly new to me, will take me now *Sits up, drops rosary.*
ENVOY	to glory you had never thought to gain
ROSEI	and lift me to the skies,
ENVOY	so you will feel.

CHORUS (*ageuta*) Entering this jewelled palanquin

Rosei steps off dais and comes to centre, where, in concert with Palanquin-Bearers, he mimes entering the palanquin. Envoy stands behind him.

> entering this jewelled palanquin,
> I set out on the way, yet unaware
> the flower of happy fortune is a dream,
> and wondering that I should rise above the clouds
> to reign as king.

Exeunt Envoy and Palanquin-Bearers.

To shin-no-issei *music, enter Dancer and Court Officials. They sit along the side of stage.*

    (*ageuta*) O how glad, how glorious a vision!
> O how glad, how glorious a vision!
> High beyond the clouds there tower now,
> bright beneath an all-illumining moon,
> the Cloud-Dragon Hall, the Abō Palace,[4]
> gleaming in a flood of radiance.
> And behold an equally wondrous scene:
> a park spread with gold and silver sand,
> walled in the four directions. Four jewelled gates
> admit or bid farewell to happy folk
> clothed in light. Surely, the far-famed
> City of Glory, or the Fair Citadel,[5]
> offer no more perfect loveliness
> than this sight so welcome to the eyes!

    (*sageuta*) Lords of a thousand or a myriad households
> pour in, bearing a thousand or a myriad gems,
> treasures innumerable, as offerings.
> Their banners paint the heavens, and on earth

4. 'Cloud-Dragon Hall' evokes an idealized imperial residence. The Abō (A-fang) Palace belonged to China's first emperor, Ch'in-shih-huang-ti (3rd c. B.C.).
5. Palaces in the Buddha Amida's Western Paradise and in the Tōri Heaven at the summit of Mount Sumeru, the central mountain of the Buddhist cosmos.

ROSEI (*uta*)   To the east, three hundred cubits high,[6]

resound like thunder; while with mighty voice
the multitude roars out tumultuous praise
the multitude roars out tumultuous praise.

CHORUS   stands a mountain all of purest silver,
surmounted by a risen sun of gold.

ROSEI   To the west, three hundred cubits tall,

CHORUS   rises a mountain made of purest gold,
surmounted by a risen silver sun.
The Hall of Life Eternal harbours
springs and autumns beyond reckoning,
and before the Gate of Everlasting Youth,
sun and moon barely move:
surely these inspired the present scene!

Envoy bows to Rosei.

MINISTER (*mondō*) Forgive my rude interruption, Your Majesty, but you have now sat on the throne for fifty years. Be good enough to drink this Elixir of the Immortals, and you will enjoy a thousand years of life. I have brought you on this occasion the Heavenly Elixir and the Goblet of Celestial Dew.

ROSEI   This Heavenly Elixir, of which you speak,

MINISTER   is the wine that the Immortals drink.

ROSEI   And the Goblet of Celestial Dew,

MINISTER   likewise, is the cup they drain in joy.

ROSEI   And this wine confers a thousand years,

MINISTER   yes, ten thousand springs in high estate,

ROSEI   the Sovereign having wealth,

MINISTER   the people, ease,

With his fan, Minister mimes pouring wine for Dancer, who then goes to Rosei and does the same. Rosei receives the wine on his fan.

CHORUS (*dan-uta*) the realm, peace, and, forever more
the realm, peace, and, forever more,
fullness of happy fortune,
joy increasing through all future time:

---

6. This scene is based on a passage in *Heike monogatari* about a palace associated with Ch'in-shih-huang-ti. The lines about the Hall of Life Eternal and the Gate of Everlasting Youth are from a congratulatory couplet in the *Wakan rōei shū* ('A Collection of Japanese and Chinese Poems for Chanting Aloud', 1013).

those blessings the chrysanthemum wine[7]
brings to all. Come, pass it lightly round!

ROSEI   Pass the cup!

Below, as Chorus sings, Dancer performs a 'dream dance'.

CHORUS   O pass the cup, I say,
that clear, chrysanthemum waters
speed on down the stream, till eager hands
dart from sleeves gay with chrysanthemums
to pick it up again:[8] a swaying dance
of graceful, sweeping gesture, as of light;
while, aloft, the round and radiant moon
circles in the everlasting sky.

DANCER   O silver dew

CHORUS   O silver dew
that from my chrysanthemums
drops day by day,
what aeons will you need
to fill the deep?[9]

Never shall these blessed waters fail,
flowing as they do from healing springs
that yield all their bounty, without end.
O how they gush forth, with might renewed!
One who drinks, savours the dews of Heaven,
waxes glad, and fain would leap for joy,
as pleasure merges night into bright day.
Happiness, delight, brilliant success:
all these here attain their pinnacle.

Dancer retires to side of stage.

(DANCE: *gaku*)

Rosei now performs a gaku *dance, first on the dais, then on the full stage. As text resumes, he continues dancing and miming.*

ROSEI (*waka*) How long shall the spring of glory last?
Forever and a day,

7. The chrysanthemum is the flower of long life.
8. An evocation of *kyokusui no en* ('the feast of the meandering waters'), at which cups of wine were set floating down a stream. A participant had to compose a Chinese poem before a cup drifted past, then pluck the cup from the stream and drain it.
9. A poem by Fujiwara no Motosuke, from the *Shūishū*, a tenth-century imperial anthology.

and longer still.
Just so, the dawn moon lingers in the sky.

ROSEI (*waka-uke*) He of the moon dances a manly measure,
feathery cloud-sleeves billowing, manifold,
while his song of joy

(*noriji*) resounds night-long

CHORUS   resounds night-long,
till sunrise bursts upon the world.
I had thought it night

ROSEI   yet day has dawned;

CHORUS   had thought day risen,

ROSEI   yet the moon is bright.

CHORUS   With spring flowers blooming on the bough,

ROSEI   autumn leaves gather their deep hues.

CHORUS   Ah, here is summer!

ROSEI   No, for snow is falling.

CHORUS   So the seasons turn before my eyes.
spring and summer, autumn, winter;
trees and grasses bloom within a day.
How beautiful, how wondrous a sight!

(*noriji*) So time passes and the years slip by
so time passes and the years slip by,
till fifty years of glory reach an end,
and melt away to nothing. They are gone,
for all these things happened in a dream.

Rosei gazes around him, races to the dais, leaps on to it, and lies down.

There upon the Pillow of Kantan,
the sleeper's dream is broken, and he wakes.

Innkeeper comes forward and raps upon the dais, by the pillow.

INNKEEPER (*mondō*) Wake up, traveller! The millet is ready for your
meal! Get up now, get up!   *Exit through side door.*

Rosei rises. He dances and mimes as appropriate throughout the final passage.

ROSEI (*uta*) From his dream, Rosei now awakens

CHORUS   From his dream, Rosei now awakens,
fifty springs and falls of glory gone
as though they had not been. Dazed, he rises.

ROSEI   How many they were, before,

CHORUS   the lovely palace ladies' murmuring voices,

ROSEI   that now are wind sighing through the pines.

CHORUS	Halls, pavilions, towers
ROSEI	were a passing lodging at Kantan.
CHORUS	All that time of glory,
ROSEI	fifty years,
CHORUS	was a dream that lasted the short while
ROSEI	millet takes to cook upon a stove.
CHORUS	A wonder, yes, and a mystery!
ROSEI	Pondering at last man's condition,
CHORUS	one sees a hundred years of happiness,

once life is done, are a dream, no more.
Fifty brilliant years are over now.
Hopes for future glory or great age,
all the joys five decades offered him,
have fled, now that he has reigned on high.
All things are a dream while millet cooks.

ROSEI   All hail, the Three Treasures! [10]

CHORUS   Now he understands: the sage he sought,
bent on liberation, was this pillow.

Kneels, presses the pillow reverently to his forehead.

How great the gift it gave him at Kantan!

Puts pillow down and goes to stand in base square, where he will stamp the final beat.

How great the gift it gave him at Kantan,
where he has seen the world to be a dream,
and, finding his hopes met, now journeys home.

10. The Buddha, his teaching, and the fellowship of monks.

Kasuga ryūjin · THE KASUGA DRAGON GOD

The Kasuga Dragon God, first mentioned in a record dated 1465, may be by Zeami's son-in-law, Komparu Zenchiku (1405–1468). Zenchiku had close ties to the Kasuga Shrine and Kōfuku-ji in Nara, the religious institutions that fostered early nō, and no doubt had several reasons to celebrate the Kasuga deity.

Kasuga was the ancestral shrine of the Fujiwara clan, which usually supplied the emperor with his consort and his regent, while Kōfuku-ji was the clan's senior ancestral temple. The two are neighbours, and in Zenchiku's time they formed an indissoluble pair that was dominated by Kōfuku-ji. According to a syncretic pattern then common, the Kasuga deity was understood as a local manifestation of various Buddhist divinities, and his sacred hill, Mount Mikasa, was therefore seen as the paradise of several different buddhas and bodhisattvas. *The Kasuga Dragon God* presents this deity as the living voice of the Buddha, Shakyamuni, and Mount Mikasa as Vulture Peak in India where Shakyamuni preached the *Lotus Sutra*.

The play's unusual historical background has to do with Myōe, the *waki*. Myōe Shōnin ('The Venerable Myōe', 1173–1232) was an outstanding monk of his time, and a man of dreams and visions. His *Yume no ki* ('A Record of My Dreams') survives. The ultimate source of *The Kasuga Dragon God* is a series of divine oracles and dreams vouchsafed to him by the Kasuga deity in 1203.

Myōe often felt despair at having been born too late, and in the wrong place, to hear the Buddha preach in person. As early as 1195, he considered going to India, to worship in the places where the Buddha had taught; and he began studying the travel account left by the T'ang monk Hsüan-tsang (600–664), who went to India in search of the true scriptures. Then, in 1202, he resolved to act. It was a brave, in fact a unique ambition for the time, and if he had gone, he probably would not have returned.

He did not go because the Kasuga deity persuaded him to desist. It is unclear why the deity should have been so concerned about him.

The stories in *Kasuga Gongen genki* ('The Miracles of the Kasuga Deity', 1309) show how assiduously the deity protected Kōfuku-ji and how eager he was to keep any Kōfuku-ji monk from leaving. Myōe, however, had only studied for a few years, in his early twenties, at Tōdai-ji, a temple near Kōfuku-ji but otherwise quite different. His bond with the Kasuga deity must have been a private matter.

The earliest record of the oracles and dreams of 1203 is dated 1205 and was written by Myōe himself. Two later, more detailed accounts by Myōe's disciple Kikai (1178–1250) provided the material for the corresponding text of *Kasuga Gongen genki*: a set of twenty painted handscrolls presented by the Fujiwara, with the full collaboration of Kōfuku-ji, to their tutelary deity. (Scrolls 17 and 18 are devoted entirely to the subject.) The story told by these documents is undoubtedly the source of the play, but the playwright changed it a great deal. All his changes emphasize Kōfuku-ji.

According to the earlier accounts, the oracles of 1203 were spoken in Myōe's native province of Kii (the present Wakayama Prefecture), in a house where Myōe was staying. The medium was a woman relative by marriage, twenty-eight years old. In the first lunar month of 1203, this lady began a spontaneous fast, and then, ten days later, mounted the crossbeam under the ceiling of her room. She then said: 'I am the Kasuga deity. Good monk, you intend to travel towards the west, and I have come down in order to dissuade you from doing so.' However, this first, relatively short oracle did not entirely convince Myōe, who sought confirmation that it had been genuine.

The second, three days later, swept away all doubt. Some seventy or eighty people witnessed it and breathed in the unknown fragrance, indescribably rich and sweet, that emanated from the medium's body. Calling himself 'this old man', the deity announced the silent presence also of the Sumiyoshi deity (celebrated in *Takasago*), and he pleaded with Myōe to give up his plan. The visitation was so powerful that the gathering, including Myōe, quickly dissolved in tears. Meanwhile, the medium sat perfectly still and dazzlingly radiant, in a profound trance. The deity spoke at great length, saying for example (in the *Kasuga Gongen genki* version):

Never before have I shown my true form this way and come down into human presence, nor will I again. I have done so now, good monk, because I have such extreme regard for you. That you should have your heart set on the mountains and forests of distant lands is wonderful as far as your own practice is concerned, but it makes those whom you might otherwise touch lose a chance to establish their link with enlightenment, and that is what distresses me so . . .

Several times he said he must leave (that is, leave the medium's body), yet could not bring himself to do so. Finally (once more in the *Kasuga Gongen genki* version):

> Lifting her head again, she [or he] addressed them for a last time. 'Now I *am* going,' he said. 'I will leave you my fragrance a while, to remind you all of me and to give you comfort. You, good monk, come quickly to Kasuga-yama!' As before, the deity prepared to leave. Then he said, 'If you undertake to gather each month on this same night, to talk and to study, I will come down and join your assembly, no matter where it may be.'

Thus, the deity not only urged Myōe to visit Kasuga-yama (Mount Mikasa), but called on him to establish a new variant of the Kasuga cult.

Myōe in time answered that call, but first he set out immediately for Nara. There, he sat in vigil at the shrine, as people did then at shrines and temples when they sought a sacred dream. In the words of *Kasuga Gongen genki*:

> On the eleventh day [of the month following the great oracle], he was before the Kasuga Sanctuaries when he dozed off a little and dreamed that he went to Vulture Peak and served our Great Teacher Shaka [i.e. Shakyamuni]. This happened half a dozen times.

These dreams are the climactic vision of *The Kasuga Dragon God*.

One imagines from the play's version of these events that Myōe's oracles and dreams had become garbled as they passed into Kōfuku-ji folklore (the temple was a varied community perhaps ten thousand strong) and had then fused with other local motifs before emerging on stage as visionary musical drama. No one knows whether any such process actually took place or whether Zenchiku (if it was he) worked the entire transformation himself; but if he did, he probably had advice from the monks.

The play annexes the whole story to Kōfuku-ji. Myōe's untidily idiosyncratic medium is replaced by 'Tokifū Hideyuki', an idealized

Kasuga Shrine priest, and the oracle occurs at the shrine itself, when Myōe comes to bid the deity farewell. However, it is the Dragon God who really gives the temple's pretensions away.

The Kasuga deity was a complex divinity, but dragons were not prominent among his many forms. It is true that much dragon lore was linked to him, but its physical focus was Sarusawa Pond at the Great South Gate of Kōfuku-ji: the pond inhabited by the Dragon God of the play. The Shido-ji legend (*The Diver*) mentions this pond as the abode of a dragon king unconnected with Kasuga. In any case, Kōfuku-ji folklore associated the temple itself with dragons, since there was supposed to be a 'Dragon Palace' under the temple's central hall. A Kōfuku-ji monk had found it by entering a hole on the slope between the Pond and the Great South Gate.

No doubt the Dragon God of the play, with his display of the life of Shakyamuni, is continuous with the Kasuga deity proper. The Kōfuku-ji monk Gedatsu Shōnin (1155–1213), whom Myōe knew, had explicitly defined the Kasuga deity's higher, Buddhist identity (*honji*) as that of Shakyamuni, and *Kasuga Gongen genki* insists on the point. Moreover, the deity particularly enjoyed the *bugaku* dance *Ryōō* ('The Dragon King'). But although dragons are not absent from Kasuga lore, nothing in this lore suggests that the deity could actually star in a play in dragon form. It is because of Kōfuku-ji that he does so in the *Kasuga Dragon God*, where he matches the type of the Dragon King in *The Diver* or *Chikubu-shima*. As the legend of Shido-ji shows, Kōfuku-ji was never shy about asserting its own pre-eminence.

In the end, Kōfuku-ji fell from its pride. Hard times came in the Edo period (1600–1868), and in 1717 much of the temple burned down. Then, after the Meiji Restoration (1868), a violent movement sought to disestablish Buddhism. Temple property was destroyed and the remaining upper-class monks of Kōfuku-ji declared themselves to be Kasuga Shrine priests. For a time, Kōfuku-ji ceased to exist. The modern visitor to Nara still sees the Kōfuku-ji Museum and Sarusawa Pond (it is not nearly as impressive as in the play), but the temple is hardly more than a wraith from the past. In contrast, the Kasuga Shrine is doing very well. Countless tame deer – the deity's canonical messengers – roam the green expanses of Nara Park, delighting scholar and tourist alike.

THE KASUGA DRAGON GOD

Persons in order of appearance

Myōe, a monk	*waki*
Two Companions, also monks	*wakizure*
An Old Man, a shrine priest (*Koushijō* or *Akobujō* mask)	*maeshite*
A Minor Deity in the service of Kasuga (*Nobori-hige* mask)	*ai*
A Dragon God (*Kurohige* mask with dragon headdress)	*nochijite*

Remarks: A fifth-category play (*kiri-nō*) current in all five schools of nō. Among several variant performance traditions (*kogaki*), one, in the Kanze school, adds to the *shite* in part one an identically costumed *tsure*, then in part two presents the Dragon Princess as *tsure* and has her dance a *tennyo-mai*. Another, in the Hōshō and Kongō schools, likewise has both *shite* and *tsure* in part one, then in part two presents seven or eight Dragon Kings in addition to the Dragon God. They are accompanied by two Dragon Princesses who dance a *chū-no-mai*. In another Kanze variant, the Dragon God gives Myōe a jewel. There are also several versions of the interlude. Present or past variants replace the minor deity by a shrine official, a citizen of Nara, or even a monkey. By no means all include the passage, given here, about the forbidding distance between Japan and India.

*   *   *

To shidai *music, enter Myōe and Companions. They stand at centre, facing each other.*

MYŌE and COMPANIONS

    (*shidai*) Thither the moon, too, makes its nightly way
              thither the moon, too, makes its nightly way:[1]
              then I will seek the land where the sun goes down.

Face audience.

1. The westward course of the moon generally recalls the soul's journey towards Amida's Western Paradise, although Myōe himself was not an Amida devotee. Here, the moon refers more explicitly to the Buddha Shakyamuni and his native land. The 'land where the sun goes down' was of course the opposite of Japan, the 'land of the rising sun'.

MYŌE (*nanori*) You have before you the monk Myōe of Toganoo.[2] My
heart is set upon travelling to China and India, and I must therefore
go before the Kasuga Shrine to bid the God farewell. I am just now
on my way down to the Southern Capital.

MYŌE and COMPANIONS

> (*ageuta*) Mount Atago[3]   *Face each other.*
> and Shikimi-ga-hara detain us no more
> and Shikimi-ga-hara detain us no more.
> Under the moon, the pine-clad Double Hills
> and deep blue heavens breathe quiet peace.
> The Miyako mountains fade behind us
> as, southward-bound towards ancient Nara,
> we cross Nara Slope, spy Mount Mikasa,
>
>   *Myōe mimes walking.*
>
> and at Kasuga Village have at last arrived
> and at Kasuga Village have at last arrived.   *Face audience.*

MYŌE (*tsukizerifu*) Having come so swiftly, we have already reached
Kasuga. I will quietly go before the Shrine.

COMPANIONS Very well.

Myōe and Companion sit in witness square.

To issei *music, enter Old Man. He stands in base square.*

OLD MAN (*issei*) Eyes that turn to the limpid sky
> see the brightness of the Tempered Light.[4]

(*sashi*) The Mountain displays an unmoving form:
the path, now as long ago, of the gods.
The Village offers a place of peace and ease,

---

2. Toganoo, in the hills north-west of Kyoto, is the site of Myōe's own temple, Kōzan-ji.
However, Myōe did not live there until he had given up his journey to India. His shrine
there to the Kasuga deity was recognized by the court as almost equivalent to the main
shrine in Nara.

3. Mount Atago (890m) rises north-west of Kyoto and Shikimi-ga-hara ('star anise
moor') is on its lower slopes; the two names were conventionally associated in medieval
linked verse. The Double Hills are Narabi-ga-oka: two low, wooded hills now surrounded by the north-western sector of the city. From Nara Slope, over the Saho Hills,
the traveller from Kyoto had his first glimpse of Nara, the 'Southern Capital' (as
distinguished from Kyoto).

4. The Buddha tempers the brilliance of his enlightenment so as not to blind and
frighten sentient beings, who might then never conceive the aspiration to enlightenment.

ringing for ever with human voices.[5]

      These in truth are the generations
      of Amenokoyane, eternally divine.[6]
      Beneath the moon rise twin columns:
      the Torii;[7]

  (*ageuta*) O how the Shrine
      showers blessings: all Four Sanctuaries[8]
      showers blessings: all Four Sanctuaries,
      heirs to divinity bequeathed of old,
      from the Age of the Gods, show, clear and pure,
      the divine intention mingling with the dust.[9]
      Yes, even the wind,
      playing through the pines of Mikasa Grove
      rustles no boughs: ah, a peaceful scene
      rustles no boughs: ah, a peaceful scene!

MYŌE (*mondō*) Please excuse me, good priest, but may I speak with you?

OLD MAN Ah, you are the Venerable Myōe of Toganoo, are you not? The God will surely be happy that you have come.

MYŌE You see, I wish to approach the Shrine today because I have set my heart upon visiting China and India, and so have come to say goodbye.

OLD MAN This is news indeed. But surely you realize how eagerly He awaits your visits for the New Year and each of the following seasons, and becomes impatient at the least delay. In fact, I understand He calls you His first-born son, and treats as his second son the Venerable Gedatsu of Kasagi.[10] You two might as well be His

5. The language of these four lines resembles that used for Chinese verse. In *Kasuga Gongen genki*, the deity describes enlightenment as 'the path of my mountain'.

6. The direct, divine ancestor of the Fujiwara clan and, more locally, of the Kasuga priestly lineages.

7. The sacred gate to the shrine.

8. In the world of nō, Amenokoyane was the chief of the deities enshrined at Kasuga, but there were three others, as well as a Wakamiya, or 'Young Prince' deity. All are encompassed by the term 'Kasuga deity'.

9. As the Buddha 'tempers' his light (n. 4, above), so he 'mingles with the dust' of the world in order to make enlightenment accessible to all sentient beings.

10. Gedatsu Shōnin (1155–1213), the most distinguished Kōfuku-ji monk of his time, received many revelations from the Kasuga deity; but the deity was vexed when, against his express wish, Gedatsu moved to Kasagi, a sacred mountain about twenty kilometres away. Gedatsu gave the deity so much trouble that the deity considered him junior to Myōe, even though Myōe was eighteen years younger.

own hands or eyes, He protects you so loyally, night and day. How, then, could it please Him to learn that you wish to leave Japan and cross the sea to China and India?

MYŌE I know you have good reason to speak as you do. However, I will be visiting China and India only in order to venerate the places linked with the Buddha's memory. How could such a plan displease the God?

OLD MAN Your words astonish me.

> Were the Buddha alive in the world today,
> one would do well to see and hear Him.
> But that noble spot where the Buddha preached
> is now Mount Mikasa, not Vulture Peak.
> Besides, good monk, when you first came
> before our Shrine, along Nara Slope
> the crowd bowed to you with folded hands;
> and not only humans, but, all insentient,

CHORUS (*ageuta*) the plants and trees of Mikasa Grove

> the plants and trees of Mikasa Grove
> bowed their branches low, though no wind blew;
> and the very deer, who each morning roam
> the happy meadows below the Mountain,
> came forth to greet you on bended knee
> their antlers lowered in meek reverence.[11]
> This prodigy your own eyes have seen,
> yet still you wonder where the Pure Land may lie,[12]
> O you of faith as vast as Musashi Plain![13]
> No, I implore you, again and again:
> Stay here instead, as the God would wish,
> and humbly submit to His Will
> and humbly submit to His Will.   *Sits at centre.*

MYŌE (*mondō*) Please tell me all you can about this noble Shrine.

OLD MAN (*sashi*) Now, it seems to me one seeks India or China
> so as to honour those antique sites

---

11. This moment, attested by the earlier records, is told and illustrated in *Kasuga Gongen genki*.
12. The final section of *Kasuga Gongen genki* insists that the Pure Lands of all the Buddhas are present at Kasuga itself.
13. A reference to a poem in the *Shinkokinshū* (1206). The poem evokes the boundlessness of autumn on Musashi Plain, the region that is now greater Tokyo.

CHORUS   where in His time the Buddha preached the Law.
                But one who hopes to worship Mount Tendai,[14]
                ought now to travel to Mount Hiei;
                and should one's goal be Mount Godai,
                then Yoshino or Tsukuba deserve the honour.[15]

OLD MAN   Of old, Vulture Peak;

CHORUS   now, for the salvation of sentient beings,
                He makes manifest our Divine Presence
                and dwells in state upon this Mountain,

OLD MAN   so that Vulture Peak, where the Buddha taught,

CHORUS   is here to worship in Mount Mikasa.

                (*kuse*) Know me as I am:
                        the Buddha Shakyamuni
                        came into this life,
                        and lo! the bright moon
                        now illumines the world.[16]

                A wonder indeed, this verse the God spoke,
                for this was His vow: that His godly virtue,
                Complete in Mercy's Works,[17] should illumine the lost.
                Concerned that beings of lesser wit
                should miss His blessing, He appeared in this guise:
                having put off His jewels, His exquisite raiment,
                He clothed Himself in a simple, patched robe;
                and the Deer Park, where once He taught
                the Four Noble Truths, is this very spot!
                Do not all the deer on the Kasuga meadows
                make this a Deer Park too?[18]

OLD MAN   And, what is more, behold our Shrine:

CHORUS   there stands Mount Mikasa, bathed in light,

14. Mount T'ien-t'ai in China, the origin of the Tendai Buddhism practised in the great
monastic complex on Mount Hiei (848m), just north-east of Kyoto.
15. Mount Godai (Wu-t'ai-shan), in China, was the Pure Land of the Bodhisattva Monju.
According to certain medieval manuals of poetry, the sacred Yoshino Mountains (south
of Nara) and Mount Tsukuba (east of modern Tokyo) were both fragments of Wu-t'ai-
shan that had flown to Japan.
16. A poem spoken to Gedatsu Shōnin by the Kasuga deity (*Kasuga Gongen genki*;
Shoku kokinshū, 1265). It affirms the deity's identity as the living presence of Shakyamuni.
17. In 937, the Kasuga deity claimed through a medium, and was given, the title
'Bodhisattva Complete in Mercy's Works'.
18. Shakyamuni first preached in the Deer Park at Sarnath, near Benares.

while beyond it rises the springtime sun.[19]
The radiance of His mercy lights all four directions:
the Kasuga meadows, the broad thoroughfare
that leads to the Shrine. Spotless, in the west,
a bright moon illumines the Great Temple,[20]
and, waxing in brilliance, the Seven Great Temples
where the Teaching flowers, as cherries do,
eightfold, to grace our own Capital.[21]
The Kasuga meadows lie at peace
in the calm of spring!

MYŌE (*mondō*) It has been a rare good fortune to meet you! I will take your words for a divine oracle and give up my journey to the continent. But who are you? Please tell me your name.

OLD MAN If you will give up your journey to China and India, then I will display upon Mount Mikasa the five regions of India, the Buddha's Birth from Queen Maya, His Enlightenment at Bodhgaya,

His Preaching on Vulture Peak,

CHORUS (*uta*) His Passing in the Sala Grove:
yes, all these things I will reveal to you.
Be patient a while and wait at this spot,   *Rises.*
he cries, giving voice to the God's decree.
I am Tokifū Hideyuki![22]
Suddenly, then, he is seen no more
suddenly, then, he is seen no more.

To raijo *music, exit Old Man.*

*   *   *

To ranjo *music, enter Minor Deity, leaning on a staff. He stands in base square.*

19. The characters 'spring' and 'sun' spell the name Kasuga.
20. The Great Temple 'in the west' is Saidai-ji ('Western Great Temple'), one of the traditionally defined 'Seven Great Temples of Nara'. Kōfuku-ji, one of these, at least claimed to rule them all.
21. The 'teaching that flowers eightfold' is the *Lotus Sutra*. The Kasuga meadows are still covered with cherry trees that have 'eightfold' (double) flowers.
22. This name combines those of Nakatomi no Tokifū (731–818) and Nakatomi no Hideyuki (713–807). (Hideyuki's own descendants, who are still priests at the shrine, read his name Hidetsura.) These two priests played a key role in the legend of the founding of the Kasuga Shrine in 768.

MINOR DEITY You have before you a minor deity in the Kasuga Dragon God's service. I am here to explain that since the Venerable Myōe of Toganoo was planning to set off for China and India, he came to the Shrine to bid the God farewell . . . [*He now repeats matters already explained in the play.*] . . . The Venerable Myōe is so holy that the God was most distressed to contemplate the thought of his absence, and did His best to persuade Myōe to desist.[23] However, Myōe remained determined to go. Considering the matter further, the God then realized that from the T'ang capital of Ch'ang-an to the Royal Palace of the King of Magadha, in India, the distance was fifty thousand leagues. Since this seemed an awfully long way, He examined the route by sea. This turned out to be an ocean voyage of one hundred thousand leagues, and the perils of wind and wave were thoroughly alarming. The land route, on the other hand, crossed precipitous mountain ranges. Any traveller there would surely be attacked by evil genii and venomous beasts. Of old, at the river of the Flowing Sands, Tripitaka Master Hsüan-tsang was robbed seven times of his life by frightful serpents. Each time, however, he revived. At last he reached the Royal Palace, brought back the miraculous scrolls of the *Sutra on the Perfection of Wisdom*, and so bequeathed them as a treasure to later generations. But what with one thing and another, the God was still very doubtful. Between China and India, the Venerable Myōe would have to pass four particularly dangerous places known as the Flowing Sands, the Pamir Mountains, the Iron Gate, and the Feeble Water. Myōe, however, kept insisting that he wished to emulate Hsüan-tsang . . . [*He evokes Myōe's resolve.*] . . . His determination aroused the God's compassion. 'No doubt,' the God observed, 'you intend to worship the sites linked with the Buddha's career. If the Buddha were still alive, your journey would not be in vain, for you would be able to see and hear Him. But as things are now, I have grave doubts about the value of your going. If you will desist, then I will in the course of this night make visible upon Mount Mikasa the Five Regions of India, the Buddha's Birth from Queen Maya, His Enlightenment at Bodhgaya, His Preaching upon Vulture Peak, and His Passing in the Sala Grove.' In this way, with many a persuasive touch, the God sought to dissuade Myōe; and Myōe, in response, did indeed decide not to go. The wonder displayed tonight will be most impressive. [*Looks up, over the audience.*] Why, the Five Regions of India are already appearing! Mountains, rivers, and the great earth are quaking! Good people, quiet your minds, and bow in reverence and awe! Bow in reverence and awe! [*Exit.*]

23. The journey from Japan to China was risky enough, but at least its dangers were understood. The Japanese knew about the more exotic perils of travelling from China to India mainly from the account left by Hsüan-tsang (600–664). They also knew that by Myōe's own time, Buddhism was all but dead in India.

*   *   *

MYŌE and COMPANIONS *(ageuta)* Awesome indeed, the Divine Oracle
                awesome indeed, the Divine Oracle,
                mightily spoken, yields to a flood of light:
                all of Kasuga, meadow and mountain,
                becomes a land of gold; the plants, the trees,
                are now the Buddha-Body, a wonder to behold
                are now the Buddha-Body, a wonder to behold!

To hayafue *music, enter Dragon God, with a 'demon mallet' in his sash. He stops
at first pine.*

CHORUS *(chū-noriji)* Does the mighty earth's rocking and quaking
                mean Dragon Gods are gathering in the Nether World?
DRAGON GOD Yes! The Eight Great Dragon Kings: [24]
CHORUS   Dragon King Nanda,
DRAGON GOD Dragon King Batsunanda,
CHORUS   Dragon King Shakara,
DRAGON GOD Washukitsu, His Dragon Majesty,
CHORUS   Dragon Majesty Tokushaka,
DRAGON GOD Dragon Majesty Anabadatta,
CHORUS   attended by an entourage, an entourage of millions,
                a surging multitude, like waves on the plain,   *Enters stage.*
                gather to attend the Buddha's assembly,   *Sits.*
                range themselves to hearken to the Law.
DRAGON GOD So gather, too,
                the Kinnara King of the Marvellous Teaching,
CHORUS   the Kinnara King of the Teaching Upheld,
DRAGON GOD King Gaku-Kendatsuba,
CHORUS   His Majesty Gakuon-Kendatsuba,
DRAGON GOD His Majesty Bachi of the Ashura,
CHORUS   King Rago of the Ashura,
                with their attendant host,
                a host as vast in number as the sands of the Ganges,
                likewise press forward to take their seats.

24. Eight Dragon Kings are mentioned in the *Lotus Sutra* as having gathered, with their
followers, to hear the Buddha preach. The 'Kinnara Kings' (deities of song) and the
other kings mentioned below are likewise from the *Lotus Sutra*. Their names (Japanese
pronunciations of Chinese transliterations of Sanskrit) are suitably impressive, but in
Japanese mean nothing at all.

Dragon God mimes and dances, below, demon mallet in hand.

(*noriji*)   The Dragon Girl dances, her billowing sleeves[25]
the Dragon Girl dances, her billowing sleeves
a pristine white: across the foaming sea
they sweep, and a spray of gleaming drops
rises from the blue of the sky reflected
upon the ocean abyss!
Now she treads the deep: the ship of the moon
sails the waters of the Saho River[26]

DRAGON GOD while the Eight Great Dragon Kings

(QUASI-DANCE: *mai-bataraki*)

Dragon God performs a mai-bataraki *circuit of the stage, and continues dancing as text resumes.*

the Eight Great Dragon Kings
incline their eight crowns.

CHORUS   Ah, the Kasuga meadows, and over Mikasa
the moon ascending through fleeing clouds!
Watchman of Signal Fires, come forth and see:[27]
the Birth from Maya, the Sermon on Vulture Peak,
the Passing in the Sala Grove:
you have watched them all, and now they are done.
Well, Venerable Myōe? Your journey to China?

MYŌE   I will stay here.

CHORUS   Your voyage to India?

MYŌE   I will not go.

CHORUS   The Buddha's holy places?

MYŌE   I will let them be.

CHORUS   Yes, for all your seeking, your pious searching,
you will never see a more exalted vision!
Now, mounting the clouds, the Dragon Girl
soars on her way towards the south,
as with lusty tread the Dragon God
churns the blue waves of Sarusawa Pond,

25. The Dragon King's daughter who, in the *Lotus Sutra*, presented a priceless pearl to the Buddha and passed on into enlightenment. (See the introduction to *The Diver*.)
26. A small river that flows not far from Mount Mikasa.
27. A figure mentioned in poetry, though still mysterious even to the poets. He was sometimes called the Watchman of the [Kasuga] Meadows.

       now a mighty Serpent a thousand fathoms long,
       swarming in the mid-heaven,
       writhing upon the earth,
       tossing the pond aloft,
       he is lost to view.

In base square, leaps into the air, comes down kneeling on one knee, flips a sleeve over his head, rises, and stamps the final beat.

Kinuta · THE FULLING BLOCK

Zeami was probably in his late sixties when, 'one quiet evening, listening to the music of *The Fulling Block*, he said: "I can't imagine anyone these days appreciating a play like this. Writing one is more trouble than it's worth." ' The passage is from *Sarugaku dangi* ('Conversations on Nō'), a record of Zeami's sayings taken down by his second son, Motoyoshi. Zeami had probably written the play quite recently, under the unhappy circumstances created by the accession of a shogun (Ashikaga Yoshimochi) who did not care at all for Zeami or his art. Elsewhere in *Sarugaku dangi*, Zeami said: 'In generations to come, no one will appreciate this play. It's a shame.'

Actually, the play is greatly admired today. It is true, however, that performances of it lapsed shortly after Zeami's time. Amateurs continued to sing it, but it was not staged again until the 1690s. Since no staging traditions for it survived, each school of nō has had to work out its own, with the result that performances of *The Fulling Block* differ more widely than usual from school to school. The play is now in the repertoire of all five schools, but the Komparu, the last to adopt it, did so only after the Second World War.

The Fulling Block certainly does not cater to anyone's taste for colourful, exciting, or even lyrical entertainment. It is what Zeami called a *hietaru nō*: a 'cold play' that avoids display in order to pursue a higher purpose. The lofty ideal of 'coldness' has been championed in modern times, but in the case of *The Fulling Block*, the issue of the play's true worth seems even now not to have been entirely resolved.

Surely *The Fulling Block* is a work of extraordinary stature. If Zeami, considering his own and future times, felt that no one could truly 'taste' it (his own word), then he must have believed men were now heartless indeed. For despite its theatrical 'coldness', the play has enormous human warmth. It is a tragedy, certainly: a wife, mistakenly believing herself abandoned, dies insane and suffers in Hell. Yet she is saved in the end by her husband's love, and, for both, the play ends in dignity.

One who admires *The Fulling Block* in this way will be deeply moved by part two: the wife returns as a spirit, describes the torments of Hell, unburdens herself to her husband of all her complaints, then, transformed by his care, finds eternal rest. Yet, even in recent times, this part has gone relatively unappreciated. There may be two reasons for this: the character of part one and the conception of the *shite* as the sole actor in the play.

In several ways, literary technique among them, *The Fulling Block* resembles *Lady Han*. Zeami imagined a commonplace misfortune and, especially in part one, embellished it with a haunting Chinese 'melody': the story of Sobu (Su Wu), supplemented by further ornaments from poetry in Chinese. The poetic style of part one, like that of *Lady Han*, seems directly influenced by the medieval songs known as *enkyoku*. Moreover, each play is a study of love and separation – romantic love in *Lady Han*, conjugal love in *The Fulling Block*; and in each, Zeami kept to his subject by avoiding the issue of fault. The woman's conviction that her love has forgotten her is entirely natural, but wrong. At the end of each play the truth emerges: the man and woman are equal in love. In this respect, these plays are unique in nō.

The poetry of part one of *The Fulling Block*, in the original, is astonishing. Nowhere did Zeami spread himself more generously as a poet. However, this beauty is of a kind easily recognizable to a modern audience and one critic (Kanai Kiyomitsu) observed that for many people, part one is enough. The spirit's complaint, in part two, can seem pale in comparison.

It may pale not only because part one is so beautiful, but because the conception of the *shite* as the sole actor obscures its value. This conception represents a trend that began shortly after Zeami's time, and it was given definitive expression in 1930 by Nogami Toyoichirō. It means that the only significant presence on the nō stage is that of the *shite*: there is only one 'actor' in the play. The other figures only set off the *shite*. As a result, nō is not 'drama' (*gikyoku*) at all. Although Nogami did not say so explicitly, this conception therefore stresses a radical inwardness: nō is not mere theatre, but a vehicle for the expression of the *shite* character's inner being. A play like *The Well-Cradle* supports this view and so does part one of *The Fulling Block*. However, part two of *The Fulling Block* is another matter. The problem is the significance of the husband, the *waki*.

The view of the *shite* as the sole actor denies any dramatic interaction between the *shite* and the *waki*. This idea can be debated even for a play like *The Well-Cradle* (can the seer be dismissed from what is seen, the dreamer from his dream?), but in the case of *Lady Han* or *The Fulling Block* it has serious consequences. A representative writer on *Lady Han* (Sagara Tōru) delicately analysed the distraught girl's feelings so as to prove that she meets her lover again because of her own purity of heart, yet ignored a much plainer explanation: the lover – as the play makes clear – is just as anxious to find *her* as she is to find him. In fact, the same writer hardly acknowledged the lover as a presence in the play, as distinguished from a presence in the girl's mind.

This is the difficulty with part two of *The Fulling Block*. Part one having already revealed the wife's innermost feelings, part two is relatively obvious if one takes it as a soliloquy – if the 'sole actor' is really alone on stage. Yet part two is not a soliloquy. It is a conversation. The husband says nothing, it is true, but his presence matters a great deal. The foremost contemporary historian of nō (Omote Akira) has warned against discussing Zeami's art on the basis of *The Fulling Block* as it is presently performed, but the text itself carefully stresses the husband's concern, and this, surely, was Zeami's intention. The husband is patient and he listens. While he listens, the chanting of the *Lotus Sutra* goes on (although not on stage), and all his love is present in this chanting. The lyric beauty of *Lady Han* would be misplaced in part two of *The Fulling Block*. The wife's words, spoken in extreme agony, are the unadorned truth. So is the husband's care. Both are so convincing that *The Fulling Block* does not fall back from the heights of part one. It rises.

It rises so high that when the wife has spoken, there is nothing left to say. Ascetics chanted the *Lotus Sutra* to 'abolish sins' (*metsuzai*). The wife's sin is of course psychological, not moral: anxiety about the husband she loves has caused her to hate him, and this hate has sunk her in Hell. Yet the voice of love, speaking through the sutra, has turned anguish to knowledge, darkness to light. Sin is exhausted and Hell dissolves. No doubt that is why the end of the play, which may seem abrupt, comes so suddenly. With pain gone, release is swift. Some scholars (especially Yashima Masaharu) have shown that Zeami accorded *The Fulling Block* his highest possible rank, that of the 'wondrous flower' (*myōka*). The term recalls the *Lotus Sutra*'s full title, 'The Sutra of the Lotus Flower of the Wondrous Teaching'. It is a rank, as Zeami said, beyond praise.

The 'fulling block' of the title was beaten to soften the silk of a robe and restore its lustre. This could be done at any time of year, but Chinese poetry associated the block's dull thud with the melancholy of autumn. The motif, as developed by Japanese poets, settled into its final pattern in about the twelfth century. By convention, the beater was a widow or a lonely wife who, with each stroke under the autumn moon, lamented her husband's absence.

The site of *The Fulling Block* is Ashiya, a locality on the north coast of Kyushu (Fukuoka Prefecture). Another Ashiya, near the present Osaka, appears in *Pining Wind* and elsewhere. Perhaps Zeami's choice alludes to this much closer, more familiar Ashiya, and so emphasizes the gravity of the wife's estrangement from a happier truth.

The Ashiya in Kyushu is at a river mouth. A few kilometres upstream stands the small Yatsurugi Jinja, formerly known as Kinuta-hime Jinja: the Shrine of the Lady of the Fulling Block. According to the legend of the shrine, the hero Yamato Takeru was passing that way when he heard someone beating a block. The beater turned out to be a lovely young woman who told him, in tears, that she had served in the imperial palace until her companions' vicious tongues so wounded her that she sought lonely refuge here. The hero made love to her and found, when he passed by again, that she was soon to give birth. Alas, he had to go on to the capital, but in memory of their liaison he planted a ginkgo tree. The shrine, now practically deserted, is in a grove of huge ginkgo trees. What this legend has to do with *The Fulling Block* is hard to say, yet its presence at the spot is very interesting. It evokes the baffling depths of history and meaning that lurk behind many masterpieces of nō.

THE FULLING BLOCK

Persons in order of appearance

The Husband, a local squire	*waki*
His Sword-bearer	*wakizure*
A Maid, Yūgiri (*Ko-omote* mask)	*tsure*
The Wife (*Fukai* mask)	*Maeshite*
A Manservant	*ai*
The Spirit of the wife, after her death	
(*Deigan* or *Yase-onna* mask)	*nochijite*

Remarks: A fourth-category play (*yonbamme-mono*) current in all five schools of nō.

*   *   *

To nanori-bue *flute music, enter Husband followed by Maid. He stands in base square while she kneels on one knee behind him.*

HUSBAND (*nanori*) You have before you a squire from Ashiya in Kyushu. Presently I am staying in Miyako, where I have a lawsuit of mine to look after.[1] Although I had not thought I would be in Miyako long, this year is already my third, and I am very worried about my wife and my home. For that reason, I mean to send my maid, Yūgiri, down to Ashiya.

(*mondō*) Listen to me, Yūgiri. I am very worried about my wife and my home, and for that reason I am sending you down to Ashiya. Please announce that I myself will surely be home by the end of the year.

MAID Then I will be on my way immediately, sir. You yourself will surely arrive by the end of the year.

Exit Husband. Maid rises and comes forward to base square.

MAID (*ageuta*) This little while,

> in travel wear the days unfold
> in travel wear the days unfold
> toward nightfall in endless inns;

1. The lawsuit probably involves land. This motif (a local squire pressing a lawsuit in Kyoto, and consequently being separated from his wife) appears in several other nō and kyōgen plays.

> dream follows dream on borrowed pillows.
>
> So days and nights go by, till soon,   *Mimes walking.*
>
> Ashiya I have reached at last
>
> Ashiya I have reached at last.

(*tsukizerifu*) How happy I am! Having come so swiftly, I have already reached the village of Ashiya. I must first announce my arrival.

(*unnamed*) I beg your pardon! Is anyone at home? It is I, Yūgiri. Please announce that I have arrived from Miyako.[2]

To ashirai *music, enter Wife. She stops at third pine, facing audience. Maid, meanwhile, retires to stage assistant position.*

WIFE (*sashi*) Snug beneath mandarin duck covers,

> lovers still grieve that they must part;
>
> fish of the deep, pillowed side by side,
>
> they yet fear the sundering waves.[3]
>
> And I, whose love has turned away,
>
> though living still, can only suffer
>
> the rush of memories; my sobs
>
> cry that I have not forgotten.   *Weeps.*
>
> Tears spill from sleeves like rain
>
> that never ends for this stricken heart!

Maid has come forward to first pine.

MAID (*mondō*) Please convey the news that Yūgiri has arrived.

Wife turns to her.

WIFE Yūgiri, you say? Why, there is no need to have yourself announced! Please come straight in. [*Wife sits before Chorus, Maid before drums.*] Now, Yūgiri, I am of course pleased to see you, but I also have reason to be most unhappy with you. No doubt his heart has changed towards me, but if so, why did you not somehow send me the news?[4]

2. In both nō and kyōgen, a servant always ceremoniously announces his or her arrival at a house, however familiar the servant may be there. Here, the Maid assumes that the news will be passed on to her mistress by another servant within the house. The response of the master or mistress is always, as here, that there was no need for such ceremony.

3. Since mandarin ducks mate for life, they are a symbol of conjugal happiness. The fish is, literally, the turbot (or sole, or flounder), which has both eyes on the same side of its body, and which therefore was thought to be unable to swim unless paired (underside to underside) with its mate.

4. The complete failure of communication between Kyoto and Ashiya is crucial in this play, but no explanation is ever given for it. Zeami seems to have radically stripped the play of any anecdotal material that might distract one's attention from his theme.

MAID You see, madam, I wanted to come home sooner, but the service I owe my master allowed me no time to do so. Quite against my will, I ended up spending three years in Miyako.

WIFE It was against your will, you say, that you stayed on in Miyako? Think of that! There in the blossoming Capital,[5] amid a wealth of consolations, it is still the heart's way to grieve.

CHORUS (*sageuta*) Village life palls as autumn ends.

> None pass the door, the grasses die;
> old loves and friendships lapse.   *Weeps.*
> What have I to trust, in time to come?

> (*ageuta*) Were they a dream, these three autumn years
> were they a dream, these three autumn years,
> I should wake from sorrow, yet do not.
> Only memories stay with me.
> The old days are changed and gone.
> O it is true:

>> Were this world of ours
>> unstained by lies
>> the heart would leap
>> to hear him speak
>> such sweet, welcome words.[6]

> O foolish heart! O foolish, foolish trust!

During the passage above, Manservant slips in to sit at villager position.

WIFE (*mondō*) How strange! I hear a noise some way away. What can it be?

MAID Someone in the village is beating a fulling block.

WIFE Why yes, in my present misery I remember an old tale.[7] In China, a man named Sobu was taken captive by the Huns. Imagining him lying sleepless through the cold nights, the wife and child he had left behind climbed a high tower and beat a fulling block. And perhaps the message of their love did reach him, for Sobu in his exile's sleep, ten thousand leagues away, heard that block beating at

5. The glories of Miyako were conventionally summed up by its cherry blossoms, which Zeami celebrated in *Saigyō's Cherry Tree*.

6. An anonymous poem from the *Kokinshū* (905).

7. The story of Sobu (Su Wu) is from the *Han shu*, the history of the early Han dynasty (206 B.C.–24 A.D.). However, the idea that his wife beat a fulling block to call him first appears in a couplet by Ōe no Masafusa, in *Shinsen rōei* ('A New Selection of Chinese Poems for Chanting Aloud', *c.* 1115).

his home. It may ease my heart to do the same. Yes, this desolate evening, I will lay upon the fulling block his bright-patterned robe[8] and beat it to comfort my own heart.

MAID Oh my dear mistress, beating the fulling block is something poor folk do! But if it will ease your pain, then I will prepare you a block.

To ashirai *music, Wife retires to stage assistant position. Stage assistant then brings on the fulling block, a light stand over which a robe might be draped, though none is draped over this one. Wife slips the outer robe off her right shoulder; this is at once a preparation for work and a sign that she is not in her right mind. She comes forward to stand in base square.*

WIFE (*kakeai*) Come, come, I shall pound the block:
　　　　　　where he and I, fond lovers, lay,
MAID 　　　　and desolate tears now stain a lonely bed,
WIFE 　　　　the beat shall tell my thoughts abroad!

Wife and Maid sit facing each other across the fulling block, with Maid at witness position. They gaze at it, absorbed.

MAID 　　　　Yūgiri joins her, till mistress and maid
WIFE 　　　　beat upon the block of angry pain.
CHORUS (*shidai*) Pine trees' sighing falls across the robe
　　　　　　pine trees' sighing falls across the robe:
　　　　　　wind with tidings of the chill of night.

Both rise. Wife moves to base square, Maid before Chorus. Below, Wife dances and mimes in consonance with the text.

WIFE (*issei*) The autumn wind tells of love grown cold,
　　　　　　the autumn wind tells of love grown cold,
CHORUS 　　　bringing me tonight nothing but sorrow.
WIFE 　　　　Others too, in far-flung villages,
　　　　　　will, no doubt, be gazing at this moon
CHORUS 　　　that never asks which watcher claims the night.[9]
WIFE (*sashi*) O the hour has its own beauty!
　　　　　　Autumn is here, and the closing dusk.

---

8. 'Bright-patterned robe' paraphrases the *kurehatori aya no koromo* of the original. These words recall the language of *Kureha*, the present text of which alludes directly to the end of the *kuse* passage of *The Fulling Block*.

9. In poetry, separated lovers often watched the moon, feeling sure the other was watching it, too. The wife assumes this of her husband, but knows that many others as well, strangers to her, are watching the moon. The moon shines equally on them all and has no comfort to give her.

CHORUS   Loud on the unseen mountain wind,
                a stag's cry quivers in the heart,[10]
                and somewhere a twig lets one leaf fall.[11]
                From desolate heavens, the moon
                shines in through grasses at the eaves[12]
WIFE   agleam with dew, while I,
CHORUS   night-long, disclose abiding grief.

    (kami-no-ei) The palace clock points aloft; the wind veers to the north.
Nearby, a block beats slow then fast; the westering moon sinks low.[13]

        (uta)   Sobu, exiled, slept in northern lands,
                while my love lies under eastern skies.
                Winds of fall, that sweep in from the west,
                blow him my message. Come,
                beat upon his robe, of weave so thin!

    (ageuta)   O pine at the eaves of this, his home,
                I beg, be kind! In your branches,
                hold back nothing of the storm's loud cry!
                Take up this block's voice, O wind,
                blow it to my husband yonder!
                Yet softly, kind wind in the pine –
                for should all of my heart
                reach him, and he dream of me . . .
                O do not break his dream!
                For if you do, this robe of his –
                who ever will come and wear it?
                But if he comes, then for all time,
                we shall cut the cloth anew.
                Ah, summer robe, so thin: so thin,
                his old promises, I hate them!
                Yes, may the man I love live long
                as those long nights the moon
                keeps me from sleep!

10. The mating call of the stag, in autumn, was a powerful motif in countless poems.
11. This sign of autumn also suggests, here as in Lady Han, that the speaker's mind is shaken and turning to madness.
12. Shinobu grasses that grow in the thatch. The name puns on shinobu 'to remember with longing'. The full moon brought back memories, and doubly so when seen through shinobu fronds gleaming with dew (tears).
13. A couplet in Chinese by Prince Tomohira, from Shinsen rōei. The clock is a water clock.

          Come, beat upon the robe!

Wife continues to dance and mime until, at the end of the kuse *passage below, she and Maid sit once more facing each other across the fulling block.*

    (*kuse*)   This promise binds the Tanabata Stars:[14]
            that one night of every year
            they shall lie, briefly, together,
            till waves of the Celestial River
            surge once more and part them.
            This poor tryst yields them nothing
            but distracted hearts; and tears,
            weak as dewdrops, wet their sleeves.
            Let them, O waves, be waterweeds
            that you might wash into close embrace
            that pair, foam on the stream.

WIFE   O dawn, the seventh of the seventh moon!

CHORUS   Come the eighth moon and the ninth,
            when the nights grow long,
            thousand, ten thousand-voiced[15]
            sorrows are the news I would send him!
            Brilliance of the moon, touch of the wind,
            frost gleaming in pale light,
            chill the heart as the block beats
            and night winds moan.
            Cries of grief, shrill insect cries
            mingle with weeping dew:
            horo horo hara hara hara,
            they go, and among them all,
            O which cry is the block's?

Maid rises, moves towards corner pillar, then goes down on one knee facing Wife.

MAID (*mondō*) I beg your pardon, madam. It appears that our lord will not be back this autumn.

WIFE (*kudoki*) I detest him, then!

---

14. This Chinese legend is still universally known in Japan. The Herd Boy and the Weaver Maid (Altair and Vega) are two stars on either side of the Celestial River (the Milky Way). Although lovers, they can meet only one night a year, the seventh night of the seventh month. The Tanabata festival is held on that evening.

15. These three lines are based on a couplet by Po Chü-i (772–846), included in the *Wakan rōei shū* ('A Collection of Japanese and Chinese Poems for Chanting Aloud', 1013).

He promised, 'By the year's end,'
and I, who well knew he lied,
still looked for him.   *Buries face in hands.*
So it is true.
His love really has grown cold.

Maid, moving behind Wife, places her hands on Wife's shoulders to comfort her.

CHORUS (*sageuta*) Never think it of him,
urged my too fond heart,
that now is breaking.

As Chorus sings on, Wife slowly traverses stage and bridge, and vanishes through the curtain. At first, Maid follows her, supporting her faltering steps. At third pine, Maid stops abruptly, withdraws her hands, and weeps.

(*ageuta*) The cries fade out. In wintry fields,
insect voices falter and die.
The tangled grasses' blossom heart
feels the wild wind's withering touch.
Sunk upon a bed of sickness,
she yields up her breath and is no more
she yields up her breath and is no more.

Exit Maid. Stage assistant moves the fulling block to front of stage.

*   *   *

Manservant rises and comes forward to base square.

MANSERVANT You have before you one who serves the squire of Ashiya in Kyushu. Now, while pressing a lawsuit for three years in Miyako, my master missed his home so badly that he very much wanted to return. When at last judgement was pronounced in his favour, he sent his maid Yūgiri on ahead to announce his arrival. She was to convey the message that he would be back at the year's end. My mistress was very happy, for since he had been away three years, she naturally was anxious to see him. The end of the year was not far off, but she could not for a moment forget her concern about him; and so it occurred to her she might at least relieve her feelings by beating a fulling block, such as the village women beat. This she did constantly, and Yūgiri with her, for Yūgiri was deeply affected by her distress and kept her faithful company. In short, Yūgiri did her best to improve her mistress's spirits. But then there came the news from Miyako that my master would not be home at the year's end after all. My mistress took it badly, as a woman is apt to do, and decided that he was not returning because he no longer cared for her. She started raving then, till at last she died. I need hardly say that the household mourned her with heartfelt tears. When in due course my master learned of her death, he rushed home at once, overwhelmed with grief. Yet the tragedy was beyond recall. He therefore had the bowstring plucked to summon her spirit, and offered to the buddhas the fulling block that she had beaten until the moment she expired. And he decided that a service should be held for her comfort and guidance. He ordered me to go to the people of this place and announce this service to them, so that all should attend it. Hear me, good people! Come now, gather for the service! Come, gather now! Gather now! [*Starts down bridge towards curtain when Husband enters, rosary in hand and followed by Sword-bearer.*] Ah! Here is my master now! [*Goes down on one knee. Husband stops. Sword-bearer too goes down on one knee.*] Excuse me, master. I announced the service, as you asked.

HUSBAND Is the fulling block still exactly as it was?

MANSERVANT Yes, sir, it is.

Husband sits before the fulling block. Sword-bearer sits behind him to one side and reverently bows.

Manservant retires to villager position; he will slip out after the Spirit's entrance.

*　　*　　*

HUSBAND (*unnamed*) It is too cruel!

        Angry that three years had gone,
        the wife I missed in separation
        now has left me, never to return.

  (*ageuta*) All in vain,

        remorse stings me a thousand times
        remorse stings me a thousand times.
        Yet from beneath the sod, I hear,
        there is a way to bring her once again,
        to call her to the curved bow's tip,
        poor soul, that we two may speak [16]
        poor soul, that we two may speak.

Husband sits at witness position, and Sword-bearer near him.

To deha music, enter Spirit, weakly leaning on a staff. She stops at first pine.

---

16. This shamanic procedure was probably done by a professional medium. Having been summoned, the spirit would then speak through the medium's mouth.

SPIRIT (*ageuta*) River of Three Crossings: [17]
              down I sank, swallowed by the waters:
              a fleck of foam consigned to a dark fate.

Below, comes to shite *spot and begins to mime in consonance with text.*

(*kuri*) Grave-marker plums bloom gaily side by side,
displaying spring to our unhappy world;
lanterns lit to guide the wandering shade
show the autumn moon, face of the truth.

  (*kudoki*) Yet love's lustful karma rules me still.
              Fires of longing smoulder night and day.
              Now as before, I have no peace: this sin,
              a heart in pain, yields me its reward:
              assaults of hell-fiends, the Ahōrasetsu,

Turns angrily to Husband, steps towards him, then weeps.

              brandishing their rods and raining blows.
              Beat on, beat (they howl), as you deserve,
              the block: [18] for all my hate

  (*noriji*) reaps me the fruit of wrongful clinging
CHORUS   reaps me the fruit of wrongful clinging.
              Anguished tears, touching the block,
              turn from tears to fire.
              Smothering in smoke and flame,
              I shriek, yet soundlessly.
              The block makes no noise, and wind
              in silence passes through the pines.
              Fiends' foul curses fill my ears, O terror!

Below, mimes and dances a passage which musically is the climax of the play.

  (*dan-uta*) As sheep loiter or a colt flicks by [19]
              as sheep loiter or a colt flicks by,
              the Six Realms [20] revolve, for karma's wheel

17. The river that the soul must cross to reach the afterworld.
18. The demon in part two of *The Damask Drum* cries the same thing to the Consort of that play, who beats a drum that will not sound. The motifs of the drum and the fulling block are here closely related, and one scholar (Yashima Masaharu) has explicitly linked these two plays.
19. A simile (derived by Zeami from Buddhist and Chinese sources) for the passage of time, either slow or fast, from birth to death and rebirth. More fully stated: slow as the gait of a sheep being led to slaughter, fast as a running colt glimpsed through a crack in a wall.
20. The six realms of reincarnation: Heaven, the human realm, the realm of warring demons, the realm of beasts, the realm of starving ghosts, and Hell.

turns on and on, and unless we drive
our carriage out the Burning Mansion's gate,[21]
we turn and turn among them,
ever drowning in the sea of birth and death.
O cruel, O unhappy world!

SPIRIT Anger, creeping like a vine

CHORUS Anger, creeping like a vine,
only spreads. My face, O shame,
is the very face of desperate clinging!
Husband I so love, it was two lives
you pledged to me, as man and wife will do,[22]
and swore devotion for a thousand ages,
till seas swallow the inviolate mountains.[23]
Yet your vows were empty.
They were lies.
Was that really all your love was worth?
'Fibber-bird', they call the crow,[24]
yet even he keeps his own faith.
What madman could call *you* true?
Plants and trees, yes, know the seasons;
birds and beasts have feelings.
How rightly I recalled Sobu
who, to a wild goose southward-bound,
tied a letter that across ten thousand leagues
carried her his message: for he loved her,
and his vows were anything but shallow.
Why, O why, my husband, far away,
if not in daylight thought, at least in dream,

21. The parable of the burning mansion, in the *Lotus Sutra*, likens the world of transmigration to a house in which children are playing. The children are so absorbed in their games that they do not notice the house is burning, and must be enticed out by their father with promises of gifts.
22. The bond between husband and wife is believed to last for two lifetimes. The parent–child bond lasted one and the bond between retainer and lord lasted three.
23. The 'inviolate mountains' are, in the original, Sue-no-matsuyama ('the pine mountains of Sue'). In a *Kokinshū* poem, a lover swears that if he is ever false, waves will sweep over Sue-no-matsuyama in the far north of Japan, and the oath became proverbial.
24. An idea based on a poem in a work of poetic criticism entitled *Toshiyori zuinō* ('The Teachings of Minamoto no Toshiyori', *c.* 1115). The reason why the crow should be a 'fibber-bird' is unclear.

did you not hear me beating on the block
and know my pain? O you are hateful!

*Spirit, above, moves towards Husband, goes down on one knee before him, strikes
stage with her fan, points left hand accusingly, and suddenly weeps. Palms pressed
together over the beads of his rosary, he greets her reverently.*

(*kiri*) So powerful, the chanted Lotus Sutra
so powerful, the chanted Lotus Sutra,
before the spirit a bright path of light
opens out straight to Buddhahood.
See, how from the block she briefly beat,
its complaint her own, a perfect flower
has blossomed: the true Teaching,
now the seed of her illumination
now the seed of her illumination.

Facing side from base square, stamps a final beat.

Kureha

Kureha is about the sacred craft of weaving. It tells how two weavers came from China to Japan and wove the emperor's robe: 'a flawless weave of honoured precedent' that sums up all of higher civilization. There are few plays in which less happens, but that is the point. *Kureha* is about a perfect world, and the fabric of such a world is without rent or incident.

The play is probably by Zeami, although neither he nor Zenchiku mentioned it in their writings. Perhaps the earliest known performance of it, in 1429, was the first. The present version has only the *shite* (Kurehatori or Shuttle Maid) in part two, but originally the *tsure* from part one (Ayahatori or Heddle Maid) must have appeared in part two as well, for her presence has left traces in the text.

Nihon shoki ('The Chronicles of Japan', 720), in the reign of Emperor Ōjin (r. 270–310), mentions the arrival of four weavers from the state of Wu (J. Go), the area of the mouth of the Yangtze River. An envoy from Japan had gone to request them. Two stayed in Kyushu to serve the Munakata deities, while two went on until they reached the site of the play. Like the pair in the play, these two were sisters. Rather than *Nihon shoki*, however, the direct source of *Kureha* is the medieval *engi* ('sacred history') of the Kureha Shrine. The *engi* extant in Zeami's time was lost in the sixteenth century, but a digest of its contents (*Kurehatori Ayahatori Daimyōjin ryaku engi*) survives in manuscript. This text states:

> Kurehatori [Shuttle Maid] and Anahatori [Ayahatori, Heddle Maid] are divine ladies. Surely they are transformations of the Great Deity Amaterasu. They passed away on the seventeenth and eighteenth days in the ninth month of the seventy-sixth year of Emperor Nintoku's reign (388). Then there came an oracle, and they descended from Heaven to the village of Kureha. Moved by this wonder, the emperor built their two shrines and scrupulously performed the rites.

The 'Great Deity Amaterasu' is the Sun Goddess, whose descendants are the line of Japanese emperors. In the myths, she is the heavenly weaver who weaves the order of the world. Her shrine at Ise has a special association with cloth offerings, and the *Engi-shiki* ('Procedures of Engi', 927) mentions two annual rites (Kammiso-sai, 'Rites of the Divine Robe') devoted to them.

In nō, the deep significance of cloth and clothing is stated more explicitly in *Kureha* than elsewhere, but it is implicit in many plays. *The Feather Mantle* is an obvious example. In *Tatsuta*, the wholeness of a poetic 'brocade' is a crucial issue, while *Takasago* celebrates poetry as an unbroken weave of language. The robes donned by the women of *The Well-Cradle* or *Pining Wind*, and the one beaten by the wife in *The Fulling Block*, are the 'worlds' inhabited by each of these women, whose every thought dwells on a departed husband or lover. When the wife in *The Fulling Block* beats this robe instead of wearing it, her mind breaks down and she dies. In this sense, *The Fulling Block* is an anti-*Kureha*.

The weaving technique brought by the weavers from China yields *aya*, 'twill'. Simple twill is a plain cloth with fine, faint diagonal lines, but there are all sorts of figured twills, including *aya nishiki* (literally, 'twill brocade'). During the early part of *Kureha*, one imagines that the cloth is fairly plain, but it turns out in the end to be extremely elaborate. Not that the play need be consistent on the subject; it is certainly vague about the loom. Perhaps Zeami had in mind the sort of draw loom (*sorabiki-bata*) used, for example, to weave nō robes; but this loom is a large, complex apparatus that did not exist in the reign of Emperor Ōjin, and in any case, nobody would dream of using one outside, under a pine tree by the sea. It is true, however, that such a draw loom requires two operators, as in the play. One, on the ground, throws the shuttle and also works a set of treadles, while the second, who lifts the heddles (the threads that control the pattern), is perched high in the superstructure. The 'loom' often used in performances of *Kureha* is pretty but small, and does not imitate any particular variety.

Apart from these technical matters, *Kureha* poses a geographical problem. The old village of Kureha is now within the city limits of Ikeda, near Osaka International Airport, and the sea is nowhere in sight; yet *Kureha* takes place on the shore. It seems that an arm of the sea did once reach that far into the land. One name for it was Karafune-no-fuchi ('The Deep of the Chinese Ships'). Although it appears in the *engi* and in other documents, it had vanished long before Zeami's time.

The fine Kureha Shrine honours Kurehatori, Ayahatori, and Inatsuhiko, the imperial envoy who went to fetch them from China. It stands about 200 metres from Ikeda Station, near the Takarazuka Line tracks of the Hankyū Electric Railway. Shuttle Maid's body was entrusted to the 'upper shrine' (now Ikeda Shrine, some distance away beyond the end of a shopping street), in a sacred grove at the foot of the mountains.

Kureha

Persons in order of appearance

A Court Official	*waki*
Two Followers	*wakizure*
Shuttle Maid (*Zō-onna* mask)	*maeshite*
Heddle Maid (*Ko-omote* mask)	*tsure*
A Villager	*ai*
Shuttle Maid (*Zō-onna* mask and celestial maiden's crown)	*nochijite*

Remarks: A first-category or god play (*waki-nō*) current in the Kanze, Hōshō, Kongō, and Kita schools. In present Kanze school usage, the play can be performed without the loom.

*   *   *

To shin-no-shidai *music, enter Court Official and Followers. They stand facing each other at centre.*

OFFICIAL and FOLLOWERS

(*shidai*) Ways in our time are no doubt the true Way[1]
            ways in our time are no doubt the true Way,
            for the provinces all enjoy peace and ease.   *Face audience.*

OFFICIAL (*nanori*) You see before you an official in the service of our sovereign. Recently, I have been on humble pilgrimage to Sumiyoshi in Settsu province. Now I will take advantage of my journey and continue on to Nishinomiya, further along the shore.

1. 'The people must each be following their own proper calling in perfect sincerity of heart . . .' The line alludes distantly to a passage in the Chinese Taoist classic *Lao-tzu*.

OFFICIAL and FOLLOWERS

    (*ageuta*) Ah, Sumiyoshi![2]   *Face each other.*
           The waves gently lap Asaka Strand,
           the waves gently lap Asaka Strand
           while seafolk, who, so poems say,
           gather sleek sea-tangle,[3]
           follow straight their own way   *Official mimes walking.*
           on Naniwa shore; beyond, lies our goal,
           Kureha Village, and we have arrived
           Kureha Village, and we have arrived.   *Face audience.*

OFFICIAL (*tsukizerifu*) Having come so swiftly, we have reached the village of Kureha. Ah, I hear the sound of a loom from that pine wood yonder. I will go and find out who the weavers are.

All sit in witness square.

Stage assistant places a loom and a stool at side of stage.

To shin no-issei *music, enter Heddle Maid, carrying a length of silk; she stops at first pine. Shuttle Maid follows, stopping at third pine. They face each other.*

SHUTTLE MAID and HEDDLE MAID

    (*issei*) O Kure weave, O patterned raiment!
           Upon this shore, lo! these many years,
           the seafolk maidens

HEDDLE MAID dwell by waves   *Face audience.*
           white-breaking, white

BOTH   thread to weave   *Face each other.*
           upon the clattering loom.

To ashirai *music, Heddle Maid comes to stand at centre, Shuttle Maid in base square.*

SHUTTLE MAID

    (*sashi*) Kureha Village, in this province of Tsu,   *They face audience.*
           has harboured us two, years beyond number,

BOTH   yet though our home may now be Japan,   *Face each other.*
           once, in Cathay,
           we were renowned among weaving women.

---

2. Sumiyoshi is a great shrine now surrounded by modern Osaka, while Nishinomiya is a coastal city between Osaka and Kobe. Between these two, in ancient times, a long arm of the sea reached up to the scene of *Kureha*. Asaka Strand was near Sumiyoshi, while Naniwa is the old name for the site of Osaka.

3. 'Seafolk [*ama*] who gather sleek sea-tangle [*tamamo karu*]' are celebrated in many poems.

Yes, those old days still come to mind.
From where the moon sets, westward over the sea,
by wave-lanes we came a far, far journey:
for we are Chinese from the state of Kure,
and this village too, with its wide renown,
broadcasts that very name!

(*sageuta*) So wise and fair are these sovereign reigns
that woven stuffs from across the sea,
accepted with pleasure, now flourish here, too:

(*ageuta*) Chinese silks of Yamato weave [4]
Chinese silks of Yamato weave,
to join with the words of poetry
in yielding blossoms for all to see,
brilliant in hue, [5]

Shuttle Maid moves to centre, Heddle Maid to corner.

and with devotion richly dyed:
sleeves so pure, so lovely to behold
sleeves so pure, so lovely to behold!

Official rises.

OFFICIAL (*mondō*) Having reached the pine wood, I now see before me
two young ladies at their loom, and they are of astonishing beauty.
One is throwing the shuttle and one lifting the heddles. Neither
resembles a simple village girl. May I ask you, young ladies, who
you are?

SHUTTLE MAID I am ashamed!
So far from the village, beneath this pine,
with tide-haze [6] veiling the evening moon,
here in the shadows, I never thought
another might hear the noise of the loom,
that merges so with waves on the shore.
Yet you have found us. I am ashamed!

OFFICIAL What is it, then, you wish to conceal?
You are no villagers, no simple folk,

4. Yamato is a noble name for Japan. 'Yamato weave' means simply 'woven in Japan',
not the cloth known as *yamato-ori* ('Japanese weave', a combination of *kuzu* thread and
cotton).
5. These lines equate the weaving of thread with the weaving of words, or poetry. Zeami
developed this theme in *Takasago*. The 'blossoms' are at once poems and the patterns on
brocade.
6. A haze that overspreads the shore as the tide comes in.

who, hidden away beneath this pine,
weave the hours away. I find this strange.
Please, I insist: tell me your names.

SHUTTLE MAID   Those who, in Emperor Ōjin's august reign,
first wove His Majesty's noble robe,
the two sisters, Shuttle Maid,
and Heddle Maid, in this happy age
have come before you, plain to see.

OFFICIAL   Why yes, of old, in a reign long ago,
two weaving maidens crossed to our shores
from the land of Cathay –

and now they make themselves visible once more, in our time!
Please tell me, then: what does this mean?

SHUTTLE MAID   How quickly you understand! Why, first of all, did
this village receive the name Kureha? Because we ourselves were
here.

HEDDLE MAID   'Heddle Maid' means the one
who lifts the threads upon the loom,
so bringing forth the figured pattern:
and so it is my name.

SHUTTLE MAID   'Shuttle Maid' means the one
whose hands work the *kureha*,
the wooden piece that draws the thread:
and so that name is mine.

HEDDLE MAID   For poets who use our two names,

SHUTTLE MAID   'shuttle maid'

HEDDLE MAID   itself means a pattern, or so tradition tells.[7]

BOTH   Since we ourselves were born in China
we hardly know Yamato speech,

SHUTTLE MAID   yet, that old poem,
'Shuttle maid' –
ah, so fine a pattern
for you my love:

7. The meaning of the word *kureha-tori*, ('shuttle maid', literally 'weaver from Wu') was
an issue in the poetic tradition. Some treatises held that the word actually designated a
particularly successful pattern devised by the weaver Kureha-tori. The proposition that
' "shuttle maid" itself means a pattern' suggests that Shuttle Maid and Heddle Maid are
indivisible, for the *aya* of Ayahatori (Heddle Maid) means 'pattern'.

accept these silks . . .[8]

in truth, speaks of us two.

CHORUS (*ageuta*) Ah, traveller,

you who wonder at weave and pattern
you who wonder at weave and pattern,
uphold with your keen eye the high renown
of those who inhabit Miyako.
Here on this spot, you well discerned
we were Chinese: a shrewd insight!
Most wise is he, that noble Lord,
whom, happily, you serve so well
whom, happily, you serve so well!

Shuttle Maid sits at centre, Heddle Maid before Chorus.

COURT OFFICIAL (*mondō*) Please go on. Please tell me all you can
about Shuttle Maid and Heddle Maid.

SHUTTLE MAID If that is your wish, we will do so gladly.

CHORUS (*kuri*) Now, patterned twill was woven first
in Wu district of China, that you call Kure,
by women devoted to that craft.

SHUTTLE MAID (*sashi*) Once Empress Jingū had bravely subdued
the three Korean kingdoms,[9]

CHORUS between Yamato and the lands abroad,
the way lay open, for in those days
even far-flung peoples bowed to Japan,
a realm of peace where the sovereign
illumined all the world;
where the land was rich, the people at ease.

SHUTTLE MAID To east and south, clouds melted away;
to west and north, mild breezes blew.

CHORUS (*kuse*) In Emperor Ōjin's reign, it was,
an ambassador from the state of Wu
first disembarked upon our shores.

---

8. This poem by Kiyowara no Morozane, from the *Gosenshū* (*c.* 951), can be taken as the poetic seed of the play, and certainly explains this discussion of the name of Shuttle Maid. The original being quite untranslatable, this rendering is only a functional paraphrase.

9. The Empress Jingū, consort of Emperor Chūai and the mother of Ōjin, is described in the early chronicles as having ruled as regent from 201 to 269 A.D. She is said to have led a successful campaign against the three Korean kingdoms of the time, Silla, Koguryo, and Paekche. It is believed that the story of her conquest was largely fabricated, in this formative period of the Japanese state, in order to glorify Japan.

> With him, two weaving maidens
> had braved a myriad leagues of ocean waves.
> The westering sun sank into night
> as they reached Kureha; and there they stayed.
> Daily the weavers toiled at their loom
> to weave the loveliest silken fabric:
> a robe the ambassador, reverently,
> offered His Majesty –
> who, be it said, was thoroughly pleased.
> Thenceforth the pattern received a name:
> Dragon Raiment [10] –
> in workmanship, perfection itself,
> in colour, the hue of the mountain dove, [11]
> striking to see, as though among clouds
> birds beat their wings: so went the weave –
> an awesome vision!

SHUTTLE MAID   Ten thousand reigns shall pass away
before such gifts gladden us no more:

CHORUS   so decreed His Majesty.
Thenceforth the fabric's Chinese name [12]
was softened to Japanese,
and the weavers dubbed, in homely speech,
Shuttle Maid and Heddle Maid.
With each New Year, colours aglow,
the rich brocade robe of Cathay
the rich brocade robe of Cathay
clothes our Lord, his billowing sleeves
a flawless weave of honoured precedent
in His reign of perfect peace.

CHORUS (*rongi*)   Yes, very wise is our Sovereign Lord
yes, very wise is our Sovereign Lord.
Come, all through the night,
weave on and on at your loom!

BOTH   Why then, we will, upon the loom,
weave bright brocade, and to our Sovereign

10. An imperial robe bearing a design of dragons, sun, moon, and stars.
11. A light olive green.
12. This name consists of two characters, pronounced *gofuku* ('clothing from Wu'), and is still a standard word for 'clothing' in modern Japanese.

offer raiment new.

CHORUS Among the gifts laid before our Lord,
ah, brocade glows

BOTH with many colours!

CHORUS Deep night[13] is past; wait now till light
first stains the sky: renewed in form,
we shall then come to you.
Farewell a while!
Shuttle Maid and Heddle Maid
withdraw for now. *Heddle Maid goes to base square.*
No cock as yet crows in the day,
for darkness lingers: kindly, wait!
Yes, darkness lingers. Please, patiently, wait!

Exit Shuttle Maid, followed by Heddle Maid. Stage assistant removes the loom.

* * *

OFFICIAL Are you there, my man?

FOLLOWER At your service, sir.

OFFICIAL Call me a villager, please.

FOLLOWER Certainly, sir. [*Goes to base square.*] Is any villager nearby?

Enter Villager, who stops at first pine.

VILLAGER Someone is calling for a villager. I will go and see what he wants.
[*Turns to Follower.*] You are calling for a villager, sir? What is it you want?

FOLLOWER Something is puzzling my superior a little. Please come closer.

VILLAGER Certainly, sir.

Both come to sit at centre.

FOLLOWER I called a villager, sir. Here he is.

VILLAGER Here I am, sir, at your service.

FOLLOWER If you are a villager of Kureha, then please tell me the story of
Shuttle Maid and Heddle Maid.

VILLAGER I am surprised you should ask me to do that, sir. I do live nearby,
it is true, but I really know very little about such things. Still, I will do my
best to tell you what I myself have heard.

OFFICIAL Please do so.

VILLAGER This is why our village is named Kureha. Of old, in the reign of
Emperor Ōjin, the sixteenth Human Sovereign, two weaver girls were

13. *Ushi mittsu*, 'the third quarter of the hour of the ox': roughly 3 a.m.

brought over to Japan. Their names were Kurehatori, or Shuttle Maid, and Ayahatori, or Heddle Maid. This is where the Chinese ship landed, and the two girls disembarked on this very shore. When the Emperor learned of the event, he was delighted. He ordered the weavers to set up their loom here and to weave him a robe. So they did. The one called Heddle Maid, by her craft, brought out the pattern; while Shuttle Maid merited her name by managing the wooden piece that draws the thread. The two together wove imperial robes and every day presented them to His Majesty. All this showed how wise a ruler our Sovereign was: so wise that all tendered him obedience, not only in our own land, but in China, too. And ever since, the realm has known such peace that the two weaver maids are honoured, each in her own shrine, as the Divine Presence of Kureha and Ayaha. Humble villagers, such as I, honour this Presence with grateful awe.

OFFICIAL Thank you for your thorough account. A short while ago, I saw here two women in Chinese dress, weaving at a loom. Their account of themselves resembled your own. Then they told me they would weave a robe for our Sovereign, but enjoined me to be patient because the night was far from done. And with those words, they simply vanished into the shadows beneath this pine.

VILLAGER That is truly a wonder, sir! Then the two weavers, Shuttle Maid and Heddle Maid, must have appeared and worked their loom before your very eyes! Do please stay here a while longer, sir, because I think you will see yet another wonder.

OFFICIAL Then I will by all means do as you suggest.

VILLAGER And if you should need me for anything, sir, please let me know.

OFFICIAL Thank you. I will not fail to do so.

VILLAGER Very well, sir.   [*Exit.*]

*   *   *

Official and Followers stand facing each other at centre.

OFFICIAL and FOLLOWERS

(*ageuta*) A happy prospect! Then, my friends, come [14]
A happy prospect! Then, my friends, come,
let us break our journey beneath this pine,
with winds sighing above, this midnight hour,
and await a word from the Gods

14. This *ageuta* may have been added to the play after Zeami's time.

and await a word from the Gods.   *Sit in witness square.*

    To deha *music, enter Shuttle Maid. She stands in base square.*

SHUTTLE MAID (*sashi*) In our Sovereign's reign,
the celestial feather mantle
rarely descends
to brush the rocks below:
unworn, they endure [15]
age upon age,
pine needles fall, yet still remain.
Their green only grows and grows,
like the *masaki* vine, the sign
of an eternal reign;
and we, as our own sign,
make a patterned weave of pristine hue,
spotless as the times.   *Begins to dance.*

CHORUS (*issei*) 'How wise the rule our Sovereign wields!'
declares above the noise of waves
the clatter of the loom

SHUTTLE MAID that weaves into bright brocade
a message, plain to see, of perfect love;
although elsewhere, with anguished stroke,
one may, upon the fulling block,
beat a robe, sounding the cry of separation. [16]

    (*issei*) Wind in the pines, noise of waves
beating upon the shore,

CHORUS loud, ceaseless clatter of the loom:

SHUTTLE MAID (*noriji*) Shuttle Maid takes up the thread tenderly spun,

CHORUS while Heddle Maid sees to the pattern,

SHUTTLE MAID loudly lifting the heddles:

CHORUS *kiri hatari chō*

---

15. This poem from the *Shūishū* (*c.* 1006) celebrates the eternity of the imperial realm, which will last as long as it takes an angel's mantle, brushing every few thousand years the rocks of the mountains, to wear those rocks away.

16. This first *issei* may be a later revision of the text. The discordant note sounded in its last three lines seems to refer to the *kuse* scene of *The Fulling Block*. The last five lines draw on a quatrain in the *Wakan rōei shū* ('A Collection of Chinese and Japanese Poems for Chanting Aloud', 1013). The quatrain speaks of one Chinese wife who wove a love poem into a piece of brocade and sent it to her husband far away; and of another wife very like the wife of Sobu in *The Fulling Block*. Originally, the *issei* that immediately follows must have been sung by the *tsure* (Heddle Maid).

SHUTTLE MAID *kiri hatari chō chō*:

CHORUS   a sound to strike demon hearts with terror!
              How lovely are the comely weaver's sleeves!

(DANCE: *chū-no-mai*)

She performs a chū-no-mai *and continues dancing as text resumes.*

(*noriji*) Yes, one recalls that weaving maid
            yes, one recalls that weaving maid
            of Tanabata, whom her lover
            so rarely joins. Equally rare,
            O traveller, we offer you this dream vision
            of the Bodhisattva of Wondrous Banners,[17]
            the spirit of dreams, night-long, night-long,
            weaving and weaving a fabric, priceless,
            for our own Sovereign: an exemplar
            for His noble reign: two weaving maids
            who throw the shuttle, lift the heddles,
            throw the shuttle, lift the heddles,
            offering our sovereign Lord a happy, happy reign.

Facing side from base square, stamps the final beat.

17. A figure mentioned in the sutra known in Japanese as *Konkōmyō saishōō kyō*, but seldom encountered in nō. His name fuses the weavers' work with the dream in which they appear, for according to *Kokin eiga shō* (1498) and other such commentaries on classical poetry, one who wishes to dream of a lover should invoke this bodhisattva.

Matsukaze · PINING WIND

Pining Wind is widely regarded as one of the most beautiful plays in the repertoire. Zeami himself seems to have felt deeply about it, since he mentioned it in his writings more often than any other. Matsukaze, the play's Japanese title, is a common word in poetry and means simply wind (*kaze*) in the pines (*matsu*). 'Pining wind', in contrast, is an unusual expression. It is made necessary by a problem of translation, because the play skilfully exploits a second meaning of *matsu*: 'to wait'. Thanks to the word 'pine' ('pine tree' and 'to pine'), a relatively faithful translation of this key poetic device is actually possible.

On the basis of remarks in Zeami's writings, *Pining Wind* was long held to be Zeami's revision of a play by Kan'ami, his father. However, meticulous analysis of these remarks and of the text itself (by Takemoto Mikio, supported by Omote Akira) suggests that Kan'ami can be connected only with the *sashi–sageuta–ageuta* sequence early in part one. This was probably an independent dance piece, with music by Kan'ami and words by someone unknown. Zeami is responsible for all the rest, although he took the *rongi* section ('Far away they haul their brine . . .') from another work that may or may not have been by him. These two passages from elsewhere contribute to an unusual variety of tone and mood in the first half of *Pining Wind*. The second half (which begins once the Monk enters the salt-house) is seamless and is one of the summits of Zeami's art.

The background of *Pining Wind* includes a play which is now lost, *Shiokumi* ('Gathering Brine'), by the *dengaku* actor Kiami, a near contemporary of Kan'ami. *Shiokumi* seems still to have been current when Zeami wrote *Pining Wind* (possibly *c.* 1412). No doubt it evoked the lives and labours of saltmakers like the ones in *Pining Wind*. Otherwise, *Pining Wind* has no obvious source, and the imaginative power it displays has been justly praised. The two sisters, Pining Wind and Autumn Rain, appear to be Zeami's inventions, and so, for all practical purposes, is their lover, Yukihira. However, Zeami drew on elements well known in the literary tradition. It is a pleasure to examine how he put these elements together, and to what effect. Many writers have discussed these topics, and the following account builds on their work.

Why did Zeami give the two sisters of *Pining Wind* the courtier Yukihira for a lover? It has been suggested (by Takemoto Mikio) that Zeami chose Yukihira because his name appears in Kan'ami's dance piece, the original nucleus of the play.

Ariwara no Yukihira (818–893) was the elder brother of Narihira, who plays a similar role in *The Well-Cradle*. In his thirties, Yukihira was exiled (or found it prudent to retire) to Suma shore, the scene of *Pining Wind*; and there he wrote a poem that colours the beginning of Kan'ami's passage. However, it does so only because Prince Genji, the fictional hero of *Genji monogatari* ('The Tale of Genji'; early 11th c.), also lived in exile at Suma, and because shortly after his arrival, the sound of the waves reminded him of Yukihira's poem. The presence of Yukihira in *Pining Wind* is therefore inseparable from memories of Genji, and it is because of Genji that he figures in the play. The language of *Pining Wind* alludes constantly to the 'Suma' chapter of *Genji monogatari*. The only direct quotations from this chapter appear at the start of the passage associated with Kan'ami, but the rest of the play is filled with images drawn from medieval manuals on how to work material from the novel into linked verse.

The central motif of *Pining Wind* is that of the courtier who goes down to the provinces, becomes briefly involved with a woman there, then leaves her yearning for him forever more. The outstanding classical occurrence of this motif is in *Genji monogatari* itself. While at Suma, Genji takes up with a lady of distinguished birth whose father has retired to Akashi, a stretch of shore west of Suma. By mentioning both place-names, the play's opening verse announces not only the appearance of the sisters at Suma, but the background presence of the Akashi lady.

After his three years of exile at Suma (the same period as Yukihira's in the play), Genji returned to the capital, leaving the lady pregnant with their daughter. She gave him for his journey a 'hunting cloak' (a courtier's normal outer garment) that she had made him. In return, he gave her his old one, fragrant with his scent. Later, when her thoughts lingered on him, she probably took it out to recall his presence. In *Pining Wind*, this cloak has become the one that Yukihira left the sisters, and Zeami has added to it a man's court hat. (The lady of *The*

Well-Cradle has the same mementoes of her love, Narihira.) The hat completed the costume worn by a *shirabyōshi*, a woman entertainer like Shizuka in *Benkei Aboard Ship*.

As Pining Wind dances in part two, wearing Yukihira's hat and cloak, she resembles a professional entertainer like the pining ladies in several other Zeami plays. One of these is the *yūjo* (singing-girl, prostitute) of *Lady Han*. Others are the *yūjo* of *Matsura* and the *shirabyōshi* of *Higaki*. Each longs for a gentleman from the capital who came to her briefly and then went away.

A different sort of woman, but with a similar preoccupation, figures in the legend of *The Diver*. Like Pining Wind, the *shite* in *The Diver* is a woman of the shore; and, like the Akashi lady, she bore a great lord's child. 'Seafolk' women (*ama*) enjoyed a romantic reputation in classical poetry, and resembled in some ways the shepherdesses of European letters. They could even be seen as a variety of singing-girl. One scholar (Abe Yasurō) cited a document dated 1297 that lists *yūjo*, *shirabyōshi*, and *ama* equally under the heading of 'entertainers'. A story about Yukihira in *Senjūshō* ('A Choice of Tales'; mid 13th c.) helps to explain why:

Of old, there was a man known as the Middle Counsellor Yukihira. Having misbehaved, he was sent down to Suma shore, where, the salt brine dripping from him [like his tears], he wandered along the beach. Among the divers on Eshima [an islet between Akashi and Awaji] there was one whom he found singularly attractive. Going up to her, he asked, 'Where do you live?' She replied [in verse]: 'No home have I of my own, for I, a diver's daughter, live beside white-breaking waves upon the ocean shore.' Then she slipped away. Yukihira, deeply moved, could not refrain from weeping. Amid the seas' thrust and ebb she dove into the waves, and although her aim was not to have the moon lodge on her sleeves [as it would have been had she been a poetically inclined courtier], those sleeves of hers were lovely indeed. Upon them, swept as they were by wave on wave, a dear face shone, illumined still more brightly by the moon. Alone, she spread her damp robe and lived aboard a boat among the divers. Yukihira was astonished to discover such a girl. Her poem was quite wonderful.

One imagines Yukihira discovering the two sisters of *Pining Wind* in rather the same way, and perhaps Zeami did, too. Though not a singing-girl, this diver had beauty, wit and mystery. Perhaps these same qualities captivated the courtier who actually took a diver back with him to the capital and married her (*Shasekishū*, 'A Collection of Sand and Pebbles', 1287). If this is what a young *ama* could do to a gentleman from Miyako, some *ama* may have cultivated the effect professionally.

The diver-girl in the *Senjūshō* story resembles Pining Wind, but as a poetic figure she also resembles the Akashi lady. This lady is no *ama* by birth, but she assumes the persona of an *ama* in her poetic exchanges with Genji, and in these poems, her preoccupations (loneliness, longing) are those of Pining Wind. Yukihira himself, in a poem that is important in the play ('Should one perchance ask after me . . .'), had assumed the persona of a male *ama*. He had addressed this poem to someone in the capital. Genji, too, assumed this persona in poems he addressed from Suma to ladies in the capital. *Ama* being the characteristic inhabitants of the shore, any lord or lady at Suma was found, poetically, to be an *ama* too. Furthermore, by calling themselves *ama*, Yukihira and Genji not only elicited sympathy but also took a suitably humble stance for men no longer welcome at court.

However, Genji is no *ama* in relation to the Akashi lady. He is of far higher rank than she, and he is only a visitor to her shore. Soon, he will leave her and return to Miyako. To her, he is as Yukihira is to the girl in the *Senjūshō* story. In other words, his poetic role is that of Yukihira. In contrast, that the Akashi lady should address Genji as an *ama* accords both with poetic practice and her own situation. Her poetic role is that of Pining Wind. The relationship between the two is deeply romantic, yet – as in the play – always imperfectly fulfilled.

Why, when there is only one Akashi lady, are there two sisters in *Pining Wind*? The initial clue can be found in a passage of *Ise monogatari* ('Tales of Ise', 10th c.), one of the canonical texts of the literary tradition. In the opening episode, a very young man from the capital, out hunting on one of his estates near Nara, spies two beautiful sisters who throw his heart into hopeless confusion. In Zeami's time, this young man was assumed to be Narihira, Yukihira's brother. An authoritative commentator (Takeoka Masao) has suggested that the presence of two girls in the story is meant precisely to heighten his romantic bemusement. Narihira knows he will have to make a choice, but he would much rather have both sisters at once; hence his excitement and confusion. The 'Uji chapters' of *Genji monogatari* evoke a young nobleman's inability to choose between two sisters who live in a country setting very like this one. Yukihira's involvement with two girls at Suma seems therefore to be a transposition of the first episode of *Ise monogatari*.

Since Zeami himself called the play *Pining Wind and Autumn Rain* (*Matsukaze Murasame*), he may have seen the two women as roughly equal; and in his time, Autumn Rain probably took more lines of the text than she does now. Her Japanese name, *Murasame*, means the kind of rain that falls hard, then gently, in fits and starts. In poetry, it evokes particularly the cold rains of late autumn. Medieval linked verse manuals taught that a mention of *murasame* could properly be followed up by a mention of *matsukaze*. Pining Wind and Autumn Rain therefore turn out to be not only sisters, but paired poetic images.

The difference between these images is developed in the play. When Pining Wind, at the climactic moment, sees Yukihira instead of the pine tree, Autumn Rain rushes to her, objecting that 'Yukihira is not there.' Autumn Rain loves Yukihira too, but she, unlike her sister, has forgotten his promise to return. She even says so.

In the complementary qualities of the sisters, one discerns the presence of the Akashi lady. This is not because she somehow embodies those qualities, but because she is a superb musician. Genji met her through her music, and, in the novel, music is at the heart of their love. The sisters are the complementary qualities of this music.

In part two of *Tsunemasa* (a play which may be by Zeami), the music of a lute calls down what sounds like a shower of rain, but proves to be only a gust of wind in the pines. The text then quotes two lines from a famous poem on the lute (*biwa*) by Po Chü-i (772–846): 'The great string is loud like autumn rain; the little string is urgent like the whisperings of lovers.' Next, it works in some even more famous lines from a poem on the *kin*, a kind of zither related to the Japanese *koto*. Po Chü-i likened the sound of the lower strings of the *ch'in* to wind gusting through pines, and of the higher strings to the voice of a caged crane, crying in the night for its children. Pining Wind and Autumn Rain are therefore, among other things, these two voices of music: one loud but intermittent, the other softer but constant and urgent with longing. The couplet on the lute fits them particularly well. The sound of the great string is Autumn Rain, that of the little string Pining Wind. The Akashi lady played both *koto* and lute.

Pining Wind's vision of Yukihira is a fascinating moment. What really happens when she sees him instead of the pine? Is Autumn Rain right when she tries to recall her to her senses, or does Pining Wind, having stood fast, then open her sister's eyes to a higher truth? The passage is so highly charged and so abstract (because stripped of nearly all anecdotal detail) that it invites comment.

The chief understanding of Pining Wind's feelings and vision speaks of attachment, delusion, and madness. The sisters' phantoms cling to the world they once knew because they cannot give up their love. That is why, near the end of part one, Pining Wind is happy to learn that their visitor is a monk: she hopes he will help them towards release. That is also why she tells her story in part two. Confessions like hers figure in many plays and are connected with the Buddhist practice of *zange*: 'confession' to exhaust attachment. Instead, however, her telling of the tale overwhelms her with memories, until she actually puts on Yukihira's hat and cloak. Now, in her derangement, she sees him before her. Autumn Rain is right. Pining Wind is mad and Yukihira is not there, even if Autumn Rain herself soon succumbs.

Within the nō tradition, the Pining Wind who sees Yukihira is clearly a *monogurui*: a madwoman. Many plays are centred on *monogurui*, either male or female. In those days, the ravings of the mad were scarcely distinguished from the antics of entertainers, and *monogurui* often *are* entertainers. It was Zeami (according to Yamanaka Reiko) who gave his female *monogurui* such depth that the pretext of their being entertainers dropped away. They became simply women in acute distress.

The oldest manuscripts of *Pining Wind* date from the early sixteenth century, some sixty to eighty years after Zeami's death. Whatever Zeami's own practice may have been, the play by then (according to Nakamura Itaru) was being performed in a style that emphasized this distress. Into the seventeenth century, Pining Wind wore the *Fukai* mask (the face of a woman of about forty), and the dances of the play evoked her disturbed state much more explicitly than at present. Thus the play was interpreted just as *The Well-Cradle* was in the same period.

Since then, conceptions of *Pining Wind*, as of *The Well-Cradle*, have become more elevated. For example, an authority on folk theatre and festivals (Honda Yasuji) wrote in 1941 that when Pining Wind dons the hat and cloak, she recalls a medium calling down a spirit; but that once the spirit (Yukihira) has appeared, she should dance with the pure serenity of one who watches the moon in the sky. Others, too, are impressed above all with the purity and beauty of the sisters' emotion.

Still, Pining Wind generally remains a *monogurui*, however attenuated. Her vision, and Autumn Rain's subsequent attunement to it, at least require a break with common reality. Yet there persists a feeling that, somehow, the truly sane one should be Pining Wind, not Autumn Rain. One writer versed in French literature (Tashiro Keiichirō) acknowledged this feeling when he likened Pining Wind's longing to 'religious passion'.

If her passion is 'religious', then the Yukihira of her vision must be less an amorous young courtier than a god. The idea has a certain appeal because, in the poetic imagination, courtiers were indeed god-like. They inhabited the heights (Miyako) of an island mountain, the shores of which were peopled by male and female *ama*. From this mountain, the emperor's divine virtue (in which courtiers shared) bestowed blessings upon the world. The God of Sumiyoshi, in *Takasago*, displays this virtue in the form of a 'god pine' on the ocean shore. Why, then, should Yukihira too not be a god?

Japanese religious lore recognizes the pine as a link between the higher and the lower realms. Gods 'descend' through pine trees, like lightning down a wire. The back wall of every nō stage illustrates this idea, since the pine painted on it is called the 'pine of the divine manifestation' (*yōgō no matsu*). Other – real – pines in temple or shrine grounds throughout Japan bear the same name. No wonder one scholar (Honda Yasuji) caught, in *Pining Wind*, echoes of a rite of divine possession. They are there.

However, they are only echoes. The play is art, not shamanic rite. Pining Wind is not a medium, nor does a medium feel 'religious passion'. Pining Wind's sole thought is love. If her passion is 'religious', then her love is divine and Autumn Rain, when she tries to stop her sister, is blind. Yukihira's farewell poem – a promise to come should the sisters pine for him – is then a divine promise, and his appearance is a god's compassionate response to the cries of his devotee. Is this possible?

Alas, no. Contemplation was certainly known in medieval Japan, but the rapture of divine love is not a motif in the religion of the time, and no divinities, native or Buddhist, were so conceived as to encourage it. Yukihira's appearance in response to Pining Wind's desire cannot be a religious event. Besides, he and the sisters are equally phantoms. Pining Wind is not flesh calling down spirit. Her yearning for Yukihira, although situated on a high imaginative plane, has nothing to do with transcendence. It is the quintessence of *human* love.

Human love returns one's thoughts to Genji and the Akashi lady. In his parting poem, Yukihira promised to come again should the sisters pine for him. Genji, on the night before his return to the capital, gave the lady a Chinese *koto* to remember him by, and she replied with a poem about its endless music being her own, ceaseless weeping. Genji's answer asked her never to re-tune the 'middle string', and promised that before she should need to, they would meet again.

Genji felt deeply for this lady. In her alone, among his varied loves, he found a personal distinction comparable to that of his wife, Murasaki. After their daughter was born, Genji urged the lady to come up to Miyako, but for a long time she refused, fearing many troubles and slights should she give in. At last, however, she moved to a property of her father's. The house stood by the wide reach of a river just west of the capital, in a grove of pines. As the novel observes repeatedly, the place resembled Akashi itself. One moonlit evening when Genji came visiting, the lady took out the *koto* he had given her there. The middle string was as it had been, and he spoke a poem about how, like this string, his own feelings had remained unchanged. 'Trusting in your promise to be true,' she replied, 'I added my own weeping music to the music of the pines.' Of course, Genji soon had to leave, his home being elsewhere – with Murasaki, in the heart of Miyako. The chapter that tells this story is called 'Matsukaze', or 'Wind in the Pines'.

To hear in part two of *Pining Wind* overtones of the Akashi lady's 'weeping music', and of the sad solace it must rarely have brought her, is to re-emerge from the play's tense, distracted vision into the more open world of the great novel. In her villa by the river the lady could see Genji now and again, but his nearness only made him seem the more distant and her longing remained. She could not have him for her own. Murasaki was (for her) the shadow between them. For Genji, these two loves perhaps resembled the sisters who so troubled Narihira's heart in *Ise monogatari*. *Genji monogatari* itself intimates that they are a pair, since it was when Genji first spied the child Murasaki that he also first heard tell of the beauty of Akashi, of the eccentric official who had retired there, and of that official's only daughter. These two ladies' rival claims surely distressed Genji, but their perilously paired love must have had, for him, a rare, exalting beauty.

Not that Pining Wind and Autumn Rain are really the Akashi lady and Murasaki; not at all. They and Yukihira describe an essential pattern of which the novel offers only one example, and in any case, they are not actually people. To the extent that they have human form, one can talk about attachment and derangement, or even, in modern terms, character and psychology. However, they do not properly have a 'psychology'; nor are they Jungian archetypes. They are purified essences of human feeling, refined through centuries of the classical literary tradition. They are the twin voices of the music of longing. Genji heard both in the Akashi lady's playing. One starts and stops, the other murmurs for ever. When the dream of the sisters is over and day dawns, only the murmuring voice remains. The other voice was the concert, and the play.

A little Matsukaze and Murasame Chapel now stands about half a kilometre from the sea, in one corner of a playground on the western outskirts of Kōbe. This is where Yukihira is said to have lived, and the sisters after him. A structure beside it shelters the ancient stump of the 'wind-bent pine'. A few kilometres away, in the hills, at a spot called Tai-no-hata, one finds 'the grave of Matsukaze and Murasame'. A scholar (Kanai Kiyomitsu) has noted that ritually pure young women from this locality used to go down to the shore and make salt to offer at their village shrine. On a plot in the village, surrounded by houses, stand stone funerary monuments large and small. Among them, a stele bears the two names of the sisters. Two gravestones, beside it, bear one name each. The names on the gravestones face towards Miyako.

PINING WIND

Persons in order of appearance

A Monk	*waki*
Pining Wind (*Waka-onna* mask)	*shite*
Autumn Rain (*Ko-omote* mask)	*tsure*
A Villager	*ai*

Remarks: A third-category play (*kazura-mono*) current in all five schools of nō.

*   *   *

Stage assistant places a small pine tree, set in a stand, at front of stage; a poem-slip hangs in its branches. To shidai *music, enter Monk. He stands in base square.*

MONK (*shidai*) Suma! and on down the shore to Akashi

　　　　　　　Suma! and on down the shore to Akashi

　　　　　　　I will go roaming with the moon.

(*nanori*) You have before you a monk who is looking at every province. Since I have not yet seen the lands of the west,[1] I have decided this autumn to make my way there and watch the moon over Suma and Akashi.

(*tsukizerifu*) Having come so swiftly, I have already reached Suma shore, as I believe it is called, in the province of Tsu. On the beach, I see a single pine with a sign placed before it and a poem-slip hanging in its branches. There must be a story about this tree. I will ask someone what it is.

(*mondō*) Is any resident of Suma shore nearby?

Villager, who has slipped in to sit at villager position, now rises and comes to first pine.

VILLAGER What do you need, reverend sir, from a resident of Suma shore?

MONK I see this pine has a tablet planted before it, and a poem-slip hanging in its branches. There must be a story about it. Would you kindly tell it to me?

VILLAGER Why, certainly. Long ago there were two young women – two saltmakers[2] – named Pining Wind and Autumn Rain. This pine stands in their memory. People who wished to honour them put this tablet here and hung in the pine's branches the poem-slip you see. Such people also give them comfort and guidance as they pass. Of course, reverend sir, you yourself have no connection with them,[3] but it would be good of you to do so, too, as you pass by.

MONK Thank you for your account. Then I will go to the pine and comfort the spirits of those two young women.

VILLAGER If there is anything else you need, reverend sir, please let me know.

1. *Saigoku*, a vague term for the region west of Kyoto and along the Inland Sea.
2. Saltmaking is so important in *Pining Wind* that it deserves a description. Workers cut seaweed offshore or raked it up from the beach, then poured brine over it repeatedly. Next, they burned this salt-saturated seaweed, mixed the ashes with water, let the ashes settle, and skimmed off the salt solution. Only then did they boil down this elaborately prepared brine.
3. Were the Monk a relative of the two sisters, he would have a natural duty to comfort their spirits. Since he is not, he could choose to pass on without doing so.

MONK I promise to do so.

VILLAGER Very well.

Exit Villager. Monk comes to centre and stands facing pine.

MONK (*unnamed*) So, this pine is the relic of two saltmakers who lived long ago: Pining Wind, one was called, and the other Autumn Rain. A sad, sad story!

There they lie buried deep in the earth,

yet their names still linger, and in sign,

ever constant in hue, a single pine

leaves a green autumn.[4]

Ah, very moving!

And now that I have comforted them by chanting the Sutra and by calling for them upon our Lord Amida, the sun – as it will on these short autumn days – has all too quickly set. That village below the hills is still a good way off. I will go instead to this salt-house and see the night through here.

Stage assistant places the brine wagon near corner pillar: a small, light evocation of a wagon, with a pail on it and a long brocade 'rope' to pull it by.

To shin-no-issei music,[5] enter Autumn Rain, who stops at first pine. She is followed by Pining Wind, who stops at third pine. Autumn Rain carries a second pail. Both are dressed in white robes over red trouser-skirts. They stand facing each other.

PINING WIND and AUTUMN RAIN

(*issei*) A brine wagon wheels meagrely

our dreary world round and round:[6]

O sorry life!

RAIN Waves here at our feet: on Suma shore   *They face audience.*

BOTH the very moon moistens a trailing sleeve.[7]   *Face each other.*

To ashirai music, both come on stage. Autumn Rain stands at centre, Pining Wind in base square.

4. The pine that stands 'in sign' of the sisters' memory 'leaves a green autumn' because it alone remains green amid the red autumn foliage. The pine's green constancy is male, as *Takasago* shows; and since the red of autumn is female, as in *Tatsuta*, the 'single pine' may refer to Yukihira between his two loves.

5. *Shin-no-issei* music is normally reserved for the entrance of the *shite* in a god play. It underscores the exceptional beauty and purity of the two sisters, who are dressed mainly in white. The adoption of this *shin-no-issei* probably dates from about 1700.

6. In Japanese, *kuruma* means both 'wheel' and 'wagon'. These two lines evoke not only the drearily repetitious cycle of their daily labour but their sufferings on the wheel of birth and death.

7. The sisters' sleeves are wet with the brine they gather, but even the moon moistens their sleeves because, seeing it, they recall the past and weep.

(*shidai*)	We of Suma, long familiar with fall
	we of Suma, long familiar with fall –
	come, under the moon, let us draw brine!
WIND (*sashi*)	Fall winds were blowing, to call forth sighs,[8] *Face audience.*
	and although the sea lay some way off,
	Yukihira, the Middle Counsellor,
BOTH	sang of the breeze from Suma shore *Face each other.*
	blowing through the pass; and every night,
	waves sound so near the saltmakers' home,
	apart and lonely. On the way to the village,
	beside the moon, there is no company.
WIND	The sorry world's labours claim us,
	and wholly wretched the seafolk's craft
BOTH	that makes no way through life, a dream
	where, bubbles of froth, we barely live,
	our wagon affording us no safe haven:
	we of the sea, whose grieving hearts
	never leave these sleeves dry!
CHORUS	(*sageuta*) So thoroughly *Face audience.*
	this world of ours
	appears unlivable,
	one only envies
	the brilliant moon[9]
	rising now, come, draw the rising tide

Pining Wind steps forward, as though towards the sea.

rising now, come, draw the rising tide!

Notices her reflection in a tide pool.

   (*ageuta*) Image of shame, my reflection
   image of shame, my reflection

---

8. This is the beginning of the *sashi–sageuta–ageuta* passage probably set to music by Kan'ami. The next six and a half lines quote freely from the 'Suma' chapter of *Genji monogatari*. Prince Genji lived in a house some way back from the sea. Finding the noise of the waves still very loud, he recalled a poem by Yukihira, who had preceded him at Suma and who (as *Genji monogatari* suggests) had lived at the same spot. Since Yukihira had spoken in verse of the breeze from Suma shore blowing through the pass (over the hills along the beach), Genji realized that this breeze must stir up the waves. This *sashi* intimates that the two sisters (there was probably only one saltmaker in Kan'ami's piece) live roughly where Genji, and Yukihira before him, had lived. This is inconsistent with the rest of the play, however, since a salt-house would need to be beside the sea.
9. A poem by Fujiwara no Takamitsu in the imperial anthology *Shūishū* (*c.* 1006).

shrinks away, withdrawing
tides leave behind stranded pools,   *Gazes at water again.*
and I, how long will I linger on?
Dew agleam on meadow grasses
soon must vanish in the sun,
yet on this stony shore
where saltmakers rake seaweed in,
trailing fronds they leave behind,
these sleeves, can only wilt away
these sleeves can only wilt away.   *Retreats to base square.*

WIND (*sashi*) How lovely, though so familiar,
Suma as twilight falls!
Fishermen's calls echo faintly;

BOTH   out at sea, their frail craft loom   *They face each other.*
dim, the face of the moon:
wild geese in silhouette,
flocks of plovers, cutting gales,
salt sea winds – yes, each one
at Suma speaks of autumn alone.[10]
Ah, the nights' long, heart-chilling hours!

WIND (*kakeai*) But come, let us draw brine!   *Face audience.*
At the sea's edge flood and ebb
clothe one in salt robes:

RAIN   tie the sleeves across your shoulders
WIND   to draw brine[11] – or so we wish,
RAIN   yet no, try as we may,
WIND   a woman's wagon

CHORUS (*ageuta*) rolled in, falls back, weak and weary

Autumn Rain goes before drums. Pining Wind advances slightly, gazes after the cranes.

rolled in, falls back, weak and weary.[12]
Cranes start from the reeds with cries

---

10. All these sights and sounds of Suma recall what Prince Genji sees in the 'Suma' chapter.

11. The long, dangling sleeves had to be tied back in order to allow freedom of movement for work.

12. The two lines beginning with 'a woman's wagon' defy translation. This is one possible paraphrase. They also contain the fleeting image of a great 'male wave' approaching the shore only to recede, and this wave might conceivably point to Yukihira.

while all four storm winds add their roar.[13]

The dark, the cold: how can they be endured?

Pining Wind looks at the moon, then glances into the buckets on the brine wagon.

As night wears on, the moon shines so bright!

Now we draw the moon's reflections!

Salt-fire smoke – O do take care![14]

This is the way we of the sea

live through the gloom of fall.   *Kneels by brine wagon.*

CHORUS (*sageuta*) Pine Islands! where Ojima's seafolk,[15]

beneath the moon,

With her fan mimes drawing brine, then gazes at the moon's reflection in her pail.

draw reflections, ah, with keen delight

draw reflections, ah, with keen delight!   *To base square.*

(*rongi*) Far away they haul their brine[16]

in Michinoku: though the name

is 'near', Chika, where workers tend

the Shiogama salt-kilns.[17]

WIND   And where the poor folk carried salt-wood:

Akogi beach, that was, and the tide withdrawing

CHORUS   on down the same Ise coast lies Futami shore,

and its Paired Rocks: O I would pair

a past life in the world with one renewed![18]

WIND

13. Storm winds from the four directions.

14. 'Take care lest the smoke of the salt fires should drift across the moon and hide it.' The motif is from classical poetry.

15. 'Pine Islands' is Matsushima, a celebrated scenic spot on the north-east coast of Honshu, near the Shiogama mentioned below. The name Ojima is associated with Matsushima in poetry.

16. *Tōei*, the play from which Zeami transplanted this *rongi* passage, is set at Ashiya, and that is why Ashiya and its environs figure in it when Suma does not. Having no continuous grammatical or narrative structure, the passage is almost untranslatable. Only its discontinuous phrases matter – to one who already knows the poetic tradition. In their aesthetic exaltation, Pining Wind and Autumn Rain play with fragments of poems that name, and hence eulogize, places associated with saltmaking.

17. Michinoku is northern Honshu, where Matsushima and Shiogama are to be found. *Shiogama* means 'salt-kiln', and the name of Chika, near Shiogama, resembles *chika*[*shi*], 'near'. Zeami developed the poetic value of Shiogama in his play *Tōru* and, to a lesser extent, in *Akoya no matsu* (no longer performed).

18. Akogi beach is near the Grand Shrine of Ise, on Ise Bay. Just off Futami-ga-ura ('Futami, or "Twice-See" Shore'), also near the Ise Shrine, two tall rocks rise from the water. They are called the Husband-and-Wife Rocks, and a sacred straw rope encircles them both. The 'poor folk' carrying 'salt-wood' (wood to fuel the saltmakers' fires) on Akogi beach recall several classical poems.

When pines stand misty in spring sun,
the sea-lanes seem to stretch away
past the tide-flats of Narumi,
Bay of the Sounding Sea.[19]

CHORUS   Ah, Narumi, that was,
but here at Naruo,[20]
beneath the shadowing pines,
no moon ever shines to touch
the village huts roofed with rushes
at Ashinoya,[21]

WIND   drawing brine from Nada seas
sorely burdens me with care
though none will tell, and I am come,
no boxwood comb in my hair,[22]

CHORUS   while in comb the rolling billows

Autumn Rain places her pail on the brine wagon. Pining Wind gazes at it.

for us to draw brine, and look:
the moon is in my pail!

WIND   In mine, too, there is a moon!

CHORUS   How lovely! A moon here, too!

Pining Wind looks into the other pail, then up to the sky, then again at the two pails. Having received the wagon-rope from Autumn Rain, she pulls the wagon up to drums, then looks back at it one more time.

WIND   The moon is one,

CHORUS   reflections two, three the brimming tide,
for tonight we load our wagon with the moon.[23]
O no, I do not find them dreary,

19. Narumi-gata is a spot on the coast near present Nagoya. Its name (if the characters used to write it are taken seriously) means something like 'Bay of the Sounding Sea'.
20. Naruo, the name of which sounds like Narumi, is along the coast east of Suma.
21. Ashinoya (or Ashiya) is a well-known locality on the coast east of Suma, now between Kobe and Osaka. Its name means 'rush houses'.
22. The line 'at Ashinoya' begins a five-line passage that is a variant of a poem in *Ise monogatari* ('Tales of Ise'; 10th c.), episode no. 87. Nada is the name of the shore near Ashinoya. The passage puns elaborately on *tsuge* ('boxwood') and *tsugeji* ('will not tell [of my plight]'); and on *sashi* ('insert' a comb in one's hair) and *sashi-kuru* ('[waves] come surging in'). In the original poem, the girl explains to her lover that she has been so busy gathering brine, she has not been able even to dress her hair with a comb before coming to meet him.
23. To 'one [moon]' and 'two [reflections]', the original adds the puns *mitsu* ('three' or 'brimming') and *yo* ('four' or 'night'). 'For' is meant to be homophonous with 'four'.

the tide-roads of the sea!

Stage assistant removes the wagon. Pining Wind sits on a stool before drums, while Autumn Rain sits directly on stage, slightly behind her and to her left. They are in the salt-house.

MONK (*unnamed*) The people of the salt-house have returned. I will ask them to give me shelter for the night.

(*mondō*) I beg your pardon, there in the salt-house! Excuse me, please!

RAIN [*Rises.*] What is it?

MONK I am a traveller, and now the sun has set. May I have shelter for the night?

RAIN Please wait a moment. I will ask the owner. [*Turns to Pining Wind, kneels on one knee.*] I beg your pardon, but a traveller is here. He says he wants shelter for the night.

WIND We could easily give him shelter, but our house simply is not fit to be seen. No, we cannot let him stay.

RAIN [*Rises, turns to Monk.*] I gave your request to the owner. She says that our house is not fit to be seen, and that we cannot offer you lodging for the night.

MONK I understand, of course, but please realize that I do not mind what condition your house is in. I am a monk, after all. Do pass on again my urgent request for shelter here tonight.

RAIN [*Turns to Pining Wind, kneeling on one knee.*] The traveller is a monk and he insists on asking again for a night's shelter.

WIND What? the traveller is a monk, you say? Why yes, the moonlight shows me one who has renounced the world. Well, it will do, this saltmakers' home, with its posts of pine and fence of bamboo.[24] The night is cold, I know. Tell him he may stay and warm himself at our rush fire.

RAIN [*Rises, turns to Monk.*] Do please come in.

MONK Thank you for your kindness.

Autumn Rain sits as before. Monk rises, advances a few steps, sits again. He too is now in the salt-house.

WIND (*mondō*) From the start I wanted to have you stay, but this house is simply not fit to be seen. That is why I refused.

MONK It is very good of you to have me. Since I am a monk and have always been one, my travels have no particular goal. On what

24. Prince Genji's house at Suma is described in this way in the 'Suma' chapter.

grounds, then, should I prefer one lodging to another? Besides, here on Suma shore, any sensitive person ought actually to prefer a somewhat melancholy life:

> Should one perchance
> ask after me,
> say that on Suma shore,
> salt, sea-tangle drops
> are falling as I grieve.[25]

Yes, that was Yukihira's poem. By the way, I noticed that pine tree on the shore. When I asked a man about it, he told me that it stands in memory of two saltmakers named Pining Wind and Autumn Rain. [*Pining Wind and Autumn Rain weep.*] I have no connection of my own with them, of course, but I prayed for them before going on. Why, how strange! When I mentioned Yukihira, both of you seemed overcome with sorrow. What is the meaning of your grief?

WIND and RAIN Oh, it is true! When love is within, love's colours will show without![26] The way you quoted his poem, 'Should one by chance inquire for me', brought on such pangs of longing! So tears of attachment to the human world once more moistened our sleeves.   *They weep.*

MONK Tears of attachment to the human world? You talk as though you were not of the living. And Yukihira's poem seems to afflict you with feelings of painful longing, I do not understand. Please, both of you, tell me your names!

WIND and RAIN (*kudoki-guri*) I am ashamed!

> As the tale rises to my lips,
> I whom none ask after, ever,
> rejoin a world gone long ago,
> where, brine-drenched, I learn no lesson
> but suffer on in bitterness of heart.[27]

---

25. According to the imperial anthology *Kokinshū* (905), Yukihira, in exile at Suma, sent this poem back to someone in the capital. The 'salt, sea-tangle drops' are at once the brine that drips from the seaweed gathered by saltmakers along the beach, and the poet's own tears.

26. A well-known saying, ultimately derived from the Chinese classic *Mencius*.

27. The brine that drenches her in her daily work also represents the memories from which she can never be free. This *kudoki-guri* passage uses language from the 'Suma' chapter. It is translated in the singular ('I am ashamed') because such sentiments are too private to make sense in the plural ('we'). The 'we' of the *kudoki* that follows is, likewise, the translator's choice.

(*kudoki*)   Yet having spoken,
            perhaps we need dissemble no more.
            Some while ago, as twilight fell,
            you kindly comforted those who lie
            under that pine, beneath the moss:
            two young women,
            Pining Wind and Autumn Rain.
            We before you are their phantoms.
            Yes, Yukihira, those three years,
            lightened his leisure with pleasant boating
            and watched the moon here on Suma shore.
            While seafolk maidens each night drew brine,
            he chose and courted us, two sisters.
            Pleased with names that fit the season,
            he called us Pining Wind and Autumn Rain.
            We Suma seafolk, familiars of the moon,
WIND   found our saltburner's clothing suddenly changed
BOTH   to silken summer robes censed with sweet fragrance.
WIND   So those three years slipped quickly by.
            Then Yukihira went up to Miyako
RAIN   and, not long after, came the news
BOTH   that he, so young, had passed away.[28]
WIND   O how I love him!
            But perhaps once, in another life,   *Weeps.*
            he again will come,
CHORUS (*uta*) pining, Wind and Autumn Rain
            wet these sleeves, helpless, alas,
            against a love so far beyond us.
            We of Suma are deep in sin:[29]

They appeal to Monk with palms pressed together.

            O in your kindness, give us comfort!
(*ageuta*) Upon passion's tangled grasses,
            dew and longing mingle wildly

Below, Autumn Rain goes to sit before Chorus while Monk moves to witness position.

---

28. Zeami invented this death. Yukihira actually died at the age of seventy-five.
29. This 'sin' is neither social (love across class lines) nor moral. It is the sin of 'wrongful clinging' (*mōshū*): the error of desiring intensely that which one cannot possibly have. Such clinging leads only to misery.

dew and longing mingle wildly,
till the heart, spellbound, yields to madness.
The Day of the Serpent brings purification,[30]
yet sacred streamers to ask the God's help
wave on, useless, wave-borne froth,
we melt into grief and lasting sorrow.

Below, stage assistant gives Pining Wind a man's hat and robe. Carrying them, she dances and mimes in consonance with the text.

(*kuse*)   Ah, as those old days return to mind,
I miss him so!
Yukihira, the Middle Counsellor,
three years dwelt on Suma shore,
then went away up to Miyako,
but left as keepsakes of our love
his tall court hat, his hunting cloak.
Each time I see them, ever more
passion grasses spring,
the pale dewdrops on each blade
so swiftly gone – might I so soon
forget this agony!

> His parting gifts,
> O they are enemies:
> were they gone from me,
> a moment of forgetfulness
> might even now be mine:[31]

so someone sang. O it is true!
My love for him only deepens.

Lowers hat and cloak, which she had clasped to her, and weeps. Below, she continues miming.

WIND   Night after night,
I remove on lying down
this, my hunting cloak,[32]

---

30. A purification rite was regularly performed on the Day of the Serpent early in the third lunar month. Evil influences were transferred into dolls that were then floated down rivers or out to sea. The same rite appears in the 'Suma' chapter.

31. An anonymous poem from the *Kokinshū*.

32. The first half of a poem by Ki no Tomonori, from the *Kokinshū*. The speaker of the poem says that just as he removes his hunting cloak each night before lying down and hangs it on a stand, he constantly thinks of his love. The key words in the poem are *kakete*, 'hang' (the cloak on its stand) and 'constantly', here rendered 'on and on'.

CHORUS   and on and on I only pray
that he and I might share our life —
but fruitlessly.
His keepsakes bring me no joy!
She throws them down but cannot leave them;
picks them up, and his own face
looms before her. Do as she may,
> From the pillow,
> from the foot of the bed,
> love comes pursuing.[33]

Down she sinks in helpless tears,
lost in misery.

(THE DONNING OF THE ROBE)

In base square, Pining Wind collapses to a sitting position and weeps. To ashirai music, stage assistant clothes her in the robe and places the hat on her head. She weeps once more.

WIND (*shimo-no-ei*) River of Three Crossings:[34]
> the grim ford of ceaseless weeping
> yet conceals a gulf of churning love!

(*kakeai*) O what happiness! Yukihira is standing there, calling my name, Pining Wind! I am going to him!

She rises and starts towards the pine. Autumn Rain comes up behind her and catches her right sleeve.

RAIN How awful! This state you are in is exactly what drowns you in the sin of clinging! You have not yet forgotten the mad passion you felt when we still belonged to the world. That is a pine tree. Yukihira is not there.

WIND You are too cruel, to talk that way! That pine *is* Yukihira!
> Though for a time we may say goodbye,
> should I hear you pine, I will return:
> so said his poem, did it not?[35]

---

33. From an anonymous *Kokinshū* poem, originally lighthearted in meaning.
34. The river that the soul must cross to reach the afterworld. It has three fords (deep, medium, or shallow) depending upon the sins that burden the soul. A similar passage occurs in *The Fulling Block*.
35. Pining Wind quotes Yukihira's poem inaccurately; so does Autumn Rain, a few lines later. It is a climactic moment when, a little later still, their mounting excitement recalls it to them perfectly.

RAIN	Why, you are right! I had forgotten!
	A while, perhaps, we may say goodbye,
	but should you miss me, I will come:
	those were the words
WIND	I had not forgotten, pining
	wind is rising now:
	he promised he will come –
RAIN	news to start an autumn rain,
	leaving sleeves a moment moistened;
WIND	yes, pining still, he will return:
RAIN	we rightly trusted
WIND	his dear poem:
BOTH (*waka*)	Now I say goodbye,

(DANCE: *chū-no-mai*)

In tears, Pining Wind runs on to bridgeway, while Autumn Rain, also weeping, goes to sit before Chorus. Pining Wind then returns to stage, pauses in base square, and performs a chū-no-mai *dance.*

WIND	bound for Inaba's
	far green mountains;
	yet, my love, pine
	and I will come again.[36]
(*noriji*)	Yonder, Inaba's far mountain pines;
CHORUS	here, my longing, my beloved lord
	here on Suma shore pines:[37] Yukihira
	back with me once more, while I,
	beside the tree, rise now, draw near:
	so dear, the wind-bent pine –
	I love him still!

(DANCE: *ha-no-mai*)

Pining Wind ceases weeping, then lifts her head and dances a ha-no-mai *around the pine. As text continues, she continues to dance and mime.*

CHORUS	In the pine a wind blows wild.

36. This poem, from the *Kokinshū*, is generally taken as a farewell addressed by Yukihira to a friend or friends in the capital, when he set out for Inaba province in 855 as the new governor. The translation corresponds to Zeami's use of it, but the original suggests nothing precise about the person or persons to whom it may have been addressed.
37. This 'pines' is meant to include the meaning 'is a pine'.

The Suma breakers rage night-long
while wrongful clinging brings you this, our dream.
In your kindness, give us comfort!
Now, farewell:

(*uta*) receding waves fall silent
along Suma shore
a breeze sweeps down from off the hills.
On the pass, the cocks are crowing.
The dream is gone, without a shadow
night opens into dawn.
It was autumn rain you heard,
but this morning see:
pining wind alone lingers on
pining wind alone lingers on.

Facing side from base square, stamps the final beat.

Nonomiya · THE WILDWOOD SHRINE

The Wildwood Shrine is based far more explicitly than *Pining Wind* on *Genji monogatari* ('The Tale of Genji', 11th c.), and, as many writers have pointed out, is similar in structure to *The Well-Cradle*. In the past, those who doubted that Zeami wrote it have still hesitated to make a positive attribution, but a case has recently been made (by Itō Masayoshi) for Komparu Zenchiku. The style is Zenchiku's, and so fine a play can only have been composed by an expert. Moreover, Zenchiku is known in other instances to have written new plays based on the general mood, theme, and structure of earlier works by Zeami.

The word used for the play's original title, *Nonomiya*, probably means 'The Shrine in the Country', referring to a shrine intentionally placed well outside the capital. It may also be taken to mean 'The Shrine on [Saga] Moor'. Either way, 'The Wildwood Shrine' is rather an over-translation. However, the shrine really was in a sacred grove, and this expression fairly conveys the spirit of the play.

In the time of *Genji monogatari*, the Wildwood Shrine was temporary, being rebuilt on a slightly different site (chosen by divination) each time the need arose. A new high priestess of Ise underwent purification there before going on to take up her duties at the Ise Shrine. Since she was a young imperial princess, she is called in English the Vestal of Ise. (By the fifteenth century, the custom of appointing a Vestal had long since lapsed.)

The lady of *The Wildwood Shrine* is a Vestal's mother: Rokujō, who, in *Genji monogatari*, is perhaps Genji's most intriguing love. She had been, before her affair with Genji began, the wife of the crown prince. That is why she is called 'the Consort' (Miyasudokoro) in the play. Then the crown prince died, and Rokujō, who should have been empress, found herself alone – but for her daughter – with the past.

Genji monogatari does not say how her affair with Genji began. A woman of extraordinary depth, elegance, and pride, she was clearly older than Genji, and of such rank that Genji should have treated her very carefully indeed. However, he was too young to understand fully what he was doing, and, as he pursued his other amours, he drifted away from her. She was hurt, and the consequences were a disaster. Even before she appears in the novel, one of Genji's loves is killed in the dead of night by a phantom woman, and one gathers in time that this phantom was the 'living ghost' of the jealous Rokujō.

Then followed the incident evoked in part two of *The Wildwood Shrine*. It was the time of the annual Kamo Festival, and the great nobles, especially Genji, were to ride in parade through the capital. Not even Rokujō, who shunned such events, could stay away. Ladies then travelled in curtained carriages and watched an event from inside them, through the curtains. One could not tell who the lady was, and Rokujō's excessively discreet carriage made her look like a nobody – at least, a nobody compared to Genji's formal wife, Aoi. Aoi arrived too late to join the front row of carriages, but her attendants, who were already drunk, quickly fixed that. They hauled Rokujō's little carriage out of the way, damaging it in the process; shoved it back among the gathering crowd; and installed their mistress in its place. Rokujō no longer had a view, nor could she escape.

It was not long before Aoi, now pregnant, became very ill. She gave birth safely, but soon afterwards she was dead – killed by an angry phantom. All the evidence pointed to Rokujō. (Aoi's death at the hands of Rokujō is the subject of the nō play *Aoi no Ue*). It must be said that Rokujō herself, in the novel, had no idea what she was doing. She only felt depressed and had strange dreams. She was horrified on learning that suspicion had settled on her. When at last her daughter was named Vestal of Ise, Rokujō decided to go with her to the Wildwood Shrine, and then to take the unprecedented step of accompanying her to Ise. She had every reason to wish to go away.

It is in the 'Sakaki' chapter of *Genji monogatari* that Genji visits Rokujō at the Wildwood Shrine. The novel does not explain his reason for doing so, but according to the medieval commentaries, he feared that if he did not placate her, her 'living ghost' might possess and kill Murasaki, his future wife, as well. (When Murasaki does die, much later in the novel, there are intimations of Rokujō's presence.) This interpretation of his chief motive is not implausible, and it tightens the link between parts one and two of the play. Apart from this, *The Wildwood Shrine* both quotes from the novel and incorporates all the appropriate images listed in the medieval manuals on how to work the novel into linked verse. However, the playwright also displayed his own poetic virtuosity and consistently heightened the melancholy of his theme.

In the past, Saga Moor (Saga-no) lay beyond the western boundary of Kyoto, although now most of it is covered by houses. One still finds there a Nonomiya Jinja, the age of which is unclear. It is in a bamboo grove, not a grove of trees, but otherwise it looks quite like the shrine described in the novel and the play.

THE WILDWOOD SHRINE

Persons in order of appearance

A Monk	*waki*
A Lady (*Waka-onna* mask)	*maeshite*
A Villager	*ai*
The phantom of the Consort, Lady Rokujō (*Waka-onna* mask)	*nochijite*

Remarks: A third-category play (*kazura-mono*) current in all five schools of nō. According to a variant performance tradition (*kogaki*) in the Hōshō, Kongō, and Kita schools, a carriage is brought on at the beginning of part two and placed in base square. The Consort then boards it and sings while the stage assistant draws it towards the curtain, leaving it at first pine. Historical records show that the play has been performed in the past with torii only, with carriage only, with both, and with neither.

*　　*　　*

Stage assistant places a torii, with a flimsy length of fence on either side of it, at front of stage.

To nanori-bue *music, enter Monk. He stands in base square.*

MONK (*nanori*) You have before you a monk who is looking at all the provinces. Lately I have been in Miyako, where I saw all the sights and monuments of the Capital. With autumn nearly over, I feel drawn to the moors of Saga, and I will therefore go to see them. Now, upon inquiring about this grove, I learned that this is where the Wildwood Shrine once stood. I will visit the place, since I happen to be passing by. [*Moves to centre.*]

(*sashi*)   I see before me, here within this grove,
     an unbarked log torii, a wattled fence,
     exactly as they were long, long ago.

Sits, presses his palms together in salutation.

     I do not understand: how can this be?
     But never mind, for now that I have come,
     it is a privilege to salute the Shrine.

(*sageuta*)   The sacred fence of Ise does not part
     Gods from Buddhas, and the way runs straight
     for the teaching of the holy Law.
     Monk that I am, in this sacred presence,
     I find the evening calm, my heart at peace
     I find the evening calm, my heart at peace.[1]

Rising, he goes to sit at witness position.

To shidai *music, enter Lady, with a fan in her right hand and a leafy sakaki branch[2] in her left. She stands in base square, her back to the audience.*

LADY (*shidai*)   O Wildwood Shrine, where once flowers bloomed
     O Wildwood Shrine, where once flowers bloomed,
     what awaits you when autumn is gone?   *Faces audience.*

(*sashi*)   And that time is nigh.
     The lonely days of fall draw to a close,
     and my sleeves wilt in the gathering dews.
     Night's slow descent pierces me with sorrow,
     while all the once gay colours of the heart
     change and fade as summer flowers die.
     So all human life shall waste away.

(*sageuta*)   Secretly, each year on this day,
     I again seek out the long-lost past

(*ageuta*)   at the Wildwood Shrine,

---

1. The Ise Shrine (actually, two paired shrines) honours above all the imperial lineage. In medieval Japan, Shinto was incorporated into Buddhism ('the holy Law'), but no outright fusion of the two occurred. A Buddhist monk did not lightly pray directly before the shrines at Ise, despite this one's affirmation that 'the sacred fence of Ise does not part Gods from Buddhas'. At the Wildwood Shrine itself, at least in the time of *Genji monogatari*, the slightest reference to Buddhism was taboo.

2. Sakaki is a broadleaf evergreen shrub or small tree sacred in Shinto. Its association with Genji's visit to the Wildwood Shrine becomes clear later on. As a hand prop, this sakaki recalls the *sasa* ('bamboo grass') traditionally carried by madwomen in nō. At the same time, however, it underscores the Consort's elevated refinement, and the difference between *The Wildwood Shrine* and a madwoman play like *The River Sumida*.

when late autumn gales despoil the grove
when late autumn gales despoil the grove,
sweeping away the joys of years gone by.
But why do I so long for those old days,
in the sad confusion of my mind?
That world is lost. It does not greet me here,
and I am bitter at this journeying
and I am bitter at this journeying.

MONK (*mondō*) As in the shadow of the grove I call the past to mind and feel my heart settling into peace, suddenly a very beautiful lady stands before me. But who are you?

LADY Who am I, you ask? I might well put you the same question. This is the Wildwood Shrine, where long ago the newly appointed Vestal of Ise was sent temporarily to live. Later on the practice lapsed, but each year on this day, the seventh of the ninth month, I come here to commemorate the past. Unknown to all, I sweep the place clean and honour the divine presence here enshrined. And while I am so engaged, you, an utter stranger, have come upon me. Your presence here is a desecration. Please leave immediately.

MONK (*kakeai*) No, no, my presence surely does no harm. My whole life is given to wandering, for I am one of those who have renounced the world. What moves you, then, to come here each year on this day, in memory of the past?

LADY Today, the seventh of the ninth month, is the day when Prince Genji paid his visit here. He happened to be carrying a sakaki branch that he had picked, and when he slipped it in through the Shrine fence, the Consort swiftly gave him this reply:

No cedars stand
to mark, for all to see,
this sacred boundary:
what error, pray,
made you pick sakaki?[3]

This is also the day when she made that poem.

3. The Consort gives Genji this poem in the novel. It is based on one in the *Kokinshū*: 'My humble dwelling is below Miwa Mountain. Come, if you love me, to the gate where the cedars stand.' Since the *sugi* ('cedar') was the sacred tree of the Miwa Shrine, the poem was generally taken as an utterance of the Miwa deity. The Consort is demanding to know what has moved Genji to come and why he should be offering a branch of the sacred sakaki when there is no one here to respond to his advances.

MONK   And a spirited poem it was, I quite agree. The sakaki branch
    you hold is just as green as his was, long ago.

LADY   Just as green as his: a witty thought!
               But only the sakaki is unchanged,

MONK   for autumn darkens over woodland paths

LADY   and alas, the golden leaves have fallen.

MONK   The sedge upon the moors

CHORUS (*ageuta*) is withered too,
               the grass laid waste around a Wildwood Shrine

Lady advances towards torii, kneels, and lays down her sakaki branch as an offering.
               the grass laid waste around a Wildwood Shrine
               neglected now, although I love it still.

Rising, she mimes looking at each sight mentioned.
               That day I honour has come round again,
               the seventh of the ninth month in the year.
               How plain it is, and low, the wattled fence;
               and the Virgin's lodge, how lightly built!
               Even now the fire-hut dimly glows,[4]
               its light the longing deep within my heart   *To base square.*
               yet plain to see without, as love must be.
               The Shrine in its grove is desolate!
               The Shrine in its grove is desolate!   *Sits at centre.*

CHORUS (*kuri*) To speak now of this Consort in the tale:
               the Kiritsubo Emperor's younger brother,
               known to all as the past Crown Prince,
               blossomed a while, as fragrant as a flower,
               and loved her deeply, as she too loved him.

LADY (*sashi*) Yet it is true: all those who meet must part.[5]

CHORUS   What matters is to waken from life's dream,
               as he too showed, when soon he passed away.

LADY   She could not weep for him for ever more.

CHORUS   Prince Genji, then, in his wilful way,
               came courting her, very secretly,

LADY   until (though who knows why?) his ardour cooled

CHORUS   and the tie between them simply lapsed.

      (*kuse*) Not that he disliked her, not at all.

---

4. The 'fire-hut' was where guards were posted. They kept a fire burning.
5. A proverbial saying still often cited in modern Japan.

And once he sought her at the Wildwood Shrine,
moved deeply on the way by all he saw.
For all the flowers were gone from the moors
and insect cries, once shrill, were faint and few.
The very wind, sighing through the pines,
tinged the path for him with loneliness.
Autumn seemed immeasurably sad.
Then at last Prince Genji reached the Shrine,
displayed for her every mark of love,
and, with lively, varied eloquence
poured forth in her presence his whole heart.

LADY   Later, at the Katsura lustration,[6]
CHORUS   when votive offerings of sakaki,
decked with paper strips of sacred white,[7]
drifted down the stream, the lady, too,
felt herself adrift and drawn away:

> O Suzuka River
> your white-leaping spray
> may wet my sleeves or no,
> but who will think of me
> in distant Ise?[8]

And off she went, she and her young daughter,
though no Vestal's mother had done so before,
down to the Vestal's residence at Take.
She made the journey with a heavy heart.

[for monk] (*rongi*) The tale you tell leaves me little doubt:
you are not a woman like all women.
I must ask you to tell me your name.

LADY   I have no wish to vex you with my name,
unworthy as I am. I am ashamed!
Yet word no doubt will leak out in the end.
I would have you know this name of mine
belongs to no one living. Comfort me!

---

6. A purification rite that took place before the Vestal's departure for Ise.
7. Sakaki branches thus prepared are fundamental ritual objects in Shinto. These are carrying away all impurities.
8. Another poem from the novel. The Suzuka River must be crossed on the way from Kyoto to Ise. Its spray on the Consort's sleeves would be her tears: 'Whatever I may feel as I go, you will not care.'

CHORUS	No one living? How strangely you speak!
	You mean, then, that this world of ours
LADY	is mine no more. I left it long ago,
CHORUS	for that Consort in the tale
LADY	was I myself!
CHORUS	Twilight deepens as the autumn wind
	sweeps through the wood. Aloft, among the trees,
	an evening moon sheds its pallid light
	on two rough, dark pillars: the torii
	she approaches now, and melts away
	into the torii, yes, she is gone.

Rises. (beside "on two rough, dark pillars: the torii")

Exit. (beside "into the torii, yes, she is gone.")

*   *   *

[The Villager comes forward, notices the Monk, and asks him who he is. The ensuing dialogue culminates in the Villager's recital of the history of the Wildwood Shrine and of Genji's visit to the Consort there. The passage is omitted because it conveys no new information of importance, and rather breaks the mood of this gently melancholy play. In the closing dialogue, the Villager urges the Monk to stay on and comfort the Consort's spirit.]

*   *   *

MONK (*ageuta*) My sleeves I spread alone,
                    a mossy robe beneath the grove's dark trees[9]
                    a mossy robe beneath the grove's dark trees,
                    green on this grassy bed's own green,
                    to think upon her tale all through the night
                    and guide her troubled spirit towards peace
                    and guide her troubled spirit towards peace.

To issei *music, enter Consort, as though borne in a carriage. She stops in base square.*

CONSORT (*sageuta*) At the Wildwood Shrine
                    a carriage decked with all the flowers of fall
                    brings me round again to times gone by.

MONK (*kakeai*) How very strange! Under a dim moon,
                    I hear the faint noise of a carriage coming:

9. By convention, a monk was said to wear a 'robe of moss' (*koke-goromo*) that, among other things, indicated his humility.

a wicker carriage with its curtains drawn.[10]
This is an extraordinary sight!
But surely one cannot doubt who it is.
Your ladyship, are you then the Consort?
And, if you will, please explain your carriage.

CONSORT You would question me about my carriage?
Why, now I remember! Long ago,
my carriage, at the Kamo Festival,
provoked a fight, though none knew it was mine.

MONK The carriages were crowded side by side,

CONSORT rich and poor, to see the festival,
when Aoi, that high and mighty lady,

MONK drew up in hers, and her men saw fit
high-handedly to clear all from her path.

CONSORT My own was small enough, and I replied
I simply could not move; so there I stayed.

MONK Her men rushed the carriage,

CONSORT front and rear,

Consort advances towards front and begins to mime and dance.

CHORUS (*uta*) roughly seized the shafts and forced me back
behind the carriage of her waiting women.
The defeat was mine. I had no view,
and understood my place all too well.   *Weeps.*
But let it be: for actions, so it seems,
call forth in time their own retribution.
Still bitter at heart, I ride my carriage
round and round. How long must I go on?

Salutes monk with palms joined in prayer.

Help me dispel, I pray, my wrongful clinging!
Help me dispel, I pray, my wrongful clinging!

CONSORT (*ei*) Remembering those days, my blossom sleeves

CHORUS turn, beneath the moon, the past to now.   *To base square.*

(DANCE: *jo-no-mai*)

Consort performs a jo-no-mai *dance and continues to dance and mime as text resumes.*

CONSORT (*waka*) Perhaps the moon, too, at the Wildwood Shrine
is overcome with thoughts of long ago.

10. This kind of carriage, made of wickerwork (*ajiro-guruma*), was for use by women.

CHORUS	How mournfully the pale light gleams
	from a dewdrop deep within the grove
	from a dewdrop deep within the grove.
CONSORT	(*noriji*) Here I lingered once, and, as of old,
CHORUS	the precincts have an air
CONSORT	all of their own.
CHORUS	The buildings are so light,
CONSORT	the wattled fence *Steps toward torii.*
CHORUS	where, brushing dewdrops from my sleeves,

I came that time, and he after me.
And it was all a dream. The shrine survives,
but I – what visitor do I await?
Faint, plaintive cries of autumn crickets,
and the fall wind's sighs, all through the night

Gazes through torii.

break the silence of the Wildwood Shrine.
O that I might be as I was then!   *Steps back, weeps.*

(DANCE: *ha-no-mai*)

As Chorus sings on, Consort performs a ha-no-mai *dance.*

(*noriji*) This spot from old, awesome to tell,
has held in honour the great Gods of Ise,
both the Inner and the Outer Shrines: [11]
as in and out the torii she goes,
one fears those Gods may righteously reject
her travels on the road of birth and death. [12]
Now she steps again into her carriage.
May she at long last find her way
forever out the Burning Mansion's gate, [13]
the Burning Mansion's gate.

In base square, Consort faces side and stamps the final beat.

11. The paired shrines of Ise. The Inner Shrine is dedicated to Amaterasu, the Sun Goddess, and the Outer to Toyouke, the male deity of increase. In medieval Japanese, deities are normally referred to by the names of their shrines; no distinction is made between the deity and the building.

12. That is, the gods may condemn her for constantly returning to the world of the living.

13. The 'Burning Mansion', a simile for the world of delusion and desire, is from a parable in the *Lotus Sutra*. The Wildwood Shrine is the Consort's Burning Mansion, and its torii is the gate.

Saigyō's Cherry Tree is surely by Zeami. In *Sarugaku dangi* ('Conversations on nō'), Zeami observed: '*Saigyō* and in *Akoya no Matsu* ['The Akoya Pine'] are rather alike. I wrote them because I don't suppose that anyone, in the future, will write nō like these.' His remark makes perfect sense if '*Saigyō*' refers to *Saigyō's Cherry Tree*. *Akoya no matsu*, which is not in the current repertoire, presents the spirit of a pine tree in the form of an old man, and brings in all sorts of places famous for their pines. *Saigyō's Cherry Tree* presents a similar cherry-tree spirit and dwells on places famous for their blossoms. Zeami loved the image of flowers blooming on an old tree and used it beautifully in *Komachi at Seki-dera*, too.

The debate between Saigyō and the spirit of the tree, over one of Saigyō's poems, resembles the one over a Saigyō poem in part one of *Eguchi*. In both cases, the monk-poet Saigyō (1118–1190) delivers himself of an irritated verse, only to receive a well-founded and quite unexpected rebuke: from a prostitute in *Eguchi* and from a flowering tree in this play. Both plays suggest that one cannot escape this world by leaving it, since there is nowhere else to go.

However, *Saigyō's Cherry Tree* is not really a philosophical play. It celebrates, in a suitably witty and elegant manner, the beauty of cherry blossoms in the Kyoto spring. The night spent by Saigyō and his visitors under the flowering tree echoes a theme in Chinese poetry, but countless people in Japan did the same thing.

The site of 'Saigyō's hermitage in the Western Hills' of Kyoto remains unclear, although it seems to have been near Mount Ogura, immediately west of Kyoto. However, a temple known as Shōji-ji now claims it. Shōji-ji is in extreme south-western Kyoto, at the foot of Mount Oshio. Beside some four hundred ordinary cherry trees, it has a young one said to be a direct successor to Saigyō's own.

SAIGYŌ'S CHERRY TREE

Persons in order of appearance

A Manservant   *ai*
The monk and poet Saigyō   *waki*
Two or three flower-viewing Visitors from the Capital   *wakizure*
The Spirit of the cherry tree, an old man (*Shiwajō* mask)   *shite*

Remarks: A third-category play (*kazura-mono*) current in all five schools of nō.

*   *   *

*Stage assistant places a cloth-covered framework, topped with leaves and flowers,
before drums. It represents the cherry tree, and the Spirit is inside it.
Enter then Saigyō, to sit on a stool at witness position. Servant follows and sits at
villager position.*

SAIGYŌ (*mondō*) Speak up! Are you there?

Manservant rises, moves to centre, and goes down on one knee facing Saigyō.

MANSERVANT Here I am, sir, at your service.

SAIGYŌ This year I have particular reason to remain quietly by myself.
Please announce that no visitors will be allowed in to see the cherry
tree in the garden.

MANSERVANT (*fure*) Very well, sir. [*Rises, goes to base square.*] Oh dear,
this *is* a surprise! The cherry tree here in the hermitage garden is
famous. Every spring, visitors high and low, rich and poor, crowd
in to see it. And now, this year, what can be the matter with him?
For he has declared that no one will be allowed in to see the
blossoms. Please, good people, keep this in mind! Keep this in
mind! [*Sits at flute position.*]

Enter Visitors from the Capital. They stand side by side along the front of stage.

VISITORS (*shidai*) The time has come at last to seek the blossoms
           the time has come at last to seek the blossoms:
               now to greet spring among the hills!   *Face audience.*

A VISITOR (*nanori*) You have before you a man who resides in the
southern district of the Capital.[1] Now that spring is here, I have been

1. In other words, this man is no aristocrat. The southern district was where ordinary
people lived.

roaming hither and thither to enjoy the flowers. Yesterday I saw the Land God's cherry blossoms at Kiyomizu, in the Eastern Hills.[2] Today, I am off with friends to Saigyō's hermitage in the Western Hills, for I hear that the cherry tree there is now in full bloom.

VISITORS (*ageuta*) A myriad little birds   *Face each other.*
         carol on while spring touches all things
         carol on while spring touches all things,
         day after day, with life renewed,
         this third moon, while the very skies
         call out, O stay, you who love blossoms!
         Friends and strangers   *A Visitor mimes walking.*
         step forth together, their hearts in full bloom
         step forth together, their hearts in full bloom!

A VISITOR (*tsukizerifu*) Having come so swiftly, we have already reached Saigyō's hermitage. Please wait here a moment, gentlemen. I will ask for permission to enter.

The group goes to stand on bridgeway.

     (*mondō*) I beg your pardon, but may we come in?

MANSERVANT Who is it?

A VISITOR We are a party of people from the Capital. We hear the blossoms at this hermitage are now at their best, and the news has brought us all the way here. Could we not just have a look?

MANSERVANT I would gladly let you in, but I have been forbidden to admit anyone. Still, you have all come a very long way. Let me try to catch him in a good mood and put the question to him. Wait a moment, please.

A VISITOR I understand. Very well, then, gentlemen, let us be patient here a moment.

Visitors go down on one knee, a posture of waiting. Servant goes to base square.

SAIGYŌ (*sashi*) Yes, the blossoms of spring, opening on the highest boughs,
         display the upward urge to true knowledge;
         the autumn moon, shining from the water's depths,
         shows light from on high transforming darkest ignorance.
         Ah, who is there who comprehends such truths?

---

2. Kiyomizu-dera, below Mount Otowa in the hills east of Kyoto, is a tourist attraction even today. The beautiful cherry blossoms there are considered to belong to Jishu Gongen (the 'Land God'), the divinity upon whose land the temple is built.

Flowing water knows no summer heat.

Wind through pines in the valley sounds the coming of fall.

So plants, trees, and all the land, of themselves,

direct our gaze to enlightenment

and guide our ears to harken to the Law.[3]

(*unnamed*) But the best of the four seasons are surely those of flower and fruit. Ah, how lovely it all is!

MANSERVANT (*mondō*) He seems in the merriest of moods. Now is the time to approach him. [*Comes to centre, kneels facing Saigyō.*] I beg your pardon, sir. Some young gentlemen from the Capital are here. They hope you will allow them a look at the cherry tree in the garden.

SAIGYŌ They have come all the way from the Capital, you say, and now they want to see my hermitage's cherry tree?

MANSERVANT Yes, sir.

SAIGYŌ What a bother! I retired to this mountain dwelling just so as to get away from the world and all its vexations. And now these blossoms have betrayed my retreat to everyone! Well, I wish those people would go away, but it is too late now. In their enthusiasm, they have come much too far for me simply to send them home again. Open the gate in my brushwood fence[4] and let them in.

SERVANT As you wish, sir.

He rises, goes to base square, and faces Visitors, who also rise.

(*mondō*) Listen, gentlemen! I caught him in a splendid mood, and he told me to let you in and show you the tree. Please, quickly, this way!

A VISITOR Very well.

Servant mimes opening gate, then withdraws to villager position and soon slips quietly out. Visitors sit in a line along front of stage.

VISITORS (*kakeai*) Ah, cherry blossoms, there you are, in full bloom,
        just as I first spied you between the hills;[5]
        and now I draw near,

SAIGYŌ   my own heart, I find,
        differs, for to me the flowers speak differently,
        telling how blossoms scatter and summer leaves fall.

---

3. No source for this *sashi* is known, but passages similar to the first four lines appear in several plays, including *Atsumori* and *Semimaru*. Perhaps these sentiments were familiar from Buddhist sermons.

4. A brushwood fence or brushwood gate is a standard accessory for a poet's hermitage.

5. These lines are adapted from a poem by Ki no Tsurayuki in the *Kokinshū* (905).

And while I quietly ponder these things,

VISITORS   a festive throng, as gaily apparelled
as ever were cherry trees in bloom,

SAIGYŌ   seems to bring back the springs of years past:

VISITORS   for this hillside spot, however secluded,

SAIGYŌ   is still the blossoming

VISITORS   Capital, too!

CHORUS (*ageuta*) How then can he who has left the world
hide himself away among the blossoms
hide himself away among the blossoms?
Let him seek refuge in the Saga hills,
but when spring calls – for so the world turns –
the very hills burst forth in a riot of fleeting hues.
No, renunciation is all very well,
but outside this world there is nowhere at all.
Where could one settle and never move on
Where could one settle and never move on?

SAIGYŌ (*mondō*) Gentlemen, gentlemen, I am deeply impressed by the zeal that has brought you here from so far away. But my hermitage boasts only this one tree, which I alone live here to enjoy; and I confess myself somewhat distressed that its flowers should have advertised the place to one and all.

'Flowers! Do let's look!' –
and on they come,
amateurs in droves.
Ah, lovely blossoms,
this is all your fault![6]

Saigyō, abandoning the stool, sits directly on the stage in preparation for the sequence that follows.

CHORUS (*uta*) Yes, lovely blossoms, shadows are falling.
Moonlight brightens the night, while beneath the tree,
we, in fellowship, forget our way home.
Tonight let us lodge here beneath the blossoms,
keeping merry vigil till night yields to dawn.

During above passage, Visitors exit through side door.

6. This poem appears in Saigyō's personal collection, *Sankashū* ('Poems from a Mountain Dwelling'). The prose preface to it says: '[Composed at a time] when he meant to remain quiet, and people came to see his flowers.'

(THE SPIRIT APPEARS)

Stage assistant removes cloth from the 'tree', revealing the Spirit seated on a stool.

SPIRIT (*sashi*) Wholly neglected, ignored by all,

the tree may perhaps be forgotten,

yet in his heart, yes, there are still blossoms![7]

'Flowers! Do let's look!' –

and on they come,

amateurs in droves.

Ah, lovely blossoms,

this is all your fault!

SAIGYŌ (*kakeai*) Astonishing! There comes forward now,

from the hollow tree in bloom,

an ancient man, chanting my poem!

A mystery, this apparition!

SPIRIT The old man has come in a dream to ask you what you meant by that poem of yours.

SAIGYŌ This old man is a dream, you say –

then you have come to me in my own dream.

And moreover, you speak of asking what I meant by the poem I made just now. It seems to have left you perplexed.

SPIRIT Why, no, reverend sir. How could your poem possibly have perplexed me? But you did say,

. . . and on they come,

amateurs in droves.

Ah, lovely blossoms,

this is all your fault!

I thought I might ask why you blame the blossoms.

SAIGYŌ Please understand that I am living alone in the mountains precisely to avoid the world of sorrows and to clear my mind of all its vexations. With a horde of visitors at my gate, I found their arrival distressing, and gave this feeling modest expression in my verse.

SPIRIT Forgive me, but it is just this feeling of yours that troubles me so. The eyes can see any spot as the world of sorrows or as a mountain retreat: that depends wholly on the seer's own heart.

7. The spirit calls himself an *umoregi* ('buried tree'), a common poetic image for one who feels himself neglected. The 'blossoms' in the heart of an *umoregi* are the person's true worth and feelings, which demand better recognition.

Surely no flowers upon a tree, which after all is insentient and without feelings of its own, can be held to blame for the vexations of the world.

SAIGYŌ I concede the point. You are entirely right. But who are you, then, who speaks so incisively? Are you the spirit of the tree in bloom?

SPIRIT Yes, I am indeed the spirit of the flowers.

            Spirit and tree have grown old together,

SAIGYŌ   and though cherries bloom, like all trees, in silence,

SPIRIT   to protest my innocence I stand before you

SAIGYŌ   with moving lips, to speak for the blossoms.

Spirit rises, comes to centre.

CHORUS (*uta*) I am ashamed! This ancient tree

            has so few flowers left; its branches are withered.

            No, lovely blossoms, this is *not* your fault,

            declare the petals whose spirit I am!

Sweeps right to base square, then back to centre. Saigyō rises, steps forward. Both go down on one knee facing each other, palms pressed together.

            Plants and trees perhaps lack feeling,

            yet in season forget neither flower nor fruit.

            Yes, all of them, with the soil and land,

            are the sacred Teaching of Buddhahood.

(*unnamed*) O precious moment! Most holy monk, drawn here by your presence, I rejoice in the dew of the Law's all-pervading blessing!

Flowers before the railing smile, yet never make a sound; birds in the wood call and call, yet their tears flow on.[8]

Spirit moves back before drums, Saigyō back to witness position.

CHORUS (*kuri*) Mornings, we tread fallen blossoms, walking out

                together;

Evenings, we follow the birds, all together, coming home.[9]

SPIRIT (*sashi*) Ninefold, the Capital blooms with cherries

            still eightfold,

8. A couplet included in a collection of Chinese verses in seven-character lines, entitled *Hyakuren shōkai*. In Chinese and Japanese, 'smile' and 'laugh' are the same word, hence the mild literary wit of the first line. Likewise, the verb *naku* is used in Japanese (although with different characters) to refer both to the calls or songs of birds and to weeping.

9. A couplet by Po Chü-i (772–846), included in the *Wakan rōei shū* ('A Collection of Japanese and Chinese Poems for Chanting Aloud', 1013).

CHORUS	reign after reign.[10]
	How many springs in all have passed?
SPIRIT	Now, to speak of places renowned for flowers,
CHORUS	one first recalls the early-blooming,
	weeping cherries of Lord Konoe.[11]

Spirit begins to dance, miming as appropriate.

(*kuse*)   Gazing afar, I see cherries and willows
so prettily mingled: a dazzling brocade
of springtime in our own Capital.
There, a thousand cherries line the avenue,
their beauty giving the place its name:
Senbon, the Thousand Cherry Trees,
now in full glory – a highroad through clouds
showering petal snow.[12]
The profusion of blossoms at Bishamon Hall,
the Four Celestial Kings' magnificent heaven –[13]
could either of these surpass this scene?
At Upper Kurodani, by Lower Riverside,[14]
of old, the monk Henjō

SPIRIT   withdrew from the world
to Flowertop Mountain[15]

CHORUS   where, moving to tell,
he came fully to know how the Blossom opened
on Vulture Peak, then in the Crane Grove

10. 'Ninefold', an epithet for the imperial palace, hence for the capital, refers to the nine gates of ancient Chinese palaces. 'Eightfold' cherries are cherry blossoms with many-layered petals.
11. The 'weeping cherry' has long, drooping fronds like a weeping willow. Those in the garden of the Konoe residence were especially famous – so much so that in 1378, Zeami's patron, the Shogun Yoshimitsu, commandeered some from Konoe Michitsugu and had them moved to his own residence.
12. Senbon ('Thousand Cherry Trees') is a major north–south thoroughfare in Kyoto. The 'elegant confusion' between cherry petals and snow is common in poetry and nō.
13. Bishamon-dō used to stand below the hills along the north-east edge of Kyoto. It is gone now. Bishamon is one of the Four Celestial Kings who, in Buddhism, guard the four directions. Prayers were offered to him for wealth.
14. Kurodani is probably a place in the eastern hills, and Lower Riverside (Shimo-gawara) is the banks of Kamo River in the vicinity of Bishamon-dō. The 'Upper' attached to Kurodani simply contrasts with 'Lower' (Riverside).
15. 'Flowertop Mountain' is Kachō-zan, a summit among the eastern hills of Kyoto. Its name recalls the 'Flower Mountain' (Hana-yama) where the poet Henjō (818–890) retired from the world.

withered and fell.[16]
Then there are, too, the Land God's flowers
by the temple at Kiyomizu,
beneath Mount Otowa's windswept pines;
and, yonder, Storm Mountain, its tumbling stream,[17]
waves and falls, white with scattered petals.
So the Ōi River runs, each weir, it seems,
arresting a mass of snow.

SPIRIT (*ei*) O hear the drums announce the coming dawn!

CHORUS The bell calling to daybreak devotions
now joins its own summons to theirs.

SPIRIT (*unnamed*) With what sorrow one sees them fade,
all the pleasures of the night!
It is so sad, the perfect moment so rare,
and the companions, too, that make it so.

A single hour of one spring night is worth a thousand in gold:
blossoms yield their pure scent, the moon gives its light.[18]

(*waka*) The spring night

(DANCE: *jo-no-mai*)

Spirit performs a jo-no-mai *dance and continues dancing as text resumes.*

(*waka*) The spring night pales first where dawn light
touches the flowers –

CHORUS ah, some partings cannot wait
till bells ring in the break of day
till bells ring in the break of day.

Spirit comes to centre, beckons to Saigyō with fan.

SPIRIT (*noriji*) Stay! Stay a while! The night is still black!

CHORUS That faint whiteness is only the blossoms!
Even now darkness claims Ogura's slopes,[19]
where night cherries still linger,
blooming on while the sleeper dreams

---

16. The 'Blossom' is the flower of enlightenment. Vulture Peak is the mountain in India where the Buddha preached the *Lotus Sutra*, but no doubt refers to one of the hills east of Kyoto as well. The Crane Grove is where the Buddha died.
17. Storm Mountain is Arashi-yama, immediately west of Kyoto, and still a famous beauty spot. The Ōi River runs below it.
18. A famous couplet by the Sung poet Su Shih (1036–1101). It is also quoted in *Eguchi*.
19. Mount Ogura is in the area of Arashi-yama.

SPIRIT (*uta*)   a dream scattered now, and gone
CHORUS   a dream scattered now, and gone.
                 The winds have laid, it seems, a carpet of snow.
                 Treading the petals. O how one longs
                 for that youthful dream, one spring night's gift:
                 a dream put to flight by day.
                 The kindly old man is gone past recall,
                 the kindly old man is gone.

Facing side from base square, Spirit stamps the final beat.

The legend of Ono no Komachi is famous in Japanese literature. Very little historical information about her survives, but she seems to have belonged to the lower-ranking court nobility and to have flourished in the first half of the ninth century. Her eighteen poems in the first imperially commissioned anthology, the *Kokinshū* (905), assured her lasting fame, although other, later anthologies include a good many more. Since the poems speak eloquently of love and hint at diverse affairs, her legend evokes her as a dazzling and passionate beauty. But alas (so the legend continues), retribution for her wanton ways struck her in due course. Advancing age ruined her looks, until she became so old and ugly that those of the capital could no longer tolerate her presence among them. She then took to wandering the roads as a beggar woman. The nō play *Sotoba Komachi* shows her in this guise.

At last, according to a story that seems to have been current in the fifteenth century, Komachi settled in a miserable hut near Seki-dera. This temple stood below the eastern slope of the Ōsaka Pass (the low pass between Kyoto and Lake Biwa that had to be crossed by all who travelled to the east of the country) and in classical times it was a prosperous institution. Presumably Komachi finished her life there, although the legend says nothing of her death.

Komachi at Seki-dera is accepted as being by Zeami, but Zeami's writings contain only a few tenuous scraps of information about it. Some authorities hold that Zeami wrote it quite late in his career, possibly even after 1430, while another (Takemoto Mikio) believes that it may be relatively early (before 1418). Takemoto has made the interesting suggestion that Zeami wrote it before *Pining Wind*, and in a rather experimental mood. However, the available evidence permits little more than conjecture.

What is certain is that in the sixteenth century *Komachi at Seki-dera* began to receive special treatment, and that by the end of the century the play was established as a vitally importance piece surrounded by 'secret' performance traditions. By the early Edo period (1600–1868), *Komachi at Seki-dera* had become what one might call the inner 'mystery' of nō. It still enjoys this reputation. Five plays in which the *shite* is a very old woman are accorded the highest 'dignity' (*kurai*) in nō (three are about Komachi), but *Komachi at Seki-dera* is supreme among them. It is felt to be exceedingly difficult to perform, for although Komachi hardly moves until the end of the play, which lasts some two hours, she must none the less convey a fully living presence. This difficulty contributes to the play's extraordinary dignity. Only an important actor, towards the end of his career, will wish, or even be allowed, to attempt the role. As a result, *Komachi at Seki-dera* is seldom performed.

Fortunately, the difficulty of the play is not obvious to a reader. On the contrary, *Komachi at Seki-dera* is wonderfully unaffected and innocent. If Zeami did write it as an experiment, then part of the experiment consisted of infusing an ancient woman (one year short of a hundred, to be precise) with the spirit of youth and having her dance in that mood. No doubt it is a difficult device to bring off, but Zeami's success with it in *Komachi at Seki-dera* seems complete. His old Komachi is thoroughly natural and touching.

The site of Seki-dera is now occupied by a deserted and dilapidated little temple named Chōan-ji. One can walk there from Ōtsu Station, at the southern end of Lake Biwa. At first, the way leads through urban bustle and noise, but one soon reaches the green mountainside, where a stone stairway rises towards the temple between the last of the houses. There is little there to see.

KOMACHI AT SEKI-DERA

Persons in order of appearance

A Boy in the temple's care	*kokata*
The resident Monk of Seki-dera temple	*waki*
Two or three Companion Monks	*wakizure*
Komachi, an old woman (*Uba* mask)	*shite*

Remarks: A third-category play (*kazura-mono*) current in all five schools of nō. Since the sixteenth century, the Hōshō and Shimogakari schools insert a dance (*iroe* or *chū-no-mai*) done by the Boy after the first line of the *ei* passage ('Tonight we feast the Tanabata Stars . . .') that precedes Komachi's own dance; and the rest of the *ei* then laments how few nights the two stars spend together.

*   *   *

Stage assistant places Komachi's hut, a simple framework surrounded by a cloth, before drums. A few poem-slips hang from it.

To shidai *music, enter Monk and Companions, preceded by Boy. They stand facing each other at front of stage.*

MONK and COMPANIONS

> (*shidai*) Long-awaited autumn is upon us
> long-awaited autumn is upon us:
> hasten now to celebrate the Stars.   *Face audience.*

MONK (*nanori*) You have before you the abbot of Seki-dera in the province of Ōmi. Since tonight is the seventh night of the seventh month, we are all planning to celebrate the Tanabata Festival[1] in front of the Lecture Hall.[2] Now, I understand that an old woman has built herself a hut nearby, below the mountain, and that she is a master of poetry. I will take the children to see her, so that we may all hear what she has to say.

MONK and COMPANIONS

> (*sashi*) Early fall, when the chill winds sigh   *Face each other.*
> and dark hair still youthful is laid waste,
> now brings the evening of the Seventh Day.

MONK   For Tanabata, we have offerings: *Face audience.*
> flutes and strings in modes many-hued,
> and words richly varied; for we pray

MONK and COMPANIONS

> (*ageuta*) to follow the Way of the Blessed Isles[3]   *Face each other.*

1. The Tanabata Festival came originally from China but has been celebrated by the Japanese since early times. The Herdboy Star and the Weaver Star, on either side of the River of Heaven (the Milky Way) are lovers, but the only night in the year when they can meet is the seventh night of the seventh lunar month, when the Herdboy Star crosses the river to be with his lady. Women and children, especially, prayed at the festival for success in poetry and in the other arts and crafts.

2. One of a temple's main buildings, dedicated to study of the scriptures.

3. The 'way of Japanese poetry'. Shikishima, here translated freely as 'Blessed Isles', is a noble name for Japan. The contrast is with poetry written in Chinese.

to follow the Way of the Blessed Isles,
our bright streamers[4] waving a brocade
of plume grass, flowers, all the autumn grasses
touched, as a pearl-strewn koto,[5] by the wind,
that plays among the pines a melody   *Monk mimes walking.*
perfect for our offerings tonight
perfect for our offerings tonight.

MONK (*tsukizerifu*) Let us pause a moment while I find out whether the old lady will receive us. Please wait here.

All sit in witness square.

(KOMACHI APPEARS)

Stage assistant removes cloth from the hut, revealing Komachi within.

KOMACHI (*sashi*) Morning brings me not a single bowl,[6]
yet I can seek no more;
straw wraps, at night, do not clothe my flesh,
yet perforce I make do.
Blossoms, as the rains touch them and pass,
lose the gay brightness of their youth;
willow trees, lured on by the wind,
soon enough let their fronds hang low.
Man is never young a second time.
Age claims him in the end, and though spring comes
with all the warbler's hundred carollings,
no autumn takes us back to times gone by.
O the old days – I do miss them so!
O the old days – I do miss them so!   *Weeps.*

Monk rises, and has Boy rise.

MONK (*mondō*) I beg your pardon, old lady.

KOMACHI   Who is there?

MONK   We all live at Seki-dera. You see, the temple children are learning poetry. When we heard you were here, we thought we

---

4. Wands with streamers of five colours attached to them were offered to the Tanabata Stars.

5. *Tamagoto* is simply a noble world for *koto*. However, *tama* ('pearl', 'jewel') also suggests the 'dewdrops' on the autumn grasses.

6. Much of this *sashi* passage is not in regular metre and resembles poetry originally written in Chinese. Parts of it do in fact use material from the *Wakan rōei shū* ('A Collection of Japanese and Chinese Poems for Chanting Aloud', 1013) or *Hyakuren shōkai* (15th c.?), an anthology of linked verse in Chinese.

might ask you to tell us how poetry should be written, and to give us any other advice you may have. [*Monk and Boy step towards Komachi and sit.*] That is why we have brought the children, too.

KOMACHI I fear this is rather a surprise. Everyone forgot me so long ago, I hardly think my grasses could again put forth their plumes.[7] Just let your heart be the seed, and suffuse the flowers of your words with colour and fragrance.[8] Then you will surely do well. [*Turns to Boy.*] How lovely that you young people should care for poetry!

MONK Now, people are unanimous in their praise of the 'Naniwa Harbour' poem, and one gathers that beginners ought to take it as their earliest model.[9] Do you agree?

KOMACHI Oh yes, certainly. Poetry, you see, began in the Divine Age, but then the count of syllables was irregular, and meaning was sometimes difficult to make out.[10] We are in the Human Age now, and the 'Naniwa Harbour' poem celebrates the happy accession of a sovereign. That is why it is so widely praised.

MONK Surely the 'Mount Asaka' poem is a fortunate one too, since it soothed the heart of a king.

KOMACHI You understand these things very well.

These two poems are the father and mother,

MONK   and the first models for all who would learn.

KOMACHI   All people of lofty or base degree,

MONK   from Miyako or the far countryside –

KOMACHI   yes, those, too, as humble as ourselves –

7. 'I hardly think I could say anything worth hearing on the subject.' An expression from the Japanese preface to the *Kokinshū* (905). Below, some of the play's effect is achieved simply by having Komachi discuss so seriously, for the benefit of the temple children, the very ABC of poetry. Her words rely on the *Kokinshū* preface and also on certain medieval commentaries on this basic text. Expressions from one of these commentaries are worked directly into the play.

8. The *Kokinshū* prefaces states that Japanese poetry has its seed in the human heart and 'becomes the myriad words'. Words are, literally, 'leaves of speech'.

9. The *Kokinshū* preface proposes this poem, and the 'Mount Asaka' poem mentioned below, as models for those who would master poetry and describes them in the terms used here. The 'Naniwa Harbour' poems runs, 'At Naniwa Harbour it blooms; this flower shut in the winter long, now spring is here, it blooms! this flower.' The 'Mount Asaka' poems amounts to something like, 'Mount Asaka! Reflecting you the rocky pool is shallow, but not this heart of mine in desire.' It was spoken in ancient times by a young lady to a royal visitor whose ill-humour instantly vanished.

10. The *Kokinshū* preface says that poetry sprang into existence as soon as heaven and earth parted (i.e. when the world as we know it came into being), but that in the age of the gods, metre and diction were too irregular to make the poetry readily intelligible.

MONK   find their hearts moved to song.

KOMACHI   In due time,

CHORUS (*ageuta*) O lake in Ōmi with your dancing waters,[11]
            all the sands may vanish from your shore
            all the sands may vanish from your shore,
            but the poets' words shall have no end.
            Green willow fronds grow on and on,
            pine needles do not all fall and die.
            Know that your own heart is the seed.
            Though times change and all things pass,
            so long as writing keeps these songs,
            the pattern of poetry shall live on
            the pattern of poetry shall live on.[12]

MONK (*mondō*) We are grateful for all you have told us. The old poets
wrote a good deal, but poems by women are rare. You, old lady,
are rather an exception.

                    Tonight, it is,
                    my love will come:
                    see the spider
                    in her web,
                    weaving me a sign.[13]

            Did a woman write that?

KOMACHI Yes, Princess Sotōri, who lived very long ago. She was the
Consort of Emperor Ingyō. It was her style I did my poor best to
master.

MONK You say you studied Princess Sotōri's style? Why, I understand
that Ono no Komachi, who more recently achieved such fame, herself looked to Princess Sotōri.

                    I am forlorn,
                    a drifting waterweed
                    cut off at the root:
                    should a current call,

---

11. The *ageuta* passage continues to draw copiously on the *Kokinshū* preface. The 'lake in
Ōmi' is Lake Biwa. The 'dancing waters' are a free rendering of *sazanami ya* ('O little
waves', although *sazanami* is also a place-name), an expression conventionally associated
with the lake in poetry.

12. The 'pattern of poetry' is, literally, the 'footprints of the birds', or 'bird-prints': the
letters with which poetry is written.

13. A poem attributed to Princess Sotōri (5th c.) in an ancient note to the *Kokinshū*
preface. The preface says that Komachi followed her style.

O I would go.[14]

That is one of Komachi's poems.

KOMACHI Yes, Ōe no Koreaki had tired of me and I was weary of the world. Then Fun'ya no Yasuhide went on down to Mikawa, to be governor there. He invited me to seek solace with him in the country, and that was when I made that poem.

    (*sageuta*) I had forgotten with the passing years,

        but now those lines bring tears to my eyes.

        I weep as the old days return to mind.   *Weeps.*

MONK (*mondō*) How strange! I hear you say *you* wrote that poem! And the poet known for having followed Princess Sotōri's style – why, she was Komachi, too. Even your age, old lady, seems to match, since you must be a hundred years old. Yes, Komachi might have lived to a very great age; and if she did, she might actually still be alive. Then there is no longer any doubt. You yourself are what became of Komachi!

    Do not struggle to hide who you are!

KOMACHI Oh, but your 'Komachi' shames me so!

    All unseen

    (so I wrote long ago)

CHORUS   the colours shift and fade:

        yes, such are we

        whose ways are the world's;

        such the heart's flower[15]

    that you now see plainly, to my shame!

        I am forlorn,

        a drifting waterweed

        cut off at the root:

        should a current call

        O (even now!) I would go.

    I am ashamed!

Monk and Boy return to sit in witness square.

    (*kuri*) Yes, it is true,

        I may keep my peace,

14. The prose preface to this poem by Komachi, in the *Kokinshū*, says that it was an answer to Fun'ya no Yasuhide's invitation. Fun'ya no Yasuhide was a poet and official of the time. The explanation about Ōe no Koreaki seems to have been drawn from medieval commentaries on the *Kokinshū*.
15. A poem by Komachi in the *Kokinshū*.

     yet glistening drops
     overflow these sleeves:
     from eyes that long for you
     the helpless tears [16]
   rain down as all my heart recalls the past.
   I whose own flower wilted long ago,
   O why must gleaming dew bedeck me still?

KOMACHI (*sashi*) Yes, I once sang,
     Lost in longing
     I lay down to sleep –
     and then he came, [17]

CHORUS   though now it suits me ill. How many years
   have come and gone since then, while I lived on,
   seeing each spring pass, with all its dews,
   and frosts of autumn come, with withered leaves,
   and shrilling insect voices that soon die.

KOMACHI And now my own life has reached its term,

CHORUS   just like the rose of Sharon's one glorious day.
   (*kuse*) The living die;
     the dead in this, our world,
     are always more.
     O when will come that time
     I cease to mourn? [18]

   That poem, too, was mine: and now, how long
   must my fading years, this ivy vine
   stripped of leaf and flower, linger on?
   Is not all of life a drop of dew?
   O how I miss the past! For long ago,
   I was that woman whom I now recall;
   and at each touch of memories like these,
   I lose myself again in the old days,
   until by now I hunger to regain
   even the earliest years of my old age.   *Weeps.*
   Alas, in the days when I was young,
   the lodging where I lay a single night

16. A *Kokinshū* poem by one Abe no Kiyoyuki (a man), addressed to Komachi.
17. A *Kokinshū* poem by Komachi. The last two lines read, 'Had I known it was a dream, I would not have awakened.'
18. A poem by Komachi included in the *Shinkokinshū* (1206).

was trimmed with tortoiseshell, and golden flowers
decked the garden fence. In every door
hung rock crystal beads, and those gay silks
that spill from the carriages of the great [19]
spread their colours about my own pillow,
in the room where I and my love lay
under coverlets of flowered brocade.
Those were my ways then, where now
a mud-daubed hut holds my once jewelled bed.

KOMACHI   The tolling of the Seki-dera bell

CHORUS   proclaims the plain truth that all things pass,
but these old ears of mine pay it no heed.
Winds that sweep down off Ōsaka Pass
bring the news that all born must die,
yet I learn nothing from them, nothing.

*Komachi takes in her left hand one of the poem-slips that hang from the hut, and
with her fan mimes writing.*

Whenever petals fly or the leaves fall,
moved as always, at my wattled door
I put ink to inkstone, dip the brush,
and trace out my salt sea-tangle lines [20]
in words soon withered, words that quickly fail:
'Affecting, certainly, but never strong,   *Gazes at her poem.*
no doubt because these are a woman's songs' [21]
and still more feeble at my present age,   *Puts the poem down.*
so miserably I have lapsed into ruin.

Monk addresses one of his Companions.

MONK (*mondō*) You know, we are going to be late for the Tanabata
Festival. Do ask the old lady to come with us.

COMPANION With pleasure. [*Stands, steps towards Komachi.*] I beg your
pardon, old lady, but will you not come to see the festival of
offerings to the Stars? We would be delighted to have you with
us.   *Sits as before.*

19. Ladies remained invisible in their carriages, hidden behind curtains, but allowed their
long sleeves to spill through the curtains, so advertising their presence, and their elegant
choice of colours, to all,

20. The calligraphic lines traced by the writer are evoked as resembling the lines of kelp
and seaweed washed up on the beach.

21. This is the appraisal of Komachi's verse by Ki no Tsurayuki, the author of the
Kokinshū preface.

KOMACHI No, no, an old woman like me could not think of imposing
that way.

MONK [*Rises.*] But it is no imposition at all! [*Goes to Komachi and touches
her.*] No, dear lady, come along with us.

*Komachi picks up her staff and then, assisted by Monk, rises and comes forth from
the hut as Chorus sings. She stops in base square, while Monk sits at witness position.*

CHORUS (*ageuta*) The streamer wands that Tanabata weaves
as offerings shall wave how many years
while Ono no Komachi fades away,
who now has touched a hundred? In the sky,
the Stars come together. So, for her,
those above the clouds forgathered once,[22]
and she was with them, brushing silken sleeves
that now are hemp. O pathetic sight,   *Sits with aid of staff.*
a spectacle too painful to be borne!

*As Chorus sings on, Monk opens his fan, turns to Boy, and mimes ladling wine. Boy
receives the wine with his own fan and goes to Komachi to serve her. Then he begins to
dance.*

(*uta*) This evening we celebrate the Stars
this evening we celebrate the Stars
with generous offerings, of many kinds.
Some pin all their hopes to streamer wands,
others send the moonlit winecup round,
while moonbeams glint on dancing children's sleeves –
a lovely scene!

*Komachi gazes at the dancing Boy, absorbed, and unconsciously beats time with her
closed fan. As the passage below ends, Boy ends his dance and sits in witness square.*

(*ei*) Tonight we feast the Tanabata Stars

KOMACHI   as always through each reign, and on in time,

CHORUS   eternally, with Music of Ten Thousand Years.[23]

KOMACHI (*unnamed*) How pretty they were just now, the children's
sleeves as they danced! Long ago, at the Harvest Vigil Feast, the
girls dancing the Fivefold Dance[24] twirled their sleeves five times;

22. 'Those above the clouds' are the courtiers who, in literary language, inhabited the
top of a metaphorical mountain.
23. *Manzairaku*, a felicitous *gagaku* piece from the old court music.
24. A banquet held in the eleventh lunar month on the day after the solemn Niiname-sai,
or First Fruits Festival. An event of the banquet was the *gosechi-no-mai* ('Fivefold
Dance'). Maidens of noble birth imitated the celestial maidens who had once, in the
seventh century, come down to dance before Emperor Temmu.

but dancing for the Seventh Night, these should no doubt have twirled them seven times! Well, they say that when a madman runs, the sane run after him. The dancing children's sleeves have lured me on, and now the madman will run!

Komachi rises, with the help of her staff.

One hundred years

(DANCE)

Komachi now performs a dance: in the Kanze and Hōshō schools an iroe-gakari no mai, *and in the other schools a* chū-no-mai. *She continues dancing as text resumes.*

One hundred years snug in a flower,
the butterfly now dances for all.[25]

CHORUS (*noriji*) O the touching scene! The touching scene!
Flowers seem to bloom on an old bough,

KOMACHI yet I forget the play of hand and sleeve;

CHORUS the skirts sweep weakly round to faltering steps.

KOMACHI A wandering wave,[26]

CHORUS risen now to dance,
tosses billowing sleeves to no avail,
for no such dance can turn back the years.

Slowly Komachi sits, helping herself with her staff, and weeps.

KOMACHI Alas for the old days, I miss them so!

CHORUS (*noriji*) Meanwhile, the short night of early fall
has begun to break. The temple bell,

KOMACHI the twittering of birds,

CHORUS announce the dawn.
Should daylight come upon me here,

KOMACHI all the trees in Hazukashi Grove[27]

CHORUS all the trees in Hazikashi Grove   *Rises painfully.*
would not suffice to conceal my shame.
Goodbye, goodbye, I am going now!   *Nods to Monk.*
And, leaning on her staff, she totters off,
home again to her hut of straw.   *Enters hut, sits.*

25. The dream of a butterfly was a motif in East Asian letters since Chuang-tzu (4th c. B.C.), although these lines do not allude to any particular work. The dance *Kochō* ('The Butterfly', a *bugaku* piece) is among the ancient dances of the court.

26. Several passages in Zeami's plays (for example the *rongi* of *Eguchi* or the *sashi* in part two of *Yashima*) similarly treat a person as a wave on the surface of the sea.

27. *Hazukashi*, the name of the grove, also means 'ashamed'. The place was known in poetry.

She whom they call 'the hundred-year-old crone'
was after all the ruin of Komachi   *Weeps.*
was after all the ruin of Komachi.

Music continues after Chorus ends, till Komachi again comes forth from the hut and stops.

Semimaru

Although consistent in every detail with the rest of nō, *Semimaru* resembles no other play. It is astonishingly abstract, since nothing about it can be explained in terms of the ordinary world, but that does not mean it is cold. On the contrary, *Semimaru* conveys at once the warmth of love and the deep sorrow of ineluctable loss. So strange, yet familiar, are Semimaru and Sakagami, his sister, that the drama seems to take place outside space or time. *Semimaru* resembles a pure theatre of the mind.

Zeami probably wrote the play, since the *Sakagami* he mentioned in his *Sarugaku dangi* ('Conversations on nō') can hardly be any other. His words show that he had performed it himself. In addition, *Semimaru* is partly based on *Ōsaka monogurui* ('The Ōsaka Madman'), a work that has not been performed since Zeami's time but is known to be by him. None the less, a few authorities still have trouble believing that *Semimaru* is by Zeami, and one recent writer (Miyake Akiko) attributed it to his eldest son, Motomasa. Like *The Fulling Block*, *Semimaru* seems not to have been staged between the late fifteenth and late seventeenth centuries, but to have survived instead as a text for amateur students of nō singing.

According to the play, Sakagami and Semimaru are the third and fourth children of 'His Engi Majesty'. This is Emperor Daigo (r. 897–930), whose reign was seen in Zeami's time as a sort of golden age. However, Daigo had no such children. Instead, a story in *Konjaku monogatari shū* ('Tales of Times Now Past', *c.* 1100) describes how a grandson of Emperor Daigo went to learn a rare piece of lute (*biwa*) music from one Semimaru, a blind musician who lived near the Ōsaka Barrier. This grandson is the Hakuga no Sammi who appears in the interlude of *Semimaru*, although this role in the play has little to do with the *Konjaku* story.

The Ōsaka Barrier, the setting of *Semimaru*, was a checkpoint or toll station on Ōsaka Pass, between Kyoto and Lake Biwa. Since all travellers to and from the eastern provinces had to pass that way, the spot was famous in poetry and in ordinary life. Beggar-entertainers clearly frequented the place, and Semimaru (whether or not he actually existed) was eventually claimed as a founder and patron by one line of blind strolling musicians. It was probably they who made him a prince. At the same time, he came to be honoured in a shrine near the Ōsaka Barrier. His cult was added to the shrine's established cult, that of the deity of the pass.

Sakagami first appears in *Semimaru* itself, but Zeami (if it was he) probably did not invent her out of thin air. Her name, as written in the play, means 'upside-down hair', but since the same syllables mean 'deity of the slope', she too alludes to the cult of Ōsaka Pass. A mountain deity often had both male and female manifestations. In addition, the divinities of roads and travel (*sae-no-kami, chigaeshi-no-kami*) were commonly conceived as male–female couples, sometimes explicitly erotic. It is true, however, that in *Semimaru*, Semimaru and Sakagami are brother and sister, not lovers. The analogy between them and the divinities of Ōsaka Pass cannot be pursued too far.

Although Sakagami is, in name, a 'deity of the slope', her 'upside-down hair' is more than a play on words. In general, hair like hers was accepted as a sign of intense, active energy. The most likely cause of this state, for a woman, was jealous rage, but spirit-possession could produce the same effect in a medium of either sex. Zaō Gongen, a mountain deity iconographically related to the wrathful divinities of Esoteric Buddhism, has similarly bristling hair. Yet even though hair bristling with jealousy or divine frenzy can actually be found elsewhere in nō, it is not easy to define a particular reason for Sakagami's startling looks or for her state of mind.

As a character-type in nō, Sakagami is a *monogurui* ('madwoman' or 'madman'). Many *monogurui* are entertainers, and because of the lore associated with Semimaru and the Ōsaka Barrier, Sakagami, too, may be connected with wandering entertainers. Several writers have associated her with a class of wandering female entertainers known as *aruki-miko* (literally, 'peripatetic mediums'). None the less, she is unlike any other *monogurui* in nō. While others rave only temporarily, when suitably provoked, Sakagami is mad in her normal state. From her madness, she visits sanity – for with her brother she is clearly sane – as others lapse into madness from ordinary life. Her mind, like her hair, is upside down.

A blind and gentle younger brother, pathetically sane, confined to a hut on a mountain pass, and an insane elder sister who wanders for ever: this is the pair in *Semimaru*. One weeps in silence, the other scolds passing children and vaticinates about what is the right way up or topsy-turvy. Music draws them briefly into each other's arms, then the winds of change inexorably part them again. Their nature and predicament seem to evoke experience far beyond the reach of any ordinary words.

There are three Semimaru shrines within the city limits of Ōtsu, on the Lake Biwa side of Ōsaka Pass. The largest of them, the Lower Shrine (Shimo-sha), still boasts the famous 'toll-station spring' (*seki no shimizu*) mentioned by Sakagami as she approaches Semimaru's hut. The little Keihan Electric Railway goes right past it, coating fence and torii with rust from the tracks.

Semimaru

Persons in order of appearance

Prince Semimaru (*Semimaru* mask)	*tsure*
Kiyotsura, an imperial messenger	*waki*
Two Palanquin-Bearers	*wakizure*
Hakuga no Sammi	*ai*
Princess Sakagami (*Masugami* or *Zō-onna* mask)	*shite*

Remarks: A fourth-category play (*yonbamme-mono*) current in all five schools of nō. A variant performance tradition (*kogaki*) in the Kanze school has both Semimaru and Sakagami as *shite*. In this case, Semimaru's hut is placed before drums.

*   *   *

Stage assistant places Semimaru's hut in witness square.
To shidai music, enter Semimaru, flanked by the two Palanquin-Bearers who hold a canopy over him. They are followed by Kiyotsura.

KIYOTSURA and BEARERS

        (*shidai*) In this fickle world, ever contrary,
                in this fickle world, ever contrary,

troubles may yet prove our surest hope.

KIYOTSURA (*nanori*) You see before you Prince Semimaru, the fourth child born to His Engi Majesty.

KIYOTSURA and BEARERS

(*ageuta*) In truth, all that befalls us (so this sad world turns)
only rewards our deeds done in the past.
Into this life he came, this prince of the blood,
thanks to virtuous conduct lived out long ago,
yet from birth has been (and why?) completely blind.
For him no sun, no moon shine in the heavens,
nor welcome lamplight in the dark of night.
Tears are his lot, falling like endless rain.

KIYOTSURA So the days of the prince went by,
until His Majesty, unfathomable in his wishes

KIYOTSURA and BEARERS

issued this decree:
Escort him now, in secret, to yonder Ōsaka Mountain.
Shave his head, in sign that he has left the world,
and there let him stay:
imperial words that cannot be retracted.
The task inspires immeasurable sorrow,
yet His Majesty has spoken. So it must be.

(*sageuta*) Unwilling steps, by secret ways,
lead us from the palace, stealthily,

(*ageuta*) while dawn stains the sky,
to take us from the Miyako we love
to take us from the Miyako we love:
for he is bound this day far, far away,
never to return,
this unhappy prince, who, now alone,
his refuge gone, has lost all future hope!
Sorrows enough afflict us in this world:
blind turtles, we, seeking through the years
a bit of floating wood to rest upon,[1]
wandering a benighted way
as clouds of delusion fill the skies

1. According to a Buddhist simile, it is as rare to encounter the Buddha's comforting teaching as it is rare for a blind sea turtle, who surfaces only once every hundred years, to come up with his head through the single hole in a bit of floating wood.

upon Ōsaka Mountain[2] we have arrived
upon Ōsaka Mountain we have arrived.

KIYOTSURA (*tsukizerifu*) Having come so swiftly, we have already reached the barrier on Ōsaka Mountain. Your Highness, this is where you are to remain.

Bearers slip out through side door. Semimaru sits before chorus, Kiyotsura in base square.

SEMIMARU Kiyotsura!

KIYOTSURA Here I am, Your Highness.   *Bows, touching hands to stage.*

SEMIMARU Are you then to abandon me upon this mountain?

KIYOTSURA Yes, Your Highness. So His Majesty has decreed. And now that I have accompanied you so far, I fear I do not know just where to leave you. Yet our Sovereign, more than any other since the time of Yao and Shun,[3] brings peace to the realm and nurtures his people! What can have made him issue this decree? I find it difficult to comprehend.

SEMIMARU Oh no, Kiyotsura, you must not talk so foolishly. I was born blind because in a former life I was lax in observing the Precepts.[4] My father, the Emperor, may seem cruel to abandon me in the wilderness, but he means to have me work through, in this life, all my karmic impediments from the past, and so to secure for me salvation in the life to come. Now *that* truly is a father's love. No, no, I shall not complain of His Majesty's decree.

KIYOTSURA Since His Majesty has ordered me to do so, Your Highness, I will now cut off your hair.

SEMIMARU What does this mean?

KIYOTSURA Your Highness, it means that you are now leaving the world to enter religion. This is a most fortune step for a man to take.

Semimaru rises. The cutting of the hair is briefly mimed. Stage assistant then removes Semimaru's outer robe and places upon him the headdress of a monk.

SEMIMARU Why yes, she did say she would cut off her fragrant hair
and pillow her head on hard sandalwood –

2. These 'clouds of delusion' are at once the physical clouds clinging to the slopes of the mountain and the clouds of misery that will surround Semimaru there. The end of *The Mountain Crone* describes how 'wrongful clinging swells to clouds, and clouds into the Mountain Crone, a fearsome demon bulk'.
3. The proverbial sage emperors of China's distant past.
4. The Precepts are the Buddhist rules of conduct.

Seishi, in the land of Cathay.[5]

I look very like her now!

KIYOTSURA   Your Highness, as you look now, there is every reason to fear you may be attacked by robbers. I will take the liberty of removing your silk hunting cloak. Please put on, instead, this rain-cloak of straw. It is called a *mino*.

Stage assistant gives Semimaru the mino.

SEMIMARU   The *mino*, perhaps, one knows from that poem
about Tamino Isle in the rain?[6]

KIYOTSURA   And to shelter you from the rain and dew, allow me also to give you this hat. It is called a *kasa*.

Kiyotsura takes kasa *from stage assistant and gives it to Semimaru.*

SEMIMARU   Surely the *kasa* one knows from those lines,
Good man, tell your master:
'Wear your *kasa*!'[7]

Semimaru puts the kasa *down.*

KIYOTSURA   And if you please, Your Highness, carry this staff to help you find your way as you walk.

Kiyotsura takes the staff from stage assistant and gives it to Semimaru.

SEMIMARU   Yes, yes, the staff of which Henjō once sang:
Leaning on this staff,
soon I shall cross
the summit of a thousand years.[8]

Kiyotsura sits once more in base square.

KIYOTSURA   That was a staff for a thousand long years;
SEMIMARU   this, the mountain they call Ōsaka,
KIYOTSURA   its barrier-hut closed, of straw with bamboo
SEMIMARU   pillars: his support,
KIYOTSURA   the Emperor, his father
SEMIMARU   has cast him out

5. In his distress, the gently bred Semimaru resorts to understanding his own situation through poetic similes. Seishi was a famous Chinese beauty. These lines seem deliberately to misread a couplet by the Chinese poet Li Ho (791–817).
6. Semimaru has never seen a real *mino*, but he knows the word from a poem by Ki no Tsurayuki in the *Kokinshū*. The island of Tamino was off the coast of what is now Osaka.
7. From another, anonymous *Kokinshū* poem. The poem urges a servant to have his master wear a *kasa* because 'the dew drips from the trees on Miyagi Moor more heavily still than rain'.
8. The poet-monk Henjō (818–890) was still a layman when the emperor gave his venerably aged grandmother a silver (or silver-mounted) staff. He composed this poem for her as a reply. The first two lines describe the staff as having been made by the gods.

CHORUS (*ageuta*) into a world of troubles
          upon Ōsaka. O friends and strangers,[9]
          look upon him now!
          See this Prince, born of our Sovereign.
          See what he has come to!
          Travellers and their horses crowd by,
          to and fro, and with showers of tears
          wet their sleeves, filled with distress
          that they, too, must leave him behind
          that they, too, must leave him behind.

Kiyotsura bows to Semimaru in farewell.

          Yet the parting has come. In the light of dawn,
          hiding his tears as best he is able,
          away he goes, homeward again,

Kiyotsura, weeping, rises and starts towards bridgeway.

          while the Prince remains, now wholly alone,
          his only possessions the lute clasps to him,
          the staff he bears.

Holding hat and staff, Semimaru moves to front and gazes after the retreating
Kiyotsura, who stops at second pine to look back before passing through curtain.

          Sinking to the ground, he sobs aloud
          sinking to the ground, he sobs aloud.

Semimaru takes several quick steps backwards as though his legs will hardly support
him, sits, drops staff and hat, and weeps.

          *   *   *

Enter Hakuga no Sammi. He stands in base square.

HAKUGA NO SAMMI You see before you Hakuga no Sammi. Prince Semimaru
has been abandoned upon Ōsaka Mountain, at the mercy of dew and rain.
And being distressed for his sake, I want to build him a hut of straw.
[*Opens the door of Semimaru's hut, then goes to stand in base square.*] At last the
hut is ready. I will tell him so. [*Bows to Semimaru.*] I beg your pardon, Your
Highness, but Hakuga no Sammi is before you. If you remain like this, you
will be at the mercy of dew and rain. I have therefore built you a hut of
straw, and hope you will condescend to accept it. If it please you, you may

9. 'O friends and strangers' draws on Semimaru's most famous poem: 'See O see!
Leaving, returning, they go their ways, while friends and strangers meet at Ōsaka
Barrier.' The poem is included in the *Gosenshū* (*c.* 951).

enter it now. [*Takes Semimaru's arm and guides him into the hut, then steps back and bows once more.*] I beg you to call upon me, Your Highness, should you need anything at all. For now, however, I must be off to serve my master. Goodbye, Your Highness, for today. [*Exit, after closing the door of the hut.*]

*   *   *

To issei music, enter Sakagami. Her robe is off her right shoulder to indicate that she is mad, but nothing about her hair imitates the description of it, below. She stops at first pine.

SAKAGAMI (*sashi*) I am the third child of His Engi Majesty.[10]

> Sakagami is my name. I was born a princess,
> yet acts of mine in some life long ago
> now, at every turn, addle my wits.
> In this madness of mine I wander far,
> my black hair bristling to the sky;
> Though I stroke and stroke it, it will not lie down.

Mimes glaring at someone nearby.

Very well, you children, what are you laughing at? You think it funny, do you, the way my hair grows straight up? Yes, I suppose my hair growing up that way is funny. But talk about things being upside down, you little guttersnipes laughing at *me* are far worse than my hair.

How fascinating! My hair and your laughter
become so well the realm of all we see.
The seeds of flowers, buried in the earth,
rise to tip the branches of a thousand trees;
the moon aloft, radiant in the heavens,
sinks to the bottom of ten thousand waters.
Which of these is the right way up?
Which is really upside down?
Born a princess, I fell among the common folk;
my hair, bristling skyward, is crowned with stars and frost.
Right way up, upside down,
things straight and things backwards:

---

10. In the original, the following monologue by Sakagami is not divided into verse and prose; it is all in prose, if anything, but at least parts of it are sung.

both are here, plain to see: fascinating!¹¹

(QUASI-DANCE: *kakeri*)

Sakagami comes on stage and performs a kakeri *which conveys her agitation.*

	The wind, combing the willow's green hair,
CHORUS	blow as it will, cannot tease out the tangles;
SAKAGAMI	nor can my hand ever smooth this hair.
CHORUS	I claw at my hair, sleeves wildly waving:
SAKAGAMI	just so the dancer looks in *Tearing Her Hair*,¹²
	a distressing spectacle!

Sakagami dances as the text continues.

CHORUS (*ageuta*) Leaving Miyako, the city of flowers¹³
leaving Miyako, the city of flowers,
across the Kamo River
(so mournfully the ducks seem to call!)
and the Shira-kawa River
(does it flow on for ever?)
through Awata-guchi, pining, I go
to labour on up steep Pine Hill,
and see now looming, though once so distant,
Otowa Mountain, that soon drops behind.
How sorely I shall miss Miyako!
Grasshoppers and crickets fill with their song
twilight shadows at Yamashina.
O you of the village, do not rebuke me!

11. Sakagami's speech on 'right way up, upside down' (*jun* and *gyaku*) appears to develop a passage in *Muchū mondō* (1339), a work by the great Zen master Musō Soseki (1276–1351). Soseki discussed the non-duality of *jun* and *gyaku*, terms which sum up a complex of ideas on 'right' and 'wrong', or 'normal' and 'abnormal'.

12. *Batō*, a *bugaku* dance of the kind brought to Japan from the continent in the eighth century. According to *Kyōkunshō* ('Teachings on *bugaku*', 1233): 'This dance evokes a T'ang empress who, overcome by jealousy, became an ogress; was incarcerated; and then smashed her prison, came forth, and danced. The mask used has long, wild hair.' Two other, quite different versions of the story behind *Batō* (which has no words) are difficult to connect with Sakagami.

13. The first eight lines of this *ageuta* passage (including the repeated line) are from a *kusemai* piece called *Tōgoku kudari* ('Going down to the East') that Zeami incorporated into *Ōsaka monogurui*. The road to the East led over Ōsaka Pass. The lines in parentheses acknowledge puns on the names Kamo and Shira-kawa, both rivers that one would cross on the way out of Kyoto via Awata-guchi. Pine Hill (Matsu-zaka) rises beyond Awata-guchi, and Otowa Mountain, which stands over Kiyomizu-dera, is another familiar feature of this landscape. Beyond Otowa lies the village of Yamashina.

Crazed I may be, yet my heart is pure,
pure as the loud rapids of Kiyotaki River:[14]
good people, let me pass on by!

SAKAGAMI   Upon Ōsaka,
the toll-station spring

CHORUS   shows him his face:
startled, he bridles,
the colt from Fullmoon[15]
keeps up a swift pace, and Ōsaka nears:
Rushing Spring's waters reflect my form
and I, even I, recoil, aghast:
the hair on my head a snarl of thorns,
eyebrows an inky tangle:
yes, Sakagami herself, in the water,
mirrored in ripples as night comes on,
the picture of madness!

Sakagami has arrived upon Ōsaka Mountain. She now sits, invisibly as it were, against the back wall of the stage. Semimaru, in the hut, opens his fan and holds it as though plucking a biwa. As he sings, Sakagami steals forward to base square, listening.

SEMIMARU   (*sashi*)   The first and second strings quaver, low,
with autumn winds sighing through the pines,
and the third, no, fourth imperial offspring,[16]
yes, Semimaru touches these strings,
while the season turns to cold autumn showers.
Ah, the heart-chilling, endless nights!

This world of ours,
O it will do,
fare one well or ill:
palace or straw hovel,
neither can last long.[17]

---

14. The *kiyo* of Kiyotaki ('Pure Cascades') River means 'pure', but the river itself is in north-western Kyoto, nowhere near Sakagami's present location.

15. A poem by Ki no Tsurayuki, included in the *Shūishū* (late 10th c.). Mochizuki (literally, 'full moon'), was a locality in Shinano province (now Nagano Prefecture) that presented tribute horses to the capital.

16. These lines allude to a poem on the *ch'in* (a zither like the Japanese *koto*) by Po Chü-i (772–846), included in the *Wakan rōei shū*. The second pair of lines goes: 'The third and fourth strings sing high: a caged crane's voice, crying for its children in the night.'

17. A poem attributed to Semimaru in the *Shinkokinshū* (1206).

SAKAGAMI   How very strange! Here is a straw hut,
           and from within I hear strings nobly plucked:
           the music of a lute!
           What playing, to come from so poor a place!
           How can this be?
           And O the fond memories that crowd in upon me!
           Rain beats on the roof, to drown my silent steps,
           as I steal close and stand, listening.

Sakagami moves to centre. Semimaru folds his fan.

SEMIMARU   Who is there? Who is making that noise outside? Are you
           the one who has been visiting me lately? Hakuga no Sammi, is that
           you?

SAKAGAMI   His voice is very close. It is the Prince's voice, my broth-
           er's! Hello, it is I, Sakagami! Semimaru, are you there?

SEMIMARU   Sakagami? My sister? Astonished, I open the door,
           [*staff in hand, rises and opens door.*]

SAKAGAMI   and a painful sight greets my eyes!

Semimaru comes forth from hut as Sakagami goes to him.

SEMIMARU   Each reaches out for the other's hand.

They place their hands on each other's shoulders.

SAKAGAMI   My brother, is it you?

SEMIMARU   O my sister, is it you?

CHORUS   Each calls the other's name, as on Ōsaka
           the cocks call to greet the dawn,
           and with freely streaming tears
           each moistens the other's sleeves.

Both weep. Sakagami then sits at centre.

CHORUS (*kuri*) The sandalwood tree, they say, smells sweet
           the moment it puts forth its first two leaves.[18]
           And so for us two, who in a life gone by
           must have sought shelter beneath one tree,[19]
           the air all around us breathes memories.
           Twin blossoms we were, on a single bough!

SAKAGAMI (*sashi*) In a land far away,
           Jōzō and Jōgen, two brothers,

---

18. A proverb meaning that genius or, as here, gentle birth are obvious from the start.
19. An expression often used to explain a bond in this life in terms of a meeting that must have taken place in an earlier one.

	led their own father to the truth;[20]
	while two others, Sōri and Sokuri,
	suffered bitter exile together.[21]
	Nearer to hand, Emperor Ōjin's two sons,
CHORUS	the Naniwa Prince and the Uji Prince,
	insisted on ceding each other the throne.[22]
	Such is the warmth of fraternal love.
SAKAGAMI	Yet, my brother, I never dreamed
	that *you* might be living in this place,
CHORUS	till through walls of straw I heard your music
	and knew your touch on the sounding strings
SAKAGAMI	that drew me on to plumb with you
CHORUS	the deep springs of a brother's and sister's love.
(*kuse*)	Fondly, I believed neither sun nor moon

could fall to earth, even when the world
has reached these latter, degenerate days.
Yet somehow we, expelled from princely state,
have fallen so far: shut out from the court,
to wander, lost, beyond the Palace skies:
one, with crazed wits roaming town and country,
one, a pitiful wretch, haunting a mountain road –
and no one to turn to but travellers
journeying through far-off lands.
Only yesterday, glowing silks were ours,
to wear in pavilions decked with jade,
on gleaming floors in halls bright with gold.
Yet today, suddenly, shelter means
bamboo posts, a bamboo fence,
gaping eaves, a rattling door,
straw to sleep on, a straw window,
and on the floor, matting of straw,
where, before, there lay brocade.

20. In the *Lotus Sutra*, they led their father to faith in the Buddha. It is actually unclear whether they (or the pair mentioned immediately below) were brothers or a brother and sister.
21. In a Buddhist tale mentioned in *Taiheiki* and *Gempei jōsuiki*, these two children of a Brahman king in southern India were cast out by their stepmother and died in the wilderness.
22. Both refused to accept the throne until the Uji Prince died. The Naniwa Prince then became Emperor Nintoku (r. 313–399).

SEMIMARU	No one comes calling. I only hear
CHORUS	monkeys crying from trees on the mountain,

as my tears fall; and the pattering showers
I tune my lute to, their sound my own
on through the hours, the long, long hours:
a music of weeping, a rain of tears
in the hut's deep silence. While straw eaves
through ragged gaps may let in moonlight,
these eyes of mine, alas, are blind.
Denied the moon, in a hovel of straw
that shuts out even the sound of rain,
day or night, my every thought
is of grief and misery.   *Both weep.*

SAKAGAMI   (*rongi*) I cannot stay. These sad farewells,
however prolonged, could last for ever.
Goodbye, then: goodbye, Semimaru.   *Both rise.*

SEMIMARU   Even those who take shelter beneath the same tree
grieve when they part. Think how I suffer,
now my sister leaves and I stay behind!

SAKAGAMI   O, it breaks my heart!   *Starting to leave.*
To me, at least, travel offers some solace.
But to stay on here! O I feel for you!
And with this cry she stops, in tears.   *Weeps.*

SEMIMARU   Hear him call on the Osaka road,
a frightened bird, as darkness falls,

SAKAGAMI   yearning still for her long, black hair.

SEMIMARU   O stop her, please, Ōsaka Barrier!

SAKAGAMI   The woods of the pass recede behind me,   *To first pine.*

SEMIMARU   her voice grows distant, fading away

SAKAGAMI   as by eaves of straw

SEMIMARU   I stand alone,

CHORUS   calling as she calls: Goodbye, goodbye!
O come again, come often to see me!

*Sakagami looks back at Semimaru from third pine, then, as text continues, again
starts away. Semimaru takes a few steps towards her, listening. Again she looks
back.*

Whisper-faint, the voices still carry:
he straining to hear, she gazing back,
weeping, weeping,

prince and princess have gone their ways
prince and princess have gone their ways.

Exit Sakagami, weeping. Semimaru weeps in place.

The Sumida River is by Zeami's eldest son, Motomasa (*c.* 1400–1432), whose early death plunged Zeami into despair. Motomasa left only a few plays that can be confidently attributed to him, but this one more than any other has assured his fame. Modern critics acclaim it, and there is no more popular play in the whole repertoire. The text of *The Sumida River* is read by all high school students, and the play is often performed for student audiences.

Compared to a work by Zeami, *The Sumida River* tells a tightly knit, easily understood story. Moreover, it develops an incident that could have happened in ordinary life. No written source for the play has been found, but unhappily there is nothing implausible about 'traders in children' stealing a woman's son. Two other nō plays, one by Zeami, treat the same theme. In Zeami and Motomasa's time, the east and north of Japan were developing regions with an acute need for labour, and children were sometimes sold into slavery there.

The Sumida River builds upon the existing tradition of *monogurui* ('madman' or 'madwoman') plays, and scholars have noted obvious parallels with an earlier work (no longer performed) named *Fue monogurui* ('The Madman with the Flute'). However, it constitutes in many ways a new departure for the genre. For one thing, although many nō plays focus on a parent separated from a child, only this one fails to end in happy reunion. Instead, the Woman in *The Sumida River* discovers that her son is dead. Zeami himself wrote that a skilfully performed *monogurui* play will make an audience cry. *The Sumida River* can certainly achieve that effect. It is so tragic that during the Edo period (1600–1868) it was felt to be unsuitable for performance at the shogun's or emperor's palace.

Zeami's writings and sayings show how interested he was in *The Sumida River*, and they record two disagreements with Motomasa about the play. First, Zeami held that the dead boy should not be represented in any way at the end of the work. Motomasa, on the other hand, insisted that the play could not stand at all unless the dead boy's phantom appeared on stage. Later actors and audiences have generally backed Motomasa.

Second, Zeami felt the play needed more 'colour' and recommended a more striking costume for the Traveller. Scholars now take his opinion to be the source of a disagreement that still persists about the Traveller's identity. The earliest extant text of the play (in the hand of Komparu Zempō, 1454–1520), has him as a merchant, and so do all modern performances except those in the numerically dominant Kanze school. In the Kanze line of texts, which can be traced back as far as a copy dated to the Eiroku era (1558–1570), the Traveller is a man from Miyako. Only such a figure, and not a merchant from the East, could wear the costume that Zeami preferred. Three other textual variants are indicated in the notes to this translation. There are a good many other, minor discrepancies not only between but within the two major lines of texts.

One scholar (Itō Masayoshi) has pointed out several instances in which Motomasa's evocation of the boy's tomb seems to draw upon the poetry of Po Chü-i (772–846). However, the only classic work indispensable for understanding *The Sumida River* is a part of episode no. 9 of *Ise monogatari* ('Tales of Ise', 10th c.). Motomasa used this passage so concertedly that the Woman's lines in the first part of the play (until she boards the ferry) can be difficult to follow unless one knows it.

Ise monogatari was assumed in Motomasa's time to tell the story of the courtier and poet Narihira (825–880). Narihira's affair with a future empress got him into such trouble at court, so the story goes, that he had to leave the capital and travel down to the East. He and his companions took the same route as the Woman of the play when she went in search of her son.

On and on they went until, between the provinces of Musashi and Shimōsa, they came to a large river. 'Sumida River' was its name. Clustering together on the bank, they groaned to think how far they had come. Meanwhile, the ferryman cried, 'It's sundown! All aboard!' They felt very downcast as they boarded the ferry and set out to cross, for every one of them had left someone dear behind in Miyako. It happened that white birds the size of snipe, with red bills and feet, were just then sporting upon the water and catching fish. They had not seen birds like that in Miyako and did not know what kind they were. To their questions, the ferryman replied that these were 'Miyako birds'. On hearing his words, [Narihira] made the poem: 'Are you true to your name? Then, Miyako birds, I put you this question: the one I love – does she live or does she die?' All on board wept.

Motomasa superimposed this episode on the Woman's own plight in order to heighten the play's artistic appeal, and the skill with which he did so has elicited much praise. Still, his use of such material seems different from his father's.

The boy's grave-mound (Umewaka-zuka) is at Mokubo-ji, on the east bank of the Sumida River in modern Tokyo. It is surmounted by a willow tree. Although near an expressway, the spot is a quiet one, cut off from the rest of the world by a huge apartment development. Scholars agree that the temple's account of its history was made up from the play itself, but at a more popular level, the account has long been accepted as genuine.

Mokubo-ji claims to have been founded in 977 as a result of the miraculous apparition at the boy's tomb, although its existence is more likely to be connected with the rise of Edo (the pre-1868 name of Tokyo), which became the shogun's capital in 1603. Many elaborate versions of the play's story were produced for Edo readers and theatre audiences, especially in the eighteenth century, and Mokubo-ji no doubt prospered as a result. The temple was razed in about 1870 in the attempt to disestablish Buddhism, and an 'Umewaka [Shinto] Shrine' was erected on the site. Within twenty years, however, it was rebuilt, and had to be rebuilt again after 1945. In 1976, it was moved slightly to accommodate urban redevelopment, but a Society to Preserve the Umewaka-zuka was then formed to protect the grave-mound. An 'Umewaka Festival' is still held at the grave every year on 15 April, and prayers are offered for the boy's spirit.

It is upon an earlier translation of *The Sumida River* that Benjamin Britten based his opera *Curlew River*.

THE SUMIDA RIVER

Persons in order of appearance

A Ferryman	*waki*
A Traveller	*wakizure*
A Woman (*Fukai* mask)	*shite*
A Boy, Umewaka-maru	*kokata*

Remarks: A fourth-category play (*yonbamme-mono*) current in all five schools of nō. The Boy can be treated in different ways. Zeami opposed representing him in any way, but the playwright, Motomasa, disagreed. The present version, in which he appears on stage, is the most popular, but his presence can also be evoked simply by a voice from within the grave-mound; or even this voice can be omitted.

*   *   *

Stage assistant places a grave-mound, with a willow branch set in its top, before drums; the Boy is invisible inside it.

To nanori-bue *music, enter Ferryman. He stands in base square.*

FERRYMAN (*nanori*) You have before you a ferryman on the Sumida River in Musashi province. Since this is an important crossing, we take the ferryman's duty turn by turn. It is my turn today. I will therefore wait for travellers to come and then ferry them across the river.   [*Sits before Chorus.*]¹

To shidai *music, enter Traveller. He stands in base square, facing back of stage.*

TRAVELLER (*shidai*)   Eastward lies the goal: in travel wear
                                    eastward lies the goal: in travel wear
                        I go, daily bound for distant skies.   *Faces audience.*

(*nanori*) You have before you a merchant from the eastern provinces.

---

1. This *nanori* passage is from the Zempō text, the earliest surviving one. The text upon which the rest of this translation is based has: 'You have before you a ferryman on the Sumida River in Musashi province. I must row on quickly today and ferry people across the water. And there is something else, as well. For a certain reason, a Great Invocation is to be held at this place. It is open to all, clerics and laymen alike. Please, good people, note the present announcement!' Dramatically, this passage of the Zempō version seems distinctly preferable. However, the whole text has not been published.

Recently I went up to Miyako, and now that I am done with my trading, I am again on my way home.[2]

(*ageuta*)   Clouds and mists
            obscure far mountains that drop behind
            obscure far mountains that drop behind,
            while tollgate by tollgate, down the long road
            I journey on, the provinces pass,
            and my way leads to the Sumida River   *Mimes walking.*
            of song and story:
            here at the crossing I have arrived
            here at the crossing I have arrived.

(*tsukizerifu*)   Having come so swiftly, I seem already to have reached the ferry crossing on the Sumida River. Yonder I see a ferry about to set out. I must hurry aboard.

(*mondō*)   Excuse me, ferryman, but I wish to board your boat.

FERRYMAN   Certainly, certainly! Please do so. But you know, that woman coming up behind you is making the most extraordinary racket. What can be the matter with her?

TRAVELLER   She is a madwoman, you see. She has come all the way from Miyako. Her ravings make a very entertaining show.[3]

FERRYMAN   In that case, I will delay sailing and wait for her.

Traveller sits at witness position, Ferryman before Chorus.

To issei *music, enter Woman, carrying a* sasa *branch as a sign of her madness. She stops at first pine, facing audience.*

WOMAN (*sashi*)   O it is true,

            A mother's heart,
            though not in darkness,
            may yet wander, lost,
            for love of her child.[4]

            This I know well, now I roam, astray,
            the highroads, among the travellers.
            How can I tell them, how shall I seek

2. This second *nanori* passage is from the current non-Kanze school texts, which descend from the Zempō text. The text adopted for the rest of the translation has: 'You have before you a man from Miyako. A friend of mine lives in the East, and I am therefore on my way to see him without delay.'

3. In medieval times, the ravings of the mad were scarcely distinguished from the antics of entertainers, and many of the *monogurui* ('mad') figures in nō actually are entertainers. In fact, a display of song and dance was the main object of many earlier *monogurui* plays. The Traveller's remark is not as heartless as it sounds.

4. From a poem by Fujiwara no Kanesuke in the *Gosenshū* (c. 951).

the place where my son has gone?

(*issei*) Ah, do you hear?
The wind, even the wind
coursing the skies,
sings welcome tidings
to the patient pines.[5]

(QUASI-DANCE: *kakeri*)

She performs an agitated kakeri *circuit of the stage.*

Frail the dew on Makuzu Moor,

CHORUS   and I, as frail, am I to live on,
ever bitter at my lot?

WOMAN (*sashi*) I lived for many years at Kita-Shirakawa, in the northern district of Miyako. One day, alas, disaster struck, for my only son,

enticed away by traders in children,
vanished from my side.
I sought him, and learned they had spirited him off
eastward, across Ōsaka Pass,
to distant lands, to unknown Azuma.[6]
News so distressing confused my wits.
The one thought left me was to go there,
to find my darling boy;
and now, in my quest, I am wholly lost!

CHORUS (*sageuta*) A thousand leagues are never far
to a fond mother's heart, they say,
when she cannot forget her child.

(*ageuta*) That bond in life
is always so fragile, yet now he is gone
is always so fragile, yet now he is gone,
when he might still have stayed with me a while,
and we are sundered, mother and son.
Just so, long ago, a mother grieved
to see her nestlings fly.[7]

5. A *Shinkokinshū* (1206) poem by Kunaikyō.
6. Azuma is the old name of the wild region of eastern Japan: in modern times the Kanto Plain, centred on Tokyo.
7. A proverbial expression derived from a passage in *Kōshi kego* (Ch. *K'ung-tzu-chia-lü*, 'The Sayings of Confucius').

This anxious heart can go no further.
Here, the road ends where Musashi stops
and Shimōsa province begins:
to the Sumida River I have come at last
to the Sumida River I have come at last.

Ferryman rises.

WOMAN (*mondō*) Please, please, let me come aboard, too!

FERRYMAN Where have you come from and where are you going?

WOMAN I have come from Miyako, and I am looking for someone.

FERRYMAN So, you are from Miyako, and you are mad into the bargain. Rave for us, then, rave and entertain us. Otherwise, I will not let you aboard.

WOMAN Cruel man! If it is you, the ferryman on the Sumida River, then you should be calling, 'It's sundown! All aboard!' Yet instead I hear, 'No, I'll not let you aboard!' Do not talk like that, for if you do, how can I believe that you are the ferryman?[8]

FERRYMAN Sure enough, you really are from Miyako. Your spirit and wit are true to the capital's name.

WOMAN And that expression you just used will not pass unchallenged, either. Here at this crossing, long ago, Narihira sang,

(*kami-no-ei*) Are you true to your name?
Then, Miyako birds,
I put you this question:
the one I love –
does she live or does she die?

(*mondō*) Come, ferryman, those white birds there are like none I ever saw in Miyako. What do you call them, then?

FERRYMAN Gulls, they are called. They are seabirds.

WOMAN What an answer! Perhaps by the sea they are gulls, or even plovers for all I care. But why do you not answer, here on the banks of the Sumida River, that they are Miyako birds?

FERRYMAN Ah, why indeed? I confess my mistake. Here I live in this famous place, and still, I dully failed in reply to call them Miyako birds.

8. This speech begins the passage in which the playwright superimposes episode no. 9 of *Ise monogatari* on the Woman's own situation. The Ferryman, in his reply, recognizes the allusion and acknowledges, as people often do in nō plays, the superior qualities of those who come from the capital.

WOMAN   Gulls from the sea? No, for evening waves[9]
             wash back to times past when Narihira
FERRYMAN   put that question:
             Does she live or does she die?
             recalling his love left in far Miyako.
WOMAN   For me, it is eastward my love goes
             to the child I seek, as Narihira sought:
FERRYMAN   he, his dear lady,
WOMAN   I, my own son.
FERRYMAN   The two loves are one,
WOMAN   and at love's urging,   *Begins to mime and dance.*
CHORUS (*ageuta*) I in my turn
             put you the question, Miyako birds
             put you the question, Miyako birds:
             the child I love, on this Azuma road,
             does he live or does he die?
             Again and again I question you,
             but you give me no reply.
             Miyako birds, your silence is rude.
             Shall I name you, then, 'rustic birds'?
             As the old song goes,
                  On the broad banks
                  of Horie River,
                  teeming with boats,
                  they settle in flocks,
                  the clamouring Miyako birds.[10]
             But that was Naniwa. Now I stand here
             by the Sumida River, in the depths of the East.
             What distances this search has led me –
             endless! But let that be.
             O ferryman, your boat may be full,
             perhaps it is small, but still I beg,
             O ferryman, take me aboard!

9. The expression 'evening waves' involves a pun, very common in nō, on *yū*, which means both 'evening' and 'say'. It appears even in passages where one does not expect to find 'evening'.

10. A poem from the *Man'yōshū* (late 8th c.), by Ōtomo no Yakamochi. Naniwa, the scene of the poem, is the site of present Osaka. The poem's function is to stress how far the Woman has come from home.

> Do me a kindness, ferryman, please,
> make room for me as well!

Ferryman, with the outer robe now off his right shoulder in preparation for work,
and pole in hand, is ready to cast off.

FERRYMAN (*mondō*) Never was there a madwoman so well-spoken.
Come aboard, then. Hurry! [*Woman sits near stage centre, towards witness*
square.] This crossing is tricky. Please make sure you stay quiet.

Traveller moves to sit slightly behind Woman, to her left. Behind them stands
Ferryman. They are in the boat.

WOMAN (*mondō*) Pardon me, but I see on the far bank a crowd gathered
around a willow tree. What are they doing?[11]

FERRYMAN They are holding a Great Invocation,[12] and the reason
why is a very sad story. Let me tell it to you while we make our
crossing.

(*katari*) Last year, on the fifteenth day of the third month – why,
that means it was exactly a year ago today! – a trader in children
came by here from Miyako. He had with him a twelve-year-old boy
whom he had bought, and he was bound for the far north. But the
boy was not used to travelling. He was exhausted and had become
very ill. Unable to walk another step, he collapsed here, on the bank
of the river. Ah, what heartless people there are in this world! The
trader simply abandoned him and went on his way. Meanwhile, the
people here noticed that the boy seemed to be from a good family.
They looked after him as best they could, but no doubt his own
karma opposed his recovery, because he grew weaker and weaker
until he clearly was dying. They asked him then who he was, and
where he was from. 'What is your family's name,' they said, 'and
which is your province?' 'I am from Miyako,' he replied, 'from
Kita-Shirakawa. My family name is Yoshida, and I am an only
child. After my father died, I stayed alone with my mother. Then I
was stolen away by traders in children, and that is how I came here.
I miss so much the sight and sound of the people of Miyako! So

---

11. In the oldest extant text, it is the Traveller who asks this question.
12. A *dai nembutsu*, or 'Great Invocation to Amida': a gathering, usually lasting seven
days, at which people called the name of the Buddha Amida, praying for his grace and
for rebirth in his Western Paradise. The participants prayed more for the benefit of
others than for themselves. The practice could be associated with the death of a child,
and the Zempō text of the play shows that this is the case here. The Woman arrives on
the last day of a *dai nembutsu* held for the spirit of her son.

please build a mound over me, by this roadside, and on it plant a willow tree.'[13] He spoke very sweetly. Then he called the Holy Name four or five times and it was all over. What a sad, sad story!

(*mondō*) Actually, I see we have people from Miyako aboard with us now. Of course, the boy was no relative of yours, but do pause, none the less, and call the Name too, for his soul's comfort and guidance. Well, what with all my chattering, we are already here.

TRAVELLER Then I will stay here today, and although I myself have no tie to him, I will call the Name for the comfort and guidance of his soul.

Traveller sits at witness position. Woman weeps.

FERRYMAN (*mondō*) Now then, madwoman, why are you not getting out too? Please go ashore. Oh, poor thing, the story I told just now has made you cry! But quickly, do please step ashore.

WOMAN Tell me, ferryman, when did all that happen?

FERRYMAN Why, in the third moon of last year, on exactly this day.

WOMAN And the boy, then – he was

FERRYMAN twelve years old.

WOMAN His given name was

FERRYMAN Umewaka-maru,

WOMAN and his family name was

FERRYMAN Yoshida.

WOMAN And after he died, no parent of his ever came looking for him?

FERRYMAN No, no relative came in search of him, ever.

WOMAN Especially not his mother. She never came, did she?

FERRYMAN No, naturally not.

WOMAN Of course no parent or relative ever came looking for him. He was the boy this poor madwoman has been seeking! Oh, am I dreaming? What horror is this?

FERRYMAN Oh, how awful! Here I had thought the story was about

13. The Ferryman's speech has been reworked a great deal over the centuries. The Zempō text does not have this request; the boy only asks to be buried beside the road so that he should be near the passer-by from Miyako. Nor does this text, unlike all subsequent ones, speak of a willow tree being planted upon the boy's grave. It mentions only a 'marker' (*shirushi*). Perhaps the willow was simply an item in the landscape nearby, clearly visible from the boat. Nevertheless, a diary entry dated 1485 precisely describes a grave-mound surmounted by a willow at the spot. Scholars suspect that, even so early, this willow was there because of the play, rather than the other way round.

someone I myself would never know, and all the time he was your own son! What a terrible, terrible thing!

(*unnamed*) But come, further lamenting will never help him now. I will take you to his tomb. Please follow me. [*Putting down his oar, he helps Woman up and leads her before the mound. He then retires to sit before Chorus.*]

(*mondō*) This is the boy's tomb. Pray for him, pray for him with all your heart.

WOMAN (*kudoki*) My eyes shall behold him –
  or so I believed, until this moment.
  For that, I travelled a weary way
  to unknown Azuma,
  only to find him gone from this world;
  only to stand here before his tomb!
  O the cruelty of it!
  For his own death, he left his birthplace.
  Deep in the East,
  he became earth by the side of the road.
  There he lies buried,
  with only the new growth of spring
  to cover his tomb.

CHORUS (*uta*) But come, good people,
  turn the earth over. One last time,
  show a mother her son as he looked in life!

  (*ageuta*) Had he lived on,
  he would have known gladness; but hope was vain
  he would have known gladness; but hope was vain,
  yes, vain as living to me now, his mother,
  for whom a while, a lovely figure,
  he glimmered and then, like all things in this world,
  suddenly was gone.
  Such sorrows lurk in the blossoms' glory,
  as storm winds of change howl with fiercer voice!
  The moon, through the long night of birth and death,
  is lost behind clouds of impermanence.
  Ah, this sad world's truth is here, plain to see
  ah, this sad world's truth is here, plain to see.

Ferryman has put his right arm back through its sleeve. Now he rises, bell in hand.

FERRYMAN (*mondō*) No lament of yours can help him any more. Just call the Name and pray for his happy rebirth in paradise.

   (*kakeai*) Now the moon is rising,
         the river breeze sighs as the night wears on.
         Invocations will surely be heard.
         In this spirit all present, urged on by faith,
         strike bells in rhythm,

WOMAN   while the mother, overcome by sorrow,
         unable even to call the Name,
         lies there, prostrate, dissolved in weeping.

FERRYMAN This is not right! Even with all the people here chanting the Invocation, it is still his mother's prayers that will give the deceased the greatest joy. [*Goes to Woman, places bell and striker before her.*]
         Please, you too, take a chanting-bell.

WOMAN   For my own dear son's sake?
         Yes, how right you are!
         I too, then, will take up the bell,

FERRYMAN cease lamenting, call with ringing voice,

WOMAN   this night of bright moon, invoking the Name
         at one with all the others,

FERRYMAN with eager heart, drawn straight to the West:

BOTH   *Hail, in Thy western Realm of Bliss!*
         Thirty-six million million worlds
         ring with one cry, one Name: Amida!

CHORUS (*unnamed*) *Hail Amida Buddha!*
         Hail Amida Buddha!
         Hail Amida Buddha!
         Hail Amida Buddha!

WOMAN   On the banks of the Sumida River,
         wind and waves now swell the chorus:

CHORUS   *Hail Amida Buddha!*
         Hail Amida Buddha!
         Hail Amida Buddha!

WOMAN   Are you true to your name?
         Then, Miyako birds, add your voices, too!

CHORUS   *Hail Amida Buddha!*
         Hail Amida Buddha!
         Hail Amida Buddha!

WOMAN (*mondō*) Listen! Listen to me! That voice, just now calling out the Name: I am certain it was my child's! It seemed to come from within the tomb!

FERRYMAN We heard it too, as you say. We others must stop calling and let the mother chant on alone.

WOMAN Oh, please, let me hear that voice again, another time!
(*uta*) *Hail Amida Buddha!*

BOY [*from within the mound*] *Hail Amida Buddha!*
Hail Amida Buddha!

CHORUS And from whence the voice came,
perhaps an illusion . . .

Boy appears from behind the mound and stands in witness square.

WOMAN Ah, my child, is it you?

BOY Mother dear, is it you?

As Chorus sings, Woman goes to Boy, touches his shoulder; he slips away from her and re-enters the mound.

CHORUS She takes his hand, his slips into hers,
but again his shape fades and is gone.
Her fond longing waxes; as in a mirror,

Boy reappears in base square. She starts towards him, but again he slips into the mound.

remembered form and present illusion
fuse, glimmering, now seen, now hidden,
till light streaks the sky and pale dawn
breaks into day. His shape has vanished.
What seemed a dear child is wild grasses
thick on the tomb, nodding in sign
over wide, grassy wastes,
O sorrow: nothing else remains
O sorrow: nothing else remains.

Facing audience, Woman weeps.

Tadanori

In the late 1160s, the Taira clan under Taira no Kiyomori (1118–1181) seized control of the capital, although they left in place the emperor and his court. Then, in 1183, the approach of the rival Minamoto forces put the Taira to flight. Taira no Tadanori (1144–1184), a much younger brother of Kiyomori, fled with them. Renowned for his courage and strength, he was by this time one of the chief Taira officers, but he had also studied poetry in Kyoto with the great Fujiwara no Toshinari (or Shunzei) (1114–1204), and was just as devoted to letters as to the art of war. *Tadanori* evokes him both as a warrior and a poet.

The play is by Zeami, who late in his life ranked it almost with *The Well-Cradle* as a work of the highest quality. As in the case of *Atsumori* and *Yashima*, his source was the epic *Heike monogatari* ('The Tale of the Taira'). In one of his treatises, Zeami wrote that a warrior play should be adorned with poetic beauty ('flowers, birds, wind, and moon'). *Atsumori* and *Yashima* both follow this principle, but *Tadanori* goes further, since its main theme has more to do with poetry than with war.

The scene of *Tadanori* is Suma shore, a setting already familiar from *Atsumori* and *Pining Wind*. There, in 1184, the Taira were routed by the Minamoto at the battle of Ichi-no-tani. Tadanori died in the encounter, and his death is evoked in the play. However, this is also where Ariwara no Yukihira (818–893) spent his poetically melancholy exile, leaving a poem that figures in both *Tadanori* and *Pining Wind*; and where Prince Genji, too, in *Genji monogatari* ('The Tale of Genji', early 11th c.), passed sad years of exile. Genji planted a cherry tree on the beach at Suma, and this tree reappears in *Tadanori* as Tadanori's own grave-marker. Since the season of the play is spring, the 'Young Cherry Tree' is in full bloom.

In *Pining Wind*, the two sisters, whose grave-marker is a pine, linger at Suma because they cannot give up their love. In *Tadanori*, Tadanori lingers on as a phantom for a quite different reason. He cannot give up his desperate desire to have a poem of his included, under his own name, in an imperially commissioned anthology.

Since Tadanori was a pupil of Fujiwara no Toshinari, who received in 1183 the order to compile the *Senzaishū*, this honour might normally have come his way. Alas, the Minamoto drove the Taira from the capital before Toshinari could finish the collection, and they quickly had the whole Taira clan branded as 'enemies of the court'. This declaration – one that the court could not have refused to make – simply sanctioned what the Minamoto were doing anyway: seeking to destroy their rivals. However, it meant that, thereafter, no work by a Taira poet could be included in an imperial anthology. Tadanori tells in the play how he turned back to Kyoto and begged Toshinari to include one of his poems after all. Toshinari was sufficiently moved to do so, but he did not feel able to record the poet's name. As a result, Tadanori's poem appears in the *Senzaishū* as 'Anonymous'.

To appreciate the weight of the issue, one must understand that inclusion in an imperial anthology meant immortality. Poetry was the highest art of classical Japanese civilization, and inclusion in an imperial anthology was an ultimate mark of recognition. The literature of the time is full of stories about people, sometimes very humble, who rose high or even saved their own lives thanks to a single, apt poem. The practice of poetry was therefore important and could be intensely competitive. In short, there is nothing eccentric about Tadanori's distress. Another poet could easily have felt the same way. Moreover, Tadanori's desire to be named in an imperial anthology is no different from the warrior's wish to leave a great name to posterity. He was already respected as a warrior, and his poetic ambition simply displays his mettle in another, higher, arena.

Zeami adopted Genji's cherry tree as Tadanori's grave-marker because of the poem found attached to Tadanori's quiver after his death in battle: 'Dark barring my way, a tree's sheltering boughs shall be my inn: tonight let blossoms stand as my host!' The poet speaks in the person of a traveller at nightfall, obliged to seek shelter beneath a tree in bloom. His poem is not strikingly profound or original, but it acquires greater stature in the setting provided for it by *Heike monogatari*. The dark that bars the traveller's way is then death, and the blossoming tree that stands host to him on the road of life is Poetry itself. Zeami certainly took the poem that way.

Perhaps the point of *Tadanori* (as Itō Masayoshi has suggested) is really that the poet is one with his work, for Tadanori is certainly one with the Young Cherry Tree. Part one of the play speaks of 'winds along the shore' that 'scatter mountain cherry petals', while the beginning of part two evokes a 'desolate, gale-swept scene'. Soon, Tadanori recounts his own death on the shore at Suma, and one gathers that he fell like the blossoms. It is ironic that the Monk, a former intimate of Toshinari, should be one who 'no longer loves even blossoms' (that is, who has now given up poetry). At Suma, he meets blossoms and poetry again, in the person of Tadanori, and no doubt realizes that poetry is not something a living being can give up. It is the song of the winds of change.

The place where Tadanori fell is said to be several kilometres west of Suma, near the present Hitomaru-mae Station in the neighbouring town of Akashi. A funerary monument to Tadanori can be seen there, and also a 'Tadanori Ude-zuka' (a funerary mound for Tadanori's arm). The Ude-zuka had to be moved a little recently because of work on the railway, but at the new site there is a little Ude-zuka Shrine as well. It has a large wooden right arm. Rubbing an ailing arm with the wooden one is suppose to help it get better.

Another funerary monument to Tadanori, in the grounds of a temple in Saitama Prefecture, east of Tokyo, was erected by Okabe no Rokuyata, the warrior who killed him. Over it stands a cherry tree. They say the present tree's ancestor was planted by Tadanori's wife in her husband's honour.

Tadanori

Persons in order of appearance

A Monk	*waki*
Two or three Companions	*wakizure*
An Old Man (*A sakura-jō* mask)	*maeshite*
A Villager	*ai*
Taira no Tadanori (*Chūjō* or *Jūroku* mask)	*nochijite*

Remarks: A second-category or warrior play (*shura-mono*) current in all five schools of nō.

* * *

To shidai music, enter Monk and Companions. They face each other along front of stage.

MONK and COMPANIONS

(*shidai*) One who no longer loves even blossoms
one who no longer loves even blossoms
cares not that clouds should cover the moon. *Face audience.*

MONK (*nanori*) You have before you one who, long ago, was in the service of Lord Toshinari. It was after Lord Toshinari passed away that I put on the habit you see. Never having visited the provinces of the West, I am setting out that way now.

(*sashi*) Then off past Their Majesties' South-west Villa,[1]
farewell to Miyako, and over the hills
to Yamazaki!

MONK and COMPANIONS

Tollgate Station, now only a name, *Face each other.*
cannot detain us: as travellers will,
we press on, weary, worn with the cares
of our sad, soiled world, across Akuta River,
through bamboo-grass brakes at Ira, and on

(*sageuta*) to where the moon in Koya Pond
so deep and clear, lodges, radiant.

(*ageuta*) That dreary wind sighing through the reeds,
that dreary wind sighing through the reeds,
we fain would ignore,
who once renounced sorrow, yet hear it too,
below Mount Arima: nowhere to hide
in this vale of tears. Folly fills the mind
with vain dreams that only fade
when distant bells from Naniwa *Monk mimes walking.*

1. This journey leads overland past the Toba Palace (Toba is a locality south of Kyoto) of Emperors Shirakawa and Toba; along the Katsura River to Yamazaki, on the border between Yamashiro and Settsu provinces; to Sekido-no-shuku (Tollgate Station) where a toll-barrier had existed in centuries past; across the Akuta River (*akuta* also means 'dirt'), a tributary of the Yodo River, that flows through the present Takatsuki city; through the Ina Moors, covered with *sasa*, in the area of modern Osaka airport; by Koya Pond on the Ina Moors; past Mount Arima (*ari* also means '[even we] have [sorrows]'); to Osaka Bay at Naniwa; on along the shore of the Inland Sea past Naruo, in neighbouring Harima province; and, finally, still further west, to Suma.

                    ring in the dawn. And now we pass on
                    to Naruo. Beyond the sands
                    dance far waves, and little boats sail by
                    dance far waves, and little boats sail by!

MONK (*tsukizerifu*) Having come so swiftly, we have already reached
    the shore at Suma. Let us rest a while and look at the cherry blos-
    soms.

COMPANIONS Very well.

  To issei *music, enter Old Man, leaning on a staff and carrying a branch. He stands
  in base square.*

OLD MAN (*sashi*) Yes, so it is with all who struggle through life,
                    inured to labour, ever benighted.
                    When not drawing brine I haul wood for salt-fires;[2]
                    dry at times, I still have no rest,
                    hastening between hill and shore
                    at Suma, by the sea,
       (*issei*) seafolk's cries ring out endlessly
                    while, far away, the plovers call.

(*sashi*) Now, Suma shore is known for lonely melancholy.
                         Should one perchance
                         ask after me,
                         say that on Suma shore
                         salt, sea-tangle drops
                         are falling as I grieve.[3]
                    Ah, the little fishing craft offshore,
                    smoke from saltmakers' fires,
                    wind through the pines . . .

Every one of these calls up melancholy thoughts. And below the
Suma hills stands a single cherry tree, in memory of someone who
died long ago.

                    Now that the season brings us spring flowers,
                    I too bring offerings, in charity:[4]

2. The process of making salt is described in note 2 to *Pining Wind*. The sharp argument,
below, about where the Old Man belongs (in the hills or on the shore) reflects a real
distinction between such local populations in pre-modern Japan. However, it probably
hints, too, that the Old Man is in fact a courtier even though he lives at Suma, and it no
doubt alludes as well to Tadanori's mastery of both poetry and arms.

3. By Ariwara no Yukihira, from the *Kokinshū* (905). Yukihira, in exile at Suma, sent it
back to someone in the capital. The 'salt, sea-tangle drops' are at once the brine that
drips from the seaweed gathered by saltmakers along the beach, and the poet's tears.

(*sageuta*) on each return journey from the hills
I add to my firewood flowering branches,
gifts for the tree on my way home,
gifts for the tree on my way home.

Monk rises.

MONK (*mondō*). I beg your pardon, old man, but are you a peasant from these hills?

OLD MAN Yes, I am. I am one of the seafolk from this shore.

MONK But if you are one of the seafolk, you should live on the shore. Yet your work takes you into the hills. Surely you ought to call yourself a hill-dweller.

OLD MAN Really? Then are the seafolk simply to abandon the brine they gather, and never boil it down?

MONK   No, I concede you are certainly right.
Smoke of salt-fires to burn sea-tangle

OLD MAN   must always rise. So woodcutters, too,

MONK   hasten along pathways not their own,

OLD MAN   to spots deserted. On Suma shore,
just beyond the beach, on hilly slopes,

OLD MAN (*ageuta*) wood grows in plenty, there for the taking

CHORUS   wood grows in plenty, there for the taking
and there they go for their precious fuel,

OLD MAN   our seafolk – ah, reverend sir,
your quibbling does not flatter you!

CHORUS   Yes, Suma shore is unlike other places:
for while most blossoms fear mountain gales
or cold winds whistling down the slopes,
here at Suma the Young Cherry Tree
stands no distance from the sea,
which is why the winds along the shore
scatter mountain cherry petals.

During the above Chorus passage, Villager slips in to sit at villager position.

MONK (*mondō*) Pardon me, old man, but the sun is already down. I would be much obliged if you would give me lodging for the night.

OLD MAN Have you no finer feelings? Where could one find a finer lodging than the shelter of these blossoms?

4. 'In charity' (*gyakuen nagara*) means that the speaker has no personal connection with the 'someone who died long ago', and therefore no obligation to make offerings at all. Actually, he is the phantom of that 'someone'.

MONK Yes, yes, I see, these blossoms do promise lodging. But then, what host will I have to thank?

OLD MAN   Dark barring my way,
                   a tree's sheltering boughs
                   shall be my inn:
                   tonight let blossoms
                   stand as my host![5]

Alas, the man who wrote those lines lies here under the moss. Even I, a simple man of the sea, often come here to pray for him. Why do you monks, out of charity, not pray for him too?

MONK   Dark barring my way,
                   a tree's sheltering boughs
                   shall be my inn:
                   tonight let blossoms
                   stand as my host!

That is a poem by the Lord of Satsuma.

OLD MAN Tadanori, for such was his name, was killed here at the battle of Ichi-no-tani. People close to him planted this tree in his memory.

MONK   This is truly a strange encounter!
                   For Toshinari loved in him

OLD MAN a friend in poetry; and destiny now,

MONK tonight, makes of him

OLD MAN a wayfarer's host: *Steps towards Monk.*

CHORUS (*rongi*) Tadanori, hearken to the voice of the Law!
                   Take your seat upon a lotus throne!

OLD MAN O precious moment!
                   A voice reaches my ears, guiding, comforting.
                   The fruit of enlightenment shall now be mine!
                   Gladness fills me!

CHORUS Astonishing! Why, that old man
                   takes my chanting as meant for himself,
                   and responds with signs of joy!
                   How can this be? What is the reason?

OLD MAN To have you, O monk, guide and comfort me –

5. This poem appears in the 'Death of Tadanori' chapter of *Heike monogatari*, under the circumstances described in part two of the play. The original is more tentative than the translation: 'Were I, still travelling as night falls, to make a sheltering tree my inn, then would my host tonight be the blossoms themselves?'

that is why I came to you here.

CHORUS   Yes, lie tonight under the blossoms,
wait and see what your dreams may bring
while I take the news to Miyako!
says he, and fades into the blossoms,
vanishing as though he had never been
vanishing as though he had never been.   *Exit.*

    *   *   *

Villager rises and comes to base square.

VILLAGER You have before you a man who lives on Suma shore. I think I will go today and look at the blossoms on the Young Cherry Tree. [*Sees Monk.*] Aha, there is a monk I have never seen before. Reverend sir, where are you from?

MONK I come from Miyako. Do you live nearby?

VILLAGER Yes, reverend sir, I do.

MONK Then would you come a little closer? I have something to ask of you.

VILLAGER Very well. [*Comes forward to sit at stage centre.*] Well, reverend sir, what is it?

MONK A rather surprising request, perhaps. Would you tell me all you know about this Young Cherry Tree, and also about how Tadanori met his death?

VILLAGER You are right, reverend sir, your request *is* a surprise. I do live here, it is true, but I really know very little about such things. Still, it would be too bad of me, the very first time we meet, to claim I know nothing at all. So I will tell you the story as I have heard it myself.

MONK That is very good of you.

VILLAGER [*Turns to audience.*] Now, among all the Taira lords, it was Tadanori, Lord of Satsuma, who excelled at once in letters and in war. They say he was a remarkable commander. And before he withdrew from Miyako with all his clan, to journey here, he went to see Lord Toshinari. 'I have always been devoted to poetry,' he said, 'and I so long to be counted among the poets!' Lord Toshinari replied, 'Since all the Taira are now under imperial censure, I fear that cannot be.' But Tadanori could not accept this verdict. When his company reached Yamazaki, he could not help turning back to the city, seeking out Toshinari again, and leaving with him a good number of verses. 'If any of these will do,' he implored Toshinari, 'please include them!' Then, so they say, he left once more. Later on, in the time of

Cloistered Emperor Go-Shirakawa, Lord Toshinari put together the *Sen-zaishū* and he did include one poem by Tadanori. But he did not put Tadanori's name to it. He only wrote in, 'Anonymous'.[6]

Now for the way Tadanori died. The Taira host was camped here when the Minamoto approached, bent on destroying them. Sixty thousand horsemen divided into two forces, one under Noriyori and the other under Yoshitsune, and charged the Taira from left and right. A great number of the Taira nobles were killed in the savage attack. Tadanori was in command of the western wing of the Taira, but he was soon driven from the camp and fled among the common warriors. That was when Okabe no Rokuyata Tadazumi spotted him and decided he had found a worthy opponent. Okabe attacked, with his group of seven or eight riders. Tadanori closed with him immediately, and with the great strength he was famous for, he soon had Okabe down. Then one of Okabe's retainers killed him. They say the tragedy of it brought tears to everyone's eyes.

As for this Young Cherry Tree, some say Tadanori planted it himself, while others say it was planted by Prince Genji. That is the story, at least as they tell it here. But may I ask, reverend sir, why you wished to hear it? I cannot help being a little curious.

MONK Thank you very much for your account. This is why I asked. I myself once served Lord Toshinari, and after he died I became a monk, as you see. Before you arrived, I talked here with an old man who told me the Young Cherry Tree's tale just as you did now. He spoke of Tadanori as though he were Tadanori himself, then said he would take the news to Miyako and at that moment vanished into the blossoms.

VILLAGER How extraordinary! Surely it was Tadanori's own spirit that appeared and exchanged words with you. You must stay here and give him comfort and guidance.

MONK Then I will do so. I will do my best to give guidance and comfort to his spirit.

VILLAGER If there is anything you need, reverend sir, please let me know.

MONK That I will.

VILLAGER Very well.   [*Exit.*]

*   *   *

6. This poem treats the familiar theme of regret for an ancient seventh-century capital on the southern shore of Lake Biwa, and celebrates the cherry blossoms blooming there now as of old.

MONK and COMPANIONS

  (*ageuta*) On a grassy couch spread with lonely sleeves
       on a grassy couch spread with lonely sleeves,
       dream pathways call; as the moon sinks low,
       shadows veil shapes of shore and hill,
       and by darkened blossoms travellers rest,
       purer of heart the deeper the night.
       Ah, the desolate, gale-swept scene
       ah, the desolate, gale-swept scene!

To issei *music, enter Tadanori. He stands in base square.*

TADANORI (*sashi*) I am ashamed! Here where death took me,
       a dream recalls my form into vision,
       real as waking. My heart roams once more
       the past, that old tale I shall tell you now:
       for this my spirit, transformed, has come.

  (*kudoki*) But O, in this deluded world
       rife with wrongful clinging,
       why, I ask, did he range my poem
       among such exalted company
       in the *Senzaishū*,
       yet, alas, invoke imperial censure
       and give the poet as 'Anonymous'?
       That supreme disappointment binds me still.
  Yet Toshinari, who chose the poems, has now passed away.
  You, O monk, were once in his service.
  Take my complaint to his son, Lord Teika![7]
  If the thing can be done, have him enter the poet's name!
  Do this, I beg you, and give my spirit peace!
       As in dream I plead, winds down Suma shore,
       blow softly, pray, wake not the dreamer!

CHORUS (*kuri*) Yes, to be born into a house of poets,[8]
  to give to poetry one's all,
  to follow the way of the Blessed Isles:
  that is the highest calling a man can pursue!

---

7. Fujiwara no Teika (1162–1241), perhaps an even greater poet than his father, did in fact include a poem by Tadanori, under Tadanori's name, in the *Shinchokusenshū* (1235).
8. Tadanori's father, Taira no Tadamori, was a poet too, and had poems included in several imperial collections.

MONK (*sashi*) And above all others, Tadanori,
    heir to the twin paths of letters and war,
    enjoyed in the world a lofty fame.
CHORUS For when Cloistered Emperor Go-Shirakawa
    took in hand the reins of government,[9]
    the imperial commission went out
    to Lord Toshinari, of the Third Rank,
    to compile the *Senzaishū*.
      (*sageuta*) Autumn, it was, in the Juei years
         when we abandoned Miyako.
      (*ageuta*) Though a cruel press of cares beset me
         though a cruel press of cares beset me,
         from Yamazaki my own heart's flower[10]
         turned me back to seek once more
         Toshinari's house and tell him, in tears,
         my hope for my songs. He heard my plea.
         Once more I took up quiver and bow,
         roamed the waves of the western sea,
         then found brief refuge on Suma shore
         where Genji, exiled, once lived a while –
         no place for the Taira, as I now see,
         though foolishly, I never saw it then!
   (*kuri*) Then came the battle of Ichi-no-tani.
    When the outcome was no longer in doubt,
    we all fled to our ships and put to sea.
TADANORI (*katari*) I too, meaning to board a ship,
    had made my way to the water's edge
    when, glancing behind me, I saw pursuers
    bearing down on me: half a dozen riders,
    their leader calling out his name,
    Okabe no Rokuyata Tadazumi.
    This was exactly the chance I craved.
    With a tug at the reins I turned my horse,
    instantly fell on Rokuyata,

9. In the twelfth century it was the retired emperor, not the reigning one, who actually ruled. An emperor generally took nominal Buddhist orders upon abdication. Go-Shirakawa abdicated in 1158 and died in 1192. The *Senzaishū* was commissioned in 1183.
10. The pure love of poetry and poetic distinction that he still had in his heart.

grappled with him, and crashed to the ground
between his mount and mine. O I had him down,
and already my hand was on my sword

CHORUS (*uta*) when one of Rokuyata's men,
circling round Lord Tadanori, who was on top,
from behind struck off his right arm.
Seizing Rokuyata with his left,
Tadanori shoved the fellow away,
knowing full well his time had come.
'Get back,' he cried, 'leave me room,
let me turn to the Western Paradise!'
And, softly, he breathed,
Thy universal radiance
fills all worlds everywhere;
sentient beings who call on Thee,
Thou dost welcome, one and all.[11]
Alas! The pitiless Rokuyata drew his sword
and that fine head, severed, fell to the earth.

TADANORI Then in his heart Rokuyata felt sorrow,
seeing the warrior was still young.
The late autumn sky, thinly overcast,
was raining a cold, fitful drizzle
such as stains the mottled fall leaves.
Just so, mottled red, was the warrior's armour,
wholly unlike any common man's.
Was it possible? Could he then be
one of the nobles from the Court?
Wishing to learn the slain man's name,
Rokuyata inspected his quiver
and, to his amazement, found tied to it
a poem-slip, with, next to the title,[12]
'A Traveller's Lodging', these lines:
　　(*kami-no-ei*) Dark barring my way,
　　　　　　　a tree's sheltering boughs

---

11. A passage from the sutra known in Japanese as *Kammuryōju-kyō* ('Sutra on the contemplation of infinite life'), a basic text of the Amida cult.
12. This 'title' (*dai*) is, more exactly, the set topic on which Tadanori had written the poem. A great deal of poetry was written on such conventional, assigned topics.

>shall be my inn:

(QUASI-DANCE: *tachimawari*)

Tadanori dances a warrior's tachimawari *circuit of the stage.*

TADANORI   this night let blossoms
                 stand as my host!

   (*uta*) Tadanori, the name was signed.

CHORUS   Then he was that warrior whose name
                 storm winds cried abroad:
                 he was the Lord of Satsuma!
                 O the pity of it!   *Turns to Monk.*

   (*uta*) These blossoms, O monk, drew you on
                 to seek lodging here, because I wished
                 that you should hear my tale.
                 For this I detained you and ended the day.[13]
                 Now you know me beyond a doubt,
                 the flower again shall seek its root.[14]
                 Guide my shade, comfort me, I pray!
                 A tree's sheltering boughs you made your inn,
                 and, yes, the blossoms were your host!

Facing side from base square, Tadanori stamps the final beat.

---

13. A rather puzzling line (*hi o kurashi todomeshi nari*) that may mean simply, 'I detained you all day long until night [when a spirit can manifest itself fully] fell.' However, a clearer example of a spirit bringing night on early occurs in Zeami's *Higaki*, and *The Mountain Crone* elaborates on the theme.

14. 'I shall return to where I came from.' A half-proverbial expression ultimately based on a couplet in the *Wakan rōei shū*.

Takasago

God plays form a special group within the nō repertoire, and because of their undramatic nature they are not always the most popular. *Takasago*, however, is the unquestioned king among them, and at least its title is known to practically everyone in Japan. The Old Man and Old Woman of part one, in the form of dolls, can be seen in countless homes and are a regular presence at weddings, where passages from the play are commonly sung. It is therefore one of Zeami's greatest successes, and his writings leave no doubt that he was proud of it.

Some (Kanai Kiyomitsu and Ochi Reiko) have suggested that Zeami meant *Takasago* to honour not only an idealized imperial sovereign but the more concrete figure of his own brilliant patron, the shogun Ashikaga Yoshimitsu (1358–1408). If so, the play has a political meaning rarely detectable in nō after the passage of so many centuries. Moreover, *Takasago* owes its pre-eminence over other god plays to political significance of another kind. Although *Kureha* was performed slightly more often than *Takasago* in the late sixteenth century, *Takasago* turned out to be the perfect vehicle for honouring the Tokugawa shoguns, who ruled Japan during the Edo period (1600–1868). The play lauds the enduring virtues of the pine (*matsu*), and *matsu* is the first character of Matsudaira, the shoguns' original clan name.

The pine is so prominent a motif in Japanese poetry and art that it is hard to say precisely what may have given Zeami the idea for *Takasago*. Perhaps, as one scholar (Kanai) has suggested, Zeami had in mind the *senshū banzai* ('a thousand autumns, ten thousand years') dances performed for the new year (the beginning of spring) by beggar musicians. At any rate, when composing the play, Zeami referred to a precise, thoroughly classical source: the Japanese preface (there is another in Chinese) to the *Kokinshū* (905), the first and most revered of the imperially commissioned poetry anthologies. This preface, by the poet Ki no Tsurayuki (868?–945?), is the earliest poetic treatise in the Japanese language.

In a review of established poetic metaphors, the *Kokinshū* preface mentions that 'the pines of Takasago or Suminoe [Sumiyoshi] are felt to be "paired" [*aioi*]'. From this statement come the two pines of the play. Zeami's understanding of the pines, however, is quite different from Ki no Tsurayuki's. The original expression means that poets evoke their own age by calling themselves 'paired' with (born or nurtured together with) such venerable pines as these; in fact, the play's first *sashi* passage contains a poem that illustrates this point. In contrast, 'paired' in the play describes the relationship between the two pines themselves.

Zeami's interpretation of *aioi* is just the sort of understanding found in the medieval commentaries on the *Kokinshū* and its preface. Like other medieval writings, these commentaries favour balanced pairs of opposite images or terms. Properly speaking (according to a late sixteenth-century dictionary), *aioi*, when applied to trees, means a tree with twin trunks growing from a single base. Such trees are still honoured at Japanese temples and shrines. However, the Takasago and Sumiyoshi pines are, according to one commentary, a three-day journey apart. Their distance from one another only makes more interesting the proposition that they are 'paired', since their mutual bond then transcends the limitations of space. Zeami stressed just this point in the play.

He also stressed that their bond transcends time. The commentaries hold that the Takasago pine stands for the age of the *Man'yōshū* (the eighth century) and the Sumiyoshi pine for the Engi era (901–923) when the *Kokinshū* was compiled. The Engi era, widely cited in medieval times as a golden age, is the present of the play. In its past, the *Man'yōshū* (the earliest, though privately compiled, collection of Japanese poetry) made an impressive prologue to the more classical tradition established by the *Kokinshū*. Since the two pines that represent these works are 'paired', the past and present of poetry are one. Their union in space and time therefore demonstrates that Japanese poetry is universal and eternal. Moreover, as the Old Woman (Takasago) and the Old Man (Sumiyoshi) carefully explain, this union is founded on a perfect marriage.

According to the *Kokinshū* preface, poetry moves the invisible powers, soothes the warrior's fierce heart, and smooths the relations between men and women. It is pure and perfect communication. No doubt for this reason, the medieval commentaries hold that poetry is continuous with good government. The *sashi* that precedes the *kuse* section of *Takasago* speaks of 'dewdrop pearls that in the heart seed polished grace until all beings alive, to the Blessed Isles, they say, draw nigh'. This statement has to do with the impulses that move one to compose poetry and so to acquire culture. To 'draw nigh' to 'the Blessed Isles' means to follow the path of Japanese poetry, hence the highest ideals of culture; and a land where all people do this – where all hearts are attuned to one another and to poetry – is a land where sovereign and subject, too, are in perfect accord. In that land dwells a wonderful virtue. This idea is stated even more plainly later on in the play.

This wonderful virtue, the sovereign's, calls into being the fabric of higher culture, exemplified by law as well as poetry. In *Kureha*, the sovereign wears 'a flawless weave of honoured precedent' woven for him by two maidens whose presence in Japan, and whose devoted work, are a response to his virtue. In *Takasago*, a 'god pine' wears a cloak of poetry: the song of the wind as it passes through the needles of the pine. In Japanese, *ha* means equally the needles of a pine and the leaves of any other plant, so that these needles are *koto no ha*, or 'leaves of speech': the words of poetry.

Part one of *Takasago* presents the spirits of the 'paired pines' of Takasago and Sumiyoshi, while in part two, the 'god pine' of Sumiyoshi – that is, the Sumiyoshi deity – appears alone. What is this deity and what is the relationship between parts one and two of the play?

As a sacred place, Takasago figures more in the poetic than in the religious tradition. There has never been an important shrine there. Sumiyoshi, however, is one of the great shrines of Japan. In classical times it stood on the shore of the Inland Sea. The deity, a patron of seafaring and poetry, had a close connection with the emperor. Music and dance (known as *kagura*, 'god music') were and still are essential at such shrines, and in part two of the play, the deity dances to *kagura* performed by the priests and maidens of Sumiyoshi. His form as he dances is that of a vigorous young man, a true *vert galant*. Curiously enough, this form is unique to part two of *Takasago*. Not only was the deity an old man in part one, but in every other such manifestation elsewhere, he is likewise an old man. Scholars therefore suspect that the play's young deity represents a later, anonymous emendation. No evidence confirms this idea, but a young god so perfectly suits *Takasago* that Zeami may have had no choice but to invent him.

Leaving aside the question of the Sumiyoshi deity's apparent age, it is odd that he should appear in part two without a consort. Part one insisted on the conjugal union of Takasago and Sumiyoshi. What, then, has become of Takasago in part two? The text, unlike that of *Kureha*, shows no trace of having been rewritten so as to eliminate an original *tsure*. If the two parts of the play are consistent with one another, then Takasago must still be present in part two, even if she is now invisible to the physical eye.

In *Kureha*, two maidens, under a pine tree by the sea, weave the sovereign his robe of kingship. In *Pining Wind*, two maidens, under a pine tree by the sea, set the pine's branches singing with the breath of their desire, and the tree is their noble lover. In *Takasago*, a 'god pine', a manifestation of the ideal sovereign, dances by the sea, surrounded by his dancing people. The felicitous marriage of the sovereign and his people is a motif so well known in myths of kingship that Takasago may plausibly be taken to have merged with those who perform the divine *kagura*. These, the sovereign's subjects, clothe him in a robe harmoniously woven of many diverse inspirations (poetry), and he, in response, confers upon them happiness and peace.

Takasago ('high sand' or 'dune') is now a zone of heavy industry along the northern shore of the Inland Sea, in Hyōgo Prefecture. The ancient shoreline is some way back from the sea. The site of the Takasago Pine is disputed by two rival shrines that probably owe, if not their existence, then at least whatever prosperity they enjoy to Zeami's play. The Sumiyoshi Shrine, surrounded by modern Osaka, is now a good way from the coast, not only because the shoreline has moved but because a great deal of new land has been built out from the natural coast in order to accommodate the growth of the city.

Takasago

Persons in order of appearance

Tomonari, a priest from the Aso Shrine in Kyushu	*waki*
Two Companions, also shrine priests	*wakizure*
An Old Man, the spirit of the Sumiyoshi pine (*Koushijō* mask)	*maeshite*
An Old Woman, the spirit of the Takasago Pine (*Uba* mask)	*tsure*
A Villager	*ai*
The God of Sumiyoshi (*Kantan-otoko* mask)	*nochijite*

Remarks: A first-category or god play (*waki-nō*) current in all five schools of nō. Variant performance traditions (*kogaki*) in all schools involve, among other things, placing a pine tree on stage.

*   *   *

To shin-no-shidai *music, enter Tomonari and Companions. They stand facing each other along front of stage.*

TOMONARI and COMPANIONS

    (*shidai*)   Now at last we don our travel wear

          now at last we don our travel wear

          day by day bound to roam afar![1]   *Face audience.*

TOMONARI (*nanori*) You see before you Tomonari, the chief priest of the Aso Shrine in Kyushu.[2] Not having yet laid eyes on Miyako, I am starting out there now. I will also have a look at the famous sights along the way.

TOMONARI and COMPANIONS (*ageuta*) Travel wear!   *Face each other.*

        Unfolding long, the Miyako road

        unfolding long, the Miyako road

        calls us forth today; waves lap the shore

        and ship lanes lie at peace, while spring's mild airs

        waft away the count of passing days.

        Behind us and before, clouds hide the path

        that stretches on and on, until at length

                          Tomonari mimes walking.

        we spy ahead the coast of Harima

        and Takasago shore: we have arrived

        and Takasago shore: we have arrived.   *Face audience.*

TOMONARI (*tsukizerifu*) Having come so swiftly, we have already reached Takasago shore in the province of Harima. Let us pause here a while and inform ourselves about the place.

Tomonari and Companions go to sit in witness square.

To shin-no-issei *music, enter Old Woman and Old Man, in that order. Old*

1. Here and at the beginning of the *ageuta* below, several *engo* ('related words') connected with clothing have been worked into the text, although the main narrative line has nothing to do with clothing. *Engo*, a ubiquitous device in poetry, are usually untranslatable, but these lines illustrate them a little.

2. The Aso Shrine honours the great volcano of that name in present Kumamoto Prefecture. An Aso priest named Tomonari was awarded a court rank (junior fifth lower grade) in 903. Zeami probably chose him because he lived precisely during the Engi era (901–923) celebrated in the play. The fact that he comes from Kyushu may have to do with the theme of bridging space and time.

Woman, who carries a broom of evergreen fronds, stops at first pine. Old Man
carries a rake; he stops at third pine. They face each other.

OLD COUPLE (*issei*)   Takasago! Here the winds of spring
play among the pines till shadows lengthen
and the hilltop bell gently tolls.

OLD WOMAN   Waves, by light mists veiled from shore,   *Face audience.*

BOTH   announce the salt tides' ebb and flow.   *Face each other.*

To ashirai music, both enter stage. Old Woman stands at centre, Old Man in base
square. They face each other.

OLD MAN (*sashi*)

In all the world,
whom am I to call a friend?
Alas, when I was young
the very Takasago Pine
stood me no company,[3]

BOTH   for countless ages come and gone
have heaped with their snows
these hoary cranes upon their perch,[4]
lingering in the light of dawn,
through frosty nights in spring,
hour after hour, the only sound abroad,
wind in the pines; and the heart –
that is the friend I call my own,
to trust in, yes, the heart alone.

(*sageuta*)   What callers come courting the pines?
Breezes from the shore, while needles fall,
making us a cloak – Come, sleeve to sleeve,
let us sweep litter from beneath the tree,
let us sweep litter from beneath the tree!

(*ageuta*)   Here at this spot, at Takasago
here at this spot, at Takasago,
the hilltop pine[5] is very old:

3. A poem by Fujiwara no Okikaze, included in the *Kokinshū* (905). The poet complains of being so old that his friends have all died by now; even the venerable Takasago Pine did not exist when he was young.

4. The crane is a symbol of long life. Snow refers to the white hair of old age.

5. As several writers have pointed out, the area of Takasago is quite flat, so that the conventional expression *onoe no matsu* ('hilltop pine') is topographically implausible; besides, the pine of the play is actually near the sea. *Onoe* may therefore, in this case, be a corruption of a local place-name.

> ripples of the years come wrinkling in,
> as all around needles fall and fall,
> and life thrives on – how much longer yet?
> The Iki Pine:[6]
> that is another tree of lasting fame
> that is another tree of lasting fame!

During the last few lines above, Old Woman moves to corner and Old Man to centre. Both stand facing audience. Tomonari rises.

TOMONARI (*mondō*) Just as I am waiting for someone from the village to appear, here come an old man and an old woman. Excuse me, old people, but I have a question for you.

OLD MAN Do you mean us, sir? What is it, then?

TOMONARI Which of these trees is the Takasago Pine?

OLD MAN Why, the one I am sweeping under now. This is the Takasago Pine.

TOMONARI The pines of Takasago and Sumiyoshi are said to be 'paired', yet this place and Sumiyoshi are a province and more apart. Why is it that they are called the Paired Pines?

OLD MAN The *Kokinshū* preface says that 'the pines of Takasago and Suminoe are felt to be paired'. But I to whom you are speaking come from Sumiyoshi, yonder in the province of Tsu. This old woman is the one from Takasago. [*To Old Woman.*] If you know anything about all this, please say so.

TOMONARI Astonishing! Old people, I see
> that you are a couple, together here,
> though Takasago and far Sumiyoshi,
> by shore and mountain a province apart
> are, so you say, your homes.
> What can you mean?

OLD WOMAN Sir, you ask us a foolish question.
> Though a myriad leagues of hill and stream
> divide them, hearts truly in touch
> do not find the way to each other long.

OLD MAN Just reflect on the matter a little.

OLD COUPLE The Pines of Takasago and Sumiyoshi   *Face each other.*

---

6. A pine said to have been planted on the coast of Kyushu by Empress Jingū (the regent for her husband, Emperor Chūai) when, in the third century A.D., she set off with her army to conquer Korea. The character used to write 'Iki' means 'life'.

bear, all insentient,[7] the name of Paired;
still more then do we, living humans
who, since time out of mind, ply to and fro
between this place and Sumiyoshi:

They turn to Tomonari and step towards him.

yes, we two live in the Pines' company,
an old couple, paired in age.

TOMONARI (*kakeai*) Your story gives me the greatest pleasure.
Tell me then: these Paired Pines
you just spoke of – do people here
draw from them no happy moral?

OLD MAN   In the old days, yes, people used to say
they signify a most blessed reign.

OLD WOMAN Takasago, you see, refers to the distant past of the
Man'yōshū,

OLD MAN and Sumiyoshi, to His Majesty who reigns in the present
Engi age.

OLD WOMAN These pines mean unfailing leaves of speech: words

OLD MAN   whose vigour endures, now as then.

OLD COUPLE Nobly they stand in praise of the reign.

TOMONARI   All you have told me fills me with joy.
No more doubts spring to mind: the sun

OLD MAN   with tempered beams[8] lights the western sea

TOMONARI   that stretches far away to Sumiyoshi

OLD MAN   and washes, here, the Takasago shore

TOMONARI   where the pines wax a deeper green.

OLD MAN   The spring is mild,   *Steps toward Tomonari.*

*Old Man faces audience, Old Woman goes to stand before drums. Tomonari sits at
witness position.*

CHORUS (*ageuta*) the Four Seas[9] calm, the realm at peace.
A timely breeze rustles no boughs

---

7. Generally, in Buddhism, plants were considered to be 'insentient', that is, without
feelings or soul. However, nō plays such as this one show the influence of medieval
Tendai Buddhist thought, which held that 'plants, trees, soil, and land' directly manifest enlightenment.

8. 'Tempered beams' refers to mild spring sunshine, but the original expression is taken
from a widely known Buddhist statement about how the Buddha tempers the radiance of
his enlightenment in order not to alarm sentient beings. The entire statement is quoted
in *Tatsuta*.

9. A conventional Chinese expression that means 'the whole world'.

in this blessed reign:

and that is why, well met indeed,

the Paired Pines display good fortune!

Below, Old Man sweeps past corner and up to base square, then turns to Tomonari.

Truly, no praise can do them justice,

for such a reign brings to us,

our Lord's subjects, all the richness

of His blessing, O the precious gift

of His blessing, O the precious gift!

Old Man sits at centre, Old Woman before drums. Meanwhile, Villager slips in to sit at villager position.

TOMONARI (*unnamed*) Please tell me more about the fortunate meaning of the Takasago Pine.

CHORUS (*kuri*) Now, plants and trees, they say,[10]

Old Man turns to audience.

are insentient beings, yet flower and fruit

never mistake their time.

Suffused with the surging power of spring,

the southern boughs put forth blossoms first.

OLD MAN (*sashi*) Yet this pine looks forever the same.

Flowers and needles distinguish no time.

CHORUS While the four seasons circle by,

the pine's millennial hue remains

deep amid the snow, and the pine's flowers

bloom, so the saying goes, ten times,

once every thousand years.

OLD MAN   For such tidings, yes, one may

pine boughs glow

CHORUS   with ever green

leaves of speech: dewdrop pearls

that in the heart seed polished grace

OLD MAN   until all beings alive,

CHORUS   to the Blessed Isles, they say, draw nigh.[11]

10. The content of these *kuri* and *sashi* passages is generally derived from Chinese poetry, especially from lines included in the *Wakan rōei shū* ('A Collection of Japanese and Chinese Poems for Chanting Aloud', 1013).

11. 'The [Way of] the Blessed Isles' means Japanese poetry. The expression 'Blessed Isles' conveys the spirit, although not the letter, of the name Shikishima, a noble name for Japan. 'Pine', above, is a 'pivot word' meant to convey the original pun on *matsu* ('pine tree' and 'to wait').

(*kuse*) For indeed, as Chōnō wrote,[12]
'All beings, feeling or non-feeling,
have a voice, and that voice is a song.'
Plants and trees, soil and sand,
wind sounds and water noises:
in each one the spirit harbours all things.
Springtime woods swaying to east winds,
fall insects crying in northern dews –
are not both song, our poetry?
The pine among them towers, lordly,
green through a thousand falls,
and shows no hue of new or old:
a tree worthy of that title, 'Marquis',
the First Emperor gave it,[13]
so that in China and in our Realm
all men sing its praise.

OLD MAN Takasago:
hear the voice
of the Hilltop Bell,

CHORUS the long night through
as hoar frost builds apace,[14]

Old Man rises, comes forward to front of stage.

and these pine boughs
yet keep their old, deep green.
Morning and night I rake beneath the tree,   *Mimes raking.*
yet fallen needles never fail, for it is true,
pine needles fall not all at once:
their green only grows
as grows the *masaki* vine,[15]   *To base square.*

12. Fujiwara no Chōnō (949–?) was in his time an arbiter of poetic taste, but no extant work of his contains this passage. A longer quotation from Chōnō, found elsewhere, contains the same one. It seems so typical of medieval thinking that the attribution to Chōnō is probably false.
13. A Chinese story tells how Ch'in-shih-huang-ti, the first emperor of the Ch'in dynasty (3rd c. B.C.) took shelter from the rain under a small pine tree, and how the pine then grew tall to protect him. The delighted emperor conferred a title upon the tree.
14. A poem by Ōe no Masafusa, included in the *Senzaishū* (1188). 'Hoar frost' alludes to the white hair of advanced age.
15. The *masaki* vine, which grows very long, often appears in poetry as a simile for 'an enduring reign'.

the sign of an enduring reign;
and among all evergreens
the Takasago Pine,
in this latter age, signals blessing.   *Sits at centre.*

Chorus sings briefly for Tomonari.

(*rongi*) Yes, justly famed, these pine boughs
justly famed, these pine boughs
tell the old tree's tale.
Now, please, let me know your names!

OLD COUPLE What further need have we for secrecy?
The Takasago and Sumiyoshi   *Turns to Tomonari.*
Paired Pines' spirits, man and wife,
stand before you.

CHORUS Astonishing!
The famed pines display a wonder,

OLD COUPLE and although plants lack sentience,

CHORUS   in this happy age

OLD COUPLE both soil and trees –

CHORUS   land that this is of our own Sovereign [16] –
under His reign wish to live on
and on now let us go to Sumiyoshi
there to wait for you to join us!
So they cry amid the evening waves, [17]
board a fishing-boat and sail,   *At side, mimes doing so.*
before a following breeze,
far, far away across the sea   *To base square.*
far, far away across the sea.   *Exit Old Couple.*

*   *   *

TOMONARI Are you there, either of you?

A COMPANION Here I am, sir, at your service.

TOMONARI Please call someone from this shore.

A COMPANION Certainly, sir. [*Rises, calls.*] Is any villager nearby?

16. This and the preceding line begin a poem cited in a medieval *Kokinshū* commentary: 'Since soil and trees are the land of our great lord, where could a demon ever hide?'
17. The expression 'evening waves' involves a pun, common in nō, on *yū*, which means both 'evening' and 'say'.

VILLAGER [*Rises.*] He's calling for a villager. I'll go and see what he wants.
[*Turns to Companion.*] You are calling for someone from here, sir? What is
the matter?

COMPANION My master wants to ask you something. Please come closer.

VILLAGER Certainly, sir. [*Comes on stage.*]

COMPANION [*Going before Tomonari.*] I have called the person you wished to
speak to, sir.

VILLAGER [*Sits at centre facing Tomonari.*] Here I am, sir, a man from this
shore.

TOMONARI I am Tomonari, the chief priest of the Aso Shrine in Higo
province of Kyushu. This is my first visit here. Please tell us the story of
the Takasago Pine, which stands upon this shore.

VILLAGER That is rather a startling request, sir. It is quite true that I live
nearby, but you see, the story you want to hear is a very, very old one, and
I am afraid I hardly remember it. Still, now that you have gone to all the
trouble of calling me, it would be too bad of me to claim that I do not
know it at all. So I shall tell it to you, sir, just as I have heard it myself.

TOMONARI Please do so.

VILLAGER [*Faces audience.*] First of all, sir, our shore is known for the Takasago Pine, which is this pine tree here. As for the pines being 'paired',
the *Kokinshū* preface states, 'People see the pines of Takasago and Sumiyoshi
as paired.' There are all sorts of trees, of course, but among them the pine
is always green, and lives particularly long. That is why our enduringly
vigorous poetry is compared to the evergreen needles of the Takasago and
Sumiyoshi Pines. Some say the Gods of Takasago and Sumiyoshi are man
and wife, so that when the God of Sumiyoshi visits Takasago, the two
converse through the Sacred Tree. In fact, when the Divine Presence of
Takasago goes to Sumiyoshi, then too, the pair converse through the
Sacred Pine. Since they have been visiting back and forth that way since
time immemorial, we who live here customarily call them 'paired'. The
God of our Shrine here and the God of Sumiyoshi are really supposed to be
one in spirit. Both confer special blessings on those who practise poetry,
and likewise promote the happiness of wedded couples. They say, concerning poetry, that 'pebbles may grow into boulders, dust may pile up into
mountains, and the sands of the shore may all be swept away, but for
poetry, there will always be words'.[18] That, at any rate, is what I have
heard. But I am afraid I do not know what 'paired' *really* means. Naturally,

18. This passage appears in the Japanese preface to the *Kokinshū*.

pines convey the highest good fortune because every inch of a pine is green for ever, and because a pine lives a thousand or ten thousand years; and so perhaps for that sort of reason both Gods planted pines, and the 'paired' refers to their having done so together. Anyway, I gather that both Gods are to go on protecting this spot for a good 5,670,000,000 years.[19] [*Turns to Tomonari.*]

TOMONARI Thank you very much for your excellent account. Actually, an old man and an old woman were here a little while ago, and when I asked them about the Takasago Pine, they told me just the same sort of thing. Then they boarded a little boat that was there on the beach and said they would wait for me at Sumiyoshi. Finally, they sailed out to sea and simply disappeared.

VILLAGER What an astonishing thing to have happened! As I told you a moment ago, sir, the God of Sumiyoshi sometimes manifests himself here at this Shrine. You must have come upon the two Gods as they were sweeping around this tree and actually spoken with them. If they got on board a boat, told you that they would wait for you at Sumiyoshi, and then just sailed away, why, you should go on pilgrimage to Sumiyoshi just as fast as you can. Fortunately, sir, I happen recently to have made a new boat and have not even launched her yet. I had been hoping to have just such a holy person as yourself aboard for my first sail. Since you are a priest of the Aso Shrine, sir, and since on top of that you have just spoken with our own God and the God of Sumiyoshi, you obviously please the divinities. Having you aboard now will mean happy and safe sailing for me for ever and ever. So please, sir, do get in. You are very welcome. I will take the helm and sail you myself to Sumiyoshi.

TOMONARI Very well, then, you others too, please get aboard. We are sailing for Sumiyoshi.

VILLAGER Oh, look! The Gods really are with us! We have a perfect following wind! Quickly, all aboard!

TOMONARI Right you are.

Villager rises, returns to sit for a moment at villager position, then slips out through side door.

*   *   *

Tomonari and Companions stand facing each other along front of stage.

19. This fanciful number is typical of *kyōgen* passages and plays.

TOMONARI and COMPANIONS (*ageuta*) Takasago!
　　　　　　　　Our light craft under all sail
　　　　　　　　our light craft under all sail
　　　　　　　　slips out with the moon
　　　　　　　　rising, the flood-tide swells
　　　　　　　　foam round Awaji Isle,
　　　　　　　　thunder upon Naruo[20]
　　　　　　　　far behind us now, for we skim on
　　　　　　　　to Sumiyoshi where we soon put in
　　　　　　　　to Sumiyoshi where we soon put in.

They sit in witness square.

To deha *music, enter God of Sumiyoshi. He stops on bridgeway, facing audience.*
Throughout this second part of the play, he dances and mimes, making full use of the
stage.

SUMIYOSHI (*sashi*) These eyes of mine
　　　　　　　　first saw you long ago
　　　　　　　　on Sumiyoshi shore –
　　　　　　　　O noble Pine,
　　　　　　　　what aeons have you seen?[21]
　　　　　　　　Ours is a close bond –
　　　　　　　　did you not know?
　　　　　　　　Within the pristine zone,
　　　　　　　　throughout the ages,
　　　　　　dance, strike up the music, and night drums
　　　　　　in rhythm beat: soothe His heart,
　　　　　　ye of the shrine!   *Comes on stage, to base square.*

CHORUS (*ageuta*)   O Western Seas!

---

20. Sailing from Takasago to Sumiyoshi (Osaka) one passes through a strait between the mainland and Awaji (*awa* means foam), a large island in the Inland Sea. Naruo (*naru* means 'to thunder') is a little further along the mainland coast, past modern Kobe.

21. A poem, like the following one ('Ours is a close bond . . .'), from episode no. 117 of *Ise monogatari* ('Tales of Ise', 10th c.). In *Ise monogatari*, the first poem is spoken by an emperor on pilgrimage at Sumiyoshi, and the second is the deity's answer. The emperor marvels at the age of the pine (the deity); while the deity assures the emperor that they are indivisible and that he has always protected the imperial line. Here, the missing last line of the second poem ('I have given you my blessing') has been replaced by 'dance, strike up the music': an appeal to perform sacred *kagura* music for which the deity, in return, will continue to bless and protect the line of emperors. Some medieval commentaries on *Ise monogatari* take the speaker of the first poem to be Narihira, who figures in *The Well-Cradle*. The second poem then means that Narihira, as the supreme poet and lover, is a manifestation of the Sumiyoshi deity.

	Up from the waves
SUMIYOSHI	of Aoki Meadows
	rises in the sight of all [22]
	the God Pine,
(issei)	bringing spring!
	Lingering snows thin down Asaka strand. [23]
CHORUS	Along the beach rich with sleek seaweed,
SUMIYOSHI	Go to a pine's stout root, rub your hips upon it,
CHORUS	and a thousand years' fresh green brims from your hands;
SUMIYOSHI	break off plum in bloom, set the flowers in your hair,
	and snows of the second moon sprinkle your cloak. [24]

(DANCE: *kami-mai*)

Sumiyoshi dances a vigorous kami-mai.

CHORUS *(rongi)*	O wondrous, O divine vision
	O wondrous, O divine vision!
	Beneath a clear moon
	the God of Sumiyoshi dances on,
	while we in awe adore His holy form!
SUMIYOSHI	Many the dances, the dancing maidens'
	voices ring clear as the moon.
	The Sumiyoshi Pine
	stands mirrored in 'Blue Ocean Waves': [25]
	that is the dance now, surely!
CHORUS	For God, for Sovereign, the road runs straight
	to Miyako in springtime,
SUMIYOSHI	when the dance is 'Home to the Palace'.

22. Most of a poem by Urabe no Kanenao in the *Shokukokinshū* (1265). According to the myth recorded in *Kojiki* and *Nihon shoki* (the two early eighth-century histories of Japan), Izanagi, the male of the primordial pair, visited the realm of the dead and then, on re-emerging, purified himself in a stream upon Aoki-ga-hara in Kyushu. From this act of purification were born the triple marine deities subsumed, at Sumiyoshi, under the name 'Sumiyoshi deity'. The 'pristine zone' (*mizugaki*) is the sacred fence around the shrine. The poem's final line (instead of 'the God Pine') is 'the deity of Sumiyoshi', and these words are retained in the Shimogakari version of the text.

23. Asaka-gata is the old name for a stretch of shore near Sumiyoshi.

24. A quatrain in Chinese by Tachibana no Aritsura, in the *Wakan rōei shū*.

25. 'Blue Ocean Waves' (*Seigaiha*) is the name of a *bugaku* dance appropriately performed, with its music, in a deity's honour. 'Home to the Palace' (*Genjōraku*), below, is another such dance. 'Ten Thousand Autumns' (*Senshūraku*), further below, is a highly felicitous *gagaku* musical piece, and 'Ten Thousand Years' (*Manzairaku*) another *bugaku* dance.

CHORUS	They bring endless happy years,
SUMIYOSHI	those dancers in sacred robes:
CHORUS	a hand thrust forth sweeps demons hence,
	an arm drawn in clasps length of days
	and happy fortune.
	'A Thousand Autumns' brings peace to all,
	'Ten Thousand Years' makes life long
	while, touched by the wind,
	the Paired Pines sing, inspiring tranquil joy
	the Paired Pines sing, inspiring tranquil joy.

Sumiyoshi spreads his arms wide towards audience, then turns towards side and stamps a final beat.

Tatsuta

According to surviving records, *Tatsuta* was first performed in 1432, well within the lifetime of Zeami, and its text was among those formally passed on by Zeami to his son-in-law Komparu Zenchiku (1405–1468). Still, the play is almost certainly by Zenchiku himself. A recent study (by Takemoto Mikio) suggests that he must have given it for approval to Zeami, who then touched it up a little and returned it with the group of his own plays. Zenchiku can have been no more than twenty-six years old when he wrote it.

Although *Tatsuta* celebrates the Tatsuta deity, it is not now defined as a god play. A female *shite* like the one in part two is rare in a god play, despite the example of *Kureha*. Moreover, a Buddhist monk is equally rare as a *waki*, and god plays are normally set not in autumn but in spring. However, *Tatsuta* is related to two god plays (*Sakahoko* and *Furu*), and its theme combines literary with profoundly religious themes.

Documentary support for the ideas and imagery in *Tatsuta* exists, but only in scattered fragments, and it is therefore remarkable that Zenchiku's treatment of his subject should have such unity and distinction. The play can be read rather as one might read an iconographically consistent syncretic (Shinto–Buddhist) painting.

A syncretic cult like that of the Tatsuta Shrine, especially by Zenchiku's time, involved a tangled weave of myth, legend, history, dream, and intuition. Buddhist doctrine had its place in the weave, and so did the subtleties of medieval yin-yang lore. The Buddhist and Shinto deities were so unlike each other, and so complex, that centuries devoted to linking them produced a result rather like that achieved by earlier centuries of effort to write Japanese with the desperately unsuitable Chinese writing system. Arbitrary phenomena flourished. Nevertheless, Japanese writing is often beautiful, both as calligraphy and as language, and the same is true of the patterns of intuition woven into cults like that of the Tatsuta Shrine. These patterns are informed above all by conceptions of sacred landscape.

Ideas about Tatsuta could be fluid precisely because what really mattered was the shrine itself, in its landscape setting. *Tatsuta* is grounded in the configuration of this landscape, although Zenchiku clearly shaped the landscape further in order to evoke an ideal. In medieval Japan, one did not use (and might not even know) a deity's name, but referred instead to the name of the place where the deity was enshrined. 'Tatsuta' is a place-name. The deity of such a place was seldom single or simple, and that is why this translation speaks of 'the Tatsuta Presence' (*myōjin*) instead of 'the Tatsuta deity'. 'Presence' is indeterminate with respect to number, as well as to many other qualities or attributes.

The Tatsuta Shrine is located at the north-west corner of the Yamato Plain, the cradle of early Japanese civilization. The traditional date for its founding corresponds to the first century B.C. To the north rise the Ikoma Hills and, to the south, the Katsuragi Mountains. The shrine stands near a gap through which travellers passed on their way between Yamato and the coast of the Inland Sea. That way, too, came the winds from the sea. The shrine was originally dedicated to the deity, or deities, of the winds – storm winds, typhoon winds, and winds that carried (or so people believed) the influences of disease.

Through the same gap flows the Yamato River, the nearby stretch of which is called, in the play, the Tatsuta River. (The modern Tatsuta-gawa, although in the same area, is a different stream.) Not far away, the Hirose Shrine honours the divinities of rain. In medieval lore, Hirose and Tatsuta were one, so that at Tatsuta, too, one could address the water and rain deities. In 1320, *sarugaku* (primitive nō) was performed at the Tatsuta Shrine, as a thank-offering for rain, by the local troupe whose descendants are the present Kongō school of nō.

In the idealized landscape of *Tatsuta*, a mountain rises beside the shrine: a *mimuro no yama*, or sacred mountain. Exactly which one this may be, in sober geography, remains unclear. There is a suitable hill near the shrine, but the play often speaks instead of Hō-zan ('Treasure Mountain'), an old name for Mount Katsuragi, some twenty kilometres to the south. One receives the impression that Hō-zan and the *mimuro no yama* of Tatsuta are identical. It contains the Celestial Spear with which Izanagi and Izanami, the primordial pair, first created the land. (The Villager tells this myth in the interlude.) No doubt this Spear is the mountain's central axis, just as a single pillar is the 'heart' of a Buddhist pagoda.

From high on the mountain, a stream tumbles down towards the valley, forming a waterfall above the shrine. The *waka* section near the end of the play even suggests that the waterfall spills from the lip of the moon. (A waterfall on 'Tatsuta-yama' was known in early poetry, but there is none at the shrine now.) Given no other information, one might wrongly assume from the play that the stream's source is that of the Tatsuta River itself. This is not so, but the misleading impression is probably intentional.

Tatsuta and the anonymous *Sakahoko* ('The Down-Turned Spear') both stress that the Tatsuta Presence protects the Celestial Spear. In *Sakahoko*, the earlier play, the *shite* in part two is an aspect of this Presence: a powerful, chthonic male deity identified as Takimatsuri-no-kami, the 'Divinity of the Rite of the Cascading Waters'. In *Tatsuta*, however, the *shite* of part two is the Presence's female aspect, and the play identifies her, the Tatsuta Lady (Tatsuta-hime), as the red leaves of fall. Red autumn leaves were a favourite topic in poetry, and those of Tatsuta were so famous that merely to mention the name was to conjure up a vision of autumn leaves.

As autumn advances (in poetry), red leaves are scattered from the heights until they cover the Tatsuta River with a seamless 'brocade' that the waters then bear away towards the sea. In the play, a Shrine Maiden warns the Monk, who is about to ford the river, not to tear this brocade. If he does, she says, the Presence will be offended. (The sovereign in *Kureha* would be equally displeased, and for similar reasons, if someone – a rebel, perhaps – tore the brocade that clothes him in his robe of kingship.)

It is significant, with respect to the Tatsuta Lady's nature, that the red leaves weave their pure brocade as they flow down the river. Since the Tatsuta Presence is of water and rain, the Lady is also a water-woman, and water and leaves join in the river-borne brocade. Although beautiful, the Lady, like any Japanese water deity, has a fundamentally dual nature, at once kind and overpowering. The 'Divinity of the Rite of the Cascading Waters' in *Sakahoko* shows her other face. A classical poem about her asks rhetorically: 'Does she become clouds and rain, the Tatsuta Lady, to stain with colour the bright autumn leaves?' (Fujiwara no Shunzei, 1114–1204). She may be the leaves, but secretly, she is also the cold rains that colour them and the wind and waters that carry them away. Her brocade clothes the Spear in time and the passing seasons.

The play shows that this is true by insisting on the cryptic proposition that the Lady 'guards the Spear, protector of the Reign, with red autumn leaves, eight-lobed in form, at the tip of the blade'. Somehow, the autumn leaves – or one ideal leaf – form a bright eight-lobed halo at the tip of the spear. ('Red' and 'bright' are the same word in classical Japanese.) This image amounts to a gloss on the meaning of the river-borne brocade.

The eight-lobed halo of autumn leaves recalls a better-known version of the same pattern: the red, eight-petalled lotus at the centre of the Taizōkai ('Womb Realm') mandala. This mandala, together with its paired counterpart, the Kongōkai or 'Diamond Realm', is a key icon of Japanese Esoteric Buddhism. In the centre of the lotus, and of the whole mandala, is the Cosmic Buddha, Dainichi, whose name means 'Great Sun'. The power present on a sacred mountain was often identified with Dainichi, and for Tatsuta this idea is affirmed in *Sakahoko* and in other medieval documents.

The play's 'Spear . . . with red autumn leaves, eight-lobed in form, at the tip of the blade' is therefore, in Buddhist image-language, Dainichi at the centre of the eight-petalled lotus of the Taizōkai mandala. Consequently, it is also the 'Great Sun' that illumines all 'eight directions' of the world. This is precisely the dream-vision seen by the Monk in part two of *Tatsuta* when, 'this midnight, a bright sun shines'.

At the same time, the Spear is the instrument with which the primordial pair impregnated the deep. The red, eight-lobed halo alludes also to the impregnated womb, or placenta, from which issued that great offspring, the world (Japan) with its ruling line of emperors.

Several of Zenchiku's plays vary freely, in pattern or motif, on plays by Zeami. Examples are *The Wildwood Shrine* (from *The Well-Cradle*), *Oshio* (*Saigyō's Cherry Tree*), or *Teika* (*Kazuraki*). In addition to the obvious connection between *Tatsuta* and *Sakahoko*, *Tatsuta*, too, is a variant on a Zeami play: *Furu*. *Furu* has never been in the active repertoire, but a manuscript of it in Zeami's own hand is dated 1428, four years before the first known performance of *Tatsuta*.

As in *Tatsuta*, the *shite* in part two of *Furu* is a female deity (or a female medium in a state of divine possession); the *waki* is a monk; and the season is late autumn. *Furu* honours the Isonokami Shrine, across the Yamato plain from Tatsuta. The scene of *The Well-Cradle* is nearby.

One day, according to the legend of *Furu*, a maiden of Isonokami was washing a divine cloth in the stream that flows near the shrine.

Behind her loomed the shrine's sacred mountain (Ryūō-zan, 'Dragon King Mountain'), and the cold wind from its slopes brought her the distant yet powerful noise of a waterfall. One recognizes, from *Tatsuta*, the landscape, the woman beside a river, and the divine weave immersed in water. Just then, a divine sword came down the stream and lodged in the cloth. This story is told in part one of the play. In part two, a female divinity dances, holding the sword (according to Zeami's express instructions) with its point enfolded by the cloth. Thus she displays, during her dance, what one can only call the moment of conception. The monk, in whose dream she appears, sees the sword illumine the world exactly as the spear does in *Tatsuta*.

Furu and the Isonokami legend identify no finite offspring from this union, and in this respect, too, *Furu* resembles *Tatsuta*. However, a related legend from the Upper Kamo Shrine in Kyoto takes that extra step. The legend is dramatized in the god play *Kamo*, which may also be by Zenchiku. As a maiden draws water from the Kamo River, intending to offer it to the deity, a divine arrow comes down the current and lodges in her pail. She takes the arrow home, hangs it on the eaves of her house, and soon gives birth to a beautiful son. When her son enters his third year, people ask him, 'Who is your father?' He points to the arrow, which then becomes a thunderbolt and rises up into the sky. The Upper Kamo Shrine honours this fertile thunder deity, who is a major protector of the imperial house. It, too, has a sacred mountain.

In short, *Tatsuta* evokes the fruitful descent of spirit into matter or of the changeless into time. The Monk all but says so in part one, on arriving at the Tatsuta Shrine, for he speaks of the Buddha's descent into the world. A *Lotus Sutra* parable describes how the life-giving rain of the Teaching nourishes all beings impartially. In the play, as in poetry, the autumn rain touches each tree, first staining the topmost leaves. The descent of autumn red towards the lower leaves therefore shows, as the play puts it, 'the divine intention mingling with the dust': the Buddha's influence descending towards the lowliest beings so as to quicken them with aspiration and bring forth from them the 'Buddha-fruit', enlightenment.

The Buddha's descent to 'mingle with the dust' is the fundamental theme of medieval syncretic faith. This faith had reached maturity by Zenchiku's time, and after the fifteenth century its complexities dissolved, slowly, into the twilight of 'folk religion'. About 1870, government decrees destroyed what remained of it by forcibly separating Shinto from Buddhism. Despite the survival of the Tatsuta Shrine itself, *Tatsuta* is a testament to a poetic and religious world now lost for ever.

Although hard to reach except by car, the Tatsuta Shrine (Tatsuta Taisha) still rewards the visitor with its delicate beauty. The 'Rite of the Cascading Waters' is held there each year on 4 April: fish taken from the river are offered at the shrine, then released again, alive. Not far away, another Tatsuta Shrine (Tatsuta Jinja) has served since the time of Prince Shōtoku (574–622) as the local protector (*chinju*) for the famous Hōryū-ji. The two shrines should not be confused. The one near Hōryū-ji is now made of yellow-painted concrete.

Tatsuta

Persons in order of appearance

A Monk	*waki*
Two Companions	*wakizure*
A Shrine Maiden (*Fukai, Zō-onna* or *Ko-omote* mask)	*maeshite*
A Villager	*ai*
The Tatsuta Lady (masked as above)	*nochijite*

Remarks: A third or fourth-category play (*kazura-mono* or *yonbamme-mono*) current in all five schools of nō.

*   *   *

Stage assistant puts a dais before drums and on it places a 'shrine' surrounded by a cloth curtain.

To shidai *music, enter Monk and Companions. They stand facing each other along* front of stage.

MONK and COMPANIONS

(*shidai*) The path of the Teaching opens before us
the path of the Teaching opens before us:
come, offer our land the scrolls of the Law.   *Face audience.*

MONK (*nanori*) You see before you a holy man who is offering the
   scrolls of the *Lotus Sutra* to sacred places throughout the sixty-six
   provinces of Japan. Recently, in Nara, I worshipped at every
   venerable temple and shrine. Now, I am hurrying on over Tatsuta
   Pass towards the province of Kawachi.[1]

MONK and COMPANIONS (*ageuta*) Hallowed in name,   *Face each other.*
                    Nara the Capital recedes behind us
                    Nara the Capital recedes behind us;
                    a daybreak moon lingers in clouds
                    as we pass on by the Great Western Temple,
                    with autumn advancing
                    by Akishino and the foothills beyond
                    to where scarlet leaves   *Monk mimes walking.*
                    glowed but lately, as always in song
                    to Tatsuta River, for we have arrived
                    at Tatsuta River: we have arrived.   *Face audience.*

MONK (*tsukizerifu*) Having come so swiftly, we have already reached
   the Tatsuta River. Let us cross the river and pay our respects to the
   Presence.

Companions sit in witness square. Monk starts to follow them but Shrine Maiden
calls to him through curtain.

MAIDEN (*mondō*) No, no, do not cross the river! There is something I
   must tell you!

MONK How strange! Just as I am about to cross the river and salute
   the Presence, I hear you admonish me to desist. What is your
   reason?

Shrine Maiden advances along bridgeway.

MAIDEN You wish to cross precisely in order to please the Presence, is
   that not so? [*Stops at second pine.*] But should you cross over thought-
   lessly, the bond between the Divine Presence and man would be
   torn. Before crossing, then, reflect carefully on what you do. [*Advances
   once more.*]

MONK Why, yes, I remember the old song:

1. This is roughly the journey taken by Narihira in episode no. 23 of *Ise monogatari*
('Tales of Ise', 10th c.) and evoked in *The Well-Cradle*. The travellers pass Saidai-ji ('the
Great Western Temple', now a major stop on the Kintetsu Electric Railway), beyond the
western confines of medieval Nara. The locality of Akishino, with its own temple, is
nearby. They then turn south-west along the hills and pass (although the play does not
say so) the famous Hōryū-ji before reaching Tatsuta.

Tatsuta River:
red leaves in profusion
follow the stream:
but cross – the brocade
will surely be torn.[2]

Are you suggesting that I should take this warning seriously?

MAIDEN I am indeed. The song means that when the red leaves fall and float away down the river, they resemble an expanse of brocade; so that if someone crosses, the brocade will be torn. But there is a much deeper meaning as well. [*Stops in base square, facing Monk.*] The red leaves of fall, you see, are the Shrine's divine treasure. The song also warns against offending the Presence.

MONK (*kakeai*) That is most interesting. On the other hand, the time of red leaves is now past, and the river is covered by a sheet of thin ice. There is not a ripple to be seen. Please let me proceed, for I do wish to cross. [*Begins walking.*]

MAIDEN No, no, that is only one more reason to take care. There is a second warning that the ice, too, will be torn.

MONK How extraordinary! And what is this warning, that if not the brocade of red leaves, then the ice will be torn?

MAIDEN The song of the red leaves was by an emperor, but there is another, later one by Ietaka:

Tatsuta River –
thin ice has arrested
the red autumn leaves:
but cross, and it too
will surely be torn.[3]

This second song, by the poet, shows that the warning applies not only to the autumn leaves.

As Chorus sings, below, Shrine Maiden moves about and mimes, using the full stage; as the passage ends she returns to base square.

CHORUS (*ageuta*) The ice as well
will surely be torn on the Tatsuta River
will surely be torn on the Tatsuta River,
spread with brocade that the Tenth Moon weaves

2. A poem included in the *Kokinshū* (905), together with the note, 'Said to have been composed by the Nara Emperor.' The identity of this emperor is uncertain.
3. Fujiwara no Ietaka (1158–1237), a major poet and one of the compilers of the *Shinkokinshū* (1206). This poem appears in *Minishū*, his personal collection.

till winter sets in: forbear a while,
lest this thin ice that arrests the red leaves
be cruelly torn.
O heartless, the man who would cross now!
Besides, they do say,
peril awaits one who treads on thin ice:
the proverb is true, as you now clearly see
the proverb is true, as you now clearly see!

MONK (*mondō*) May I ask you who you are?

MAIDEN I am a shrine maiden in the service of the Presence. If you wish to worship at the Shrine, I will gladly guide you there.

MONK How wonderful! Then I will follow you.

Monk and Shrine Maiden go to stand before the shrine.

MAIDEN (*mondō*) You see before you the Divine Presence of Tatsuta. Worship, then, with all your heart.

Shrine Maiden sits at centre, Monk at witness position.

MONK How very strange! This eleventh month is the month of frosts, when all the leaves are gone from the trees and the Shrine is left stark and bare; yet here I see a single maple[4] covered with glorious red leaves. Is this the Shrine's Sacred Treasure?

MAIDEN Yes. You see, at the Miwa Shrine in this same province, the cedar is the Sacred Tree;[5] while here at our own Shrine, the Divine Presence favours red leaves. Revere this maple, then, as our Sacred Tree.

MONK How fortunate I am, that my travels through the provinces should have brought me today to encounter this noble Divinity! Oh, how wonderfully fortunate! 'The Tempering of the Light and the Merging with the Dust initiate the Link with Enlightenment; the Achieving the Way through all Eight Phases finishes accomplishing all creatures' weal.'[6]

4. The original does not name the tree, but one cannot translate the sentence without doing so. 'Maple' is the inevitable choice in English. In fact, however, the tree is probably a *hahaso*, a species of oak often mentioned in poems about Tatsuta. The *hahaso*, too, reddens nicely in autumn.
5. The Miwa Shrine honours a sacred mountain across the Yamato Plain from Tatsuta and south of Isonokami. Its 'cedar' is the *sugi* (cryptomeria).
6. This statement is often quoted, in whole or in part, in medieval literature. It is from fascicle six of *Makashikan* (Ch. *Mo-ho-chih-kuan*, 'The Great Treatise on Cessation and Contemplation'), by Chigi (Chih-i, 538–597), the Chinese founder of Tendai (T'ien-t'ai) Buddhism. It means that the Buddha tempers his light so as not to blind and confuse sentient beings with the full radiance of his enlightenment. Instead, he manifests himself

CHORUS (*uta*)   The red autumn leaves low on the trees
are the divine intention mingling with the dust,[7]
while the Tempered Light deepens in hue –
O Divine Presence, protect us now!

(*ageuta*)   Now I am come at last into the Presence
now I am come at last into the Presence,
yet with no streamer wand, alas, to offer,[8]
be kind, rushing winds, spare these red leaves,
themselves offerings fit to please the God,
a Divine Presence breathing pure peace,[9]
Tatsuta Mountain looms dimly yonder,
the River tranquilly murmurs on
amid the shades of evening.

Below, Shrine Maiden moves around stage as though visiting each sanctuary of the Shrine. Monk remains in place, although he is felt to move with her.

(*uta*)   Come! let us start our round of the Shrine!
Far-famed in song, ah, Tatsuta Mountain:
as once red leaves, the maiden now holds
glossy green sakaki boughs,
bright skirts asweep, gay sleeves displayed,
leading the round from altar to altar,
with reverent mien, until, strange to tell,
she who had seemed to serve the Shrine
declares: In truth, I myself am the God.
Yes, I am the Tatsuta Lady.   *Turns to Monk.*
Now she is known, she blazes with light.
Veiled behind her scarlet sleeves,
she flings the sacred portals wide
and at last withdraws into the Shrine
and at last withdraws into the Shrine.   *Does so.*

---

in various familiar forms (such as the native divinities of Japan) and so makes the thought of enlightenment accessible to all. Then, by accomplishing the eight phases of a buddha's career (descent from the Tosotsu Heaven, conception, birth, taking religious vows, conquering illusion, attaining enlightenment, teaching, and entering nirvana), he extends his enlightening influence to all beings.

7. These two lines are from a verse by the linked-verse poet Kyūsei (1284–1378).

8. A visitor to a shrine would normally offer *nusa* or *gohei*, sacred objects composed of paper streamers attached to a wand or to a branch of the broadleaf evergreen sakaki. The sacred tree with its red leaves is itself a sort of *gohei*.

9. This line goes with the lines both above and below it.

*   *   *

Villager enters and stands in base square.

VILLAGER You see before you a man who lives in the village of Tatsuta. It has been ages since I last went to the Shrine, so today I am on my way there. [*Sees Monk.*] Ah, there is a monk I have not seen before. Reverend sir, where are you from?

MONK I am a holy man, and I am offering the scrolls of the *Lotus Sutra* to sacred places throughout the sixty-six provinces of Japan. Do you live nearby?

VILLAGER Yes, reverend sir, I do.

MONK Then please come closer. I have a request to make of you.

VILLAGER By all means. [*Sits at centre.*] Now, what is your request?

MONK A rather curious one, perhaps. The red leaves of fall are greatly honoured at this Shrine, you see, and I would like you to tell me all you know about the reason why.

VILLAGER You are right, reverend sir, that is a curious request. Even we villagers who live near the Shrine know very little about such things. Still, it would be too bad of me, the very first time we meet, to claim I know nothing at all. So I will tell you the story as I have heard it myself.

MONK I will be very grateful.

VILLAGER Here, then, is an account of the Divine Presence of Tatsuta, in the province of Yamato. The Presence issues from the City of Primordial Light, tempers the radiance of Enlightenment, becomes manifest at this spot, and protects our Sovereign Lord. They say also that Izanagi and Izanami, the divine pair who were the seventh generation of the Celestial Gods, stood on the Floating Bridge of Heaven, and from there thrust down the Celestial Spear. As with the Spear they probed the depths of the sea, it struck against something that proved upon inspection to be a reed. Drops from the Spear congealed into islands: those we call the Land of Reed Plains, or the Land of Yamato.[10] Now, having conjoined, the divine pair engendered one daughter and three sons. These we call Kuninushi, that is, Sovereign over the Land – meaning the Heaven-Illumining Goddess of Ise.[11] The Spear we name Ame-no-sakahoko, or Heaven's Down-Turned

10. Yamato is a noble name for Japan.
11. Kuninushi ('Lord of the Land') is well known as a separate deity. The proposition that he is somehow the three children of the divine pair, and that these children are somehow Amaterasu (the Sun Goddess enshrined at Ise) is thoroughly confusing.

Spear. It is stored nearby in Treasure Mountain, and they say the Presence of our Shrine protects it.

Now, you wish to know why the maple in red autumn foliage is our Shrine's Sacred Tree. The Spear's tip was eight-lobed, you see, so that the maple leaves follow the same pattern and have eight lobes as well. That is why the Divine Presence so favours the red maple tree.

Furthermore, we have here at Tatsuta a spot well known as Mimuro-no-kishi, the Riverbank of the Sacred Dwelling. In late autumn, the red leaves, which fall only to be borne away on the waters of the Tatsuta River, look just like an expanse of brocade. No one crosses the river then, for to do so would displease the Presence. Actually, our Shrine rules the four seasons. Spring is the Saho Lady, summer the Lady of Ikuta, and winter Kasuga, Complete in Mercy's Works; while our Shrine especially governs autumn.[12] At any rate, all this is what I have been told. But what makes you ask? I do find your request surprising.

MONK Thank you very much for your excellent account. This is why I questioned you. A short while ago, when I was about to cross the Tatsuta River and salute the Divine Presence, a young woman appeared as it were from nowhere. She recited several old poems for me and led me round the Tatsuta sanctuaries. Then she declared that she herself was the Tatsuta Lady and vanished into the Shrine.

VILLAGER What an astonishing thing to have happened! Then the Divine Presence of our Shrine must have taken temporary form as a shrine maiden and come before you to act as your guide. You must stay here a while longer, reverend sir, for I think that you will soon see another wonder.

MONK Then I will do so.

VILLAGER If you should need anything at all, please let me know.

MONK Thank you very much.

VILLAGER Very well.   [*Exit.*]

*   *   *

Monk and Companions are seated as before.

MONK and COMPANIONS

(*ageuta*) In night-long vigil before the Presence

12. The source for these associations with the seasons is unclear. The nō play *Saho-yama*, which celebrates the Saho Lady, resembles *Tatsuta* in style and may also be by Zenchiku. Saho is close to Kasuga, while the Ikuta Shrine is in modern Kōbe.

in night-long vigil before the Presence,
let us await now the promised vision,
spreading lonely sleeves in uneasy rest
spreading lonely sleeves in uneasy rest.

To deha *music, Tatsuta Lady speaks from within the shrine.*

LADY (*kuri*)   The Gods accept no breach of the rites.
How pure thy source, O Tatsuta River!

CHORUS   Powerfully the sanctuary creaks and quakes[13]
as shrine priests beat resounding drums.

LADY   Moon in the dawn sky, brilliance of torchlight,

CHORUS (*noriji*)   tempered light mingling with the dust,
gleam warmly on the vermilion fence[14]
as the Sacred Treasure stands revealed anew.

(THE LADY APPEARS)

Stage assistant removes curtain from shrine, revealing the Lady within, seated on a stool.

LADY (*sashi*)   To this very day, since time began,
in these Dragonfly Isles[15] I make this place mine,
guarding the Spear, protector of the Reign,
with red autumn leaves, eight-lobed in form,
at the tip of the blade.
Such dharma-might does he display,
the Ascetic who bears the Sword,[16]
that, this midnight, a bright sun shines.[17]

CHORUS (*kuri*)   Now, in the God of the Divine Cascade
we have the Sacred Presence of our Shrine.
Of old, the Ancestor aloft in the Sky[18]

13. This is a well-attested sign of divine pleasure in offerings of music and dance.

14. Many shrines, including Tatsuta, have red-painted sacred fences around their sanctuaries.

15. A possible meaning of Akitsushima, a poetic name for Japan.

16. This 'Ascetic' appears to be the Monk, whose 'dharma-might' (spiritual power) has called this fortunate vision into being. The expression is from *Furu*, where the identity of the *waki* explains it. In *Tatsuta*, however, it is excessively cryptic. The sacred object of the Isonokami Shrine is a sword.

17. This line recalls Zeami's image (in *Kyūi shidai*, 'The Nine Grades of the Actor's Art') for artistic perfection: 'Silla [i.e. Korea] at midnight: the sun is bright.'

18. The 'Ancestor aloft in the Sky' is the deity Kunitokotachi who decreed that Izanagi and Izanami, the divine pair, should rule the land, and who gave them the Spear. The story appears in *Jinnō shōtōki* ('A Chronicle of Gods and Sovereigns', 1339) by Kitabatake Chikafusa.

gave a decree bright with hope for our land.

LADY (*sashi*) So to Treasure Mountain at last the Spear came,

CHORUS witness to a Reign when peace prevails
in Heaven as on Earth.
Tranquil the people, and prosperous withal:
the thanks for this blessing belongs to our Shrine.

LADY The colour of fall upon trees far and wide
displays ten thousand autumns [19] before our eyes.

Tatsuta Lady rises, comes forth from the shrine, dances to the singing of the Chorus.

CHORUS (*kuse*) Year after year
the red leaves flow,
O Tatsuta River:
do you then run
down to the haven of fall? [20]
The Mountain rises, still, while the sea,
all along the coast, heaves with gentlest swells:
such autumn scenes inspire pure joy.
Known in song and story, the mountain wind
down Tatsuta's slopes blows quietly now.
Age upon age, the poets of old,
suffused their hearts with the red of the leaves.
Morning mists upon Tatsuta Mountain,
rising in spring, have nothing of fall,
yet a poet, in love with scarlet, wrote:
Ah, how this morning
the Tatsuta cherries
glow with rich colour,
dyed in long sunsets,
like leaves in autumn rains! [21]
Lines like his betray a heart touched,
like the leaves themselves, with autumn's bright hue.

LADY Below the Mountain,
the God's Riverbank
must be crumbling now:

19. In other words, an eternity of bountiful harvests.
20. A poem by Ki no Tsurayuki, included in the *Kokinshū*.
21. A poem by Fujiwara no Motoie (1203–1280), included in *Shirin saiyō shō* (*c.* 1365).

CHORUS   the Tatsuta River
                    is running clouded,[22]
                yet the Tempered Light as always shines
                clear, the moon of truth illumines as ever
                the Tatsuta River, where not long ago
                red leaves ran in rich profusion.
                Brocade they were then, now fall leaves frozen over –
                and O how lovely, aglow with what colours,
                the red maple leaves overlaid by thin ice!
                Should anyone cross,
                ice and leaves at once will surely be torn.
                Who then could bear to be so cruel?

LADY *(suso-guse)* So through the hours the God's night-music
CHORUS   so through the hours the God's night-music
                rings out till soon the last note is played;
                the priests' drums cease their beat and fall still.
                Moonlight on frost: the snow-white wands
                wave on aloft, while voices resound:

In base square, Lady shakes a gohei *(sacred streamer) wand.*

LADY   *(ei)* *We offer with all respect*
CHORUS   *obedience renewed . . .*[23]

    (DANCE: *kagura*)

Lady dances a kagura *dance, first holding the wand, then simply her fan.*

LADY *(waka)* From lofty heavens the Divine Cascade
                spills, with bright moonlight,
CHORUS   dashing waves high
LADY   before the Tatsuta Presence[24]
CHORUS   before the Tatsuta Presence

Lady comes to front of stage. She dances and mimes throughout final passage.

       (noriji) as red leaves fall.
LADY   Offering wands
CHORUS   stream in the wind that, down Tatsuta Mountain,

22. A poem by Takamuku no Kusaharu, included in the *Shūishū* (late 10th c.).
23. A formula of salutation to the gods. It appears also in *Lady Han*.
24. These waves that splash high before the Tatsuta Presence suggest the motif of a waterfall reversing its flow in the presence of intense spiritual power. The reversed flow, or rising aspiration to enlightenment, complements the descent of saving influence emphasized elsewhere in *Tatsuta*.

	sweeps the sound of autumn rain.
LADY	Bell-rattles, jingling,
CHORUS	ring out over the river,[25]
LADY	the rapids white as festival flowers.
CHORUS	A divine wind, a wind in the pines

A divine wind, a wind in the pines
gusts and whirls,
gusts and whirls, and the red leaves fly.
Sacred cocks, paper streamers trailing,[26]
flutter past billowing sacred robes:
We offer with all respect obedience renewed,
obedience renewed,
countless voices cry;
as with mountains, rivers, plants, and trees,
all the land at peace,
the God ascends[27] and is gone.

Facing side, stamps the final beat.

25. 'Bell-rattles' are *suzu*, still an essential instrument in dances performed for Shinto deities.
26. Cocks were sacred to the gods at Tatsuta, as well as at Ise and elsewhere. At Tatsuta, sacred paper streamers really were attached to cocks on the occasion of important festivals.
27. This is the standard expression used to describe the departure of a deity from a medium's body.

Yamamba · THE MOUNTAIN CRONE

There is no serious doubt that Zeami wrote *The Mountain Crone*. In fact, in *Sarugaku dangi* ('Conversations on nō'), he mentioned having performed it for the Shogun at the Shogun's special request. Some scholars have doubted that he also wrote the *shidai–kuri–sashi–kuse* sequence in part two, since the play itself describes this as an existing *kusemai* (a dance-and-song form popular in Zeami's time). However, the weight of opinion now holds that the whole play, including the *kusemai*, is a fiction made up by Zeami himself.

One scholar (Nishino Haruo) described the entire play as a model of Zeami's late style, since it so clearly manifests his principle (mentioned in his late treatises) of *kyakurai*, or 'returning'. Zeami came to hold that the actor who has mastered the highest flower of his art should then return to disport himself among the lower, less refined styles of nō. For him, one of these styles was that of the *oni* ('ogre' or 'demon') play. The earlier Zeami had little use for *oni* plays, despite their popularity, because an *oni* is neither beautiful nor elegant. In *The Mountain Crone*, however, he gave a female *oni* figure awesome dignity and linked her with the very sources of art.

In *Sarugaku dangi*, Zeami described *The Mountain Crone* as a play 'with detours', as distinguished from a 'straight' play like, for instance, *The Well-Cradle*. It is not hard to grasp, in general, what he meant, or to see that these 'detours' help to create an impression of massive richness unique among Zeami's works. Another aspect of this richness is intellectual. Not that Zeami's plays do not often have intellectual depth, but *The Mountain Crone* comes close to having a message. The play's *kusemai* sequence, like that of *Eguchi*, is profoundly Buddhist. Towards the end of his life, Zeami became more and more interested in Zen, and *The Mountain Crone* seems to show this influence. However, the play does not preach, and Zeami's statement, if he really meant to make it, clearly goes beyond words. One shrinks from defining what *The Mountain Crone* is about. The following discussion, like a particular route up a mountain, is only one approach.

What is the 'Mountain Crone'? The Japanese term, *yama-uba* or Yamamba, appears to mean (judging from the character used to write *uba*) 'old woman of the mountains'. In fact, however, an *uba* may be a good deal livelier than an 'old woman', or 'crone', as the play itself shows. One authority (Origuchi Shinobu) connected Yamamba with a possessed female medium and wrote that *uba*, when applied to a medium, should actually refer to a fairly young woman. The Yamamba of the play wears the *Fukai* mask, the face of a woman in her forties, but it is obvious in any case that no mask could show all her faces.

Legends about Yamamba occur in many regions of Japan. An early mention of her, roughly contemporary with Zeami, includes a major trait that Zeami left out: she gives birth to strange children in the mountain wilderness. These may be goblin-like beings (*tengu*) who then rule certain peaks and leave giant, mysterious footprints in the snow. Mountain deities in Japan are often understood to be female, but they need not have human form. The motif of childbearing (according to the folklorist Yanagita Kunio) connects the Mountain Crone with wolf deities that also bear their pups in secret places in the mountains. Sometimes such a wolf manifests itself to humans as an old woman. Legends about Yamamba usually occur together with legends about Yama-otoko, the 'Man of the Mountains', but Zeami omitted any allusion to this figure. Yamamba sometimes does terrible things and merits the term 'ogress' (*kijo*) that describes her in the play. At other times, however, she bestows good fortune, and she certainly allows herself to be honoured in village festivals.

Yamamba's most interesting single trait in the play is that she sometimes leaves the mountains in order to lighten the woodcutter's load or to speed on the work of the weaver. Zeami may have invented this idea. A single eighteenth- or early nineteenth-century document (cited by Yanagita Kunio) says the same thing in a few words, but this work is an archaizing forgery that may well draw on the play.

The mountains are thought in Japan to be 'another world' inhabited by the spirits of the dead and of other trans-human or non-human powers. When Yamamba comes down from the heights to help people, she crosses a critical boundary. The same boundary is crossed, in the opposite direction, by the Dancer of the play when she enters the mountains on her pilgrimage to Zenkō-ji. In these mountains, the Dancer meets Yamamba. However, the Dancer's name is also Yamamba. What is going on?

Any answer should fully acknowledge the Dancer's role. As explained in the introduction to *The Fulling Block*, Japanese critics tend not to do this because it is understood that the *shite* (here, the Mountain Crone) is the 'sole actor' in a play. The result is an exclusive concern with the *shite* figure's own mental or spiritual state. A recent interpretive essay on *The Mountain Crone* (by Sagara Tōru) ignores the Dancer, except as a sort of prop, and discusses Yamamba's 'wrongful clinging' that keeps her from enlightenment. The conception of the *shite* as 'sole actor' compelled the essayist to treat Yamamba as though she were a person, when she is not.

However little the Dancer may have to say, she and Yamamba are counterparts of one another. They are paired opposites. Medieval Japanese Buddhism was intensely concerned with the play of paired opposites (such as delusion and enlightenment) and constantly affirmed their non-duality. Its vocabulary supplies several paired terms with which to discuss the issue. 'Subject and object', 'emptiness and form', 'true dharma and dependent dharma', and 'seed and fruit' are all possibilities. They are not all the same, but all would do equally well in the present case, since *The Mountain Crone* is art, not a technical treatise.

'Seed and fruit' make a good choice. 'Seed' (*in*) refers to pattern, potential, and the aspiration to enlightenment; 'fruit' (*ka*) to matter, manifestation, and the realization of enlightenment. Which precedes the other is a matter of opinion, since different Buddhist lines took opposite positions on the issue.

The Dancer from the capital corresponds roughly to this 'seed'. Her *kusemai* about Yamamba has won her Yamamba's name, but she has never seen Yamamba's world. Her dance apparently conveys the true pattern of Yamamba's existence, but she is understandably overwhelmed when faced with the full manifestation of what it so artfully evokes. However, she began, unknowingly, to seek this confrontation when she conceived the aspiration to enlightenment and set out on her pilgrimage. The play makes her religious seriousness quite clear.

Yamamba, for her part, is rather like the 'fruit'. Being all the mass and variety of untamed nature, she has never been to the capital or seen the pattern of her own existence. She is angry with the Dancer for having taken her name without due acknowledgement, but, at the same time, she is eager to 'hear the power of my own name' – this name being, in truth, the *kusemai* itself. Yamamba even promises the Dancer that she will 'shadow' her dance, that is, dance beside her, perfectly imitating her. Her wish to know the dance has its counterpart in the Dancer's religious aspiration.

In the play, the Dancer does not actually dance at all. Instead, Yamamba dances (for the audience) the great *kusemai*. Still, she learned it from the Dancer. How did the Dancer conceive it? At the prompting of the mountains' majesty, even if she knew this majesty, like enlightenment, only at second hand. And how did the mountains give birth to her dance? By finding a mind to have it born from . . . It is hard to say which has precedence, Yamamba or the Dancer.

None the less, Yamamba complains of suffering from 'wrongful clinging', and the opening lines of the *kusemai* speak of her 'rounds of the mountains, made in pain'. Rather than invoke Buddhist maxims like the non-duality of suffering and enlightenment, it is better to admit that existence really does involve pain. Yamamba exists, and although she seems at one point to be only 'clouds and waters', even clouds and waters may labour in their rise and fall. The Dancer, too, has suffered, or she would not take the difficult road over The Tops and meet Yamamba. Moreover, when at last she sees the mountain wilderness, she surely realizes with mingled terror and awe that she had never known what her own *kusemai* was actually about. Yamamba herself then appears – she who, in part two, seems less to suffer from 'wrongful clinging' than to *be* this clinging, as conjured up in a sentient being's mind.

To what does a deluded sentient being cling? To sights, sounds, and so on: the objects of sense and desire. Of course, it is not the fault of these objects ('nature') if sentient beings become attached to them. But what of sentient beings who *create* objects of sense – singers and dancers? Are they not doubly sinful for being attached to the senses themselves and then seducing others into the same attachment?

This was a critical question for medieval Japanese artists and poets, who often recalled, as Zeami did at the end of *The Mountain Crone*, a statement written by the T'ang poet Po Chü-i (772–846) when he presented a copy of his works to a Buddhist temple: 'I pray that the karma of profane letters in this life, and the error of foolish words and pretty language, shall turn and become, in my future life, the seed of praising the Buddha and the occasion of turning the Wheel of the Law.' Po Chü-i hoped that his poems were not, at heart, just glittering vanities, speaking only of himself or of themselves, but that they contained, after all, a redeeming seed of selfless truth.

Perhaps the Dancer, when she sees the wilderness, suddenly knows with awful certainty that her *kusemai* is only 'foolish, pretty words', a bauble and nothing more; then Yamamba is before her, terrifying. But when she and Yamamba dance, and Yamamba sings the Dancer's song, seed and fruit conjoin. The song becomes transparent, praising the Buddha and turning the Wheel of the Law (proclaiming the Buddha's message). Still, this turning of the wheel is not different from the Dancer turning her sleeves, or Yamamba turning round the mountains. The *kusemai* is still a 'song that takes us round this world with all its sorrows': the song of one whose work, however painful, is still praise and testimony to higher truth.

No wonder the woodcutter's load is lightened when Yamamba, invisibly, joins him, and no wonder the weaver's shuttle flies. They, too, are singing. They are like all the figures in these plays who, through their work, come to know beauty – like the saltmakers in the *rongi* of *Pining Wind*, who 'draw [the moon's] reflections, ah, with keen delight!' Yet if the weaver actually saw Yamamba (as Yamamba herself says), she would be terrifed. She would have stepped back from her song and seen, suddenly, only herself. The difference between the error of foolish words and pretty language and turning the Wheel of the Law is that between the bounded and the open view, and it is all the difference in the world.

No sentient being can sustain for ever the open view. As the *kusemai* says, 'Once [there is a] Buddha, then all beings; and once all beings, the Mountain Crone.' Work goes on, whether or not with a song. Doubt and attachment go round and round. But sometimes the clouds clear, the view opens up, and work and worker are one. The Dancer sees at last the truth of her own dance, and once the Mountain Crone has seen that same dance, her rounds of the mountains become pure poetry, as she pursues blossoms and the moon. The fusion of her labour with the beauty of the seasons, in the closing lines of the play, sums up the aim and nature of classical poetry. In *The Mountain Crone*, Zeami showed that the poet or dancer's work, despite all doubts, really does bring comfort to us all.

Agero (The Tops), the site of the play, is a little basin in the mountains of extreme south-western Niigata Prefecture, about seven kilometres from Sakai-gawa (Border River). Beyond the mountain to the north-west, sheer cliffs plunge down to the Japan Sea. On the mountain, but visible from Agero, Yamamba's Dancing Rock affords a magnificent view. Nearby is Yamamba's Cave. Down in the tiny hamlet, shrines honour Yamamba and Tengu-sama, her husband. The fame of *The Mountain Crone*, combined with folkloric nostalgia, seem to have drawn renewed attention recently to Agero. A trail is being cleared up to Yamamba's Cave, and in 1984, a stele was erected at the entrance to the hamlet. It reads, 'The home of Yamamba'.

A newspaper article on the local Yamamba legend (summarized by Nakamura Kyōzō) states that Yamamba wandered to Agero from the capital in the Tengen era (978–983) and settled down to live in the cave, together with a fabulous boy named Kintoki. She was so ragged and dishevelled when she reached the hamlet that the people feared her, but her elegant dancing won her their admiration. As they watched her from below in the hamlet, dancing before her cave, they thought she must be an elegant Miyako courtesan or perhaps a great lord's wife. Presumably this legend is inspired by the play itself – unless, to the terror of those who write essays on *The Mountain Crone*, the truth is really the other way round.

THE MOUNTAIN CRONE

Persons in order of appearance

A Dancer from Miyako (*Ko-omote* mask)	*tsure*
Her Attendant	*waki*
Two or three Servants	*wakizure*
A Woman of the mountains (*Fukai* mask)	*maeshite*
A Villager	*ai*
The Mountain Crone (*Yamamba* mask, long black wig)	*nochijite*

Remarks: A fifth-category play (*kiri-nō*) current in all five schools of nō. A variant performance tradition (*kogaki*) in the Kanze school changes the play into a god play: to the *shidai* sung by the Chorus in part two are added the words, 'The blossoms and autumn leaves of Yoshino and Tatsuta, the moon and snow of Sarashina and the Northern Marches'; after which the Mountain Crone dances a *chū-no-mai*. In the Kanze, Komparu and Kongō schools, the Mountain Crone may wear a white wig rather than a black one, in which case the play acquires greater dignity since the *shite* is then truly an ancient woman.

There is also a variant interlude tradition in which the Villager tells a different set of stories about the origins of the Mountain Crone.

*   *   *

To shidai *music, enter Dancer, Attendant and Servants. They stand facing each other along front of stage.*

ATTENDANT and SERVANTS

(*shidai*)   Thou Good Light! Thy glow we trust

Thou Good Light! Thy glow we trust,

Lord Buddha, whose temple is our goal.   *Face audience.*

ATTENDANT (*nanori*) You have before you a man who resides in Miyako, and the lady whom you see, too, is Hyakuma Mountain Crone,[1] a dancer renowned far and wide. The young men of Miyako dubbed her Hyakuma Mountain Crone because she made up a *kusemai* song and dance piece about the Mountain Crone's rounds of the mountains. Now she has declared her wish to go on pilgrimage to Zenkō-ji, the Temple of the Good Light. We are therefore setting out with her for Zenkō-ji this very day.[2]

ATTENDANT and SERVANTS

(*sashi*)   Miyako drops behind, and ripples now   *Face each other.*

1. Zeami invented the courtesan's sobriquet, Hyakuma Yamamba. Hyakuma (or Hyakuman) was the name of the founder of the line of woman *kusemai* dancers, and would naturally have been passed down to the dancer of the play. 'Yamamba' would then have been added to her name because of her own accomplishments.
2. Zenkō-ji, a pilgrimage centre dedicated to Amida (the Buddha of Infinite Light), is in present Nagano City, Nagano Prefecture (old Shinano province). The travellers leave Miyako over Ōsaka Pass and descend to the southern Shiga coast of Lake Biwa. (*Sazanami ya*, 'O ripples', is a set phrase attached to the name Shiga in poetry.) A boat takes them to the lake's north-east corner, whence they continue on into Fukui Prefecture (Echizen) over the Arachi mountains. Descending the Hino-gawa valley, they pass modern Fukui City (Tamae Bridge, the *tama* of which means 'dewdrop') and reach the Japan Sea at Shiokoshi, a river-mouth on the border with Ishikawa Prefecture (Kaga). The pines of Shiokoshi had been sung by Saigyō. On the coast near the present Komatsu City in Ishikawa Prefecture, they pass the Ataka Barrier, made famous by an incident in Yoshitsune's flight towards the north. Eventually, at the level of modern Kanazawa City, they turn east, cross the steep Kurikara Pass below Mount Tonami (a tunnel now cuts under it) and come down into Toyama Prefecture (Etchū), thinking all the time of their long road through the Three Marches (Mikoshiji), the provinces of Echizen, Etchū, and Echigo. They cross Toyama Prefecture, eventually reaching Toyama Bay and following the coast on to Boundary River (Sakai-gawa) on the border with Niigata Prefecture (Echigo). From there, they could continue along the coast and turn south toward Zenkō-ji up the valley of the Hime-gawa, but instead, they will take a path over the mountains via Agero (The Tops).

　　　　　lap the Shiga coast we sail along,
　　　　　on to Arachi and pass the mountains,
　　　　　with dewy sleeves cross Tamae Bridge
　　　　　while, still ahead, to the northern marches,
　　　　　our thoughts fly down an endless road.

(ageuta)　Through the trees, waves break on Shiokoshi
　　　　　through the trees, waves break on Shiokoshi,
　　　　　while the pine of Ataka, at evening, looms
　　　　　in smoke that lingers like our sorry lives,
　　　　　tangled with sin that Amida's sword alone
　　　　　cuts: sharp soars Mount Tonami, above,
　　　　　urging us on by pathways through the clouds
　　　　　across the Three Marches, an exhausting road,
　　　　　until we ask what place this is:　　*Attendant mimes walking.*
　　　　　yes, Miyako is far behind us now
　　　　　for Boundary River is where we have come
　　　　　Boundary River is where we have come.　　*Face audience.*

ATTENDANT *(tsukizerifu)* Having travelled so swiftly, we have already reached Boundary River, between the provinces of Etchū and Echigo. From here on, there are several ways we might take, I must ask someone from the locality for advice. [*To Dancer.*] Please sit down here.

Dancer sits at witness position, Servants nearby. From base square, Attendant calls to Villager, who by now has slipped in to sit at villager position.

ATTENDANT *(mondō)* Is anyone from Boundary River nearby?

Villager stands.

VILLAGER You wish to speak with someone from Boundary River? What is it you want?

ATTENDANT We are a party of people from Miyako, and we would be most grateful if you would tell us the way from here to Zenkō-ji.

VILLAGER Oh, I see. There are three ways to go from here: the high road, the low road, and the passage over The Tops. The Buddha himself blazed the trail over The Tops, which means that one trip that way is worth any number of trips by another route. The passage over The Tops, you see, puts you in touch with the Buddha's own inner illumination. On the other hand, it's a much rougher and steeper way than the others. Ah, I see you have an elegant lady with you. You can't possibly get a litter up there, I'm afraid.

ATTENDANT Thank you for your kind help. Please wait a moment while I ask my mistress's opinion.

VILLAGER Please do so.

Villager returns to villager position. Attendant sits at centre, facing Dancer.

ATTENDANT Excuse me, but I asked about the way to Zenkō-ji and was told that there are three routes: the high road, the low road, and the passage over The Tops. The trail over The Tops was blazed by the Buddha himself, but unfortunately, one cannot possibly get a litter up it.

DANCER In truth, the Western Paradise we hear of so often is said to lie some hundred billion leagues from here.[3] So if this passage over The Tops is a direct path to Amida's welcome, then it is the route we must take. It is a penance after all, this pilgrimage of mine. I will leave my litter here and continue on foot. Please be my guide.

ATTENDANT I will transmit your message. [*Returns to base square.*] Is the man I just spoke to still there?

VILLAGER [*Rises.*] Here I am, sir.

ATTENDANT I told the lady what you said. She answered that she would leave her litter here and proceed on foot. She would like you to be her guide.

VILLAGER Of course, you don't know the way, so you need a guide. But I have urgent business to look after. I'm afraid I can't help you.

ATTENDANT Despite your refusal, I really must repeat my request. Please, will you not be our guide?

VILLAGER Well, I understand your difficulty. I'll drop everything and guide you after all. Let's be on our way.

ATTENDANT Thank you very much. [*Once more sits at centre facing Dancer.*] We have our guide. Let us start immediately.

Dancer and Servants stand in witness square, Villager in base square, and Attendant before Chorus.

VILLAGER Look! Isn't the path even steeper than I said?

ATTENDANT It certainly is.

VILLAGER This is why I told you you could never get a litter up here. Goodness, how strange! It seems somehow to be getting dark!

ATTENDANT So it is.

VILLAGER But it's not *supposed* to get dark now. How very strange!

3. Amida's Western Paradise was conventionally said to be a vast distance away, but a counter-convention, well known in medieval times, had it here, 'within us'.

ATTENDANT Do you think we might find lodging somewhere nearby?

VILLAGER Oh no, there's nowhere to stay anywhere near here.

Woman's voice calls from behind curtain.

WOMAN Come, come, travellers! I will give you lodging!

VILLAGER Wonderful! She'll give us lodging, she says.

Villager sits at villager position. Woman comes through curtain and starts down bridgeway.

WOMAN They call these mountains The Tops. The nearest settlement is far away, and since the sun has set, please be good enough to pass the night in my modest hut.

ATTENDANT That is very kind of you. We will be happy to do so.

Woman comes on stage and sits at centre. Attendant, Servants, and Dancer sit in place. They are in the hut.

WOMAN I have a particular reason for offering you lodging tonight. Please sing me your song about the Mountain Crone! For years and years I have longed to hear it. Think how a countrywoman like me will treasure this memory! It was for this that I made the sun go down and offered you my hospitality. Do please sing me the song.

ATTENDANT I can hardly believe my ears! Who on earth do you think we are, that you should now wish to hear *The Mountain Crone*?

WOMAN Why are you keeping it a secret? Is not that lady over there the celebrated dancer known as Hyakuma Mountain Crone? Now, the song begins,

> Well then an ill way,[4] Mountain Crone's
> rounds of the mountains . . .

Wonderful, wonderful! Of course, the lady's name is a nickname taken from the song. But do you know, sir, what the real Mountain Crone is like?

ATTENDANT The Mountain Crone is an ogress who lives in the mountains, as the song itself makes perfectly clear.

WOMAN 'Ogress' means a female ogre, I suppose. Well then, ogre or

---

4. The song begins, *Yoshi ashibiki no yamamba . . . Yoshi* means 'Well!' or 'Fine!' or 'Come now!' and suitably prefaces a vigorous dance piece; but it is also the adjective 'good'. *Ashibiki no* is a conventional epithet, of uncertain meaning, attached to the word *yama* ('mountain'), which is a part of the name Yamamba; however, *ashi* by itself is the adjective 'bad'. The syllables *yoshi ashi . . .* therefore mean also 'well and ill', 'good and evil'. The same play on words occurs elsewhere in nō, and in *The Mountain Crone* it is much more important than the more obvious meanings of *yoshi* and *ashibiki no*. This translation attempts at least to hint at it.

human, as long as I am female and live in the mountains, the song is about me, is it not?

> Year after year, your words, bright-hued,
> leaf out, dew laden, while in your heart
> you care not one drop for *me*.

[*Turns to Dancer.*] I resent it, and have come to tell you so. [*Faces forward again.*] You have reached the peak of your art and made a great name. For you, the marvellous flower of worldly glory has opened wide, and all – you must agree – thanks to this one song. But had you given me comfort and guidance, and with the magical sounds of dance, song, and music commended me to all the Buddhas, why should I myself not have escaped the wheel's turning[5] and attained to the bliss of perfect knowledge?

> (*sageuta*) Yes, anger will out over darkling ranges
> bird and beast cries rise: the Mountain Crone,
> an ogre phantom, is now before you.

DANCER (*kakeai*) An astounding speech! In short, the real Mountain Crone has come to this spot?

WOMAN
> In my rounds of the mountains from land to land,
> this day I have come, to hear the power
> of my own name.
> Sing then, I beg you, if only in kindness:
> dispel the gloom of my wrongful clinging!

DANCER After such an appeal, I cannot refuse. I tremble to think what horrors might assail me, should I even try.

> This is all so sudden! Yet I will catch
> the right mode for the hour,[6] and strike up the beat . . .

WOMAN
> No, please stop! Since you are willing,
> wait for the dark, and with moonlight voice,
> sing to me then: for if you will,
> I will show my true form.
> Ah, look there! The moon is rising;

> (*ageuta*) and not only the moon,
> for over these mountains that night soon must swallow
> over these mountains that night soon must swallow,

5. The turning of the wheel of transmigration.
6. The mode of music was to be adjusted according to the time, season, and setting. The same expression, at a similar moment, occurs in *Benkei Aboard Ship*.

Woman rises. Henceforth, her movements powerfully underscore the text.

> clouds are building: gaze upon them
> as, the night through, you sing the song
> of the Mountain Crone:
> for I, the while, shall show my true form,
> and, sleeve to sleeve, shadow your dance![7] –
> cries she (does she not?) and suddenly,
> like a flame snuffed out, is gone
> like a flame snuffed out, is gone.   *Exit.*

*   *   *

Villager stands in base square.

VILLAGER Well, I was right after all! The night's over. What a very strange thing to have happened! I knew the sun oughtn't to have set as it did a while ago, and sure enough, there it is, high in the sky! I've never seen such a thing before. It's a mystery, that's what it is! [*Sits at centre facing Attendant.*] I beg your pardon, sir, but the night is over.

ATTENDANT So it is. How very strange!

VILLAGER I *knew* it was too early for sunset, and there you are: the sun is still high in the sky. When it got dark a while ago, I was sorry I hadn't put you up in Boundary River. I was afraid my bringing you up here had caused you a good deal of trouble. But now the night's over, I feel much better.

ATTENDANT Is this something that happens from time to time in these mountains? And, by the way, can you tell me what the Mountain Crone actually is?

VILLAGER Oh no, sir, I live right by these mountains, and I've never seen anything like this before. As to the Mountain Crone, Boundary River is close to the heart of the mountains, as you know, but I'm not much up on all that. Still, I *have* heard a few stories, and I'll gladly pass them on to you. The most popular theory is that the Mountain Crone is a mixture of all sorts of things. Her head, first of all, is an old crocodile gong that's hung far too long in a neglected mountain shrine.[8]

ATTENDANT Really? How can that be?

---

7. The Woman promises to dance an *utsuri-mai* with the Dancer: a dance in which she will follow the Dancer's every movement.

8. A 'crocodile gong' (*waniguchi*) was hung at a shrine or temple associated with mountain ascetic practice (*shugendō*), and mountain ascetics dealt with magic and the occult. An old shrine with a *waniguchi* would have been particularly spooky.

VILLAGER Well, sir, a crocodile gong, as I'm sure you're aware, is called that because of its big, grinning mouth. That mouth makes the mouth of the Mountain Crone. Her eyes are acorns, her nose is a walnut, her ears are toadstools, and her hair is vines. Her body, they say, is rather peculiar. Balls of pine resin from up on the high peaks all tumble together, then gales bowl them along till they bump into the crocodile gong head I just told you about, and stick. After that, the whole thing rolls on some more, picking up dust and trash, till it becomes simply enormous. And that, they say, is what turns into the Mountain Crone. To me, the idea sounds quite plausible.

ATTENDANT I find it highly implausible.

VILLAGER But people insist it's true, as far as I know. Personally, though, I can't say whether you're right or wrong to doubt it. Anyway, they also say that what turns into the Mountain Crone is the egress of fortifications built back in the mountains.

ATTENDANT Really? Why is that?

VILLAGER Well, you see, first they build themselves a gate for egress, and then they don't maintain it. They just let it go, with the doors and everything all rotting away till nothing's left but the posts. Then moss grows on the posts; eyes, nose, mouth, ears, arms, and legs pop out; and there you have the Mountain Crone. To me, that sounds convincing.

ATTENDANT Preposterous is the word I would choose.

VILLAGER No, no, because that's why they describe the Mountain Crone as an egress in the mountains.

ATTENDANT Surely you mean an *ogress* in the mountains.

VILLAGER Oh dear, oh dear, I had it all wrong, didn't I! I'm so glad to have met a Miyako man and at last got the story straight. Anyway, there's supposed to be one more thing that turns into the Mountain Crone, but I've forgotten what it is. Ah, now I remember! It's a wild yam.

ATTENDANT A wild yam?

VILLAGER Yes. Day or night, you see, whenever there's a downpour, some- where in the mountains there's bound to be a landslide. The slide leaves a nubbin of yam exposed, and as the nubbin weathers, its whiskers – yams have whiskers, you know – its whiskers bleach into white hair. The yam itself makes the body, and bit by bit the eyes, ears, nose, arms, and legs stick themselves on too, till you have the Mountain Crone. I don't doubt that's the way it happens.

ATTENDANT I hardly think so.

VILLAGER You don't believe that one either? People insist it's true, but I must admit that the part about the yam is pretty hard to swallow. Anyway, I don't know where the Mountain Crone comes from, but I certainly wonder what's the name of that lady over there.

ATTENDANT That is the celebrated dancer known as Hyakuma Mountain Crone.

VILLAGER Hearing that name reminds me of something. You know the woman we saw a little while ago? The last thing she said was that if this lady would sing her *The Mountain Crone*, she would show her true form. If you'll excuse my giving you advice, sir, I think the lady ought to go ahead and sing. Then you may see the real Mountain Crone.

ATTENDANT Thank you very much for your suggestion.

Villager withdraws to villager position and soon exits.

*   *   *

DANCER (*unnamed*) She whose strangeness so perplexed me,
I was unable to think her real,
surely now will keep her word,

ATTENDANT and SERVANTS
(*ageuta*) for wind through the pines
joins flutes blowing limpid notes
all along the stream,
where hands detain the drifting cups:[9]
moonlit music, pure, across deep ranges
moonlit music, pure, across deep ranges.

To issei *music, enter the Mountain Crone, leaning on a stout staff. She stops at first pine.*

CRONE (*unnamed*) Awesome they are, the plunging chasms
Awesome they are, the plunging chasms!

(*sashi*) In charnel grounds demon phantoms
scourge their own bones, weeping, weeping,
raging at their past lives' deeds;
in graveyards thankful angel beings
offer flowers, suffused with gladness

---

9. An allusion to *kyokusui no en* ('the feast of the meandering waters'), at which cups of wine were set floating down a stream. A participant had to compose a Chinese poem before a cup drifted past, then pluck the cup from the stream and drain it.

at the bliss of truth attained.[10]
No, good and evil are not two:
why then feel anger, why rejoice?
All is of this world before our eyes:
quick rivers stretch away,
mighty scarps soar sheer.
(*kuri*) Mountain upon mountain:

(QUASI-DANCE: *tachimawari*)

To music, the Mountain Crone performs a slow but powerful tachimawari *circuit of the stage, still leaning on her staff, and ends in base square. (Some modern performances omit this* tachimawari.)
what craftsman sculpted the green crags?
Water upon water:
in whose house was dyed the blue abyss?[11]

DANCER (*kakeai*) O terror!
        Moon-hidden deeps of mountain gloom
        now yield a shape alien to see!
        Are you then the Mountain Crone?

CRONE   Some time past my words leafed forth
        to bear first fruit: a sketch of me
        you doubtless recognize.
        Do not be afraid!

DANCER   Come, then, though I tremble still,
        through the jet-black veil of darkness,
        you, human in form,

CRONE   yet crowned with a snarl of snowy weeds:

DANCER   whose pupils shine like stars,

CRONE   whose face in hue

DANCER   glows ruddy bright

CRONE   as any red-daubed demon tile
        glowering from the eaves.[12]

DANCER   My eyes have not seen this sight before,

10. The six preceding lines appear to be drawn from a Buddhist sermon, although no source for them is known. This *sashi* passage is sung but is not in verse.
11. This *kuri* passage is a poem in Chinese by Ōe no Sumiakira (d. 950), included in the *Wakan rōei shū* ('A Collection of Japanese and Chinese Poems for Chanting Aloud', 1013).
12. A 'demon tile', adorned with a frightening monster's face, terminated each ridge-line of a roof, at the eaves. It was supposed to repel evil influences.

CRONE	and it recalls
BOTH	how long, long ago
CHORUS (*ageuta*)	a demon in one gulp, that stormy night
	a demon in one gulp, that stormy night,
	swallowed a cowering girl as thunder roared [13] –
	ah, terrifying!
	Her feelings now are mine, her fate my own,
	and soon my sorry tale, like hers, will be,
	to my shame, upon the lips of all
	to my shame, upon the lips of all!
CRONE (*kakeai*)	A single hour of one spring night
	I would not trade for a thousand in gold:
	so the poet sang, to praise
	the scent of flowers and pure moonlight.[14]
	For now, by rare good fortune,
	my long-held wish is met:
	you, this hour, are here with your song.
	Come then, quickly, sing!
DANCER	Your urging leaves me no excuse.
	O beyond words, this mountain scene
CRONE	where piping birds beat their wings,
DANCER	drums are waves of cataracts,
CRONE	sleeves, gleaming white
DANCER	snow swirling down from trees in bloom!
CRONE	What is there that is not the Law?

Stage assistant now takes the Crone's staff and gives her a fan. She goes to base square.

CHORUS (*shidai*)	Well then an ill way, Mountain Crone's
	well then an ill way, Mountain Crone's
	rounds of the mountains, made in pain!

Crone moves to centre and sits on a stool.

CRONE (*kuri*)	Now, mountains rise from dust and mud,
	till drifting clouds embrace thousandfold peaks;

13. An allusion to episode no. 6 of *Ise monogatari* ('Tales of Ise', 10th c.). Narihira (if it was he) had made off in the dead of the night with a noble lady. When a storm broke, he put the lady in a ruined storehouse that happened to be nearby and stood guard in the doorway. Alas, when the storm was over, he found the lady gone. A demon had eaten her. (Another, excessively complicated allusion to the same story has been omitted.)

14. The poet was the Sung poet Su Shih (1036–1101). These famous lines are quoted also in *Eguchi* and in *Saigyō's Cherry Tree*.

CHORUS oceans drip from dewy moss
    till billows crease the multitudinous seas.

CRONE *(sashi)* Calls from the valley, wholly empty,
           scatter echoes from each twig,

CHORUS   till through sound the ear hears silence.
           'Give me a valley not ringing with calls':
           a wish, surely, for this place.[15]

CRONE   Witness the view from these, my mountains:
           noble summits and, close by, the sea;
           deep-cleft valleys and distant streams.

CHORUS Before, the ocean rolls its boundless waters,
    the moon aloft lifting high the light of truth;
    behind, huge pines tower from beetling crags,
    their wind's song shivering dreams of eternal bliss.

CRONE Bulrush whips rot away till fireflies rise free;

CHORUS alarm drums gather moss till birds take fright no more:[16]
           lines like these speak of this place, too.

        (kuse) Among the hills
                where near and far
                to the eye seem one,
                a little bird
                calls mournfully,[17]
        its note quivering in the heart;
        or perhaps an axe rings out
        and the mountain stillness grows.[18]

Still seated, the Crone begins to underscore words with miming movements.

        Peaks that are Truth, soaring aloft,
        display the upward urge to perfect knowledge;
        lightless valleys, cleft to awful depths,

15. A wish expressed in a Buddhist text known in Japan as *Shichinyo-kyō*, 'The Sutra of the Seven Women', and included in several Zen collections. The god Indra gave seven wise women each a wish. The first asked for a tree without root, branch, or leaf . . . and the third for a valley where the ear heard no calls. Indra was unable to grant such wishes.

16. The six preceding lines are based on a passage in *Gempei jōsuiki* ('The Rise and Fall of the Minamoto and Taira', early 14th c.), an epic text related to *Heike monogatari*. The last two of them quote from a poem in the *Wakan rōei shū*. The 'bulrush whips' are those used to punish criminals.

17. An anonymous spring poem in the *Kokinshū* (905).

18. These two lines are from a single line of a poem by the great Chinese poet Tu Fu (712–770).

show the Teaching pouring from on high
to touch the golden disc beneath the world.[19]

She stands, then begins to dance and mime.

Now, to speak of the Mountain Crone:
born nowhere, she has no home.
Clouds and waters bear her on
to seek out each mountain's last recess.

CRONE   See her, then, as alien,
CHORUS   and clouds that screen the distant view
shift their form:
for a while their nature changes
and as one thought transmutes existence,
an ogress looms from them to fill your gaze.
Yet, see the unity of right and wrong,
and 'Form is emptiness'[20] is obvious.
For once there is a Buddha's Law,
there is a Worldly Law;[21]
once suffering, highest knowledge;
once Buddha, then all beings;
and once all beings, Mountain Crone.
Willows are green, yes, and flowers red.[22]
And when she tarries in the human realm,
she may, as on a forest trail
woodcutters rest beneath the blossoms,
shoulder their heavy load and, with the moon
rising, leave the hills to see them home.
Or she may pass in through the window
where a weaving maid has stood her loom
and, nightingale, the willow-weaver,[23]

19. According to Buddhist cosmology, the world rests upon a golden disc. 'Peaks that are Truth' (*hosshō mine*) are mountains that directly demonstrate the truth of the Buddha's teaching.
20. A statement from the highly philosophical *Heart Sutra*, a short Buddhist text widely known in Japan.
21. The Buddha's Law is his 'way' or teaching; the Worldly Law is the 'way' of the profane world.
22. A well-known Buddhist saying, known in China as well: things simply are as they are.
23. An anonymous *Kokinshū* poem evokes the image of the *uguisu* warbler (the poetic counterpart of the nightingale) weaving a spring hat of willow fronds and plum blossoms.

                    seat herself in the spinning room,
                    only to help the work along —
                    invisible, though were she seen,
                    an ogress, certainly.

CRONE   World-worn and
                    cicada-shell hollow
                    gown of Cathay![24]

CHORUS   Unswept sleeves gather glistening rime,
                    moon-frosted the cold night long,
                    as flagging beaters break to rest, still,
                    thousand, million-voiced,
                    the fulling blocks beat as before:
                    the Mountain Crone, toiling on!
                    Go home to Miyako and tell the tale!
                    Or is this wish still wrongful clinging?
                    Then let it be, for all, in truth, is
                    well then an ill way, Mountain Crone's
                    rounds of the mountains, made in pain!

CRONE   (*ei*)   Yes, those endless rounds of mountains . . .

   (QUASI-DANCE: *tachimawari*)

   In base square, the Mountain Crone receives her staff, then does a vigorous
   tachimawari *circuit of the stage.*

   (*unnamed*)   One tree's shade, one river's flow:
                    both are links from other lives!
                    And our bond is closer still
                    when my name beneath the moon
                    I hear the song that takes us round[25]
                    this world with all its sorrows:

   At centre, she drops to one knee, facing Dancer.

                    the path of foolish, pretty words
                    that leads us on to praise the Buddha's Way![26]

24. These all but untranslatable lines convey the weariness and sorrow of those who, in autumn under the full moon, beat a robe upon the fulling block. Frost gathers, unhindered, on the beater's sleeves that shine white in the moonlight, until, worn out, the beater pauses to rest — yet the block beats on.

25. 'I hear' goes with both 'name' and 'song'.

26. These two lines are discussed in the introduction. They refer to lines by Po Chü-i (772–846), included in the *Wakan rōei shū*.

O how I hate to leave you!

Below, she dances out the final lines.

CRONE   Now I must be off, back to the mountains,

CHORUS   in spring to watch, with bated breath,
               every tree for those first signs

CRONE   of the blossoms I pursue
               all around the mountains;

CHORUS   in autumn to seek glorious light

CRONE   and the best view of the moon
               all around the mountains;

CHORUS   in wintertime, to welcome cold,
               the lowering rainclouds,

CRONE   then the snow, all around the mountains,

CHORUS   round she goes, as ever bound
               to the wheel of birth and death,
               for wrongful clinging swells to clouds,
               and clouds into the Mountain Crone,
               a fearsome demon bulk.
               That you might see her well,
               she soared up peaks, echoed down valleys,
               and just now seemed present here,
               yet mountain after mountain, mountain rounds
               mountain after mountain, mountain rounds
               she follows and is lost to view.

Facing side from base square, she stamps the final beat.

Yashima

Yashima is almost certainly by Zeami, and its beauty is matched only by the thoughtfulness with which it treats the theme of war. Just as Hanago, in *Lady Han*, rises above the usual limits of the 'madwoman' role, so the Yoshitsune of *Yashima* rises above his counterparts in other warrior plays – not because he is braver than they, but because he is still more universally human.

In *Yashima*, as in *Atsumori* and *Tadanori*, Zeami developed a passage of the epic *Heike monogatari* ('The Tale of the Taira', 13th–14th c.). The Taira clan had ruled in Kyoto for a generation when, in 1183, the approach of the rival Minamoto forces put them to flight. The next year, Yoshitsune led a daring attack to rout them from their camp on the shore at Ichi-no-tani (*Atsumori* and *Tadanori*). The Taira took to their ships and sailed across the Inland Sea to Yashima, on the northern coast of Shikoku, where, early in 1185, Yoshitsune's courage and cunning routed them again. This time, they fled south down the Inland Sea. Later that year, a fleet under Yoshitsune attacked them at Dan-no-ura, at the southern tip of Honshu, and destroyed them for ever. Dan-no-ura is evoked briefly at the end of *Yashima*.

Not only *Heike monogatari* but other, specialized, oral narratives made the battle at Yashima famous. Before Zeami's time, there was probably a *dengaku* play (an early variety of nō) on the theme. An incident told in part one of *Yashima*, the death of Satō Tsuginobu, appears in several nō plays and in various folk performing traditions as well. The struggle between Mionoya no Shirō and Kagekiyo, also told in part one, was equally well known. So was the feat of the Minamoto archer Nasu no Yoichi who, from horseback, shot a fan displayed on a Taira ship offshore. Although *Yashima* omits this incident, it may be told in a special version of the interlude known as *Nasu no katari* ('The recital of Nasu's feat'). *Nasu no katari* is a show-piece for a virtuoso *kyōgen* actor and can easily overshadow the main play.

Zeami's treatment of such familiar material is unique. In *Heike monogatari*, the relevant incidents occur in this order: the death of

Tsuginobu, Nasu no Yoichi's feat, the encounter between Mionoya and Kagekiyo, Yoshitsune's dropped bow. The play, however, has Mionoya and Kagekiyo, the death of Tsuginobu, (Nasu's feat), the dropped bow. Moreover, Zeami eliminated most details of the action. His editing suggests a special purpose.

In *Heike monogatari* (Book 3, the 'Ariō' chapter), a man who has landed on the shore of a remote volcanic island quotes to himself a phrase from the *Lotus Sutra*, 'The Ashuras dwell beside the vast sea', then goes on to reflect that 'the hellish realm of the Ashuras lies between great mountains and the ocean'. The Ashuras are the warring demons of Buddhist teaching. They inhabit a realm of transmigration immediately below the human, and their struggles, endlessly poised between victory and defeat, take place (according to the passage just quoted) between the peaks and the abyss. Their landscape is therefore that of *Yashima*, which is set on the shore beside steep volcanic hills. A gentler version of this landscape is seen in *Pining Wind*. *Yashima* resembles *Pining Wind* in structure and language; it is like a transposition of *Pining Wind* into a different key. *Pining Wind* evokes romantic longing, *Yashima* the martial calling; one, a quintessentially feminine life between 'the seas and mountains of birth and death' and the other, a life quintessentially male.

The playwright carefully demonstrates in *Yashima* the hopeless symmetry of Ashura conflict. The Taira–Minamoto encounter, as told in part one, proceeds as though the two forces were mirror images of one another. (This is true of Tsuginobu's death as well, although the mirror-symmetry is not fully stated in the play.) When Noritsune (the Taira commander) tried to shoot Yoshitsune, Satō Tsuginobu, one of Yoshitsune's cherished lieutenants, interposed his own body and was killed. Then Noritsune's equally cherished page, Kikuōmaru, rushed to take Tsuginobu's head but was shot in turn by Tsuginobu's brother. At this, 'Perhaps because sorrow had touched both sides, the fleet withdrew to sea, the army to camp . . .' It is as though sorrow has dispersed the mirror of war, leaving emptiness and silence. However, the mirror reappears near the close of the play, when Yoshitsune cries (remembering Dan-no-ura): 'Who today is my Ashura foe? What? Noritsune, Lord of Noto?' One expects a direct encounter with Noritsune, and the text does go on to evoke the 'thundering clash, counterclash' of the two fleets. However, what actually happened between Noritsune and Yoshitsune was quite different (see note 12, below). Zeami took what he needed from his source and left the rest.

Between the two scenes of symmetrical conflict, at Yashima and at Dan-no-ura, Zeami placed the moment when Yoshitsune dropped his bow into the sea, then risked his life to keep it out of enemy hands. This is another side of war: not the clash of balanced forces but a man's insistence on honour. The bold Yoshitsune was physically small, and his bow was one that any man could draw. According to *Heike monogatari*, he told his men after the incident that if his bow had been as powerful as his uncle's, he might even have dropped it into the sea on purpose, just to impress the enemy.

The hero of a warrior play normally triumphs or, more often, dies in battle; but in *Yashima*, Yoshitsune does neither. Instead, he gallantly risks all for a slight purpose: to prevent the enemy learning the banal truth about his physical strength. In the battle scenes of *Yashima*, and in the closing words of the play, Zeami suggested that final victory or defeat elude the warrior for ever. Thanks to the scene of the dropped bow, however, the play conveys both the absurdity of the warrior's struggle and the generosity of his motives. It is no mean feat.

Yashima is a steep volcanic peninsula, 282 metres high, that juts out into the Inland Sea between modern Takamatsu City and Shido Bay (the scene of *The Diver*). A long inlet runs down the peninsula's east side, and beyond it the rock rises precipitously once more to over 300 metres. The inlet is now known as Dan-no-ura; perhaps the name alludes to the much greater sea battle fought far to the south. The events of the clash at Yashima took place near the head of this inlet, on the east side. Monuments great and small still commemorate them. Yoshitsune entrusted the care of Tsuginobu's soul to a priest of Yashima-dera, high on the peninsula, and the graves of Tsuginobu and Kikuōmaru are not far away. A stele marks the spot where he dropped his bow.

Yashima

Persons in order of appearance

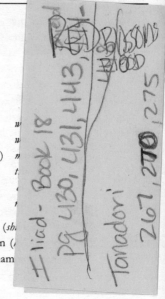

A Monk
Two Companions
An Old Man, a Fisherman (*A sakura-jō* mask)
A young Fisherman (not masked)
A Villager
Minamoto no Yoshitsune (*Heida* mask)

Remarks: A second-category or warrior play (*sh...*
schools of nō. A variant performance tradition (*...*
the Villager narrate a celebrated feat by the Minam...

*   *   *

To shidai *music, enter Monk and Companions. They stand facing each other along front of stage.*

MONK and COMPANIONS

(*shidai*)   Southward the moon over ocean plains
southward the moon over ocean plains
sails and we follow to Yashima shore.   *Face audience.*

MONK (*nanori*) You have before you a monk lately come from Miyako. Never having seen Shikoku, I have set my heart on a pilgrimage through the provinces of the west.

MONK and COMPANIONS

(*ageuta*)   Mists of spring!   *Face each other.*
Waves dance while our ship skims on
waves dance while our ship skims on
westward towards glowing sunset clouds,
and we sail, intent on distant skies,   *Monk mimes walking.*
down sea lanes that seem never to end,
until we reach at last Yashima shore
until we reach at last Yashima shore.   *Face audience.*

MONK (*tsukizerifu*) Having come so swiftly, we have already reached Yashima shore, or so I understand it is called, in the province of

Sanuki. Now that the sun has set, we might as well go up to this salt-house and spend the night here.

They sit in witness square.

To issei music, enter Fisherman followed by Old Man. They stop at first and third pines and stand facing audience. Both carry fishing-poles.

OLD MAN (*sashi*) Such beauty! Moonlight on the sea
          turns billows to night fires.

FISHERMAN An old fisherman, with dark, puts in to the west bank;

OLD MAN At dawn, he draws water from the Shō and lights bamboo of So:[1]

BOTH   a scene now come alive.   *Face each other.*
            The rush fire's glow
            hints at eerie sights, half-seen.

    (*issei*) Moonrise, flood tide, the rolling sea:

FISHERMAN in mist our skiff glides with the oar   *Face audience.*

BOTH   till seafolk's voices reach us: *Face each other.*
            the village is at hand.

To ashirai music they come on stage, Fisherman to centre and Old Man to base square. They face audience.

OLD MAN (*sashi*) A leaf-like skiff roams ten thousand leagues –
          for will, only the wind in its one sail.

FISHERMAN In the twilight sky, cloud billows

BOTH   vanish with the moonrise; through the mist *Face each other.*
            pine woods loom, mirrored in deep green.
            Sea and shore fuse, on and on
            to Tsukushi this same ocean runs.[2]

    (*sageuta*) Here at Yashima, along the beach,
            seafolk's homes crowd, numberless,

    (*ageuta*) while fishing keeps us tossing on the waves
            fishing keeps us tossing on the waves.
            All veiled in haze the ocean deep
            where fishing-craft gleam, vague in lingering light.
            The shore winds blow on, soft and mild,
            as to the heart spring comes beckoning
            as to the heart spring comes beckoning.

1. A couplet quoted from a poem by the T'ang poet Liu Tsung-yüan (773?–819). The Shō (Hsiang) River is a tributary of the Yangtze, and So (Ch'u) is the name of the region through which it flows.
2. Tsukushi is a poetic name for Kyushu.

OLD MAN (*tsukizerifu*) Let us go straight back to the salt-house and rest.
Old Man sits on a stool before drums, Fisherman sits directly on stage just behind him to the right. Monk rises and faces audience.

MONK (*mondō*) The owner of the salt-house has returned. I will go and ask him for lodging. [*Turns to Old Man.*] I beg your pardon, there in the salt-house! May I disturb you?
Fisherman rises and steps forward.

FISHERMAN Who is it?

MONK I am a monk on pilgrimage through the provinces. My companions and I would appreciate lodging for the night.

FISHERMAN Please wait a moment. I will give the owner your request. [*Turns to Old Man and goes down on one knee.*] I beg your pardon, but a traveller is here. He says he and his companions need lodging for the night.

OLD MAN What is that? A traveller is here and says he wants lodging for the night?

FISHERMAN Yes.

OLD MAN That would be simple enough to grant him, were it not that the interior of our salt-house really is too poor. No, please tell him that we cannot have him and his companions to stay.
Fisherman rises and turns to Monk.

FISHERMAN Excuse me, but when I asked about lodging for you, the owner said the interior of our salt-house really is too poor. He said we cannot have you and your companions to stay.

MONK No, no, we have no objection to the poverty of the place. We are from Miyako, you see, and this is our first visit to this shore. Now that the sun is down, we hardly know what to do. Please try asking once more.

FISHERMAN Certainly. [*Turns to Old Man, goes down on one knee.*] When I passed on your answer, the traveller said he was from Miyako and begged me, since the sun is down, to try asking you again.

OLD MAN What? You say the traveller is from Miyako?

FISHERMAN Yes, he is.

OLD MAN Why, that is most distressing! [*To Monk.*] We will give you lodging.

FISHERMAN So poor a place, this rush-thatched hut –

OLD MAN   but let it pass for your wayside rest.

FISHERMAN Still, recall:

Neither shining clear

OLD MAN	nor clouded quite,	
	a veiled moon	
BOTH	makes a spring night	*Face each other.*
	peerless in all the world,[3]	

though comfortless our rough-made home

Old Man, abandoning stool, sits directly on stage facing Monk.

CHORUS (*uta*)   at Yashima, the mighty pines
spread the forest floor
with a simple mat of moss.

Monk steps forward a little and sits. He is now in the hut. Old Man turns to audience while Fisherman goes to sit before Chorus.

(*ageuta*)   Yet we have pleasures: there, down Mure Shore
yet we have pleasures: there, down Mure Shore
cranes cluster in flocks – see, them, see!
Will *they* not return to their cloud dwelling?[4]

Ah, travellers, when I hear your home	*Faces Monk.*

is no less than Miyako, I am so stirred!
We ourselves, long, long ago . . .

But choked with tears, he can say no more	*Weeps.*
choked with tears, he can say no more.	*Faces audience.*

During these last lines, Villager slips in to sit at villager position.

MONK (*unnamed*)   Please forgive me – I know this is hardly a subject a monk ought to bring up, but I understand that the Minamoto and the Taira fought a battle on this spot. Would you pass the time tonight by telling us the tale?

OLD MAN   I would not have expected your request, no. But since I can offer you no better entertainment, I will gladly tell you the story. [*Sits at centre on a stool, facing audience.*]

(*katari*)   Now, it was the first year of Genryaku,[5]
the third moon, the eighteenth day.
The Taira fleet was riding a hundred yards offshore
when the Minamoto burst on to the beach.
Their field marshal, in red brocade,
and clad in armour bound with purple cords,

---

3. A poem by Ōe no Chisato (late 9th c.), included in the *Shinkokinshū* (1206).

4. This 'cloud dwelling' (*kumoi*) is not only the sky, but a poetic name for the imperial capital or palace. The Old Man and the Fisherman envy the cranes their freedom to return to the heavens. Mure shore is a stretch of shore at Yashima.

5. Most of the passage that follows, down to the *rongi*, is in the epic prose style of *Heike monogatari*.

He draws himself erect, glares ahead, then relaxes after Yoshitsune is named.

rose in his stirrups and declared his name:

His Cloistered Majesty's Envoy,

Field Marshal over the Minamoto Forces,

Censor of the Fifth Rank,

Minamoto no Yoshitsune!

Ah, I remember his mighty presence,

how great a commander he clearly was,

as though the scene were before me now!

FISHERMAN (*kakeai*) Then among the Taira all quarrelling ceased.

One ship of theirs put into shore,

and there, on the wave-washed strand,

their warriors defied a land-based foe.

OLD MAN From the Minamoto, in quick response,

there raced forth fifty mounted men,

and among them, shouting out his name,

sped Mionoya no Shirō at the point of the charge.

FISHERMAN Of the Taira, Kagekiyo

roared out his name and closed with Mionoya.

OLD MAN Their fight shattered Mionoya's sword.

Helpless, he fell back a bit to the water's edge,

FISHERMAN where Kagekiyo pursued him,

OLD MAN seized the neckpiece of his helmet,

FISHERMAN and dragged him backwards, while Mionoya

OLD MAN struggled forward to get away.

Old Man, still seated, begins to mime action; below, at 'rode down to the water', he rises and begins to use the whole stage. Monk, meanwhile, retires to witness position.

FISHERMAN Tug and heave,

OLD MAN they pulled with brute force

CHORUS (*uta*) till neckpiece tore from helmet and,

one to one side and one to the other, they hurtled headlong.

At the sight, Yoshitsune rode down to the water.

Just then, Satō Tsuginobu in his stead took an arrow

aimed by the Lord of Noto, and crashed from his horse;

while among the Taira, Noto's page was struck down.

Perhaps because sorrow had touched both sides,

the fleet withdrew to sea, the army to camp.

The battle tide ebbed, war cries died away.

Silence fell, but for the sighing

of waves on the shore and wind in the pines.

Old Man sits at centre. Chorus now speaks for Monk.

(*rongi*) How very strange! You fisherman
How very strange! You fisherman
give me an account far too exact!
If you please, now, tell me your name!

OLD MAN and FISHERMAN My name – but why need you know
now evening waves[6] ebb with the tide . . .
Were this, of course, His Majesty's
Log Palace at Asakura
I might, as I pass by, say my name . . .[7]

CHORUS No, the more you speak, the more I long
to learn your name. Tell me, old man,

OLD MAN and FISHERMAN the past: yes, many signs show who I am[8]

CHORUS this very moment, when

OLD MAN and FISHERMAN the spring night

CHORUS tide will soon ebb low, near dawn:
then comes the hour of the Ashuras.
Then I shall tell my name.   *Old Man gazes at Monk.*
But whether I do so or not,   *Rises, to base square.*
in this sad life's field marshal your dream:
wake not nor let it fade,
wake not nor let your dream fade!

Exit Old Man, followed by Fisherman.

*   *   *

Villager comes to stand in base square.

VILLAGER I am a saltmaker and my home is on Yashima shore. It has been
ages since I last made salt, so today I will go to the salt-house and get to
work. [*Looks towards Monk and Companions.*] Goodness! The door of the

6. Nō poetry often puns on the homophonous *iu* ('say') and *yū* ('evening'). Here, 'Why
should I *say* my name when the *evening* waves are withdrawing on the night tide . . .'
7. An allusion to a poem by Emperor Tenchi (r. 668–671), included in the *Shinkokinshū*
(1206): 'Since I am the one who inhabits the Log Palace of Asakura, whose daughter [or
son] are you, who call your name to me as you pass by?' This Log Palace (built at
Asakura, in present Fukuoka Prefecture, by Empress Saimei, r. 655–661), is the scene of
The Damask Drum.
8. Since the Fisherman has no identity of his own, it would be inappropriate to drop the
first person singular even when he speaks with the Old Man.

salt-house is open! [*Sees them.*] Well, you monks, what are you doing in there?

MONK The owner said we might stay here.

VILLAGER No, no, that's quite impossible. We saltmakers here never borrow a salt-house from anyone else, or lend our own. This place is mine, and I'd never let anyone else use it. Reverend, you're making this up.

MONK I am not. This salt-house is yours?

VILLAGER It certainly is.

MONK Well then, I have something to ask of you. Please come closer.

VILLAGER Very well. [*Sits at centre.*] What do you want to ask?

MONK Something a bit surprising, perhaps. I hear the Minamoto and the Taira fought a battle on this beach. Would you tell me the story?

VILLAGER Your request certainly is a surprise. We who live nearby really know very little about such things, but I will give you the rough account that I myself have heard people tell.

MONK I will be very grateful.

[The Villager relates only the encounter between Mionoya and Kagekiyo, mentioning neither Yoshitsune nor the symmetrical deaths of Tsuginobu and the Lord of Noto's page. His garrulous recital has no poetic or heroic touches, but dwells instead on concrete matters – elements of the opponents' armour, for example, or parts of the broken sword – and indulges in some humour: 'They say Kagekiyo went flying, face up, and got a big lump on the back of his neck. Mionoya, now, went flying face down. This was the third moon, mind you, when the flowers fall, and he certainly lost the bloom off the end of his nose.']

VILLAGER That's the story, at least as I myself have heard it. But why in the world, reverend sir, did you want me to tell it? I am a bit mystified.

MONK Thank you very much for your account. I asked for it because two men, one old and one young, were here before you came, and they claimed the salt-house was *theirs*. It was they who gave us permission to spend the night. When I questioned the old man about the battle, he told the story very much as you just did. 'In this sad life's field marshal your dream: wake not nor let it fade,' he said, and they suddenly vanished.

VILLAGER How extraordinary! Why, surely you saw Field Marshal Yoshitsune's phantom. You must stay here and meet Yoshitsune himself.

MONK Then I will stay, chant the holy Sutra, and wait to witness a new wonder.

VILLAGER If you will, then please accept lodging in my house, since I live nearby – though it is a very humble place.

MONK I will do so gladly.

VILLAGER Very well.   [*Exit.*]

*   *   *

MONK (*unnamed*) How very strange! The old man now,
                when I asked to learn his name,
                gave me this reply:
                in this sad life's field marshal your dream:
                wake not nor let it fade –

MONK and COMPANIONS

    (*ageuta*) his voice, through the hours, shore winds
                his voice, through the hours, shore winds
                whispering through pines, as we,
                pillowed below on beds of moss,
                dispose our hearts
                patiently to wait, to dream again
                patiently to wait, to dream again.

   To issei *music, enter Yoshitsune in full battle-dress. He stops in base square. At
   key moments, below, he turns to Monk, but otherwise faces audience.*

YOSHITSUNE (*sashi*) The fallen flower returns not to the bough;
            the shattered mirror never more will shine.[9]

                And yet, enraged by wrongful clinging
                back I come once more where demon souls,
                of their own will, torment their flesh:
                to the Ashura field of carnage
                sweeps an angry wave,[10]
                hardly shallow, karma of such power!

MONK (*kakeai*) Soon dawn will stain the sky,
                and from this spot where I lie wakeful,
                I see one approach, clad in armour.
                Are you the Field Marshal of the Minamoto?

YOSHITSUNE I am Yoshitsune's phantom. Wrongful clinging, brought
        on by fury, has me roaming, still, the waves of the western ocean.

9. Based on a passage of the Zen classic *Dentōroku* (Ch. *Ch'uan-têng-lu*). The original
passage is a master's answer to the question, 'Does an enlightened person return to
delusion?'

10. Several passages in Zeami's plays (for example the *rongi* of *Eguchi* or the *noriji* near the
end of *Komachi at Seki-dera*) similarly treat an individual as a wave on the surface of the
sea. It is a Buddhist simile.

I have foundered in the sea of birth and death.

MONK   O foolish man! It is your mind
that displays for you the sea of birth and death.
Purest truth, the moon

YOSHITSUNE shines this spring night, unsullied:
the mind clears, and the broad heavens,

MONK   recalling the old days to present vision:

YOSHITSUNE how it was we fought between ship and shore,

MONK   here at this place:

YOSHITSUNE I cannot forget

Yoshitsune's movements during the following passage show his mounting agitation.

CHORUS *(ageuta)* the stalwart warriors
Yashima-bound and bow in hand
Yashima-bound and bow in hand,
true companions, who ever cleaved
to the path of war, yet went astray,
caught by the seas and mountains of birth and death;
back I come to Yashima shore, bitter at heart!
On all that happened, this, my clinging,
lingers; deep, the night tide floods in again
as in your dream I begin the tale.
as in your dream I begin the tale   *Sits on a stool at centre.*

(kuri) There is no forgetting:
I left my home, the world where humans toil,
many long years ago,
yet as breakers pound the shore,
tonight, down the path of dreams,
I come to show you the Ashura Realm.

YOSHITSUNE *(sashi)* O how it does come back, that spring of old!
The moon, as now, was bright and clear,

CHORUS   and that shore this same shore.
Minamoto and Taira stood, arrow to string,
fleet in formation, horses abreast.
Then, at each stride dashing seas up to our bridles,
we pressed the assault.

YOSHITSUNE *(kakeai)* That moment, as chance would have it,
Yoshitsune dropped his bow –
away it floated, rocked on the waves,

CHORUS   for then the tide was on the ebb;
swiftly it drifted towards the open sea.

YOSHITSUNE I'll not let the enemy have my bow,
          thought I, and braving the waves,
          swam my horse nearly to the foe's ships.

CHORUS   The enemy saw me, and, sailing close,
          readied a grappling hook.
          Though all but lost,

YOSHITSUNE I yet blocked the hook, broke it,
          got back my bow,
          and safely returned to the beach.

CHORUS (*sashi*) Kanefusa then made bold to protest:
You should never have done that, sir. Kagetoki meant precisely this, at Watanabe.[11] Would you trade your life for a bow, even one worth a thousand in gold?
          So, with tears in his eyes,
          he reproached his commander.
          Yoshitsune, listening, made this reply:
No, no, it is not at all that I clung to the bow.

(*kuse*) Yoshitsune among all the warriors
of the Taira and Minamoto
takes up the bow for no selfish motive.
My full fame, however, is not yet half won;
and if, with his bow in the enemy's hands,
Yoshitsune were laughed at, called 'Little Lad',
the hurt would be more than a man can bear.
I might have been killed, I know, but could do nothing else.
Think how my glory hung in the balance!
As I live, I'll not let them have it, thought I,
for he who takes up the bow,
does he not leave his name to all who come after?
So I pleaded, and Kanefusa, yes, each man present,
shed tears of heartfelt assent.

YOSHITSUNE The wise man remains unconfused,
Stands, comes to stage front and begins to punctuate his words by stamping the beat.

CHORUS   the brave knows no fear.

---

11. In the second lunar month of 1185, when Yoshitsune was about to set out from the harbour of Watanabe towards Shikoku in pursuit of the Taira, his lieutenant, Kajiwara Kagetoki, urged that 'reverse oars' be fitted to the Minamoto ships so that they could retreat more easily. When Yoshitsune angrily rejected the suggestion, Kagetoki accused him of hot-blooded rashness, as Kanefusa does here.

             With valiant heart he holds to his good bow,
             lest the foe rob him of it, and this he does
             for honour's sake; but to life clings not,   *To base square.*
             for, giving it up, he leaves to history
             a glorious name, worthy of record.

YOSHITSUNE (*ei*) Again, war cries from the Ashura Realm
CHORUS   and archers' yells shake the earth.

   (QUASI-DANCE: *kakeri*)

Yoshitsune performs a vigorous kakeri *circuit of the stage, and is in base square as text resumes.*

YOSHITSUNE (*unnamed*) Who today is my Ashura foe? What? Noritsune, Lord of Noto?[12] Aha! A great one, and well-tried, I know!
[*Now moves about, miming.*]
             On the mind's eye bursts Dan-no-ura,
CHORUS (*chū-noriji*) that mighty sea fight whence I now come
             that mighty sea fight whence I now come
             back to this world, back to birth and death.
             The sea and mountains quake.
             From the ships, war howls;
YOSHITSUNE ashore, shields like waves;
CHORUS   glinting, moon-struck,
YOSHITSUNE the fire of swords;
CHORUS   salt-side mirrored,
YOSHITSUNE helmet stars.[13]
CHORUS   Water and sky,
             sky running on in cloud billows,
             thundering clash, counterclash,
             the fleet's struggle, sally, retreat,
             lift and plunge, rage on
             until the spring night waves yield up dawn.
             Foemen the eye saw were flocking gulls,
             war howls the ear heard,

12. During the battle of Dan-no-ura, Noritsune went looking for Yoshitsune, but when at last he managed to board Yoshitsune's ship, Yoshitsune leapt nimbly on to another. Knowing he could not follow, Noritsune stopped short and defied all comers. When three Minamoto warriors attacked him, he kicked one overboard, then clamped another under each arm and leapt into the waves.
13. 'Helmet stars' are the polished studs on a warrior's helmet.

wind down the shore through tall pines rushing
wind down the shore through tall pines raging:
a morning gale, no more.

Facing side from base square, Yoshitsune stamps the final beat.

Bibliography
and Comments on Texts Translated

This bibliography includes only works consulted for the specific purpose of preparing the introductions, notes and translations in this book. (Although some of these left no direct traces in the book, all were read and considered.) It is not a general reading list. Many writings on nō and on Zeami's critical essays, in English and other languages, are omitted, and so are previous translations. For this I apologize. I do not mean to slight the achievements of other scholars; on the contrary. However, the literature on nō, in Western languages alone, is by now quite large, and to cite one work for the reader would only be to neglect another. Many of the foundations of *Japanese Nō Dramas* remain unseen. I can only thank all those who built them.

1. General

Nō texts

Itō Masayoshi, *Yōkyokushū*, 3 vols. Tokyo: Shinchōsha (Shinchō Nihon koten shūsei), 1983, 1986, 1988.

Koyama Hiroshi, Satō Kikuo, and Satō Ken'ichirō (eds), *Yōkyokushū*, 2 vols. Tokyo: Shōgakkan (Nihon koten bungaku zenshū, vols 33, 34), 1973–5.

Nihon Meicho Zenshū Kankō Kai (ed.), *Yōkyoku sambyaku gojūbanshū*. Tokyo: Nihon Meicho Zenshū Kankō Kai, 1928.

Sanari Kentarō (ed.), *Yōkyoku taikan*, 7 vols. Tokyo: Meiji Shoin, 1930–31.

Yokomichi Mario and Omote Akira (eds.), *Yōkyokushū*, 2 vols. Tokyo: Iwanami Shoten (Nihon koten bungaku taikei, vols. 40, 41), 1960.

Separate interlude texts

Tanaka Kazuo (ed.), *Jōkyō nenkan Ōkura-ryū-ai-kyōgen bon nishu*, 2 vols. Tokyo: Wanya Shoten (Hōsei Daigaku Nōgaku Kenkyūjo (ed.), Nōgaku shiryō shūsei, vols. 15, 16), 1986, 1988.

Other

Miyake Noboru, 'Nō no tokushu enshutsu', in Nogami Toyoichirō (ed.), *Nōgaku zensho*, vol. 4, pp. 192–254. Tokyo: Tōkyō Sōgensha, 1979.

Nakamura Kyōzō, *Yōkyoku to shiseki*. Tokyo: Yōkyoku Shiseki Hozon Kai, 1988.

Nishino Haruo and Hata Hisashi (eds.), *Nō, kyōgen jiten*. Tokyo: Heibonsha, 1987.

2. The General Introduction

Bethe, Monica, and Karen Brazell, *Nō as Performance: An Analysis of the Kuse Scene of* Yamamba. Ithaca: *Cornell University East Asia Papers*, no. 16, 1978.

Hare, Thomas B., *Zeami's Style: The Noh Plays of Zeami Motokiyo*. Stanford: Stanford University Press, 1986.

Itō Masayoshi, *Yōkyokushū*, vol. 1. Tokyo: Shinchōsha, 1983. (The stage diagram is adapted from this source.)

Keene, Donald, *Nō: The Classical Theatre of Japan*. Tokyo and Palo Alto: Kodansha International Ltd, 1966.

Konishi Jin'ichi, 'The Art of Renga', in *Journal of Japanese Studies*, vol. 2, no. 1, Autumn 1975, pp. 33–61.

Tashiro Keiichirō, *Yōkyoku o yomu*. Tokyo: Asashi Shimbun Sha (Asahi sensho, no. 332), 1987.

Zeami, 'Yūgaku shudō fūken', in Omote Akira and Katō Shūichi (eds.), *Zeami, Zenchiku*. Tokyo: Iwanami Shoten (Nihon shisō taikei, vol. 24), 1974, pp. 162–7.

3. The Plays: Introductions and Notes

Ama (THE DIVER)

The author attribution follows Horiguchi Yasuo.
Text: Yokomichi and Omote, *Yōkyokushū*, vol. 1. *Interlude:* Sanari, vol. 1.

Horiguchi Yasuo, '*Ama*', in Horiguchi Yasuo, *Sarugaku nō no kenkyū*.
   Tokyo: Ōfūsha, 1987, pp. 70–81. (First published in *Kanze*, February
   1979.)
Itō Masayoshi, 'Kaidai', in Itō, *Yōkyokushū*, vol. 1, pp. 399–402.
Nakamura Kyōzō, *Yōkyoku to shiseki*, pp. 460–64.
Yokomichi Mario, '*Ama*', in Yokomichi Mario, *Nōgeki shōyō*. Tokyo:
   Chikuma Shobō, 1984, pp. 81–4.

Atsumori

Text: Yokomichi and Omote, *Yōkyokushū*, vol. 1. *Interlude:* Sanari, vol. 1.

Heike monogatari, various editions.
Kanai Kiyomitsu, '*Atsumori*', in Kanai Kiyomitsu, *Nō to kyogen*, pp.
   194–207. Tokyo: Meiji Shoin, 1977.
Nakamura Kyōzō, *Yōkyoku to shiseki*, pp. 335–41.
Sagara Tōru, '*Atsumori*', in Sagara Tōru, *Zeami no uchū*. Tokyo: Perikan
   Sha, 1990, pp. 143–9.
Takashima Motohiro, 'Nō ni okeru takai kan to jujutsu no imi:
   Atsumori o megutte', in *Kikan Nihon shisō shi*, no. 24, 1984, pp. 24–
   41.
Yabuta Kaichirō, '*Atsumori*', in Yabuta Kaichirō, *Nōgaku fudoki*.
   Tokyo, Hinoki Shoten, 1972, pp. 75–90.

Aya no tsuzumi (THE DAMASK DRUM)

Text and interlude: Koyama Hiroshi *et al.*, *Yōkyokushū*, vol. 2.

Sanari Kentarō, 'Shutten ["Sources"] for *Koi no omoni*', in Sanari,
   Yōkyoku taikan, vol. 2.
Waley, Arthur, 'The Damask Drum' in Arthur Waley, *The Nō Plays of
   Japan*. London: George Allen & Unwin, 1921 and subsequent
   reprints, pp. 171–8.

Chikubu-shima

Texts: Koyama Hiroshi *et al.* (eds.), *Yōkyokushū*, vol. 1; Yokomichi and Omote (eds.), *Yōkyokushū*, vol. 2. *Interlude:* Sanari Kentarō (ed.), *Yōkyoku taikan*, vol. 3.

Chikubu-shima engi, in Gorai Shigeru (ed.), *Shugendō shiryō shū*, vol. 2 (Nishi Nihon hen), pp. 26–9. Tokyo: Meicho Shuppan (Sangaku shūkyō shi kenkyū sōsho, vol. 18), 1984.

Kōsai Tsutomu, 'Sakusha to honzetsu: *Chikubu-shima*', in *Yōkyoku shinkō: Zeami ni terasu*. Tokyo: Hinoki Shoten, 1972, pp. 158–61. (First published in *Kanze*, January 1962.)

Miyake Noboru, 'Nō no tokushu enshutsu'.

Nakamura Kyōzō, *Yōkyoku to shiseki*, pp. 240–45.

Sawa Jitsuei, *Chikubu-shima shi*. Hikone: Hōgon-ji Jimusho, 1976.

Eguchi

Text: Yokomichi and Omote (from Zeami's ms.), *Yōkyokushū*, vol. 1. *First dialogue with villager:* Sanari, *Yōkyoku taikan*, vol. 1. *Interlude:* mainly from *Jōkyō Matsui bon* as published by Tanaka Kazuo; supplemented from Itō, *Yōkyokushū*, vol. 1 and Zeami's own text as included in Yokomichi and Omote, *Yōkyokushū*, vol. 1. Zeami's manuscript provides the earliest extant text of an interlude monologue and is therefore doubly precious, but Zeami's version is shorter than more recent ones and seems not to correspond to Edo-period and modern staging.

Abe Yasurō, 'Seizoku no tawamure to shite no geinō: *Eguchi*', in Moriya Takeshi (ed.), *Geinō to chinkon*. Tokyo, Shunjūsha, 1988, pp. 174–82.

Horiguchi Yasuo, '*Eguchi* no kōzō', in Horiguchi Yasuo, *Sarugaku nō no kenkyū*. Tokyo: Ōfūsha, 1987, pp. 82–101.

Itō Masayoshi, 'Kaidai', in Itō, *Yōkyokushū*, vol. 1, pp. 413–15.

Nakamura Kyōzō, *Yōkyoku to shiseki*, pp. 263–8.

Ochiai Hiroshi, '*Eguchi* no kōsō to seiritsu: keisei no mondai o chūshin ni', in *Nō: kenkyū to hyōron*, no. 15, 1987, pp. 1–10.

Tyler, Royall, *Japanese Tales*. New York: Pantheon, 1987, pp. 56–7.

Funa Benkei (BENKEI ABOARD SHIP)

Text: Yokomichi and Omote, *Yōkyokushū*, vol. 2, except as indicated in note 12 to the play.

Itō Masayoshi, 'Kaidai', in Itō, *Yōkyokushū*, vol. 3, pp. 477–9.

Kanai Kiyomitsu, *'Funa Benkei'*, in Kanai Kiyomitsu, *Nō no kenkyū*. Tokyo: Ōfūsha, 1969, pp. 598–623.

Miyake Noboru, 'Nō no tokushu enshutsu'.

Nakamura Kyōzō, *Yōkyoku to shiseki*, pp. 302–9.

Yamamoto Wakako, 'Nobumitsu no sakunō hō to ai kyōgen o meguru shiron: *Tamanoi* to *Funa Benkei* o chūshin ni', in *Jissen kokubungaku*, no. 29, March 1986, pp. 105–15.

Hagoromo (THE FEATHER MANTLE)

Text: Koyama Hiroshi *et al.*, *Yōkyokushū*, vol. 1.

Akimoto Yoshirō (ed.), *Fudoki*. Tokyo: Iwanami Shoten (Nihon koten bungaku taikei, vol. 2), 1958.

Horiguchi Yasuo, *'Hagoromo* shōkō: sono seiritsu to ichihaikei ni tsuite', in Horiguchi Yasuo, *Sarugaku nō no kenkyū*. Tokyo: Ōfūsha, 1987, pp. 34–45. (First published in *Kanze*, March 1974.)

Kōsai Tsutomu, 'Sakusha to honzetsu: *Hagoromo*', in *Yōkyoku shinkō: Zeami ni terasu*. Tokyo: Hinoki Shoten, 1972, pp. 137–40. (First published in *Kanze*, January 1961.)

Miller, Alan L., 'The Swan Maiden Revisited: Religious Significance of "Divine-Wife" Folktales with Special Reference to Japan', *Asian Folklore Studies*, vol. 46, 1987, pp. 55–86.

Miyake Noboru, 'Nō no tokushu enshutsu'.

Nakamura Kyōzō, *Yōkyoku to shiseki*, pp. 152–7.

Sanari Kentarō, 'Shutten' ["Sources"] for *Hagoromo*', in Sanari, *Yōkyoku taikan*, vol. 4.

Satoi Rokurō, *'Hagoromo'*, in Satoi Rokurō, *Yōkyoku hyakusen: sono shi to dorama*, 2 vols. Tokyo: Kasama Shoin, 1954, 1957, vol. 2, pp. 125–9.

Yasuda, Kenneth, *'Hagoromo'* (introduction), in Kenneth Yasuda, *Masterworks of the Nō Theatre*. Bloomington and Indianapolis: Indiana University Press, 1990, pp. 133–72.

Yokomichi and Omote, *Yōkyokushū*, vol. 2: notes to the play.

Items related to Mount Fuji

Fujisan ki by Miyako no Yoshika (834–879), in Hanawa Hokiichi (ed.), *Gunsho ruijū*, 24 vols. Tokyo: Zoku Gunsho Ruijū Kansei Kai, vol. 6, 1938–9, pp. 318–19.

Nippon Hōraizan, in Yokoyama Shigeru and Shinoda Jun'ichi (eds.), *Kojōruri shū*, vol. 1. Tokyo: Koten Bunko (Koten bunko, vol. 169), 1961.

Fujisan engi, in Gorai Shigeru (ed.), *Shugendō shiryō shū*, vol. 1, pp. 411–17. Tokyo: Meicho Shuppan (Sangaku shūkyō shi kenkyū sōsho, vol. 17), 1983.

'Fuji Asama Daibosatsu no koto', in *Shintōshū*, kan 8. Kondō Kihaku (ed.), *Shintōshū*. Tokyo: Kadokawa, 1967. Translated as 'Princess Glory' in Royall Tyler, *Japanese Tales*. New York: Pantheon, 1987, pp. 46–7.

Mills, D. E., '*Soga monogatari, Shintōshū* and the Taketori Legend', in *Monumenta Nipponica*, vol. 30, no. 1, 1975, pp. 37–68.

Nara Kokuritsu Hakubutsukan (ed.), *Suijaku bijutsu*. Tokyo: Kadokawa Shoten, 1964, plates 91–4.

Taketori monogatari. Various editions.

Hanjo (LADY HAN)

Text: Yokomichi and Omote, *Yōkyokushū*, vol. 1. However, the end of the Madam's opening dialogue with Hanago, after she snatches away the fan, is from *Jōkyō Matsui-bon*, edited by Tanaka Kazuo.

Itō Masayoshi, 'Kaidai', in Itō, *Yōkyokushū*, vol 3, pp. 461–4.

Kōsai Tsutomu, 'Sakusha to honzetsu: *Hanjo*', in *Yōkyoku shinkō: Zeami ni terasu*. Tokyo: Hinoki Shoten, 1972, pp. 221–6. (First published in *Kanze*, July 1964.)

Nakamura Kyōzō, *Yōkyoku to shiseki*, pp. 188–93. The story on the temple sign is quoted from p. 189.

Tokue Motomasa, '*Hanjo yokyō*', in *Kokugo to kokubungaku*, September 1967, pp. 28–43.

Izutsu (THE WELL-CRADLE)

Text: Yokomichi and Omote, *Yōkyokushū*, vol. 1. *Interlude dialogue:* Sanari, *Yōkyoku taikan*, vol. 1. *Interlude monologue (katari):* Itō, *Yōkyokushū*, vol. 1.

Hare, Thomas B., 'Nyotai: The Woman's Mode', Ch. 4 in Thomas B. Hare, *Zeami's Style: The Noh Plays of Zeami Motokiyo*. Stanford: Stanford University Press, 1986, pp. 131–82.

Horiguchi Yasuo, 'Matsu onna: *Izutsu* no shuhō', in Horiguchi Yasuo, *Sarugaku nō no kenkyū*. Tokyo: Ōfūsha, 1987, pp. 102–14. (First published in Katagiri Yōichi *et al.* (eds.), *Taketori monogatari, Ise monogatari*. Tokyo: Shūeisha (Zusetsu Nihon no koten, vol. 5), 1978.)

Ise monogatari. Various editions.

Itō Masayoshi, 'Kaidai', in Itō, *Yōkyokushū*, vol. 1, pp. 403–5.

Itō Masayoshi, '*Ise monogatari* to yōkyoku', in Katagiri Yōichi (ed.), *Ise monogatari, Yamato monogatari*. Tokyo: Kadokawa (Kanshō Nihon koten bungaku, vol. 5), 1975, pp. 359–68.

Itō Masayoshi, 'Yōkyoku to *Ise monogatari* no hiden: *Izutsu* no baai o chūshin ni shite', in Nihon Bungaku Kenkyū Shiryō Kankō Kai (ed.), *Yōkyoku, kyōgen*. Tokyo: Yūseidō, 1981, pp. 106–14. (Originally published in *Kongō*, no. 64, May 1965.)

Kōsai Tsutomu, 'Sakusha to honzetsu: *Izutsu*', in *Yōkyoku shinkō: Zeami ni terasu*. Tokyo: Hinoki Shoten, 1972, pp. 194–8. (First published in *Kanze*, September 1963.)

Nakamura Kyōzō, *Yōkyoku to shiseki*, pp. 292–7.

Nishimura Satoshi, '"Hito matsu onna" no "ima" to "mukashi": nō *Izutsu* ron', in *Kōgakkan Daigaku kiyō*, vol. 18, January 1980, pp. 95–112.

Sagara Tōru, '*Izutsu*', in Sagara Tōru, *Zeami no uchū*. Tokyo: Perikan Sha, 1990, pp. 59–68.

Takeoka Masao, *Ise monogatari zenchūshaku*. Tokyo: Yūbundō, 1987.

Ueda Tetsuyuki, '*Izutsu* ni miru inishie no kōzō', in Kikan *Nihon shisō shi*, no. 24, 1984, pp. 55–64.

Yashima Masaharu, '*Izutsu* no nochiba no nekkyō: *Kinuta* to rōjō mono ni oyobitsutsu', in Yashima Masaharu, *Zeami no nō to geiron*. Tokyo: Miyai Shoten, 1985, pp. 470–75.

Yasuda, Kenneth, '*Izutsu*', in Kenneth Yasuda, *Masterworks of the Nō Theater*. Bloomington and Indianapolis: Indiana University Press, 1990, pp. 186–226.

Kantan

Text: Itō, *Yōkyokushū*, vol. 1. However, the *tsukizerifu* and the Innkeeper's final speech are taken from Koyama *et al.*, *Yōkyokushū*, vol. 2, since Itō only summarizes them.

Itō Masayoshi, 'Kaidai', in Itō, *Yōkyokushū*, vol. 1, pp. 433–4.

Itō Masayoshi, '*Kantan*: yume no yo zo to satoriete', in Itō Masayoshi, *Yōkyoku zakki*. Osaka: Izumi Shoin, 1989, pp. 99–102. (First published in *Kannō*, no. 249, January 1983.)

Kōsai Tsutomu, 'Sakusha to honzetsu: *Kantan*', in *Yōkyoku shinkō: Zeami ni terasu*. Tokyo: Enoki Shoten, 1972, pp. 125–8. (First published in *Kanze*, July 1960.)

Omote Akira, '*Kantan* no rekishi', in *Kanze*, July 1960, pp. 8–10.

Kasuga ryūjin (THE KASUGA DRAGON GOD)

The author attribution follows Itō.
Text: Itō, *Yōkyokushū*, vol. 1. However, the *tsukizerifu* and the Companion's brief reply have been inserted from Sanari, *Yōkyoku taikan*, vol. 1. *Interlude:* Sanari, *Yōkyoku taikan*, vol. 1.

Itō Masayoshi, 'Kaidai', in Itō, *Yōkyokushū*, vol. 1, pp. 426–8.

'*Kasuga ryūjin o megutte*' (a round-table discussion between Kageyama Haruki, Katayama Keijirō, and Nomura Kōji), in *Kanze*, April 1980, pp. 14–27.

Miyake Noboru, 'Nō no tokushu enshutsu'.

Morrell, Robert E., 'Passage to India Denied: Zeami's *Kasuga Ryūjin*', in *Monumenta Nipponica*, vol. 37, no. 2, Summer 1982, pp. 179–200.

Omote Akira, '*Kasuga ryūjin* no ai-kyōgen', in Omote Akira, *Nōgakushi shinkō*, vol. 2. Tokyo: Wan'ya Shoten, 1986, pp. 289–94. (Originally published in *Tessen*, no. 186, February 1971.)

Tanabe, George Joji, 'Myōe Shōnin (1173–1232): Tradition and Reform in Early Kamakura Buddhism', doctoral thesis submitted to Columbia University, 1983.

Tyler, Royall, *The Miracles of the Kasuga Deity*. New York: Columbia University Press, 1990.

Kinuta (THE FULLING BLOCK)

Text: Yokomichi and Omote, *Yōkyokushū*, vol. 1. Interlude *katari:* Sanari, *Yōkyoku taikan*, vol. 2.

Kanai Kiyomitsu, 'Kinuta', in Kanai Kiyomitsu, Nō no kenkyū. Tokyo: Ōfūsha, 1969, pp. 464–80.
Kanze Hisao, 'Kinuta to Zeami', in Kanze Hisao, Kokoro yori kokoro ni tsutauru hana. Tokyo: Hakusuisha, 1979, pp. 161–5. (First published in Tessen, no. 256, June 1977.)
Miyake Akiko, 'Zeami kara no shuppatsu: Motomasa, Zenchiku no jidai', in Nō: kenkyū to hyōron, no. 16, 1986, pp. 12–30.
Nakamura Kyōzō, Yōkyoku to shiseki, pp. 469–75.
Nogami Toyoichirō, 'Nō no shuyaku ichinin shugi', in Nogami Toyoichirō, Nō: kenkyū to hakken. Tokyo: Iwanami Shoten, 1930, pp. 1–42.
Nose Asaji, 'Kinuta', in Nose Asaji chosaku shū, vol. 6. Kyoto: Shibunkaku Shuppan, 1982, pp. 131–81.
Omote Akira, 'Kinuta no nō no chūzetsu to saikō', in Kanze, October 1979, pp. 19–24.
Omote Akira, 'Koi no omoni no rekishiteki kenkyū', in Omote Akira, Nōgakushi shinkō. Tokyo: Wan'ya Shoten, 1986, pp. 173–201. (First published in Hōsei Daigaku Bungaku-bu kiyō, no. 8, March 1963.)
Sagara Tōru, 'Hanjo' and 'Kinuta', in Sagara Tōru, Zeami no uchū. Tokyo: Perikan Sha, 1990, pp. 91–8 and 119–33.
Yashima Masaharu, 'Kinuta e no michi: oni to mujō mumi naru kurai', in Yashima Masaharu, Zeami no nō to geiron. Tokyo: Miyai Shoten, 1985, pp. 348–67.
Yashima Masaharu, 'Sakuhin kenkyū: Kinuta', in Kanze, September 1979, pp. 4–12. (Reprinted in the work cited above.)

Kureha

The author attribution follows Itō.
Text: Itō, Yōkyokushū, vol. 2.

Bethe, Monica (an expert on both nō and Japanese weaving). Personal conversation, Kyoto, May 1989.
Itō Masayoshi, 'Kaidai', in Itō, Yōkyokushū, vol. 2, pp. 433–4.
Itō Masayoshi, 'Kureha: na o etaru Kureha no sato', in Itō Masayoshi, Yōkyoku zakki. Osaka: Izumi Shoin, 1989, pp. 160–64. (First published in Kannō, no. 261, May 1985.)
Miller, Alan L., 'Ame no miso-ori me (the Heavenly Weaving Maiden): The Cosmic Weaver in Early Shinto Myth and Ritual', in History of Religions, vol. 24, no. 1, 1984, pp. 27–48.

Miller, Alan L., 'Of Weavers and Birds: Structure and Symbol in Japanese Myth and Folktale', in *History of Religions*, vol. 26, no. 3, 1987, pp. 309–27.

Nakamura Kyōzō, *Yōkyoku to shiseki*, pp. 259–63.

Yamaguchi Noh Costume Research Center (ed.), *The World of Noh Costumes*. Kyoto: Yamaguchi Noh Costume Research Center, 1989.

Matsukaze (PINING WIND)

Text: (1) The opening *shidai*, *nanori*, and *tsukizerifu* are from the manuscript in the hand of Komparu Zempō (1454–1532), as published by Nakamura (see below), p. 49. The Zempō manuscript seems to be the ancestor of the version of the play still current in the Shimogakari (Kongō, Komparu, and Kita) schools. It is unclear whether the Zempō or the Motohiro text (mentioned below) is closer to what Zeami himself may have written, but the former, with its more explicit description of the pine tree in the opening lines, is more helpful to the reader.

(2) The *mondō* that follows is the *Ai shimai tsuke* version published by Itō Masayoshi, vol. 3, pp. 239–40. It accords with the *Kōetsu-bon* text of the play, adopted by Itō. (This early seventeenth-century version is in the Shimogakari line.)

(3) The *shidai* that immediately follows the *shite* and *tsure*'s opening *issei* is also from the Shimogakari line of texts, starting with Zempō's, and was published as a variant by Yokomichi.

(4) The rest of the play is translated from the manuscript of Kanze Motohiro, dated 1517, as edited by Yokomichi Mario, vol. 1. It is continuous with the later Kamigakari (Kanze and Hōshō) school texts. There are no significant discrepancies between the two textual lines in part two of the play.

Abe Yasurō, 'Seizoku no tawamure to shite no geinō: *Ama*,' in Moriya Takeshi (ed.), *Geinō to chinkon*. Tokyo: Shunjūsha, 1988, pp. 190–98.

Genji monogatari. Various editions.

Honda Yasuji, '*Matsukaze* no sakui', in Honda Yasuji, *Nō oyobi kyōgen kō*. Tokyo: Nōgaku Shorin, 1980, pp. 121–3. (Reprint of the 1943 edition.)

Itō Masayoshi, 'Kaidai', in Itō, *Yōkyokushū*, vol. 3, pp. 483–5.

Kanai Kiyomitsu, 'Matsukaze', in Kanai Kiyomitsu, Nō no kenkyū. Tokyo: Ōfūsha, 1969, pp. 411–25.

Kōsai Tsutomu, 'Sakusha to honzetsu: Matsukaze', in Yōkyoku shinkō: Zeami ni terasu. Tokyo: Hinoki Shoten, 1972, pp. 129–32. (First published in Kanze, September 1960.)

Koyama Hiroshi, 'Sakuhin kenkyū: Matsukaze', in Kanze, September 1975, pp. 3–8.

Nakamura Itaru, 'Matsukaze no henbō: Muromachi makki shodenbon o chūshin ni shite', in Gengo to bungei, no. 7, May 1974, pp. 47–66. (Reprinted in Nihon Bungaku Kenkyū Shiryō Kankō Kai (ed.), Yōkyoku, kyōgen (Nihon bungaku kenkyū shiryō sōsho). Tokyo: Yūseidō, 1981.)

Nakamura Kyōzō, Yōkyoku to shiseki, pp. 325–31.

Nose Asaji, 'Matsukaze', in Nose Asaji chosaku shū, vol. 6. Kyoto: Shibunkaku Shuppan, 1982, pp. 329–73.

Omote Akira, 'Kan'ami den saiken' (part 2), in Kanze, May 1984, pp. 4–13.

Sagara Tōru, 'Matsukaze (nochi no dan)', in Sagara Tōru, Zeami no uchū. Tokyo: Perikan Sha, 1990, pp. 107–13.

Shasekishū, ed. Watanabe Tsunaya. Tokyo: Iwanami Shoten, 1966. (Nihon koten bungaku taikei, vol. 85.) The story referred to is on p. 230.

Takemoto Mikio, 'Sandō no kaisaku reikyoku o meguru shomondai', in Jissen kokubungaku, no. 19, March 1981, pp. 19–35.

Takeoka Masao, Ise monogatari zenchūshaku. Tokyo: Yūbundō, 1987.

Tashiro Keiichirō, 'Yōkyoku Matsukaze ni tsuite', in Hikaku bungaku kenkyū, no. 48, October 1985, pp. 61–73 (part 1); and no. 50, April 1986, pp. 37–70 (part 2).

Yabuta Kaichirō, 'Matsukaze', in Yabuta Kaichirō, Nōgaku fudoki, pp. 107–16. Tokyo: Hinoki Shoten, 1972. (First published in Kanze, September 1966.)

Yamanaka Reiko, 'Nyotai nō ni okeru "Zeami fū" no kakuritsu: Matsukaze no hatashita yakuwari', in Nō: kenkyū to hyōron, no. 14, 1986, pp. 1–11.

Nonomiya (THE WILDWOOD SHRINE)

Text: Koyama *et al.*, *Yōkyokushū*, vol. 1.

Itō Masayoshi, 'Kaidai' in Itō, *Yōkyokushū*, vol. 3, pp. 450–53.

Nakamura Kyōzō, *Yōkyoku to Kyōto*, 1978. (No publisher indicated.)
Shimonaka Kunihiko (ed.), *Kyōto-shi no chimei*. Tokyo: Heibonsha (Nihon rekishi chimei taikei, vol. 27), 1979, s.v. 'Nonomiya'.
Kanai Kiyomitsu, '*Nonomiya*', in Kanai Kiyomitsu, *Nō no kenkyū*. Tokyo: Ōfūsha, 1969, pp. 450–63.
Kōsai Tsutomu, 'Sakusha to honzetsu: *Nonomiya*', in *Yōkyoku shinkō: Zeami ni terasu*. Tokyo: Hinoki Shoten, 1972, pp. 176–9. (First published in *Kanze*, September 1962.)

Saigyō-zakura (SAIGYŌ'S CHERRY TREE)

Text: Yokomichi and Omote, *Yōkyokushū*, vol. 1.

Itō Masayoshi, 'Kaidai', in Itō, *Yōkyokushū*, vol. 2, pp. 440–41.
Nakamura Kyōzō, *Yōkyoku to Kyōto*, 1978. (No publisher indicated.)

Seki-dera Komachi (KOMACHI AT SEKI-DERA)

Text: Yokomichi and Omote, *Yōkyokushū*, vol. 2.

Doi Hiroko, 'Koshū no uta to kokoro: Sekidera Komachi no shite o megutte', *Kikan Nihon shisō shi*, no. 24, 1984, pp. 65–77.
Itō Masayoshi, 'Kaidai', in Itō, *Yōkyokushū*, vol. 2, pp. 463–4.
Nakamura Kyōzō, *Yōkyoku to shiseki*, pp. 212–17.
Takemoto Mikio, 'Sakuhin kenkyū: *Sekidera Komachi*', in *Kanze*, November 1986, pp. 48–56.
Yokomichi Mario, '*Sekidera Komachi* nōto', in Yokomichi Mario, *Nōgeki shōyō*. Tokyo: Chikuma Shobō, 1984, pp. 209–27.

Semimaru

Text: Sanari, *Yōkyoku taikan*, vol. 3. This text indicates only the main *shōdan*. *Semimaru* has not been published in a post-war, fully annotated edition.

Amano Fumio, 'Sakagami no tanjō', in *Kanze*, December 1985, pp. 3–8.
Hattori Sachio, 'Sakagami no Miya: hōrō geinōmin no geinōshin shinkō ni tsuite', parts 1, 2, 3a, 3b, in *Bungaku*, vol. 46, April 1978, pp. 44–59; vol. 46, May 1978, pp. 84–103; vol. 46, December 1978, pp. 80–90; vol. 47, August 1979, pp. 32–53.

Kanai Kiyomitsu, 'Mōjin no nō to kyōgen', in Kanai Kiyomitsu, *Nō to kyōgen*. Tokyo, Meiji Shoin, 1977, pp. 337–51.

Kōsai Tsutomu, 'Sakusha to honzetsu: *Semimaru*', in *Yōkyoku shinkō: Zeami ni terasu*. Tokyo: Hinoki Shoten, 1972, pp. 167–71. (First published in *Kanze*, May 1962.)

Matisoff, Susan, *The Legend of Semimaru, Blind Musician of Japan*. New York: Columbia University Press, 1978.

Miyake Akiko, 'Zeami kara no shuppatsu: Motomasa, Zenchiku no jidai', in *Nō: kenkyū to hyōron*, no. 16, 1986, pp. 12–30.

Nakamura Kyōzō, *Yōkyoku to shiseki*, pp. 207–12.

Tashiro Keiichirō, '*Semimaru* o yomu', in Tashiro Keiichirō, *Yōkyoku o yomu*. Tokyo: Asahi Shimbun Sha (Asahi sensho, no. 332), 1987, pp. 244–323.

Yabuta Kaichirō, '*Semimaru*', in Yabuta Kaichirō, *Nōgaku fudoki*. Tokyo: Hinoki Shoten, 1972, pp. 153–86.

'Zeami no nō' (a round-table discussion between Omote Akira, Kanze Hisao, Kanze Motomasa, Kōsai Tsutomu, Konishi Jin'ichi, Saitō Tarō, Enoki Jōtarō, and Yokomichi Mario), in Kōsai Tsutomu, *Yōkyoku shinkō: Zeami ni terasu*. Tokyo: Hinoki Shoten, 1972, pp. 284–338. (First published in *Kanze*, October 1963.)

Sumida-gawa (THE SUMIDA RIVER)

Text: Yokomichi and Omote, *Yōkyokushū*, vol. 2, with these exceptions: (1) the *waki*'s *nanori*, from the Zempō text (quoted by Amano Fumio), and (2) the *wakizure*'s *nanori*, from the current Shimogakari and Hōshō school texts (quoted by Kanai).

Amano Fumio, 'Sakuhin kenkyū: *Sumidagawa*', in *Kanze*, March 1979, pp. 3–11.

Itō Masayoshi, 'Kaidai', in Itō, *Yōkyokushū*, vol. 2, pp. 458–60.

Itō Masayoshi, 'Sumidagawa; ningen urei no hanazakari', in Itō Masayoshi, *Yōkyoku zakki*. Isaka: Izumi Shoin, 1989, pp. 139–42. (First published in *Kannō*, no. 256, May 1984.)

Kanai Kiyomitsu, '*Sumidagawa*', in Kanai Kiyomitsu, *Nō no kenkyū*. Tokyo: Ōfūsha, 1969, pp. 555–77.

Kōsai Tsutomu, 'Sakusha to honzetsu: *Sumidagawa*', in *Yōkyoku shinkō: Zeami ni terasu*. Tokyo: Hinoki Shoten, 1972, pp. 117–20. (First published in *Kanze*, March 1960.)

Miyake Akiko, 'Zeami kara no shuppatsu: Motomasa, Zenchiku no jidai', in *Nō: kenkyū to hyōron*, no. 16, 1986, pp. 12–30.

Nakamura Kyōzō, *Yōkyoku to shiseki*, pp. 44–8.

Omote Akira, 'Sakuhin kenkyū: *Sumidagawa*', in Omote Akira, *Nōgaku shinkō*, vol. 2, Tokyo: Wan'ya Shoten, 1975, pp. 275–84. (First published in *Kanze*, March 1968.)

Tadanori

Text: Yokomichi and Omote, *Yōkyokushū*, vol. 1. *Interlude:* Sanari, *Yōkyoku taikan*, vol. 3.

Hare, Thomas B., 'Guntai: The Martial Mode', Ch. 5 in Thomas B. Hare, *Zeami's Style: the Noh Plays of Zeami Motokiyo*. Stanford: Stanford University Press, 1986, pp. 185†224.

Itō Masayoshi, 'Kaidai', in Itō, *Yōkyokushū*, vol. 2, pp. 476–8.

Kami Hiroshi, 'Sakuhin kenkyū: *Tadanori*', in *Kanze*, March 1975, pp. 3–8.

Murakami Takashi, '*Tadanori* no kōzō', in *Kikan Nihon shisō shi*, no. 28, 1987, pp. 46–57.

Nakamura Kyōzō, *Yōkyoku to shiseki*, pp. 346–53.

Sagara Tōru, '*Tadanori*', in Sagara Tōru, *Zeami no uchū*. Tokyo: Perikan Sha, 1990, pp. 162–71.

Takasago

Text: Yokomichi and Omoto, *Yōkyokushū*, vol. 1. *Interlude:* Sanari, *Yōkyoku taikan*, vol. 3.

Hare, Thomas B., 'Rōtai: The Aged Mode', Ch. 3 in Thomas B. Hare, *Zeami's Style: The Noh Plays of Zeami Motokiyo*. Stanford: Stanford University Press, 1986, pp. 65–128.

Itō Masayoshi, 'Kaidai', in Itō, *Yōkyokushū*, vol. 2, pp. 475–6.

Itō Masayoshi, 'Yōkyoku *Takasago* zakkō', in *Bunrin*, no. 6, March 1972, pp. 111–25.

Kanai Kiyomitsu, '*Takasago*', in Kanai Kiyomitsu, *Nō no kenkyū*. Tokyo: Ōfūsha, 1969, pp. 290–308.

Kōsai Tsutomu, 'Sakusha to honzetsu: *Takasago*', in *Yōkyoku shinkō: Zeami ni terasu*. Tokyo: Hinoki Shoten, 1972, pp. 205–9. (First published in *Kanze*, January 1964.)

Miyake Noboru, 'Nō no tokushu enshutsu'.

Nakamura Kyōzō, *Yōkyoku to shiseki*, pp. 353–9.

Ochi, Reiko, 'Buddhism and Poetic Theory: An Analysis of Zeami's *Higaki* and *Takasago*', doctoral thesis presented to Cornell University, 1984.

Raz, Jacob, *Audience and Actors: A Study of Their Interaction in the Japanese Traditional Theatre*. Leiden: E. J. Brill, 1983.

Sagara Tōru, '*Takasago*', in Sagara Tōru, *Zeami no uchū*. Tokyo: Perikan Sha, 1990, pp. 35–40.

Yabuta Kaichirō, '*Takasago*', in Yabuta Kaichirō, *Nōgaku fudoki*. Tokyo: Hinoki Shoten, 1972, pp. 1–32.

Yashima Masaharu, '*Takasago* keitai no sōshi o megutte', parts 1 and 2, in Yashima Masaharu, *Zeami no nō to geiron*. Tokyo: Miyai Shoten, 1985, pp. 694–709.

Yokomichi Mario, '*Takasago* no hanashi', in Yokomichi, *Nōgeki shōyō*. Tokyo: Chikuma Shobō, 1984, pp. 97–115.

Tatsuta

Text: Itō, *Yōkyokushū*, vol. 2. *Interlude dialogue:* Sanari, *Yōkyoku taikan*, vol. 3. *Interlude katari:* pieced together from Sanari, *Yōkyoku taikan*, vol. 3; Itō, vol 2, and *Jōkyō Matsui-bon* as edited by Tanaka Kazuo. The aim of my editing was to produce a text that touches on all the main issues in the background of the play.

Furu no nō, in *Yōkyoku sambyaku gojūbanshū*, ed. Nihon Meicho Zenshū Kankō Kai. Tokyo: Nihon Meicho Zenshū Kankō Kai, 1928, pp. 655–8.

Itō Masayoshi, 'Kaidai', in Itō, *Yōkyokushū*, vol. 2, pp. 478–80.

Nakamura Kyōzō, *Yōkyoku to shiseki*, pp. 379–83.

Kanai Kiyomitsu, '*Furu*', in Kanai Kiyomitsu, *Nō no kenkyū*. Tokyo: Ōfūsha, 1969, pp. 309–23.

Kanai Kiyomitsu, '*Tatsuta*', in Kanai Kiyomitsu, *Nō to kyōgen*. Tokyo: Meiji Shoin, 1977, pp. 70–76.

Kobayashi Kenji, '*Furu* to Furu engi', in *Kanze*, December 1984, p. 3.

Ponsonby-Fane, R. A. B., 'Tatsuta Jinja', in R. A. B. Ponsonby-Fane, *Studies in Shintō and Shrines*. Kyoto: The Ponsonby Memorial Society, 1953, pp. 249–61.

Sangō-chō Shi Henshū Iinkai (ed.), *Sangō-chō shi*. Nara-ken Ikoma-gun Sangō-chō: Sangō-chō Yakuba, 1976.

'Tatsuta Daimyōjin no on-koto', in *Zoku gunsho ruijū*, ed. Hanawa Hokiichi and Hanawa Tadatomi, vol. 2b, pp. 543–55. Tokyo: Zoku Gunsho Ruijū Kansei Kai, 1923–30.

Takemoto Mikio, 'Sakuhin kenkyū: *Tatsuta*', in *Kanze*, November 1979, pp. 22–8.

Yamamba (THE MOUNTAIN CRONE)

Text: Yokomichi and Omote, *Yōkyokushū*, vol. 2. '*Waki* speeches in dialogue with *ai*': Sanari, *Yōkyoku taikan*, vol. 5.

Bethe, Monica, and Karen Brazell, *Nō as Performance: An Analysis of the Kuse Scene of* Yamamba. Ithaca: *Cornell University East Asia Papers*, no. 16, 1978.

Itō Masayoshi, 'Kaidai', in Itō, *Yōkyokushū*, vol. 3, pp. 500–501.

Kōsai Tsutomu, 'Sakusha to honzetsu: *Yamamba*', in *Yōkyoku shinkō: Zeami ni terasu*. Tokyo: Hinoki Shoten, 1972, pp. 199–203. (First published in *Kanze*, January 1963.)

Miyake Noboru, 'Nō no tokushu enshutsu'.

Nakamura Kyōzō, *Yōkyoku to shiseki*, pp. 80–87.

Nishino Haruo, 'Zeami bannen no nō: *Nōhon sanjūgoban mokuroku o megutte*', in *Bungaku*, vol. 39, May 1971, pp. 37–48.

Origuchi Shinobu, 'Usogae shinji to yamauba', in *Origuchi Shinobu zenshū*. Tokyo: Chūō Kōron Sha (Chūkō bunko), vol 16, 1976, pp. 417–29.

Sagara Tōru, '*Yamamba*', in Sagara Tōru, *Zeami no uchū*. Tokyo: Perikan Sha, 1990, pp. 232–47.

Tyler, Royall, 'A Critique of "Absolute Phenomenalism"', in *Japanese Journal of Religious Studies*, vol. 9, no. 4 (December 1982), pp. 261–83.

Yanagita Kunio, 'Yama no jinsei' and 'Yamamba kibun', in *Teihon Yanagita Kunio zenshū*, vol. 4. Tokyo: Chikuma Shobō, 1963, pp. 59–171 and 377–80.

Yashima Masaharu, 'Aishō no kyokushu o megutte: *Yamamba* no koto nado', in Yashima Masaharu, *Zeami no nō to geiron*. Tokyo: Miyai Shoten, 1985, pp. 675–87.

Yashima

Text: Yokomichi and Omote, *Yōkyokushū*, vol. 2.

Ikeda Hiroshi, 'Sakuhin kenkyū: *Yashima*', in *Kanze*, May 1968, pp. 3–9.

Itō Masayoshi, 'Kaidai', in Itō, *Yōkyokushū*, vol. 3, pp. 496–8.

Kanze Henshū Bu, '*Yashima* no iseki to tazunete', in *Kanze*, May 1968, pp. 29–32.

Nakamura Kyōzō, *Yōkyoku to shiseki*, pp. 451–60.

Miyake Noboru, 'Nō no tokushu enshutsu'.

READ MORE IN PENGUIN

In every corner of the world, on every subject under the sun, Penguin represents quality and variety – the very best in publishing today.

For complete information about books available from Penguin – including Puffins, Penguin Classics and Arkana – and how to order them, write to us at the appropriate address below. Please note that for copyright reasons the selection of books varies from country to country.

In the United Kingdom: Please write to *Dept. EP, Penguin Books Ltd, Bath Road, Harmondsworth, West Drayton, Middlesex UB7 0DA*

In the United States: Please write to *Consumer Services, Penguin Putnam Inc., 405 Murray Hill Parkway, East Rutherford, New Jersey 07073-2136.* VISA and MasterCard holders call 1-800-631-8571 to order Penguin titles

In Canada: Please write to *Penguin Books Canada Ltd, 10 Alcorn Avenue, Suite 300, Toronto, Ontario M4V 3B2*

In Australia: Please write to *Penguin Books Australia Ltd, 487 Maroondah Highway, Ringwood, Victoria 3134*

In New Zealand: Please write to *Penguin Books (NZ) Ltd, Private Bag 102902, North Shore Mail Centre, Auckland 10*

In India: Please write to *Penguin Books India Pvt Ltd, 11 Community Centre, Panchsheel Park, New Delhi 110017*

In the Netherlands: Please write to *Penguin Books Netherlands bv, Postbus 3507, NL-1001 AH Amsterdam*

In Germany: Please write to *Penguin Books Deutschland GmbH, Metzlerstrasse 26, 60594 Frankfurt am Main*

In Spain: Please write to *Penguin Books S. A., Bravo Murillo 19, 1°B, 28015 Madrid*

In Italy: Please write to *Penguin Italia s.r.l., Via Vittorio Emanuele 45/a, 20094 Corsico, Milano*

In France: Please write to *Penguin France, 12, Rue Prosper Ferradou, 31700 Blagnac*

In Japan: Please write to *Penguin Books Japan Ltd, Iidabashi KM-Bldg, 2-23-9 Koraku, Bunkyo-Ku, Tokyo 112-0004*

In South Africa: Please write to *Penguin Books South Africa (Pty) Ltd, P.O. Box 751093, Gardenview, 2047 Johannesburg*